BY WILL DURANT

The Story of Philosophy
Transition
The Pleasures of Philosophy
Adventures in Genius

BY WILL AND ARIEL DURANT

THE STORY OF CIVILIZATION
I. Our Oriental Heritage
II. The Life of Greece
III. Caesar and Christ
IV. The Age of Faith
V. The Renaissance
VI. The Reformation
VII. The Age of Reason Begins
VIII. The Age of Louis XIV
IX. The Age of Voltaire
X. Rousseau and Revolution
XI. The Age of Napoleon

Interpretations of Life
The Lessons of History

A Dual
AUTOBIOGRAPHY
by
Will and Ariel Durant

SIMON AND SCHUSTER • NEW YORK

DESIGNED BY EVE METZ
MANUFACTURED IN THE UNITED STATES OF AMERICA

1   2   3   4   5   6   7   8   9   10

LIBRARY OF CONGRESS CATALOGING IN PUBLICATION DATA
DURANT, WILLIAM JAMES, 1885–
    A DUAL AUTOBIOGRAPHY.

    INCLUDES INDEX.
    1. DURANT, WILLIAM JAMES, 1885–   2. DURANT, ARIEL.
3. HISTORIANS—UNITED STATES—BIOGRAPHY.   I. DURANT,
ARIEL, JOINT AUTHOR.   II.   TITLE.
D15.D87A33   973'.07'2022 [B]   77-24590
            ISBN 0-671-22925-7

We are grateful to the following: Norma Millay Ellis for permission
to quote from "Sonnet 42" by Edna St. Vincent Millay; Mercantile-
Safe Deposit & Trust Company, Trustees for the Estate of H. L.
Mencken, for permission to quote from his letters; *The New York
Times* for permission to reprint: Book Review by J. H. Plumb, September 15, 1963; Letter from Will Durant, October 6, 1963; Letter
from J. H. Plumb, October 27, 1963; Book Review by Orville Pres-
cott, September 28, 1963; May Sarton for permission to quote from
the letters of George Sarton; *Saturday Review* for permission to re-
print "Interpreting the Orient" by James H. Breasted, July 13, 1935;
"Letter to the Editor" by Will Durant, August 3, 1935; Society of
Jesus for permission to quote from the letter of Joseph d'Invilliers,
S. J.; University of Pennsylvania, The Charles Patterson Van Pelt
Library, for permission to quote from the letters of Theodore
Dreiser.

Every effort has been made to trace the ownership of all copyrighted
material and to secure the necessary permissions to reprint these
selections. In the event of any question arising as to the use of any
material, the editor and the publisher, while expressing regret for
any inadvertent error, will be happy to make the necessary correction in future printings.

To
ETHEL, JIM, AND MONICA

Contents

Picture section follows page 93.

Explanatory

OF COURSE every autobiography is a form of exhibitionism. In writing his *Confessions* Rousseau was yielding to that impulse just as definitely as when he displayed his buttocks to the women at the well. There is a pleasure in talking, or hearing talk, about ourselves, even if the talk is hostile; and if in these pages we quote some of the adverse reviews that our books have received, it is partly because we would rather be attacked than ignored.

So we have shamelessly reveled in reminiscing about our past, shady or glorious, and in gratefully commemorating the friends who brightened our days, or in sadly recalling those who have disappeared at the end of the path. We have tried to redeem our immodesty by giving the reader a fairly honest picture of a man and a woman.

Chapter I was written by the younger of us; other sections ascribed to her were dictated to her collaborator, and received from him their final form. Each of us has revised and sanctioned the whole.

WILL AND ARIEL DURANT

CHAPTER I

The Anarch

1898–1912

1 • CHILD OF PROSKUROV

Ariel:

My hand shakes as I grope into the jungle of the past to find the sources of that troubled stream which is my life. There has been so much chaos in me, there have been so many absurdities and mistakes, so many un-reconciled elements of good and bad—how shall I find an order and channel for this turbulence, and bring myself out of a Jewish ghetto in Russia to this spot of peace on a California hill? A thousand ideas rush to my head and confuse my memory.

I was born in Proskurov May 10, 1898, of a mother who was stranger than fiction, and of a father as subdued and gentle as my mother was aggressive and strong. I'm not a happy compromise of these qualities, but rather take after my mother alone. What was left out of my hereditary makeup my husband has been trying to supply these last sixty-three years.

I do not remember my birthplace, but I am told that Proskurov (now Khmelnitski) is the capital of the Kamenets region in the West Ukraine, which was part of the territory seized by Catherine II in the Third Parti-tion of Poland (1795–97). Pogroms and Cossack raids were frequent in that area. There, too, was one center of the Hasidic movement, which consoled the fears and hardships of our people with religious hopes and dreams.

11

My sisters tell me that at birth I had an unusually plump body—a condition with which I still do daily battle. I was named Chaya, which means life, and became Ida in English. Will for years called me Puck, from one of Shakespeare's flighty fairies; but in his premature autobiography, *Transition* (1927), he rechristened me Ariel, from another fairy—forgetting that they were both male. This has become my legal name, and I shall so call myself in these pages.

There were several scholars among my relatives. My uncle Moishe Lebe loved philosophy and mathematics, and hated war. Knowing that the life of a Jewish soldier in the Czar's army was a daily torment of humiliation, he starved himself almost to death to avoid conscription. He died at an early age, perhaps as a delayed result of this drastic expedient.

My maternal grandfather suffered from a family heritage of religious purity. He took these ascetic traditions so literally that he would reprove his neighbors for the slightest indulgence; once (I am told) he moved his residence because a woman visible through the windows of a neighboring house bared her arms to the elbow. He burdened his children with ritual observances and moral prohibitions that made them poorly adapted to an increasingly pagan world.

My mother, Ethel Appel, born in 1870, was the daughter of a Biblical scholar. She was the belle of her district; she dressed so sumptuously that my father found it difficult to finance her tastes; however, much of her expenditure came out of her dowry. She was of a poetic and romantic nature, high-spirited, proud, and passionate. She read a great deal, especially in Tolstoi and the Russian radical literature. The stories that she told us mingled passages from the Bible with incidents from the lives of Russian rebels against the czarist regime.

My father at the age of two (1862) lost his father, and was thereafter brought up by his mother and his brother Luzar. My maternal grandmother owned a wholesale and retail grocery store; above this were several rooms, some of which she turned over to my father as part of my mother's dowry. She also contributed to the support of our family, for my father was earning only twelve rubles (six dollars?) per week by his work as salesman in a clothing store. His employer wondered how he could support so elegant a wife on so modest a wage. Father became restless under the spreading innuendoes. By 1900 he had begotten six children, one yet unborn. Harassed with poverty and lured with dreams of a rich New World, he decided to emigrate to America. He promised to send for all of us as soon as he had made a way for himself in Eldorado.

I can hardly understand how my mother kept all of us alive during the next year and a half. Her parents were beset with the illnesses of old age and the decline of their earnings. Mother put aside her finery, and our living costs were reduced to bare necessities. Shortly after my father's departure she gave birth to a sixth child, Mary. We waited fretfully for letters from America; some came, but at ever longer intervals, and never with money.

Finally, in the late summer of 1901, my mother, unwilling to remain a burden on her parents, packed her movable goods and started out, with five of her children, for America. Harry, aged nine, was left behind with his grandfather, who dreaded America as a godless country, and wished to keep the boy until the solemn ceremony of bar mitzvah ("man of duty") would usher him into responsible manhood.

I can imagine something of the hopeful-fearful excitement that must have agitated us—besides seasickness—as, crowded on deck or in the steerage, we moved over the Baltic and North Seas and the English Channel to Liverpool. On the ship I contracted an eye ailment; this worsened till it almost blinded me; for a time all seemed darkness and pain, and I was nicknamed *blinde katutka*—blind cockatoo. The disease spread to other members of the family, and at Liverpool we were put off the ship for treatment or quarantine. While we were absorbed in this the ship sailed for New York, bearing nearly all of Mother's baggage, including her beloved linens, flowered quilts, and silver heirlooms. She never recovered them.

We took a train, third class, to London, hoping to find medical and financial aid; for Mother, having paid full fares to America, was now almost penniless. In London we followed her desolately as she walked the streets from one address to another, with newborn Mary in her arms. Suddenly a passerby accosted her. "In God's name, aren't you the daughter of David Appel, my beloved teacher in Proskurov?" He reminded her of how in her youth she had sat quietly in a corner in her father's class, for girls were not admitted to Talmudic studies. My mother, touched in both her pride and her wretchedness, replied, "Alas, this is what I have come to." He took us to the Baron de Hirsch Society, which secured board, lodging, and medical care for us, and arranged for our passage to New York.

2 • CHILD OF MANHATTAN

On a misty morning in November, 1901, we emerged from our steerage prison to join the tumult and excitement of the passengers as they greeted, with tears and prayers, the Statue of Liberty. An hour later we were a tiny part of the chaos at Ellis Island. Would we be admitted to the land of our dreams? I can imagine the torture my mother passed through in going from desk to desk and answering, through interpreters, a hundred questions about herself, her husband, and her excited, anxious brood. Unable to understand her uncertain replies about the birth dates of the children, the immigration officials listed all the four girls as born on May 10 two years apart. To this day we four sisters celebrate our birthdays together.

Touching the sacred soil at last, Maurice, the oldest child, went looking for Father at the address he had sent us. He was there, and soon we were together, with no end of hugging and questioning. Our joy was moderated when he explained his situation and his prospects. He had found no gold in the streets; on the contrary, handicapped by his ignorance of English, he had to live by selling newspapers at a small stand that gave him hardly any protection from the weather. He must have wondered how, on his meager earnings, he could feed and house us in his two-room apartment at 228 East Forty-third Street.

To help him my mother, though she was soon pregnant again, went to work selling newspapers at the main entrance to the old Grand Central Station. Every morning, from six o'clock to eleven, she stood there in rain or shine, sleet or snow, summer's heat or winter's winds. She met with sturdy resistance the insults and harassments of her male competitors; sometimes she responded with passionate blows, feeling that she was fighting for her children's food. Some protection was given her by the stationmaster and the local policeman, who admired her courage, her temper, and her good looks.

In 1902 there were five of us children. Maurice was a hard-working lad of thirteen, who soon had a newsstand of his own. He was always good, patient, and ready to help; though his left arm became disabled in his youth, he made his right arm do the work of two, and bore the labor of the day without a word of complaint throughout his eighty years.

Flora, then eight years old, was the prettiest of us, so much so that Will later compared her to the dark-eyed beauties of Italy. When my parents and Maurice went out to earn bread for us, Flora became head of the family and served as little mother, watching over us with a fear-full love. Though we were and are so different—she patient and rational, I impetuous and emotional—we have been very close to each other through more than seventy years. She is still beautiful at eighty.

Sarah, born in 1896, was only two years older than myself, but we always seemed aeons apart. I was everything she was not: open, brash, loud, simple, and talkative. She absorbed eagerly and fervently the radical ideas that circulated around us, and entered an intellectual world that I was too young to share. Only when I fell sick and noted her patient care for me did I realize the silent depth of her affection and loyalty.

Next after me came Mary, born in Proskurov in 1900 and soon a frisky child of two, blessed with a pretty face that still brings Will's kisses. Indeed, I was jealous of all my sisters, for their features were finely molded, while mine were quite plain. Once, when my mother was asked where and when I had been born, she answered, "We found her in an ashcan." Doubtless the remark was meant to tease the questioner, but it rankled in my memory. For some time I brooded over the doubt—was I truly my mother's daughter, or had she picked me up as a waif from the streets? Seeing me downhearted, she touched me gently, bent down, and said, "You are mine, my child; now go out and play."

In August, 1902, she gave birth to her seventh child, Michael, who is now one of the joys of our old age: a man patient, loyal, self-reliant, ever cheerful through whatever trials. When Mother's pains came she sent us out of the room. Some of us stayed on the fire escape. Peering through a rent in the window shade, I tried to find out what was happening; I could make no sense of the turmoil, and I was frightened by the cries of suffering. After that ordeal—the seventh birth in fourteen years—my mother, who probably knew nothing then of contraceptives, discouraged the attentions of my father, and their alienation began.

In 1903 my brother Harry arrived from Russia after many tribulations on the way. Already eleven, he was soon assigned a part in selling the newspapers that kept us alive. He worked hard, carrying heavy batches through crowded streets and any weather. He eased his labor with whimsical humor and elfish pranks, and exalted the day's routine with excited betting on the horse races at Belmont and other tracks. He had a perfect little body, ate what he liked when he liked, slept at the foot of Mother's bed, worshiped her, and embezzled a few pennies from her every day. He never married; he is still a carefree and jolly bachelor at eighty-five. My husband is beguiled by Harry's humor, and calls him a philosopher, for humor, says Will, is based on perspective, which is the secret of philosophy. We all love Harry, for he has stuck with us through every adventure and trial, and his fun-loving disposition has redeemed many a troubled day.

Burdened beyond her great strength, Mother became cross, and sometimes gave way to wild passion—tearing garments to pieces and then moaning with regret, beating us vigorously and then trying to atone with love. As she rose at five in the morning and then worked till eleven—on Sundays till twelve—she came home exhausted and had to sleep in the afternoon, while we played or quarreled in the streets or in the next room. Father too came home quite spent, and could not be very attentive to his children or his wife. We grew up, but we were not brought up.

We moved from place to place: to Forty-first Street, Ninety-eighth Street, One Hundredth Street and Amsterdam Avenue, 193 East Broadway, 171 Henry Street. I recall Forty-first Street as populated by poor "shanty Irish," mixed with French, Greek, or Hungarian shopkeepers or lower-middle-class office workers. The Irish were a tough lot, used to fighting, full of pep and blarney, and were our natural theological enemies. We were often beaten or sniped at by the older of the Christian children, who were told that we were Christ-killers. We held ourselves aloof, and won respect, as well as anger, by our resolute pride. Some of our neighbors came to like us; they sent us on errands, gave us pennies or goodies, invited us into their homes, had us watch their babies, and spoke for us when, unable to produce our parents, we were in danger of being taken away by the Gerry Society for the protection of children.

New York at the beginning of the twentieth century was a bustling chaos of movement and energy, poverty and hope. I can still visualize the horse-drawn streetcars that added their warning clangor to the din. Electric lighting was in its infancy; we burned gas, kerosene, or candles. Heating was by coal, creating smog before we knew the word. We bathed in a washtub, and shared a toilet in the hall. We talk now about the "Gay Nineties," but their reality included dirt, disease, degradation, and almost uncontrolled exploitation.

Most of us youngsters found outlets for our vitality and natural competitiveness through games in the streets. Sometimes we were taken, usually by boat, to Coney Island, where we rode breathless in "Shoot the Chute" cars while we clung to our parents or the railing. Since arms and legs are sufficient for happiness in childhood, we seldom realized that we were poor, and we probably found more pleasure in life than the children of the rich.

Jewish youths, and many other people on the East Side, seized every opportunity for self-development. The Educational Alliance on Henry Street gave a start to such later notables as David Sarnoff, Eddie Cantor, Morris Cohen, Jacob Epstein, and Jo Davidson. There were lecture courses and evening schools; and radical orators like Josef Yanofsky and Chaim Zhitlovsky almost roused us to revolution by their flaming eloquence.

In 1905 my uncle Maurice Appel arrived from Russia with his wife and child and heady ideas of social revolt. He had read Nietzsche, and discarded all traditional morality. He passed on to Artsybashev's *Breaking Point* and *Sanin;* he made Sanin his model; he denounced all laws as outrageous violations of individual freedom, and adopted anarchism as the only true political and moral philosophy. As in Spain in the 1930s, and as in France in 1968, the anarchist doctrine in the New York of 1905 was an active competitor with socialism for the allegiance of rebellious youth. My mother's brother admired her, took her to radical meetings, told her that her life was a shameful drudgery for so beautiful a woman, and proclaimed that a rational morality did not require persistent, self-immolating monogamy. He asked us intimate questions never before heard by any of us girls. My innocence and simplicity disgusted him.

In our childhood we were physically strong but culturally blank. The stimulations of our growth and our environment far outran the elements that made for stability of character and life. The laws meant no more to us than hindrances to elude or ignore. We received no sex instruction,

16

and had to pick this up distorted and haphazard in the streets. Neither my mother nor my sisters gave me any information about the changes to be expected with puberty. There was a puritan strain in my parents, especially in my father, and even in my mother despite her later waywardness. Will teases me about a puritan element in myself, quite contrary to his Latin jollity about sex.

We had some religious training. We were taken to temple on the holydays, and we learned to say our prayers in Hebrew. In our first years in America my mother carried out briefly the domestic rituals of her religion. On the Sabbath she covered her head with a shawl and murmured the prayers required by a sacred tradition. She told us stories from the Old Testament, the Talmud, and the Cabala; some of these gave me violent dreams. However, our religion was not one of fear or celestial promises; we heard no doctrine of heaven or hell, but we were given, at least weekly, a sense of that cosmic mystery which we personified as God. Some part of our people's rich heritage in consoling myth, prophetic fervor, and noble poetry came down to us. We never deserted our faith for any other, but we lost most of it as we rubbed against a harsh and increasingly secular world.

I picked up many superstitions. Sleeping with head exposed to the moon would make you go "loony." To point at the moon was a sin for which I was supposed to step upon my hand five times. To break wind in the presence of others was a sin for which I was to wash my hands a hundred times. To tell a lie, to shout, to get angry, to call anyone hard names, were all sins that required specific penalties. I believed in a God who would punish us, here on earth, sooner or later, for sins for which we had not properly atoned. To be on the safe side I performed some extra penances. My Uncle Maurice helped to free me from such nonsense, and awoke in me a desire to read books and enter the world of thought. He liked to tease me with lofty questions, as "What is God?" I replied from a phrase I had seen in a book—"The Light of the World." He and his skeptic friends applauded, but I heard him whisper to them, "She doesn't understand what she is saying; she's only a child." I moved away from them to some privacy where I could think over his question and his discouraging remark. What did it mean to say that God is the Light of the World? I worried my little brain with such queries, and in search of answers I began to seek the company of older and smarter people.

Our home environment did not encourage thinking or reading. Privacy was almost impossible. There was some benefit in this: we were never bored or lonely; something was always happening; we had to keep on our toes. Mother taught us—and we taught one another—how to fend off attacks or insults from other children. But even across ethnic divisions there were acts of kindness that brightened our days. I remember how Mrs. Moffet and Mrs. Jones protected us against some boys who liked to tease us because we had inherited a different faith than theirs. These social difficulties bound our family more closely together. The world seemed against us, but we loved it nevertheless, and we had hopes of overcoming its hostility and finding a place in the fascinating maze.

Love for my mother was my chief solace and support, but she was away half the day and often in the evening. I could seldom fall asleep before her return. She gently reproved me for staying awake so late, but I told her, "Until you come home and I see you are safe and with me I can't close my eyes. I love you so much and worry about you." Indeed, if I understand myself rightly, I loved my mother above all other persons as long as she lived, but it was with a love that did not detract from my affection for my husband or my child; it was just different, in a category marked by a sharing of blood and years. My mother was my religion; she almost took the place of God in my devotion; she was my creator, my life; she, to me, was the light of the world. Even now, as I remember her years of labor and self-sacrifice, her full and intense personality, I seem to lose myself in her, and cease to feel myself a separate person.

She had no time to be a good housewife. She knew how to cook and sew and clean, but she came home too tired to attend to household chores. So we ate once a day in a restaurant, and at home we relied on rye bread seasoned with garlic. Every Sabbath, however, Father went shopping for food and goodies, Mother blessed the candles over our little feast, and we were gorged and happy for a day.

Neglected and undisciplined, I ran wild, and for the most part I had to take care of myself. I was free to learn in the school of experience. I developed a corresponding character: positive, lawless, ready to answer back, to dodge or strike, to fight my way. I roller-skated, skipped rope, tramped the street, ran up and down stairs, fought and made up, and avoided school as much as I could.

Imagine such an imp trying to sit still in a public school. I believe that the first of my childhood prisons was on Forty-second Street between Second and Third Avenues, and between two saloons. (I remember going into one of these to fetch a jug of beer for Mrs. Murphy, and snatching a pretzel as I came out.) Sarah, who had lost two terms through illness, was in the same class as I. The contrast between the poor and untidy dress of the two of us with the better appearance of luckier children made me uncomfortable. One of these came to school escorted by a maid; she wore a starched pink dress with lace trimmings; she never spoke to us, but she smiled discreetly when she left—a bit ahead of the rest—to be escorted home.

Our teacher, Miss Conn (?), was tall and beautiful. Generally she wore an elegant white blouse and neat black skirt. Her left arm was of wood, covered by a long sleeve cuffed at the wrist, where it met a soft kid glove. We soon got used to seeing her write, erase, and do everything with her one sound arm. Sometimes she let me stay after school and play with the oddities she had confiscated from her pupils or had received from them as gifts. My favorite was a crystal cup of colors so varied and sparkling that I hugged it close and could hardly be persuaded to part from it; finally she gave it to me, and I prized and guarded it through many years.

It was in this Public School 27, though probably with another teacher, that an unpleasant incident occurred which still bothers my memories. One day Sarah came to class late, with hair unbrushed. Asked the excuse for her tardiness, she covered her confusion by giving a reason which further questioning proved false. The teacher slapped her face; Sarah fled from the room and ran to our apartment in tears. Mother came back to the school with her, entered the class, and accused the teacher of having "a dirty heart," by the side of which Sarah's unkempt curls were a very minor blemish. "She is clean in heart," cried my angry mother; "a little water can wash off her dirt, but you have dirt in your heart." She then took Sarah, Flora, and myself to the principal, Mr. Zabrisky, told him the story, and announced that she was removing her children from so barbarous a school. He listened patiently; we found out later that he had many tribulations of his own, and that they had increased his understanding and tolerance of others. He proposed that, instead of our wholesale exodus, Sarah should be enrolled under another teacher. It was so done, and all were pacified. For many years thereafter Mr. Zabrisky bought his morning paper at Mother's stand and always greeted her with a courteous word.

We moved almost yearly. Dragged from school to school, I barely remember one that I liked. I found it exasperating to sit still in a room while life seemed to be passing me by as the vibrant street noises came through the windows, moving me restlessly. It became a major sorrow of my childhood that every day was a schoolday except Saturday and Sunday, which passed so quickly, leading inexorably to Monday and school.

On Sundays and holidays I took my own bundle of newspapers and went out, sometimes as early as 4 A.M., to help my mother at her Grand Central Station post. We used the steps of the closed Westcott Express Company for stacking and sorting the papers. I enjoyed much of this work; I liked the fresh air, though I can remember how, some mornings, my feet nearly froze. And there were pleasant surprises. One day a man came out of the depot carrying a bouquet of peonies, my favorite flower. He must have seen me eying them, for after passing me he turned back and insisted on giving them to me. I learned to tell, from a glance at an oncoming commuter, what paper he would want. The *Sun* appealed to the leisurely aristocrat with his spats and cane; the *Tribune* to the conservative businessman; the *Times* to alert and enterprising men of affairs; the *Telegraph* to the sporty man with tilted hat; the *Morning Journal* to the

19

average man or woman. When, years later, I heard that the *Sun* had faded out, I saw the event as symbolizing the passing of the type that had loved it—men who felt themselves to be Anglo-Saxon gentlemen who had inherited the manners and culture of England.

In the evenings my mother often attended the meetings of radical groups. From these assemblies she returned hot with ideas, dreams, and news of the European—especially the Russian or Jewish—literary world. She spoke to us about Tolstoi, Gogol, Chernyshevski, Gorky, and other rebellious authors. When, in 1910, she told us that Tolstoi had just died, it seemed to me that the world had lost half its soul. We heard her, too, about Walt Whitman and his paeans to the body electric and to universal brotherhood; and the theories of Freud were crossing the Atlantic to loosen the puritan traditions of America.

Maurice Appel often accompanied my mother to radical lectures. His talk about free love made my mother wonder whether she had deserved, in this land of promise and opportunity, the hard life that she had been living for the last seven years. She was still beautiful, and many men desired her. My father was good and faithful; he brought home all his earnings, laid them out for the family expenses, and seldom strayed from our sight except to go to his newsstand. He seemed resigned to remain all the rest of his life in almost the same lowly position in which we had found him on our arrival in New York; hard work had burned out ambition. He was becoming stout and bald, and careless in his dress. He had only one desire—to hold on to his wife, who was both his pride and his sorrow. For now he saw her slipping away from him into a world of ideas and associations that he could not understand.

My mother felt that she had been locked out from all the possibilities of a full or developing life. She thought that her family was now old enough to take care of itself. Son Maurice was eighteen; in that year 1907 he was marrying and making his own home. Harry was fifteen, and acknowledged no master. Flora was only thirteen, but she was already steady, even conservative, accustomed to care for all of us, and consequently a bit critical of Mother for neglecting some of the obligations of motherhood; later she made up for this resentment by self-sacrificing care of Mother in her ailing years. Mary clung to Flora as a pillar of stability in a chaotic world. As for myself, a child of the streets rather than of the home, I resisted Flora's authority, and went my own way.

What mystic rapport or secret fate had held together this unhappy family, uprooted, wind-tossed, moving from house to house, from school to school, a burden or a nuisance everywhere—yet hanging loosely together, eagerly clutching any hand held out to it? Was there in us a sustaining unity of blood, memories, and sufferings, or an obstinate belief that we would someday find or make a place for ourselves in this cruel but inviting, hard yet malleable world?

We were now (1907) to experience our deepest division and our most serious blow. Mother had absorbed the radical views of the East Side lecturers to the point where she resolved to apply them to her own life. She had read Ibsen's *A Doll's House,* and though hers was anything but a doll's house, she agreed with Nora that sometimes a woman might be justified in leaving her husband and home. "I came to this country," she cried, "at the age of twenty-six[?], already with five children, one an infant in my arms. I went out every day to sell papers to support my children; I still do this, every day in the week. Is this all that this country can give me? Am I never to have any freedom, never a day of happiness or rest?"

I was the only one in the family who sympathized with her. I accepted her heterodox ideas, and defended them passionately in arguments with my sisters and brothers. They harassed and insulted the radical friends who came to visit my mother in our apartment. They warned her that such an open break as she was contemplating would put a brand of shame upon us, and that all would condemn her as a heartless home-wrecker. The break came when my brothers Maurice and Harry battered into a pulp the face of a bust made of Mother by an East Side sculptor. Horrified, Mother packed a few belongings, marched out of our rooms and house, and did not rest until she had found another apartment. She made no move for a divorce, but she felt free now to form new attachments.

Our neighbors soon learned of the breakup, and leaped at the opportunity to look down upon us as immoral and disgraced. No decent home was any longer open to us. Even the schoolchildren knew that we were outcasts. My dear friend Dinah Melicov told me that her parents had forbidden her to play with me. Flora and Sarah, already thinking of marriage, feared that potential suitors would be frightened away by our evil reputation. As for my father, the blow to his hopes shared in breaking his spirit and his health. He said hardly a word, but wore out his heart in silence and alone.

I remained with him, but I wanted to live with my mother. I begged her, "I will cook and clean for you, and I'll do nothing wrong to worry you."

She gently dissuaded me. "No, my child. I am away part of every night, and it is not good for a child to be alone. Someday things may be better, and then you can come to me. But now you must go back to your brothers and sisters and try to get along with them."

I burst out crying. "You don't know how miserable I am. No one wants me or loves me. Papa has never anything to say to me. But you, Mother, would understand everything. I would lock the door when you went out at night, and would stay till you came back, and I would never be sad or angry no matter how scared or lonely I'd be."

I pleaded in vain. Mother would not give up her new-won freedom to take care of me, nor would she show favoritism among her children. I would have to go back to my family and fight my own battle.

Even so, my conversations with my mother, before and after the separation, were a great stimulus to me. From her I had taken the habit of reading: at first old fairy tales—Grimm, Andersen, Perrault; then *The Arabian Nights;* then Tolstoi, Gorky, Gogol. Often I hid from the family so that I might read without interruption. I began to go to lectures, and there I listened with such wide-open eyes and ears that the speaker was inspired or amused. Usually, however, I still took most of my education from the give-and-take of the streets. I was restlessly curious. I pestered old and young with questions about this and that, and naturally about sex above all.

I can't remember when my first menstruation came, but I well remember how it frightened me. I grew dizzy, and for a moment so weak that I fell against the edge of the bathtub. I ran to my mother and told her that I was bleeding between the legs. When she realized that this was my menstrual flow she was relieved; she brought me a sanitary napkin, and assured me that now I had become a woman. My discomfort was almost lost in my pride. Now I felt mature enough to engage my mother in earnest discussions of literature and life.

From my special dependence upon her some elements in my character were intensified. Like her I have a warm, sometimes hot temper, a passionate willfulness, and a tendency to be impatient with people or opinions that go against my grain or judgment. I admire those ideal souls who rise above jealousy and hostility, who open their hearts to all the world; but sometimes such people seem to me characterless, mere putty in the hands of environment and circumstance; and I do not regret having approached with a wilder spirit a reality that did not deserve a supine acceptance. And so, in 1912, aged fourteen, I was just ripe for the Ferrer Modern School, and the almost revolutionary experiences that marked a turning point in my life.

3 • AMONG THE ANARCHISTS

I must not disguise or play down this part of my story, however shocking it will seem to the well-behaved friends I have today. I was for three years an excited fledgling in a nest of New York anarchists. The new development was due in large part to one of those accidents that play so great a part in history. In 1912 my family moved from the Lower East Side to 64 East 107th Street. In the same year the Francisco Ferrer Association transferred its headquarters and school from East Twelfth Street to 63 East 107th Street. That chance proximity determined the rest of my life.

By 1912 I had had some seven years of public schools—of what seemed to me a stifling incarceration, and of lessons that appeared irrelevant to the needs and actualities of life. During those confinements I dreamed of action and freedom, and longed for the time when I would be allowed to go to work, even if it would be in another prison, another discipline. Often I thought of running away from home.

One day, playing truant from school, I sat disconsolate on a bench in Central Park. The sound of children laughing aroused my attention. I looked up and saw a scene that seemed to be some wishful dream: a group of youngsters playing merrily under the guidance of an attractive woman. As my eyes followed them jealously she sat down on the grass, and began to tell a story to the children squatting in various postures around her. I moved up diffidently, and sat near enough to hear the tale. Later the teacher explained to me that she and the children constituted the Ferrer Modern School, an experiment in libertarian education. Her name was Cora Bennett Stevenson, and she was taking care of the school while its regular teacher was on a vacation in Europe. The next morning I joined her class, and my second life began.

Gradually I learned that the school was part of the Francisco Ferrer Association, which included also a social center, an art class, and a lecture hall. I was delighted to find there was no compulsion in the school: no child had to listen to the teacher if he wanted to do something else; he might at any time leave the room and go out into the yard and play, though he was not free to go into the street. There were no punishments, no examinations, no report cards. Here, for a natural anarchist like me, was a sudden paradise.

Will:

But who was Francisco Ferrer? Year by year we gathered his story. He was born near Barcelona in 1859. To his education in censored Spain he added travel in free France. He met Anatole France and the genial old geographer Élisée Reclus; he corresponded with the German biologist Ernst Haeckel and the Russian anarchist Peter Kropotkin. Returning to Spain, he attacked the control of education by the Catholic Church; how, he asked, could the Spanish mind ever grow up in such swaddling clothes? Risking his life, he opened at Barcelona in 1901 the first Escuela Moderna, or Modern School, offering an education independent of Catholic doctrine or power. The Church and the monarchy watched for a chance to destroy him.

Like so many Spanish radicals then as now, Ferrer was an anarchist rather than a socialist; knowing the state chiefly in its Spanish form, he distrusted it as a monster of irresponsible power, and aspired to a social order in which there would be little government or none at all. However, like Kropotkin, he was a "philosophical anarchist"; he repudiated violence as a means to social reform. So he wrote:

> Time respects only those institutions which time itself has played a part in building up. That which violence wins for us today, another act of violence may wrest from us tomorrow. Those stages of progress are alone durable which have rooted themselves in the mind and conscience of mankind before receiving the final sanction of legislators. The only means of realizing what is good is to teach it by education and propagate it by example.

Some of Ferrer's friends were not so patient or optimistic. In 1906 one of them, Matteo Morral, threw a bomb at the King and Queen of Spain on their wedding day. Morral was arrested with many others, and the opportunity was seized to arrest Ferrer too. Ferrer protested that he had had nothing to do with the violent act, but he was quickly convicted, and was put to death by a firing squad in the fortress of Monjuich in Barcelona in October, 1909.

Protests against the execution took many forms. In New York a medley of freethinkers organized in 1910 the Francisco Ferrer Association, with its first headquarters at 6 St. Mark's Place. When I became acquainted with them in their third home I was astonished by the diversity of their origin and background. At first they had included socialists, anarchists, single-taxers, trade unionists, IWW's, and syndicalists. When I arrived the anarchists predominated, and acknowledged Emma Goldman as their chief.

She may well go down in history as one of the strongest voices that cried out against the development of the United States from an agrarian republic into a semi-authoritarian empire. She was born in 1869 in Kovno, Russia. She went to Vienna in 1895, heard Freud, and received diplomas in nursing and midwifery. Moving through Europe, she met Peter Kropotkin, enemy of violence, Errico Malatesta, friend of violence, and Louise Michel, the "Red Virgin" of French anarchism. In London she fell in love with Hippolyte Havel, a Czech revolutionist, and in 1900 she took him with her to America.

The anarchist movement was at that time in hot ferment in the United States. On May 4, 1886, fifteen hundred workingmen gathered in Haymarket Square, Chicago, and demanded an eight-hour day. Policemen attacked the crowd; someone threw a bomb; seven policemen and four other men were killed; over a hundred persons were wounded. Eight alleged anarchists were arrested; none of them was convicted of throwing the bomb; seven were convicted of inciting to violence; four were hanged; one blew his brains out on the day appointed for his execution. In 1893 Governor John Peter Altgeld pardoned the survivors.

Emma Goldman and Alexander Berkman were among the many immigrants who protested against the treatment of the "Chicago anarchists";

it seemed to them that the United States was going the way of czarist Russia. Emma was not deterred in her propaganda by the news that Leon Czolgosz, who had assassinated President McKinley in September, 1901, claimed that he knew her and had learned his anarchism from her. Meanwhile she supported herself by lecturing in various cities, chiefly on the contemporary drama; she found in Ibsen and Strindberg, in Chekhov, Gorky, and Andreev, in Sudermann and Hauptmann, in Brieux, Yeats, and Shaw, abundant ammunition for her war on capitalism. She expounded her views in *Anarchism and Other Essays* (1911); it went beyond the campaign for woman suffrage to argue that a wider economic and social experience for women, including sexual freedom, was more vital than participation in the quadrennial circus of sham elections. She herself took a succession of lovers, and outwore them all.

We were a bit frightened by her, for she was the most authoritarian of all the libertarians we have known. Far more likable was her current comrade, Alexander Berkman. He too was born in Russia (1870). Coming to America, he worked in the mines of the Carnegie Steel Company; he became a leader in the strike of its employees at Homestead, Pennsylvania, in 1892; he shot Henry Clay Frick, chairman of the board of the company, and was condemned to twenty-two years' imprisonment. Released after fourteen years, he came to New York, where he was soon the beloved "Tio Sasha" of the anarchist movement. When I met him he seemed subdued, almost mild, certainly courteous—to all but capitalists. He was unrepentant, and still believed that when other avenues of social protest were blocked by the power of wealth, the oppressed were justified in resorting to violence. His *Prison Memoirs of an Anarchist* (1912) is a bitter and vivid record of his years in jail.

We fell in love, as nearly all did, with the third leader of the Francisco Ferrer Association—Leonard Dalton Abbott. He was an Englishman by birth and manners, and had imbibed his anarchism not from the background of desperate revolt against czarist despotism but from the nonviolent libertarianism of William Morris. He was as handsome as a Pre-Raphaelite angel; indeed, we called him "the angel of the radical movement"; his picture, fondly preserved through sixty years, still adorns a bookcase in our hall. In 1911 he was literary editor of *Current Opinion;* his articles in that magazine had attracted me while I was in the seminary. He believed, with a sadly diminishing faith, in the power of reason to remedy the ills of personal passion and social tyranny. I doubt if he ever raised his voice to anyone. He was always slow to condemn, always ready to listen, understand, and help. I have never met a finer man.

Ariel:

I was too young to get close to these leaders, but I reveled in the new friendships that I made at the Ferrer Center. There I met Manuel Kom-

25

roff, later our rival in letters but a loyal friend through all the vicissitudes of our ideologies. And Anton Rovinsky, who was the Paderewski of the group, rousing us with his piano artistry. And Walter Groth, carpenter, philosopher, and saint, who could not hurt a fly but built a two-story house almost entirely with his own hands. And Christine Ell Hovden, whom Emma Goldman had brought to New York from Denver, and whom Eugene O'Neill took as his model for Anna Christie. I treasure a photograph taken in 1912, which shows her on the left, and myself on the right, of Walter Groth; you may judge from this picture that I was, at the age of fourteen, a buxom and ebullient lass. I spent a night as Christine's guest in that year; she and her friend Mylius (I remember his name imperfectly) came back that evening rather "high"; Mylius tried to get into bed with me (Christine was too drunk to care), and promised me unprecedented delight; I doubt if I knew what he meant; in any case I found it easy to push him out of my bed.

At the Center, too, I first met Marie Yuster, later known as Romany Marie. A gypsy by origin, she had all the pride and restlessness of her tribe, all the flair for colorful dress and the dance; and her throaty voice sang of both the joy and the sadness of love and life, of wandering from enemy to enemy under the open but incalculable sky. She took me in tow, and taught me some of the tricks of getting safely around the pitfalls of a maid among men. She did not accept the moral code that was preached but not practiced in the United States; she was a penniless woman in a man-made world, and she felt justified in believing, like nature, that anything that makes for survival is good. I imbibed a part of that philosophy. I was not above lying now and then, even pilfering a bit, in those sink-or-swim days. I had little shame of body or nakedness, and when I joined the art class at the Center it seemed to me quite natural that the model should be nude.

The art school was the most successful and fruitful of the Ferrer Association's many experiments. Robert Henri came to teach it once a week, and when he could not come he sent George Bellows to take his place. These two were among the famous "Eight"—with Arthur Davies, William Glackens, John Sloan, George Luks, and others—who rebelled against the traditional, seemly, "academic" style of painting; they chose to represent the grimmer as well as the proper side of American life, and were at first belabored as the Ashcan School. In February, 1913, they shocked the older generation with their exhibition at the Armory; in the end they won their battle.

Man Ray, Willie Gropper, and Benno Greenstein were among the pupils at the Center's art school. Marie Yuster served as manager, and it was only through her influence that I was allowed to attend. Henri brought famous personalities like Isadora Duncan and John Sloan to talk to us and spur us on. His own lectures almost set us on fire: he made us believe that the human body is a very temple of divinity, and that every part of it is a miracle; so art became a sacrament. When our fees proved inadequate to pay for a professional model, Henri proposed that we take turns in posing. I had no idea then that discretion is the better part of valor; I was among those who agreed, and I played a modest part in the history of the school by disrobing and mounting the pedestal. Henri painted a portrait of me as *The Laughing Girl*, which won some acclaim when it was exhibited. I kept up my interest in painting till 1952, when Will seduced me into the rival art of words.

Why is it that today, so many years since I discovered the Ferrer Center, I still have a warm spot in my heart for the people I met there?— though I have long since grown skeptical of their ideas, and I no longer have the stimulus of poverty to overthrow "the Establishment." Perhaps because the impressions I received there—after those of the streets themselves—were the most startling and vivid that fell upon my malleable mind. So many striking figures, thoughts and ways; such a procession of dreamers, poets, artists, musicians, and philosophers; capable managers like Harry Kelly, kindly old men like Dr. Charles Andrews, tense, devoted souls like our silent and incorruptible treasurer, Stewart Kerr . . .

Add to these living spirits the dead or distant notables we were told of in the lecture hall: Bakunin, Kropotkin, Reclus, Louise Michel . . . There, too, I heard of the IWW, of "Big Bill" Haywood, Carlo Tresca, Elizabeth Gurley Flynn, and Terry Carlin—who became one of the lasting inspirations of Eugene O'Neill. Clarence Darrow came to the Center and lectured on Voltaire. Joseph McCabe, brilliant polymath of the Rationalist Association in England, visited us during his engagement at Columbia University. And Margaret Sanger, one of the most heroic and successful reformers in history, was sending her two boys to the Ferrer School.

I made sure to attend the school when it reopened in September, 1912. I expected Cora Stevenson to be our teacher as before. I was disappointed to find, in her place, a young man of twenty-seven, awkward and shy, not at all handsome, with a pimple here and there, and an annoying defect of speech—he did not open his mouth enough when he spoke. How could so innocent and diffident a youth handle us wildcats of liberty? I didn't like him. Who was this man who had taken the place of our beloved Mrs. Stevenson?

Let him reply.

CHAPTER II

The Atheist

1885–1912

Will:

I, William James Durant—so baptized by parents who had never heard of the philosopher William James—was born on November 5, 1885, in North Adams, Massachusetts, of French-Canadian parents. My father, Joseph Durant, had been born in 1854 in a suburb of Montreal. He received no schooling, and never learned to read or write. His education was almost entirely of character and by experience. From Roman Catholic priests, and from his parents, he imbibed a moral code which, as far as I could see in fifty-eight years of knowing him, he practiced faithfully till his death in 1943. I have known some gracious gentlemen, but I have never known a better man. Thinking of him, I wonder whether an illiterate person of good character, who becomes a good husband and a good father, is of more worth to a community than a man of much education, assiduous reasoning, and ten thousand books.

My mother, baptized Marie Allors, was born in Champlain, New York, in 1856. I believe that her father operated a barge on the lake. The town was still rich in Durants when, in 1917, Ariel and I, proud of our first car, drove my parents up to Champlain to visit Abram Lavalley, the septuagenarian husband of my father's sister Caroline.

I do not recall loving my mother more than my father; there was no sign of any Oedipus complex in our family. Father had the advantage of retaining and gently exercising paternal authority, and it was he who gave us children a weekly nickel or dime for candy or peanuts. My

28

mother had the disadvantage that the task of spanking us fell almost entirely to her. She did not presume that her little savages could reason philosophically about right and wrong; she administered ethics with discriminating care, and with arms and fingers hardened by work; and each of us learned to be grateful for her loving discipline.

She had been beautiful in her youth, and remained so, in my eyes, even under her white hair. She changed, without audible complaint or regret, from blooming girlhood into industrious housewifery. I shudder when I think of her labors. She bore eleven children, saw three of them die in childhood, raised the others through every stage of mess, measles, mischief, tribulation, joy, and pride; bathed them, clothed them, cooked for them, washed and ironed their clothing, prayed for them, taught them religion and decency, and wept when they went from her into marriage or apostasy. Meanwhile she designed and made dresses for herself and her daughters, knitted blankets and comforters, made molasses candy and root beer, and, on Christmas and New Year's, without help except from her daughters, she prepared superb dinners for her multiplying progeny. All the crimes and tragedies daily gathered for my breakfast by an enterprising newspaper cannot destroy my respect for a species that can show, in millions of women, such self-consuming love. What is the itching of a boy for a girl compared to that devotion?

Her first child was Joe, the only one of us who lived an unhappy life. Then Leah, who became a good wife to a good husband (a genially skeptical Dane), and gave him a fine brood. Then John, who alone, among my brothers, cared for books; I never forget that (about 1900) he introduced me to Taine's *History of English Literature,* which I have since read two or three times over. Then Frank, whom I envied for his good looks, his practical skills, his resemblance to our father in appearance and conduct; cancer took him in 1951, when he was sixty-eight. Then myself. Then Sam, who stood by me through all the turmoil of my leaving the seminary, secretly followed me into heresy, and was killed at thirty-eight (1927) by a hunter's careless shot. Then Eva, who became a nun, perhaps to atone for my failure to become a priest, and who died in sanctity in 1966. And finally Ethel, who at seventy-eight is still beautiful, and bears with me lovingly as if I were not, on the most apostolic authority, damned to everlasting hell.

We received our first formal education in parochial schools operated by French-Canadian nuns in North Adams and Chicopee, Massachusetts, and in Readsboro, Vermont. If I remember rightly, these Sisters of Charity used French as the language of instruction in the morning, and English in the afternoon. At home (till about 1900) we spoke the Canadian patois. In 1892 the family moved to Kearny, New Jersey, and, about 1898, to Arlington, closer to the celluloid mills (later taken over by Du Pont) where my father was advancing to the position of superintendent of the "specialty" department. Brothers Joe and John went to work there to help feed all of us. Frank and I were sent to public schools in Kearny until 1896, when we were transferred to a new parochial school attached to St. Cecilia's Church.

I have made much, in *Transition*, of my exploits in school and in fisti-cuffs, and how the saintliest man I ever knew, Father James Mooney, joined with my mother in plans for changing me from a troublesome and conceited brat into a model priest. I was pleased by their belief that such a transformation was possible, and I was touched by her silent but fer-vent hopes that she might give a son to the Church. What moved me to fall in with their plans was the example of excellence and dedication as I saw it, almost daily, in Father Mooney. What could be nobler than to be like him?—sinless, laborious, busy all the working day with administer-ing the parish, visiting the sick, reading his breviary, and saying Mass as devoutly and distinctly as if every word had really come from God. I have never forgotten how, when my mother seemed near death, he hur-ried up from the rectory a mile away, knelt beside her bed, and prayed aloud while my father and the doctor stood aside, and how Mother seemed to take courage and strength from his prayers. From that day I loved Father Mooney, as I once scandalously put it, "this side of homosexuality."

I passed through the wonderments, imaginings, and experiments usual in sexual development. I puzzled over the secrets of the female form, whose plentiful concealment stimulated my curiosity; I can remem-ber when I thought that women had the same penetrating apparatus that men carry so absurdly between their legs. My imagination, always easily excited and hard to control, aroused my glands, or my glands aroused my imagination, in a marvelous interaction which Hobbes considered the most obvious proof that mind is a form or operation of matter. By the age of twelve—probably earlier—I had become an expert in masturba-tion; by the age of fourteen I was carrying this manual art to an extreme that alarmed my confessor—that same beloved Father Mooney who had nominated me for the priesthood. I did not dare hide these terrible sins in my weekly confession. This perfect priest seemed not much surprised by my first avowals; he let me off with a gentle reproof and an easy penance; but when, as my fever progressed, I confessed to him that I had broken all my records by relieving my congestion eighteen times in the week, he refused me absolution—without which I could not receive the Eucharist. Even so he spoke with sympathy, and when we met a few days later he greeted me with his usual quiet friendliness. My addiction to baseball, running, and other sports helped me to moderate the habit, but not to overcome it. Nature will out, with or without aid.

In the spring of 1900 Father Mooney took me to the Jesuits at St. Peter's College, Jersey City, and entered me into a contest for a scholarship. I was one of the winners—perhaps by merit, perhaps by Father Mooney's hint that I was sacerdotal raw material. The other victors were Kevin Lynch and William McLoughlin. I remember Kevin especially, because he was what I secretly longed to be—triumphant both in class and on the athletic field. (Just the same, I beat him in handball.) Together we went through the eight-year course (academy and college) in seven years, rivaling each other amiably in everything from baseball and canoeing to Aeschylus and chemistry. Those wonderfully patient and scholarly Jesuits labored over us, five hours a day, five days a week, as if we were a hundred geniuses destined to be pillars of the Church as doctor, lawyer, or priest. Kevin was resolved to become a good physician; he succeeded; and he put aside as beyond his purpose those airy problems of theology and philosophy that were to become my passion.

Literature preceded these as my intellectual predilection, fitly mingled with more tangible endearments. Irene Walsh, aged twelve, had lent me, aged twelve, during our calf-love idyl, her copy of *Pickwick Papers;* from that revelation dated my craze for books, which alarmed my parents and my teachers. St. Peter's College had a library temptingly rich in English literature; I prowled hungrily among those treasures, and then in the public libraries of Jersey City and Newark; in those avid seven years I must have read over two thousand books, some skippingly, some over and over again. I read almost every poem of Byron's, relished some wicked lines in *Don Juan,* and prayed to God to release him from hell; surely eighty years of burning were enough.

I have before me now a tattered notebook of 248 pages, dated November 30, 1904, containing, in my handwriting, a "Chronological List of the World's Literature," with a thousand entries, and a "List of English Writers" with 729 entries, and a "List of American Authors" with 180. Apparently I proposed to read all these predecessors, and then join them among the immortals of the pen. I made a hectic start: pages 216–17 of the notebook list forty-eight volumes as having been read between December 1, 1904, and January 12, 1905, including six volumes of Gibbon, six of Merivale's *History of the Romans under the Empire,* three of Hallam's *Middle Ages,* and six of Guizot's *History of France.* I suspect that I mistook intentions for accomplishments, and fingering for reading.

Page 139 of the same notebook proclaims a wild resolve: "I must some day, when I have made a closer study of the subject, and shall have learnt the arts of style and criticism, write a series of 'Literary Lives,' on the plan of Plutarch. Vol. I might treat of Asiatic Literature; Vol. II of Greek; Vol. III of Roman," and so on through twenty-five volumes.* Then (December 10, 1904) ninety pages of notes for Volume II: a discussion of ways of translating Homer; a powerful argument for translating

* This program was carried out, on a tiny scale, in *The Story of Philosophy* and *The Story of Civilization.*

him into dactylic hexameters, as in the original; a footnote claiming that this argument antedated my reading of Matthew Arnold's *On Translating Homer;* then the Greek text of the *Iliad,* VIII, 542–61, with my *rendering* of those lines into English hexameter verse. I remained for thirty-five years so proud of that performance that I used it on page 57 of *The Life of Greece.* Page 244 of the notebook confessed that I had read some "little obscenities" in Balzac and Musset, but expressed confidence that they had done no harm to my virgin purity. At the head of the book stands the Jesuit motto, A.M.D.G.—i.e., *ad majorem Dei gloriam,* "to the greater glory of God." I was still, in 1904, pious, orthodox, and headed for the priesthood.

My purity was questionable. It had suffered somewhat from onanistic fantasies. There was in those days a burlesque theater in Jersey City—the Bon Ton; it advertised its Aphrodites on posters displayed in saloon windows along the route that I daily walked from the Erie station to St. Peter's College. I would stop, as unnoticeably as I could, to view these alluring anatomies; the picture of a woman with exposed calves was then a veritable apocalypse—a prophetic revelation. Finally, probably in my nineteenth year, I paid a month's savings (twenty-five cents, I believe) to enter the Bon Ton shrine, and, from the gallery I gazed breathless at those magic calves. I was never the same again.

As for my orthodoxy, it could not survive the 1909 volumes. By the end of my sophomore year I had discovered, through Darwin and other infidels, that the difference between man and the gorilla is largely a matter of trousers and words; that Christianity was only one of a hundred religions claiming special access to truth and salvation; and that myths of virgin births, mother goddesses, dying and resurrected deities, had appeared in many pre-Christian faiths, and had helped to transform a lovable Hebrew mystic into the Son of God. These learned discoveries alarmed and exalted me. They alarmed me because I could no longer think of becoming a priest, and must soon reveal my unwillingness to my beloved mentor, Father Mooney, and to my mother, who was looking forward to my ordination as the reward of countless sacrifices, and the summit of her earthly happiness. They exalted me because they made me superior to nearly all those around me (except Kevin Lynch), who seemed to be dupes of childish legends and fears. No sensual pleasure could compare with the intellectual pride of belonging to the elite few who had liberated themselves from the falsehoods that had kept most Europeans and Americans in bondage for fifteen centuries. I took no notice of the utility of those myths in checking the unsocial nature of the trousered ape; on the contrary, I began to resent the use which churches and governments had made of them in dulling the edge of economic discontent and political revolt.

So, as I relinquished my belief in heaven, I turned with religious fervor to faith in a socialist utopia. I read Edward Bellamy's *Looking Backward* (1888), and dreamed of a time when men would be equal, and Beethoven would at the touch of a button issue from a box or a wall. (He does.) I read Upton Sinclair's *The Jungle* (1906), and raged at the brutal and poisonous operation of American capitalism. I shouted my support of William Randolph Hearst in his campaign for the mayoralty of New York City in 1905, and when he lost I was convinced that he had been cheated of election through ballot-box drownings by Tammany Hall. In 1907 I sent a powerful pro-socialism letter to the Jersey City *Evening Journal*, with the result that my Jesuit teachers threatened to refuse me graduation. I wrote to Arthur Brisbane, told him of my enthusiasm for Mr. Hearst, and asked him to find a place for me as a cub reporter on the New York *Evening Journal*. He discouraged the idea, but agreed to give me a trial.

Meanwhile I concealed my theological denudation from all but a few radicals in Arlington. One was Harry Kemp, the "tramp poet," whom I named Harvey Keap in *Transition*. Another was Dave Howatt, with whom I pursued physical culture on evenings and weekends. He was a devotee of Bernarr Macfadden's *Physical Culture* magazine, which converted me to vegetarianism by scandalous and delectable means. The vegetarian gospel was interspersed with pictures of splendid women naked to the waist—perhaps to advertise mother's milk. I liked the lovely protuberances so much that I accepted the gospel, and took to seeds, roots, leaves, vegetables, nuts, and fruits.*

Dave and I, in my college years (1903–07), met almost every night for hundred-yard dashes or long walks; and on Daylight Saving evenings we played baseball on the diamond where, on Saturday afternoons, our local team was good enough to meet the Cuban Giants and other tough competitors. We two were distant but ardent supporters of the New York Giants, in the heyday of John McGraw. I gathered nickels and dimes by selling newspapers, and used some of my savings to finance an occasional trip to the Polo Grounds, where I gloried in the pitching, good looks, and good manners of Christy Mathewson. Now I dreamed of being a pitcher rather than a priest.

I dreamed also of Marie Coyne. In *Transition* I called her Esther, but I slyly emphasized her coyness. She played the organ in our church, and I sang tenor parts in the choir (1906–07). She was lovely, modest, and demurely gay; I was twenty and throbbing. I fell in love with her, and earned the privilege of taking her home after rehearsals. I do not remember getting further with her than a breathless kiss. Then suddenly she

---

* I have not adhered to it with incorruptible fidelity; there were carnivorous interludes, as in the seminary and on planes. I am now adding, hebdomadally, chicken or fish. My dietetic record is so irregular that I cannot derive from it any conclusions clear enough to constitute an evangel.

shunned me, and her mother closed the door to me when I called. I later learned that my mother had begged Mrs. Coyne not to let her daughter's beauty divert me from my priestly vocation. Marie is still my friend, and sends me Christmas cards warm with Catholic piety, which I answer with tender memories.

The entire parish in Arlington, knowing little of this brief romance, and less of the books I was reading, took it for granted that I would soon enter the seminary at Seton Hall, South Orange, New Jersey. Father Mooney had lately been made rector of that seminary and president of the college. I dreaded the ordeal of telling him that I could not realize his hopes of making me a priest. Finally, some time before my graduation, I went out to South Orange and revealed to him, as coherently as I could, both the failure of my vocation and the demise of my faith. I shall never forget the forgiving sympathy with which he greeted these seismic upheavals. He told me that such lapses of religious belief had become common, and were often temporary. He asked me to say nothing of my doubts to anyone but my confessors; to go to Mass daily, receive Communion frequently, and pray that my faith would return. I promised, and kept my promise, but my doubts grew.

Meanwhile those good Jesuits at St. Peter's had decided that the best way to deal with my socialist letter was to ignore it; and so, in June, 1907, I was graduated with my first degree. The hero of that commencement was Kevin Lynch; he took most of the prizes, but so modestly that my jealousy did not diminish our friendship. His parents celebrated his triumph by giving a party in their Hoboken home. I was invited, and enjoyed myself to the brink of matrimony. Cider was served; I drank several glasses; they loosened my inhibitions; I proposed marriage to one of the girls present, and was accepted; she too was susceptible to cider. I took her home near midnight; I stumbled my way back via three trolley cars to Jersey City to Newark to Arlington. When I awoke the next day I could not remember the name or address of the maiden to whom I had proposed. I have never seen her again.

Soon afterward I went to work as a reporter for the New York *Evening Journal* at ten dollars a week, and for the first time I came into contact with the ugly side of contemporary life; I have detailed elsewhere that daily diet of filth and crime. I continued to live with my parents, who still assumed that I would enter a seminary in September. Between rapes and murders I brooded over ways of breaking to my mother the news that I was a lost soul. Father Mooney eased the situation by offering me a place at Seton Hall College as teacher of Latin, French, and geometry. I gladly accepted. Now, instead of revealing my awful secret, I could tell my parents that I was a bit hesitant about entering the seminary, and would spend a year as a teacher while I made up my mind about my fitness for the priesthood.

So in September, 1907, I began my new career. I shared a room and a mouse with Hugh Jennings, who proved to be a kindly associate, tolerant of my peculiarities, but frowning upon any hint of heresy. (I believe he continued to teach there for some forty years more, and died in harness and honor.) Another teacher shocked my innocence by greeting me, occasionally, with a formula of tender solicitude: "How's your joy-prong today?" A third teacher invited me to join him in a visit to Manhattan; he took me to a brothel, where he relieved himself while I waited, retaining my virginity less through virtue than through fear of infection or incompetence.

In my first year as a pedagogue I developed a close friendship with a senior-class student, seminary bound, whom I must still disguise as Charley McMahon. I walked with him so frequently that Father Mooney gently cautioned me, saying that such intimacy between a teacher and a pupil would arouse talk. I had no notion of what he meant; I had not yet heard of homosexuality. Charles fascinated me because he too was inclined to socialism, and to some doubts about theology. It was a comfort to me that I had found someone to whom I could at least suggest my infidelity.

Stimulated by this friendship, I now conceived an idea worthy of the most imaginative lunatic: I would please my family and Father Mooney by entering the seminary; I would pretend to have abandoned my heresies; I would become a priest, and would then work from within to lead the Catholic Church in the United States to cooperation with the socialist movement. After all (I reasoned), most Catholics in our country were then poor, and most millionaires were Protestants; and had not Pope Leo XIII spoken sympathetically of proletarian grievances? Had not Father Edward McGlynn openly and persistently supported Henry George's social-welfare campaign for the mayoralty of New York in 1886? Would not an entente between the Church and socialism be a powerful force for economic and political reform? In the enthusiasm of my realpolitik I risked everything at the outset by asking McMahon to join me in the enterprise. He was skeptical, but agreed, and he never betrayed my confidence. In September, 1908, we entered the seminary.

I was not unhappy in my first year there. My parents, rejoicing in what they thought to be my return to sanity and sanctity, visited me as often as the rules would permit, overwhelming me with gifts and love. Father Mooney showed his affection by calling me down to his office, every now and then, to recite the breviary with him in alternation. My fellow seminarians were nearly all fine men; they forgave my scandalous acquaintance with non-Catholic literature, perhaps because they found me a helpful partner in handball and tolerable in baseball. I became accustomed to the rigorous schedule of rising at five, hearing Mass before breakfast, attending classes in theology, ethics, church history, and liturgy, continuing to teach in the college, eating meals in silence, reciting the rosary together in the open air, enjoying the daily periods of recreation, studying after supper till nine, murmuring evening prayers in the chapel; going to bed at nine-thirty. By that time I was so tired that (though I do not trust my memory) I can't recall having any sexual desires or fantasies while in the seminary. Perhaps those wise old theologians had put some antaphrodisiac in our coffee. And each of us had a roommate to watch him. We slept two in a bed, but I never heard any mention of homosexuality.

I was beginning to adjust myself to a life of vain hyprocrisy when I encountered Baruch Spinoza. I had been made librarian, and was allowed to wander freely among those precious shelves. There I came upon Hale White's translation of Spinoza's *Ethics Demonstrated in Geometrical Order* (1674). I took the book to my room and studied every word of it. No other book (barring the Bible) ever impressed me so lastingly. Not only by its metaphysics (which I probably failed to understand and now generally accept), but even more so by its logical order, its stoic conclusions, and its obvious goodwill to all men. Its arguments for determinism convinced me then, but leave me skeptical now. Probably Spinoza's character affected me as much as his philosophy, and I found them more concordant than in most thinkers.

In any case the picture and record of that profound and noble Jew shared in awakening me to the absurdity of my dream of a socialist Catholic Church. I brooded now, amid study, prayers, and hymns, over the dilemma that confronted me: should I continue in pretenses that were growing ever more complex and difficult, or inflict another blow upon a mother who had so movingly rejoiced over my renewed vocation? Finally, in January, 1910, I announced my second defection to Father Mooney. He bore with me with saintly patience; and as if to ease the transition for me and my parents he asked me to resume my former duties as a lay teacher in the college. I gladly agreed, for I loved Seton Hall, and dreaded a return to a disappointed family and a gossipy parish, or a mad leap from rural isolation to the physical and mental chaos of New York.

In the next half year I slowly renewed contact with the outside world. I am amused when I recall how soon the sexual impulse resumed its itching, brooding, prowling urgency. Now that I was free to go to Newark on weekends, I became conscious of feminine clothing, colors, contours, and graces. Before I quite realized it I was involved, to the verge of betrothal, with a gentle Kathleen. I was lured from her by a buxom brunette who disconcerted me by exposing her breasts after two meetings. I was unprepared for such a confrontation. I retreated into a milder affair with a schoolteacher who cooled my blood by proposing marriage; this too was more than I could manage. I remained virginal.

Some of my ardor went into reading. In the seminary I had had little time for literature; now, eager to play a part in the literary world, I frequented the bookstores and public library of Newark, and carried away armfuls of Ibsen, Hauptmann, Shaw, Wells, Arnold Bennett, Flaubert, Maupassant, Anatole France, Whitman, Jack London, Upton Sinclair . . . I joined other swelling spirits in forming a Social Science Club, at whose meetings one or another of us read a prepared paper as the cue for a general discussion.

The most brilliant member of the club was Timothy Cairns, a Presbyterian minister tolerant of heresies and bubbling with vitality and wit. He was a little older than the rest of us, so we affectionately christened him "Uncle Tim." When he was asked about his origins he began solemnly with "I was born in Ireland when I was a boy." He had never kissed the Blarney Stone, finding it superfluous. He called his home "Blarney Castle"; there our club held some of its most hilarious sessions. I became especially attached to him, and fond of his wife, "Toby," his lovely daughters, and his handsome son John. My long friendship with Tim Cairns was one of the many blessings of my life.

It was through this Social Science Club that I met another providential friend. At a session in the home of William (?) Smith in East Orange I read a rebellious paper on "The Bondage of Tradition." Our host had invited a neighbor, Alden Freeman, who had recently signalized his freedom from tradition by having Emma Goldman, an avowed anarchist, lecture on the modern drama in the barn of his home at the corner of Grove and Central Avenues. Alden was a homosexual, ill at ease in the heterosexual society that gathered about him as the son of a Standard Oil millionaire. He sympathized with other rebels, and contributed to their projects. He liked my paper, and invited me to visit him. I did, with no harm to my morals, but with powerful influence upon my life.

At the end of the semester (June, 1910) I bade farewell to Seton Hall, and took a small room in the YMCA building in Newark. Father Mooney, endlessly helpful, gave me a letter to Mr. Poland, city superintendent of schools, who offered me employment as substitute teacher at two dollars per day of actual work. My parents took pity on me, and invited me to share my old room with my brother Sam in the house which they had bought at 524 Forest Street, Arlington. (They still knew nothing about my loss of faith.) I paid them a now forgotten amount for shelter and breakfast, and ate a vegetarian lunch and dinner in sundry restaurants—chiefly in Macfadden's Physical Culture cafeteria in Newark. My career as substitute teacher began in the summer of 1910, and continued till January, 1912.

It was a difficult and precarious interlude. I can hardly understand how I managed on ten dollars a week, but probably that sum was worth, in purchasing power, fifty dollars today. Perhaps my service improved, and my payment was increased. I added to it by giving twelve weekly lectures on "The Philosophy of Herbert Spencer" in the home of Tim Cairns, to some ten or twelve stoics who paid three dollars for the course. My parents did not interfere with my intellectual activities; they knew nothing of Herbert Spencer; and, as I went to Mass, confession, and Communion, they presumed that I was still a faithful Catholic. Meanwhile I continued to play baseball, and eat vegetables, with Dave Howatt. In the summer of 1911 I spent a week with him at Macfadden's Physical Culture City in New Jersey; there he and I subsisted entirely on fruits and nuts; our bungalow stank of rotting bananas, for Dave thought them best when their skin was black.

Somehow (perhaps through Alden Freeman) my fame as a budding philosopher reached New York. From the Francisco Ferrer Association at 104 East Twelfth Street I received an invitation to address its Sunday evening audience on "The Origins of Religion." I was not prepared on that subject, but I was attracted by the five-dollar fee, and by the hope that from that foot of earth I might rise to fame and move the world. So, in January, 1912, I faced with trepidation some sixty anarchists, social-ists, single-taxers, and free-lovers, and told them just how religion had begun. They were glad to hear me dilate on sex as one of the sources of religion, and to learn that the phallus had in many places and forms been worshiped as a symbol of divine power.

On the following Friday, while I was teaching in the Montgomery Public School in Newark, I was called to the telephone by my brother Sam, who worked as a novice architect in a nearby office. He informed me that the front page of that excellent journal the Newark *Evening News* carried a story to the effect that the Catholic bishop of the diocese had issued against me an "episcopal excommunication" on the ground that I had proclaimed sex worship to be the chief origin of religion. Since I had recently taught at Seton Hall College, the bishop felt an obligation to warn all Catholics that I was no longer connected with that institution, that my words and actions had placed me outside the pale of the Church, and that no Catholic should henceforth associate with me in any avoid-able way. I went home nevertheless, hoping that the news would not reach Arlington.

I summarize here the story told at length about "John Lemaire" in *Transition*. When my mother went to Mass on Saturday she was privately informed about my condemnation. I was with my young sisters when she returned. She went to her bedroom, fell face downward on the floor, and cried so hysterically that I feared for her reason. I tried to comfort her, but she did not seem to recognize me. My sisters were terrified. I ran to the factory to summon my father. He too had heard the news. He said little, but his stern face showed that he had given me up as a lost soul. After seeing my mother's condition he bade me leave the house within three days. I left the next morning, carrying a suitcase on one arm and an old typewriter under the other. I shall never forget my mother's cry as, awaking, she heard me leave: "Don't send him away! Don't send him away! He's my boy!" I was too young to understand that I was flesh of her flesh, blood of her blood, soul of her soul, and that I had torn her apart. To this day I am not sure but that her faith and love were not wiser than my brash and ego-swelling revolt.

I found my way to New York, searched for a room until I was exhausted, and then took a bed in a cheap hotel. My memory is especially confused at this point. Why did I go to New York, when I was due to teach in Newark the next day? Perhaps I supposed that I would be at once dismissed from my post, and that I would be safe hereafter only in the anonymity of a metropolitan multitude. Nevertheless I remember quite clearly my night in an unheated room in Nineteenth Street. On Monday morning, when I returned to the hotel after breakfast nearby, an old man asked me, "Do you live here?"—and when I replied, "Yes," he queried, sternly, "Do you know that this is a whorehouse?" I could hardly believe it, though during the night I had heard noises in the room above mine; probably the hotel allowed some ladies of the street to amuse their clients there. In any case, doubtful of the place and frightened by the noise and tumult of New York, I toiled back to Newark, and engaged half a room in the home of Dr. Butcher, chiropractor, at 28 Hill Street, near the City Hall.

I shared the room with a friend whom I remember only as Monte. He was a handsome Neapolitan, with the figure of Michelangelo's *David.* There must have been a trace of the homosexual in me, for I enjoyed looking at him, especially when he undressed for a bath; all the proportions seemed perfect, the limbs well formed, the skin unblemished. I suppose I must have surprised my intimates as often by my admiration for the male body as by my claim that I had often been moved by the loveliness of a woman without feeling any desire to do more than thank her for existing.

When I reported to the principal at the Montgomery Public School, he amiably accepted my excuses for being a day late, and restored me to my desk as teacher of the graduating class. The pupils were well-behaved (it was not then customary to assault teachers or imprison principals), and I looked forward to receiving in June a license and salary as an accredited teacher. Till then, if I remember rightly, I had to continue on ten dollars per week.

That was my situation when Manuel Komroff (I am here relying on his memory) came to me with an offer from the Francisco Ferrer Association to take me as teacher of their libertarian school in New York. When Alden Freeman told me that he was helping to finance the school, and would be responsible for my proposed salary of twenty-five dollars a week, I moved toward consent; but when I went to New York to get a closer look at the "Ferrer Center" and the "Modern School," I was a bit scared.

Francisco Ferrer, as explained in the foregoing chapter, was an anarchist—"philosophical," yes, but active enough to get shot; and I was a timid socialist who would take to his heels at any prospect of violence. Though the Association had been founded by a many-shaded mixture of radicals, it was visibly dominated by anarchists who were not averse to acting. The man officially designated as "organizer" was Alexander Berkman. Another "director" was Emma Goldman, the doughtiest rebel of all; I had heard her lecture in Alden Freeman's barn; I did not relish her dogmatism, but I respected in her the energy and courage that inspired hundreds of followers with unquestioning devotion.

More to my liking were some others active in the Association. Stewart Kerr was a Scot of somber spirit, proud integrity, and rare speech; a volcano seethed under his tight-lipped self-control. — Dr. Andrews was an elderly bearded dentist, who dressed with all the care of an Englishman but made you love him even while he was drilling your tooth. — Dr. Benzion Liber lived up to his name as a lifelong devotee of Israel and liberty; he was also a good physician, whose honesty and amiability had a more curative effect than some antibiotics. He made the mistake of naming his son Amour, so that the lad grew up as an unintentional embodiment of *amour libre*—free love. — Konrad Bercovici composed music and fiction, and humorously listed himself with the great B's; he was a kind of amateur Nietzsche, mustachioed and braggadocious, scorning morals, forgetting debts, and sprouting a flowing black tie. — Manuel Komroff played the piano well, and wrote excellent books; he was one of several Ferrer members who chose their mates without benefit of clergy or magistrate, and he remained faithful to his through every shift of fortune.

Above all was Leonard Abbott. Amid a crowd of excitable spirits denouncing Western civilization and demanding a proletarian paradise, Leonard never, to our knowledge, uttered one bitter note, never hated, never advocated—though he could forgive—violence. He went his quiet way, teaching less by words than by the example of his patient understanding, tolerance, and goodwill. Through all the ups and downs of the Ferrer Association he maintained his active loyalty to the fantastic enterprise. But when I saw him shortly before his death he acknowledged sadly that his philosophical anarchism had been an impossible dream. "I'm afraid, Will," he said, "that we exaggerated the ability of men to endure freedom."

I hardly deserved the "we," either as a friendly or as an ideological embrace, for I had disappointed him and his associates by explaining to them that a considerable amount of law was necessary in any but the simplest societies, and that if they chose me to teach their school they must not expect me to transmit an anarchist philosophy. However, they were so confident in their beliefs that they pardoned my old-fashioned socialism as the expression of an immaturity that would pass when I had read Proudhon, Bakunin, Edward Carpenter, Kropotkin, and Emma Goldman's magazine, *Mother Earth.*

Almost as lovable as Leonard was the secretary of the Association, Lola Ridge. It was she who received me into her tiny office and persuaded me to burn all bridges behind me. It was rash of me, but who could resist her? She was beautiful, gentle, consumptive, frail, and wrote poetry; I was as helpless in her slender, almost transparent hands as Robert Browning lost in the eyes of ailing Elizabeth Barrett. With warm sincerity and no perceivable guile, she told me how her associates had looked into my past and had found me not only a freethinker but an enthusiastic teacher. I made my last defense, weaker than her weakness: "I'm not an anarchist; I am a socialist." "Never mind," she said; "you believe in libertarian education, don't you?" I could not deny it, though I had never thought the matter out to any clarity. Strange to say, while doubting that adults could be persuaded to civilization without the compulsion of the law and fear of the police, I responded warmly to the view that children are angels too heavenly to be spanked, or to be subjected to any discipline but example, persuasion, and reason.

And so—partly because I fell in love with Lola Ridge at first sight, but also, no doubt, because of the gap between ten dollars and twenty-five—I became, in January or February, 1912, the "sole teacher and chief learner" of the Ferrer Modern School. It was one of those days that determine many years.

All my twelve pupils were delightful, even when troublesome. I remember particularly Stuart Sanger, the eight- or nine-year-old son of Margaret Sanger; Amour, the aforesaid son of Dr. Liber; Revolte and Gorky, the bright offspring of Konrad Bercovici; Nanette, Magda, Sophie, and Ruth. They were not obliged to listen to my lessons; the obligation was on me to interest them. So I played games with them, especially those that involved some arithmetic; I showed and explained mechanisms; I told stories of great men and women, living or dead. (When Ariel and I humanized history with vignettes of its protagonists we were only continuing this trick of bringing history to life with occasional biographies.) Usually my pupils listened absorbed, and protested when I stopped.

Sometimes I led them out to Stuyvesant Park at Fifteenth Street and Second Avenue, frolicked with them, or sat on the grass amid them and told another story of someone who had made history. In 1973 the New York Public Library showed me a tattered little brochure, the first published product of my pen, entitled *The Ferrer Modern School,* published by the Ferrer Association in 1912—eight pages of idealistic ecstasy for five cents. On the cover is a faded picture of nine pupils and of "Wm. J. Durant, Principal," standing near a tree in the little park. I look like an innocent rustic youth misty with Rousseau.

A year later I wrote for the *Modern School Magazine* an article describing a day in the school:

> Have you been present some morning and seen the children greet me? They come to school before me, most of them; and when I arrive they recognize my step, and come tumbling out of the classroom to meet me on the stairs; hardly a morning but I must mount those stairs with ten or twelve incorrigible angels hanging on my neck, my arms, my coat, and even on my legs. . . .
>
> What do I teach them? Everything under the sun. . . . One of my children is beginning algebra; . . . another is flirting with improper fractions. . . . In our reading lessons we kill two birds with one stone by reading, except in the case of the youngest children, from history. We have lessons in correct English every few minutes, when mistakes are made by the children or by myself. . . . And then we have lessons in French, for the few who have asked for them; we have writing lessons, music lessons, exercises in skill, and what I call industry lessons—as when we exhausted the article on the match-making industry, in the encyclopedia which Mrs. Sanger has given the class. And of course we have our "art class": Mr. Wolff comes every Thursday afternoon and develops the frail, easily crushed artistic, creative spirit of the children. . . .
>
> So the day passes; and when the time comes to separate you hear touchingly affectionate good-byes from everybody to everybody else. One little fellow persists in coming to me before he goes and putting his hand upon my face; others expect me to put an arm around them and give them a parting paternal touch; and still others demand that they be allowed the holy rite of the kiss. . . .
>
> I thank whatever gods there be for sending me such children. Clean children, bright, reasonable, generous, affectionate; children of the sort that overwhelm the bachelor with remorse. . . . I owe an immense debt to these children; they have given me the spiritual ecstasies of fatherhood without its burdens; they have taught me a thousand wonderful lessons that only children can teach; and they have given me that for which one hungers—not admiration, but affection. . . .

There was a modest line in the pamphlet of 1912: "One thing I lack in this matter of [teaching] geography, and that is the experience of travel." I wonder did Alden Freeman see that wishful confession. In any case, just as I was finishing my first half-year at the Modern School, I received from him a letter postmarked Vienna, asking would I like to tour Europe at his expense. I need not describe my reply. On June 25, 1912, I received a cablegram: "Meet me at the Hotel Europa, St. Petersburg, July 10–12.—Alden." I withdrew from a Newark bank nearly all the three hundred dollars I had saved since leaving the seminary. I went to Arlington to seek some reconciliation with my parents before entrusting myself to the awesome Atlantic. I found my mother in the back yard, hanging up the weekly wash. I must not repeat the pages in *Transition* that tell that story; there is enough sentiment in that book to serve for this one too. On July 1 I sailed on the beautiful *Mauretania*, all wonder and hope and trepidation.

I reached St. Petersburg about July 12, and found Alden after some tribulations. I traveled with him and his friend, Dave Newman, and our guide, Piotr Ochremenko, by rail to Moscow; then to Nizhni Novgorod, and by boat down the Volga to Tsaritsyn; then to Sevastopol; then by a wild ride in a troika (a three-horse carriage) to Yalta; then by steamer to Odessa (where a policeman advised one of our party as to the best brothel); then by night boat to Constantinople. As we moved out into the Black Sea Alden inquired could I guide myself through the remainder of Europe; he and David had seen that continent plentifully, and would like to venture into Asia. He trusted me to calculate how much money I would need to see the major cities and get passage to New York. I reckoned that six hundred dollars would do; he gave it to me in gold coins, and a few days later I sailed off on my unescorted ventures. I spent an excited week in Athens. Then by boat to Brindisi; across Italy to Naples, Rome, Florence, and Venice; on to Vienna, Frankfurt, and Mainz; by steamer down the Rhine to Cologne; by train to Brussels and Antwerp; by Channel boat to Hull—the most emetic trip I have ever made. Then to London, Oxford, Stratford, Edinburgh, Dublin, Killarney, and Blarney Castle (where I was too impatient to wait my turn to kiss the stone).

Back in London I spent a morning hour with the anarchist philosopher Peter Kropotkin. He was short, stout, bald, and saintly. He asked about my plans for the afternoon; I answered that Havelock Ellis had consented to let me interrupt his studies in the psychology, history, and morality of sex. Kropotkin smiled. "So you're interested in sex?" "Of course," I replied. "Yes, naturally," he said, "but I find that those who make a special study of sex are abnormal either at the start or at the finish."

Ellis did not at first sight seem in any way unusual. His beautiful white beard could be matched in any town in England. However, there was something feminine in his hands and his movements, and his voice was as melodious and modest as a girl's. This did not deceive me as to his courage; I knew with what energy, and against what obstacles, he had pursued and published those carefully erudite researches which had shared with Freud's theories in transforming Christendom's attitude toward sex. Then his wife entered with martial stride and masculine voice, announced that she was going off to lecture, and asked Ellis could he prepare his evening meal himself. He thought he could. I inquired what her subject would be. "Homosexualism," she answered.

At my hotel I found a message from Alden inviting me to join him and David in Paris. I went, and with them I toured the châteaux and cathedrals of the Loire region in a pleasant open-air charabanc. In Paris I took a Cook tour of "Paris by night," and after an exciting evening at the Bal Tabarin I yielded to the charms of a young woman who took nothing from me but my virginity. In September I sailed for New York, and rejoiced like a poor immigrant as the Statue of Liberty came into view.

That first of my trips to Europe, though I had come to it jejune and unprepared, taught me something more than geography and coitus. In my still narrow but broadening perspective I saw my country as a novice nation, with all the vigor, swagger, and crudity of youth—incomparable in inventiveness and enterprise, greedy for the potential wealth that invited courage and industry, and naturally demanding a form of government that would interfere as little as possible with a laissez-faire, high-risk economy needed for opening up a continent; here the profit motive was unabashedly crude and unprecedentedly productive. I vaguely felt how inevitable were our new religions, our psychological crazes, our rush to adopt and exaggerate the latest ideas in morals, philosophy, and art. I could not expect to find here any profound literature or polished style—any Dostoevski or Flaubert; nor any vision of the depths and heights in painting or music or architecture—no Rembrandt or Beethoven or Notre Dame. Even in that hectic race through countries and centuries I gained a more cautious concept of the fragile complexity of human affairs, of the ambivalent roots in man's character, and of the role of human nature in building economic and political institutions, and in determining the rate and possibilities of change.

I wondered how, trailing clouds of gore and glory from Europe and the past, I could adjust myself to the unfettered spirit of the Ferrer Center, and its utopian aims and theories of education. Nevertheless, in September, 1912, I resumed my place as "principal" of the Ferrer Modern School. In the classroom I found a new pupil, sprightly in body and mind, who asked me uncomfortable questions, and became my wife.

CHAPTER III

The Lovers

1912–13

Ariel:

My new teacher looked a bit ridiculous. He was unimpressively short—
five feet five and a half inches. He had nice black hair, but his pink face
was blotched. He was timid, awkward, shy; too gentle to keep us in
order. Often, as he tried to teach, we walked or ran about the room, and
generally we did as we pleased. I led the others in making fun of him.
He singled me out as chief mischief-maker, and asked me to remain
when the class was dismissed.

"Why do you make it so hard for me?" he asked. "You know it's
awfully hard to teach without using compulsion. You're older than any
other of the pupils. Won't you help me instead of making it harder?"

I had never heard a teacher make such an appeal. I couldn't resist it.
"All right," I said; "from now on I'll be on your side. If anybody makes
trouble I'll get after him." He smiled gratefully.

I began to feel a certain bond with him now that I was his secret
weapon in keeping order. I sensed a certain courage behind his timidity.
I was struck by the simple directness with which he answered our questions. "Where do babies come from?" asked a girl pupil, who probably
knew the answer but wanted to see him squirm. "From the mother's
womb," he replied, and then explained just what and where the womb
was—which made the questioner squirm. Fortunately none of us had the
nerve to ask him what the father had to do in the affair. In any case we
felt that here was a teacher we could trust.

45

When I heard that he was going to lecture at the Center on free love, I made up my mind to get into that lecture over whatever obstacles of age or cost. One obstacle was my father, who had forbidden me to leave the apartment after dark. But on the scheduled evening I escaped his eye, ran across the street to the Center, and importuned Marie Yuster: how could I get into the lecture without paying the admission fee? She thought she could arrange it if I promised to stay quietly in a corner of the hall.

"Do you think he believes in free love?" I asked her—for those two words seemed delightful.

She did not know, but she suggested, with mischief in her eyes, "Why don't you put the question to him yourself? He's upstairs."

I found him preparing his lecture. I broke in upon him with outlandish suddenness: "Would you live in free love?"

He blushed; a hurried word from him might lead this child of fourteen into surrendering herself to the first itching male. He dodged. "I'll answer you when you're three months older. Now I must hurry down to my lecture."

I followed him to the lecture room, and drank in his discourse without understanding more than half of it. If I remember rightly, he presented the arguments for and against free love, and then rejected it as giving too much advantage to the male; reproduction laid so many burdens upon the woman that she should receive some assurance of protection before risking pregnancy or disease. Many of his listeners were living in free love at the time, and neither the men nor the women seemed to relish his views. Already the divergence was widening between Will's moral conservatism and the ethical radicalism prevailing at the Ferrer Center.

Day after day, as a pupil in the school, I came to admire this thoughtful rebel, who seemed more a poet than a teacher. I noticed so many instances of his patience, kindness, and sensitivity that I, who had long resented the rough men of our neighborhood, warmed to him with every new experience until, not quite knowing it, I was in love. All the hidden forces of youth and growth coursed in my excited blood.

I had no sense of decorum. Once, taking advantage of a lively moment of play in the yard, I tried to embrace him. He reproved me. I brooded for a day, and then wrote him a letter addressed to his home in Newark. I kept his reply. It is dated January 15, 1913.

> I am answering your letter at once. . . .
> It is beautiful of you to feel for me as you do. I am so far from thinking it—as you thought I would think it—"a little matter," that I am deeply grateful for receiving such affection. I have hungered for affection; since I was compelled to leave mother and sisters, a year ago this week, because of my socialism and atheism, I have met with too much admiration, but too little affection. Whether your affection will last long is doubtful; but while it lasts I am grateful for it.

Our first love affairs are almost always with persons much older than ourselves. When I was fourteen I raved over a woman of twenty-eight. Most girls and boys go through such experiences; and these feelings almost always pass away with the lapse of a few months' time. . . . I think we should let time enlighten us; perhaps, four months from now, we shall know each other better, and I shall no longer appear lovable to you. . . .

So for four months let us study each other. Meanwhile try to remember that I am in rather a difficult situation because I am defending you against everybody; remember that every time you try to kiss or embrace me you will arouse a world of talk endangering the very existence of the school. . . .

You have been very unhappy of late; so many different people have turned against you despite the things you did for them. I want you to be happy now, caring nothing about these others who do not understand you. Those who understand you know your worth, and think the world of you.

Sincerely,
WILLIAM

Without this letter uncomfortably facing me I should hardly believe now that I was such a ninny then. But the letter did not hide from me the indication that Will was beginning to return my love. After all, he craved affection, and I offered it. He longed for some brightness to cheer a life that had been saddened by his loss of faith and family. I thought he was still an innocent youth, but surely he must have felt the rising warmth of those desires that had been so long suppressed by the moral echoes of his piety. And here I was, close at hand, crazy with life and energy, and physically in full bloom.

Five weeks after that letter his resistance had quite broken down. He took me for private walks in Central Park, and ventured upon an occasional kiss. One day, as we sat on the grass below a secluded tree in Bronx Park, he stooped so low—or rose to such courage—as to kiss my unresisting breasts. He still remembers that day—February 22, 1913—and celebrates it with ritual repetition.

These explorative trips were made possible by my having gone to live with my indulgent mother, who had trysts of her own. One Sunday, after a strenuous morning selling papers, Mother and I were resting in bed in her apartment, when her brother Maurice entered. Seeing my best clothes laid out on a chair, he asked me, "Where are you going?" I answered, "I have an appointment to meet my teacher." He turned angrily to my mother. "Etta, you must stop this, or your headstrong child will ruin herself. We must break it up before it is too late. Before you leave you must lock up her clothes." Mother refused to do this, but Maurice gathered up my dress, shoes, and stockings, locked them in a closet, and put the key into his pocket. I cried out in anger and grief; I begged him to relent; I protested that Will was a gentleman, who would do me no harm; but my uncle merely smiled in unrelenting triumph. Meanwhile my mother, murmuring a sad apology to me, left for her own rendezvous.

Maurice remained, and tried to soothe me. "Foolish child, don't be unhappy. It is for your own good that I have stopped you from keeping this appointment. Your teacher is not one of our people. He would seduce you and leave you." Then, as if proposing to take my education into his own hands, he jumped into bed beside me. I rolled myself up in the blanket, and moved as far as possible away from him. He came closer, and tried to embrace me. I stepped over him to the floor, still holding the blanket around me. He rose, smoothed his clothing, brushed his hair, and left—taking the closet key with him.

Desperate, I donned my mother's garments—a long green dress trailing to the ground but not always concealing her high-heel shoes—and went out to keep my appointment with Will. He was shocked by my appearance. "What whim is this?" he asked. "I've waited an hour for you, and now you show up like this. Do you think it's Halloween?" I told him of my perils and stratagem, and of my hard choice between disappointing him and anticipating Halloween. He embraced me. "I must soon go to your mother," he said, "and explain matters to her." We parted; I returned miserable to my bed.

Some time later I brought him to my mother. He assured her that he would not injure me in any way, and begged her to trust him. His innocent face and diffident tone must have appealed to her. She agreed to rely upon his word of honor, and she let him kiss her as his substitute for swearing on the Bible.

Shortly thereafter word was brought to me that my father positively forbade me to see my teacher outside of school; to which was added a warning from my brothers and sisters that Will would forfeit his life if he were caught alone with me. Uncle Maurice returned the closet key, but renewed his remonstrances. Had I forgotten the centuries during which Christians had persecuted, humiliated, and killed Jews?—and would I now offer myself to an uncircumcised heathen? Will thought that he could quiet this storm with a specimen of his English style. I have before me a letter which he sent to my father on March 15, 1913, and which was scornfully turned over to me without a reply:

DEAR SIR:

Will you permit me a few words about Ariel?

She came to me a few months ago and told me that she loved me. I admired her for her frankness, but I told her that I did not love her, and that I was too old (I am almost twice as old as she is) to have any more "love affairs." I knew that she was passing through a period—the age of puberty—at which it is customary for girls to "fall in love," usually with men much older than themselves, and I expected the matter to pass over in a month or so. But Ariel came to me a month later and told me that she loved me more than ever. I told her that her love for me would die out in another month; but that month and another went by, and today Ariel seems to love me more strongly than before. Meanwhile my own affection for her has increased daily; I can't help admiring her for her courage, her honesty, her independence of character, and for a hundred other beautiful traits. Several persons have said of her that she was the kindest and most generous girl they had ever met. All the time she has been in our school she has spent in helping me or in doing little kindnesses to the children entrusted to my care. Her affection for you is beautiful; she says that the one thing that keeps her from being very happy is that you have a bad opinion of me.

Now I fear that you have been worried of late by my relations with Ariel; and I am writing this to try to make you understand that you have no reason to worry. Remember that I am twenty-seven and that she is only fourteen. As she comes to know a greater variety of young men her fancy will change; and as she comes to know me better she will see in me so many things not to her liking that her affection will soon pass to another. Ariel is so affectionate a girl that she will almost certainly always be in love with somebody; and you are perhaps lucky that she has hit upon a man who knows enough to appreciate her affection. Indeed, I feel deeply honored by it; and I think so much of Ariel that if, when she has grown older and wiser, and knows her mind better, she should still care for me as she seems to do now, I should be very happy . . . [some words faded out] giving her a comfortable little home. But I know too much of human nature to expect that I shall have that privilege; it will not be long, I am afraid, before Ariel will give to someone else the place that I now hold in her affections.

Meanwhile I ask you to believe that I am a gentleman, and that I should be the last man in the world to take advantage in any way of Ariel's love. I want you to trust me, and to feel that I love her as a brother whose only desire is to keep her from bad influences, help her in her mental and physical development, and make her as happy as I can.

Sincerely yours,
WILLIAM J. DURANT

Will now smiles at this jejune letter, at his assumption that he had the wisdom of a philosopher and the purity of a saint. In any case, he wrote to me, only a day later, a letter which abandoned all pretense of a merely fraternal affection.

28 Hill Street,
Newark, N. J.
March 16, 1913

MY DEAR, SWEET, TERRIBLE BELOVED:

Do you remember in [Upton Sinclair's] *Love's Pilgrimage*, the letters of Thyrsis to Corydon? Hard letters, weren't they, love—full of the determination that in this one case love should not be blind. I want to write you such a letter, dear, full of little hard things that I should not have the courage to speak to you. I love you so much. A lover never thinks clearly in the presence of his beloved! . . . [There follows a paragraph about some tiff now quite unintelligible.]

I have worked hard today, traveling far out to Allentown and lecturing; but I have made the work easier by remembering that now it is for you, and not only for me, that I am working.

No more classroom kisses, dear; we must kiss outside when not too many of the world are looking. Love thrives on difficulties.

I love you, dear, for what you are and for what you are going to be,—my wild, sweet, radiantly healthy, divinely terrible, Walt Whitman girl!

WILL

That night I could not sleep, tossing about in wonderment, happiness, and doubt. I felt a new source and surge of life in me, a new freedom. I need no longer fear my father, my sisters, or my brothers; I could face them confidently now that I knew I was loved such as I was, and for myself alone. But what miracle was this, that had brought this lovable man, so recently a Catholic seminarian, across all barriers of time and creed, to offer his love to a penniless Jewish girl just entering her teens? How had two such diverse, even hostile, lines of development come through a thousand accidents to meet in so strange a school and love? But I did not feel anything wrong in it, and I would have cried out in protest at any suggestion that all that had happened was that a sexually starved man had met a nubile girl.

What did he see in me? Was it that I was so different?—so intellectually innocent, and so heedlessly passionate?

Will:

Now I will tell you, Ariel. I had been buried in books, and you came to me as the breath of life. I looked at my bachelor's room in Newark, and winced at the thought that it could be the shape of all my years. I admired Spinoza, but I pitied his solitude. I saw you play with boys or girls indifferently, jumping, running, skipping rope, dancing, and all with a wild abandon that accepted your instincts without questioning. I loved your round arms, your shapely legs, your disheveled hair, your laughing eyes, your leaping breasts. I loved your agile mind, so eager to grow and learn and understand. I compared you with Shelley's wild west wind, "tameless and swift and proud." And I told you some of this in the poem that I dedicated to you on the first Christmas after our marriage. I may have outgrown that poetry, but not any of its sentiments.

> *O Love with the wildness of winter,*
> *O Love with the summer's fire,*
> *O Love with the tender eyes gleaming,*
> *O heart of my heart's desire!*

Lonely my world when you came, Love,
   Out of the unforeseen;
Broken my heart when you healed it,
   Smiling your smile serene.

Dreams I had dreamed of your kind, Love,
   Dreams that I thought untrue;
Visioned you, limned you, unthinking
   My dreams were but visions of you.

Out of the pages of Walt,
   "Tenderest lover" of all,
Out of the Pheidian marble,
   Sweetness and strength withal.

Dreams give no beauty so rich, Love,
   Marble no graces so fair,
Body ineffably wondrous,
   Soul with the freshness so rare!

O Love with the wildness of winter,
   O Love with the summer's fire,
O Love with the tender eyes gleaming,
   O heart of my heart's desire!

Ariel:

Having discovered that he was playing Abélard to my Héloïse, Will decided that the proprieties required him to resign. At some unstated date in March, 1913, he sent the following letter to Leonard Abbott, his nearest friend on the board of directors of the Ferrer Association. He gave me the rough draft of his letter, unsigned; of this draft the following is a faithful copy of the now relevant parts:

DEAR LEONARD:

   I shall not come to the meeting of the Ferrer School Board. I have things to say which I can put more coherently in writing than in fragmentary talk; I have other things to say which will seem to show such conceit that you will understand why I prefer to write them. . . .

   Until a few weeks ago I posed to myself as a student of life and thought, dedicated to Truth with a capital T, and ready to pursue Truth with ascetic and celibate devotion. That I should ever again love a woman, or that I should think of fettering the wings of my aspiration with the holy bonds of matrimony, seemed to me as remotely possible as that I should ever return to the infallible Church. . . . The Ferrer Association has a right to know that the opinions I expressed in a letter to its secretary some six weeks ago are not my opinions now. I said in that letter that my feelings for Ariel were those of fatherly or brotherly interest; I say now that I love the girl. . . .

I am aware of the face absurdities of the matter, and I have made Ariel understand that, love her as I do, I do not expect her love for me to survive her greater knowledge of me and her wider acquaintance with others; and that I should not think of living with her, or having intercourse with her, till our affections have proved themselves by the test of four years' waiting. Meanwhile I shall remember that the school is not a trysting place; but meanwhile too I must ask the forbearance of what friends I may have in the Association. I trust that they forbear believing that the only motive that a man of my age can have in professing love for a girl of Ariel's age is the desire of sexual intercourse; I protest that such an assumption would do me wrong, and would do Ariel wrong. That these and other imputations will be made I am—sentimental as I may appear—too disillusioned a man to doubt. But the inevitable has lost its power to make me unhappy, and I put up with these little things as small price to pay for this second springtime of my soul. Rather I chant Te Deums hourly, and batter heaven with Magnificats.

I ask forbearance in another matter. I have ambitions which even my friends will think the height of absurdity and conceit; I aspire to do for my generation what Spencer did for his; I desire to synthesize the best thought of my time in biology, sociology, psychology, and ethics. I make rather a large order on myself, but the task calls not for genius so much as for understanding. I may need fifteen years more of study before I begin to write; but I shall need all my time in those fifteen years. . . .

I propose to leave the school about the middle of May. . . . I hope that in taking myself away from the work of teacher I shall not be compelled to discontinue the other work I have done. I shall be glad to lecture for the Association—particularly on the subject of education—as long as I can draw a sufficient audience; and always without fee. . . . I shall use what influence I have with Mr. Freeman to secure his continued support of the school.

The discovery that my teacher had become my lover brought me a strange mixture of happiness and doubt. I did not take very much to heart those words about "four years' waiting." But I asked myself was I (not yet fifteen) ready for marriage, or for the sexual experiences that seemed imminent? What could I bring to Will except my body and my eager but ill-furnished mind? I was penniless, and depended upon my mother for shelter, food, and clothing.

I am conscience-stricken, at this late date, when I recall how hard she worked. In that year 1913 she sold her cherished diamond ring, and with the proceeds and her savings she bought a newsstand at Third Avenue and Forty-second Street. There, morning after morning, in heat or cold, rain or snow, she took in a penny for every paper she sold, and kept her feet from freezing by feeding coke into a tiny stove. Harry came to relieve her every morning, but he gave away too many magazines to the girls who smiled at him, and he spent his savings in uninspired bets on uninspired horses. Perhaps I should have gone to work every day instead of only on Sundays.

Heretofore I had given myself almost entirely to physical living, to joy in the play of arms and legs; now a new anxiety agitated me—the desire to grow in knowledge and understanding. Will overflowed with talk about Whitman, Keats, Shelley, and Shakespeare—and I had never read a word of them, though I knew some writings of Gorky and Tolstoi. He brought me books, and pointed out the passages that especially deserved my attention. I took readily enough to Whitman; his joyous welcome to the "body electric" and the "open road" merged with my mood, though some of his catalogues wearied me. I played truant from these books now and then, but I made every effort to learn.

Will met me halfway by joining in my passion for physical sports. I was delighted when he proposed that I should borrow a bicycle and pedal beside him down to the Twenty-third Street Ferry, and then across the Jersey Meadows to Singac; there he could use a friend's canoe, and we would exchange vows while paddling leisurely on the Passaic River, like Thoreau on Walden Pond. But the letter which contained this invitation added that that trip must wait a few days till he recovered from a cold. He kept my reply, dated May 1, 1913; I have it before me now, and I expose to a brief posterity my cry of happy, childish self-surrender:

> DEAREST:
> I love the part of the bicycle and the canoe. Please get better and hurry in doing so, because I am not satisfied in writing to you and getting an answer. I must see your dear face and hear those wonderful lips of yours, that give out all the knowledge your brain takes in, talk to me. . . . We move today to 103 East 111th St. Write to me every day, for every word is life to my dying heart. . . . Dear boy, my life is turning towards you, I can only now feel what you are to me, and how much I love you. . . .

Summer came, and Will ended his teaching at the Ferrer School. An invitation came to him to visit his old friend Dave Howatt in Leominster, Mass. He wanted to go, but refused to leave me. He proposed that I should accompany him, and I readily agreed. I knew nothing then, and perhaps Will had forgotten, about the Mann Act by which Congress (1910) had made it a federal offense to take a woman across a state border "for immoral purposes." In any case we sailed off on a steamer to Boston. No one will believe me when I say that Will went no further on that trip than some warm embraces; the Marquis of Queensberry rules were carefully observed. Dave Howatt took our arrival philosophically, and smiled indulgently when Will assured him that I was still intact.

When we returned to New York Will saddened me by arranging to bicycle all the way to Albany (150 miles), alone. Later he confessed that he had wanted a week in which to think, in quiet solitude, just what our relationship should be in the coming years. He had decided to spend four years in graduate studies at Columbia University; should he complete those years before venturing on marriage? He has told, in *Transition*, how he pedaled his way to Albany, climbing so many hills that he had no time to think of me; how, at Albany, he exchanged his bicycle for a canoe; how he paddled his way 150 miles down the Hudson, facing so many buffets from the waves made by steamboats and winds that he had no time to weigh all the pros and cons of marriage. In any case, he arrived in a storm, lodged his canoe at 186th Street on the Hudson, and came to me so exhausted that he collapsed at my feet with his head on my knees, and fell asleep. When he awoke we quietly assumed that we were pledged to each other forever.

In September, 1913, I resumed attendance at the Ferrer School. Our former teacher, Cora Bennett Stevenson, again took charge, and I was happy with her, as you can see from the picture taken of the class at that time; I am the plump lass standing behind the teacher, with a white ribbon in her hair and a black ribbon on her blouse. In the evenings, sometimes with Will, I attended lectures, art school, or other affairs at the Ferrer Center.

About the same time Will began his graduate work at Columbia. Alden Freeman, who had paid Will's salary of twenty-five dollars a week at the Ferrer School, did not abandon him when he resigned; he offered to pay Will seventy-five dollars a month toward his tuition costs at Columbia. With this, and some one hundred dollars a month earned by lectures, Will felt that he could now take care of a wife. So, on October 31, 1913, we sallied down to the New York City Hall, accompanied by my mother and Frank Haughwout, associate professor at Columbia. I must not repeat the jolly and scandalous story that Will told in *Transition* (pages 266–71)—how I carried my roller skates into the matrimonial sanctum of the Board of Aldermen, and how he, at the critical moment, found himself without a ring to put upon my finger.

Nevertheless, I came out radiant with happiness. I had no clear conception of the responsibilities I had undertaken. Gaily I proposed, almost in sight of City Hall, to teach my husband how to roller-skate. He tried, floundered from one side to another, fell on his rear, and gave it up as much harder than Plato. We spent our wedding night in my mother's apartment, having as yet no rooms of our own. Everything went well until Will took me into his bed and asked for his marital rights. I was not quite prepared for this, and raised objections, until my mother, hearing my protests, came to us and assured me, "It's all right, my child; don't be afraid." I could never resist my mother.

CHAPTER IV

The Young Sophist

1913–16

Ariel:

Late in 1913 Will and I, with my mother and my eleven-year-old brother Michael, moved to a four-room apartment at 506 West 136th Street, near Amsterdam Avenue. Mother helped us by paying half the rent, which amounted, in those halcyon days of the dollar, to twenty-five dollars per month. Will allowed me seven dollars per week to feed him, myself, and Michael (Mother ate outside). From that sum I found it possible to prepare meals of dark bread, cheese, fruit, rice, and thick vegetable soup with enough beans and other proteins in it to sustain us; Will belonged to what H. G. Wells, disliking Shaw, called "those windy vegetarians." Will harks back to that soup now with idealizing memory, and mourns that I can't seem to duplicate it today. However, I sneaked a chicken into the soup occasionally—which was probably what gave it the flavor that he liked so much.

Our marriage began amid an economic depression that continued into 1914. It was in that winter of hunger and discontent that Frank Tannenbaum (a frequent visitor at the Ferrer Center) led a group of the unemployed on a march to the Church of St. Alphonsus, on Fifth Avenue, where they demanded food and shelter. In the excitement of those days Will sent to the New York *Call*, organ of the Socialist Party, a fiery letter which he insists on my recording here, though he regrets it as the most foolish thing he ever wrote:

> A boy striker dead, two strikers dying, fifty-six strikers injured—one day's toll paid by the workers in the Bayonne strike.

55

If you are a worker and have the soul of a worker, you can see that dead boy lying in his own blood, those dying men being borne away by their brothers in the face of the fire of hired thugs. "The roof leaks with the blood of Ludlow," said Robert Minor about the war lord's mansion; you know that the whole edifice of capitalism, the world over, leaks and grows rotten with the blood of the workers.

Suddenly you grow ashamed of your safety, your own comfort, such as it may be; you long to throw yourself into the class war at the point where the fighting is hottest; you throw prudence—the old man's cowardice—to the winds and—

And you are told, "Wait—be calm; when November comes you can vote."

Perhaps—if you take care not to be among the workers slain before November comes! Five years ago we believed in waiting; we thought discretion the only part of valor; we thought that if we behaved ourselves, if we adhered virtuously to the ethics laid down for us by our masters, we should be rewarded suddenly by the capitulation of the enemy and the inauguration of the millennium. And so we turned the other cheek.

"Life is sacred," you were told; and that same day the war lord's gunmen, pitilessly and without cause, killed sixteen women and children. "Violence and sabotage degenerates the workers," one of your leaders told you; and you seemed to believe him, though you must have known in your heart that violence against the suppression of human rights is an act of highest self-sacrifice, of noblest idealism. "Think more and act less," you were admonished; and you reflected so long that you never acted at all. "Let us rely on the law," your lawyers told you; and the same day John Lawson was sentenced for life. "Violence is immoral," you heard it said, even by those whom you had trusted to lead you well; and that same day strikes were being put down by violence, government tyranny was being upheld by violence, churches were being closed to hungry and sleepless poor by violence, and Police Commissioner Woods was saying that he could not rid New York City of gangs because the politicians needed them for election day!

Perhaps it is time to reconsider all this.

Men are dying in Bayonne. Must we wait till November to help them, to protect them?

I am a timid man, much given to counsel against violence except as a last resort. I know that violence itself is not a solution, but only a voice crying out to heaven for a solution. And I hope that the Battle of Bayonne (as perhaps our children will call it) can be won without further shedding of blood on either side. But I say now that we should go to Bayonne, line up with the strikers, and fight by their side for their right to picketing and public assembly; that we should organize ourselves at once to parade the streets of Bayonne in all our strength of numbers; that if violence is used upon us we should arm ourselves, law or no law, to resist it; and that, if these means fail us, if more murderers shall be found in the ranks of pelf than victims for them in the ranks of labor, then we must put aside all Utopian nonsense about non-resistance and legality, and, resorting to the only revolutionary argument which the war lord can understand, let him feel the persuasive caress of lyddite.

For that is what we have come to. There is no longer any other cheek to turn.

WILL DURANT

We date that letter uncertainly to 1914. Will has cooled down considerably since then. Today (May 10, 1969) he is preparing a commencement address to be given at Akron University on June 15; in it he advises the rebellious students to avoid violence as inviting superior violence, leading to a police state and forfeiting all the advances made by democracy. And I agree with him. So much can fifty-five years and a rising income do to our philosophies.

I believe that it was in that bitter year 1914 that Caron, Hansen, and Berg demolished the fourth (?) floor of an apartment house on Lexington Avenue by accidentally dropping a bomb that they had prepared for the home of John D. Rockefeller in Pocontico Hills. Will, writing *Transition* as a novel and not (as the publishers wrongly called it) an autobiography, pictured his fictitious hero, John Lemaire, as present at the explosion. Actually Will and I were with Leonard Abbott at the home of J. William Lloyd in Westfield, New Jersey, when a tattered and frightened man came to Abbott, saying that he had been near death in the explosion, had had no share in preparing the bomb, but now feared that the police would arrest him as an accomplice. Leonard hid him, and when the refugee felt safe he told us the rest of the story. Fourteen years later Will made the last meeting of the conspirators the *mise-en-scène* for a discussion of anarchism.

He was still an ardent socialist, but philosophy was beginning to win his predominant attention. In the fall of 1913 he organized a "Philosophy Club" at the Ferrer Center. He was already presenting Spinoza as his philosophical favorite, for I find in an old magazine a poem by Adolf Wolff—painter, poet, and sculptor:

On a Talk on Spinoza

Durant spoke of Spinoza yesterday
And I sat list'ning, feeling, meditating.
And now and ever afterwards will feel
And live and think more deeply than before,
For having heard Durant speak on Spinoza.

Spinoza! what a mighty, mighty name!
All Alexanders, Caesars and Napoleons—
Mere specks of dust upon a polished lens,
Compared to this poor polisher of lenses.
He polished lenses for myopic eyes;

57

The World's myopic eyes have need of them—
And long will need them—poor, myopic world.

My own sight seems improved since I heard
Durant speak of Spinoza yesterday.

Strange to say, Will found his first substantial audience for philosophy in a Presbyterian church at Fourteenth Street and Second Avenue, in the heart of New York's East Side. As a result of immigration, that church had lost nearly all its Presbyterian congregation, and found itself surrounded by a sea of Jews, Poles, and Italians. About 1910 Dr. Charles Stelzle persuaded the Presbyterian Board of Home Missions that instead of abandoning the stately old edifice they should allow him to make it a community church, theoretically dedicated to converting the immigrants to Presbyterian Christianity, but actually serving as a social and educational center for the pullulating neighborhood. Dr. Stelzle was succeeded (1912) in this generous enterprise by Jonathan C. Day, whose enthusiasm for reform later made him commissioner of markets in the mayoralty (1918–25) of John Hylan. Dr. Day cast about for speakers who could make themselves intelligible to audiences with little formal education. By one of those fortunate chances that have persistently favored our lives, he mentioned this need to Will's friend Tim Cairns, who, of course, recommended Will.

So, in the fall of 1913, Jonathan Day, tall, handsome, and reckless, mounted the four flights to our apartment in 136th Street, took one look at Will, fell for his innocent eyes, and invited him to deliver a lecture at Labor Temple. Will proposed Spinoza as a subject; luckily the good doctor knew little of Spinoza, and agreed; and late in 1913 Will made his debut before an audience of some five hundred new Americans plus a handful of surviving Presbyterian church members. Dr. Day escorted him to the lectern, introduced him, and then took a seat behind him.

When Will had finished, a man in a front row rose and protested to Dr. Day, "What do you mean by letting this young radical preach an anti-Christian philosophy in this Christian church?" Dr. Day replied, in substance, that as long as he remained in charge of Labor Temple it would be open for the study of any philosophy that did not preach violence against the government of the United States. (Again fortune was with us: he had not read Will's letter on the Bayonne strike.) Then he turned to Will and—taking care to be heard by all—invited him to return to Labor Temple in the following season for a course of twelve lectures. I still have the simple leaflet announcing those lectures for Sundays at 5 P.M. from January 3 to March 21, 1914, on the history of philosophy from Socrates to Bergson.

So began his career at Labor Temple. For thirty or forty Sundays and Wednesdays, each year from the fall of 1914 to February, 1927, he lectured there to audiences varying in number from four hundred to seven hundred, and on almost every major subject: forty lectures on biology, forty on psychology, forty on the history of art, forty on music in the nineteenth century, forty on the history of science, forty on sociology, and probably 160 on political and economic history. I wondered how he could become so quickly an expert (or so it seemed to us) in so many fields; he confessed the absurdity, and pictured himself (like the tortoise pursued by Achilles and never caught) as keeping just a day ahead of his audience. I hardly realized then how wide, persistent, and careful had been his reading, and how zealously he had made and kept notes. Every week he brought home an armful of books from libraries; every day he studied, classified his gleanings, and typed mnemonic aids for his lectures. Because his audience was mostly composed of men and women who had never gone beyond elementary schooling, he was compelled to be clear, to humanize his material with vignettes of creative personalities, and to bring it into some connection with current affairs; here was the happy compulsion that forged the order and clarity of his later exposition and style.

I tried, so far as my housework allowed, to keep up with him in his studies, but I always lagged behind. At his Labor Temple lectures, except when I was pregnant, I was an attentive and admiring listener; there I received a part of my education. I grew with him as a student while he grew as a teacher.

Several members of those audiences developed a personal fondness for Will and, in some measure, for me; and often, after a lecture, they would lure us to coffee and knishes or strudels at the Café Royal at Twelfth Street and Second Avenue, or to more elegant and less savory dishes at Lüchow's Restaurant on East Fourteenth Street. To this day some of these Knights Templar, as we called them, stop us on the streets of Los Angeles and reveal themselves, changed like us by time, as former devotees of Labor Temple, and many recall gratefully the informal education they received there from Will as a "one-man university."

There were other popular teachers on the East Side in those hopeful days, and sometimes we went to hear them. We liked the learned and humanistic discourses of Everett Dean Martin at Cooper Union, and the stoutly socialistic lectures of Scott Nearing at the Rand School. Max Eastman we knew chiefly through his brilliant editorship of *The Masses* and *The Liberator*; occasionally we heard him speak; Will never quite forgave him for being so handsome. Add to these eloquent men the Yiddish lecturers who were the idols of my mother, and you get some echo of the radical oratory that almost set lower New York on fire in the second decade of this century. When I think of them, and particularly of Will, I am reminded of the Sophists who traveled through Greece in the years before Socrates, criticizing the state of the nation, the absurdities of supernatural belief, and the general unreasonableness of men.

We were still friends with the less dogmatic of the anarchists at the

Ferrer Center, especially with Leonard Abbott, Arthur Samuels, Manuel Komroff, and Anton Rovinsky. To their little magazine, *The Modern School*, sometime in 1914, Will contributed an essay on the war that had just begun in Europe; the United States, he urged, should not allow itself to be drawn into it by racial sympathies. I suspect that Leonard, still cherishing his memories of England, was not resigned to seeing England swamped by German power. Certainly he was disappointed with a pamphlet, *Socialism and Anarchism*, authored by Will, and published by Albert and Charles Boni in 1914 at the price of fifteen cents. The aim of all reforms, Will argued, should be socialism—governmental control of all major industries; and this, of course, would require a powerful, not a Jeffersonian, state, much less an anarchist utopia.

Early in the summer of 1914 my mother received an angry letter from a Russian relative whom all my forebears revered—Moishe Lebe Kaufman. Apparently my father had informed him of the family breakup, and of my marriage to a Christian. The letter ran:

> DEAR ETTA:
> What is this I hear, that you have given one of your daughters to a Godforsaken Gentile? You cannot any longer be the beautiful and innocent young mother I loved to see as all goodness and devotion. Is it America, that Godless country, that has so changed you that you no longer love Joseph or protect your children? I cannot believe that it is about you that I hear these heartbreaking stories. Write to me and tell me what has happened.
>
> Your devoted
> MOISHE LEBE

That letter made my mother frantic with misery. She could not bear that the good Moishe Lebe should think ill of her. She resolved, cost what it might, to go back to Russia and tell him her side of the story. We tried every argument to dissuade her; all the children pled with her, fearing that if she went we would never see her again. She insisted, and I gave her half my savings to help pay her expenses. So she departed, and Michael, who had lived with us, went back to his father. Soon after her arrival in Proskurov Germany declared war on Russia (August 1, 1914), and my mother found herself practically a prisoner in the Ukraine.

We had now to pay all the rent on our apartment. Will's future at Labor Temple was uncertain, for several attempts were made, by conscientious Presbyterians, to have him dismissed from his incongruous pulpit. He received twenty-five dollars for each of his lectures there in 1914, and earned precarious increment with other talks. We began to look about for smaller and less expensive quarters. We remembered a bungalow that we had seen in New Dorp, Staten Island, a stone's throw from the sea; we heard that it could be had for nine hundred dollars.

We went down to examine it. It had a small screened porch, with winter remnants of a morning-glory vine; only two rooms, heated by a coal stove in the kitchen; a little back yard with a coal bin; half a lot of mud and dirt. We had six hundred dollars available after a year of stinting and saving; we borrowed three hundred from Ed White, a Philadelphia chemist whom Will had met on the *Mauretania* in 1912; Ed would charge no interest, and I took him to my heart. He remained, till his recent death, our oldest friend, in whom—and his vivacious wife Lena—we have never been able to find a fault. Will must be thinking of them, and others like them, when he says that he has met so many good people that he has almost lost his faith in the wickedness of mankind.

So, on a cold morning in December, 1914, we put all our belongings on a small truck pulled by one horse; we sat on the front seat beside the driver as we ambled from 136th Street to South Ferry; then over the harbor to Staten Island, and seventeen miles more to our hermitage. Our feet froze on the way, but we were young and gay, and knew that utopia would come soon. We helped the driver to carry in our furniture. Will made a fire in the little stove, I put together an impromptu meal, and we young socialists went to bed proud that we were now property owners.

Three or four days a week—sometimes through snow as high as his knees—Will walked the mile to the railway station, and took train, ferry, and subway to 116th Street and Columbia University. Occasionally he would bring back with him some of his biology and tennis friends— Hermann Muller, James (?) Sturtevant, Calvin Bridges; their jolly companionship kept us warm, and they helped me cook the meal and wash the dishes. Otherwise winter was quite an ordeal. Cold winds and the roar and hiss of the irreconcilable sea came through a hundred cracks of our cottage night and day. Sometimes we had to thaw out the sheets before getting into bed. We interpreted the equality of the sexes so literally that I had to take turns getting up first in the morning and restoring the banked fire in the stove.

We tried to make an adventure of the winter, and even to challenge it with boastful daring. I can't recall, but I suspect that it was Will who, one afternoon during a January thaw, proposed that we should find out how the North Atlantic feels in winter. We hurried to the beach, threw off all our clothing (nobody else being in sight), and ventured, inch by inch, into the water, rubbing ourselves madly, and shouting to keep up our spirits. Then we struck out, and swam some twenty yards. The cold water pricked our flesh as with a thousand needles. Emerging, we raced naked up and down the beach, slapping each other vigorously till our shocked blood circulated properly again. When we returned to sanity we found a solitary spectator—an old woman looking at us with a frown that had all the Puritan heritage in it.

In the spring, tempting fate a hundred times, we reclaimed the canoe that Will had left at 186th Street; we paddled it down the Hudson and the East River, dodging a dozen ferries, climbing and descending the waves they made, and under the bridges and across the harbor to New Dorp Beach. In the summer we had plenty of company, for we provided access to the beach and a tennis court. My sister Flora stayed with us for a time; and (perhaps because she was now full grown in her dark beauty) Robert Minor came to spend a week with us during his campaign against the capitalist system. I think he was the greatest cartoonist of his generation. He had made his mark with his powerful, heavy-figured, heavy-inked drawings for the New York *World*. Protests against his merciless caricatures of "malefactors of great wealth" poured into the offices of that enterprising journal; finally the editor asked Robert to depart. He transferred his podium to the socialist New York *Call*, and dealt sledgehammer blows with his brush and pen. Yet he was himself as gentle a person as I have ever known. Tall, strong, balding but still handsome, he broke as many girlish hearts as moneyed heads. I can still picture him sitting at his drawing board in our kitchen, delivering his message with a few sure, powerful lines and some cutting captions. He relaxed by courting Flora, but she was frightened by his long, strong arms, which could have crushed her with a hug; and Robert went off after other prey.

Sometimes I joined Will in social gatherings at Columbia. Usually I was poorly dressed, and uncomfortable in the presence of those alert graduate students and their well-educated girl friends. When we returned from such affairs Will would comfort me with assurances that I had enough vitality to overcome all handicaps, and that my eagerness to improve myself would soon make up for my lack of formal schooling. He had already gathered some two hundred books, including nearly all the classics of ancient and modern literature. I attacked them resolutely on my days of solitude; and when my housework allowed me I would sit near him reading, while he pored over tomes on biology, psychology, philosophy, and history, or made meticulous drawings of biological specimens (I still have those sheets), or prepared his next lecture for Labor Temple. Ed White came up now and then from Philadelphia, and sat beside me, patiently correcting my mispronunciations, as we read together a play of Shakespeare. I worked my way through Romain Rolland's *Jean Christophe*, Pater's *The Renaissance*, and Royce's *The Spirit of Modern Philosophy*. I tried Spinoza's *Ethics*, but it was too much for me. I liked better Nietzsche's *Thus Spake Zarathustra*, which finished my belief in the God of my childhood. I picked up morsels of Dante, Cervantes, and Goethe. But I am proud to say that I was an hour or two ahead of Will in discovering Dostoevski. One summer day in 1915, as we sat on the porch of our cottage, Will suddenly exclaimed, "I'm reading the greatest novel ever written." "What is it?" I asked. "*Crime and Punish-*

ment." "But," I retorted, confidently, *"I* am reading the greatest novel ever written." "What is that?" *"The Brothers Karamazov."* I think I won that deal.

In retrospect it seems that we were happy in that far-out-of-the-way Eskimo retreat. A picture taken of us in 1915 shows no sign of misery, though it surprises me by proving that Will had already grown a beard— perhaps through unwillingness to shave himself in the cold mornings of those New Dorp winters. But looking back now I wonder that Will, usu- ally considerate, could leave me alone through so many bitter days, with only one neighbor in the street—an old Victorian lady who never seemed to make up her mind whether I was a legal wife or a tramp who had found a winter's lodging with a fool. In any case I soon came to dread those occasions when Will would go off to Columbia, or to lecture in Brooklyn or the Bronx, or Philadelphia or Bethlehem, Pennsylvania. On such days I hardly dared move more than a few feet from the stove. I missed the wild freedom of Manhattan streets, and the exciting contacts and events at the Ferrer Center.

After reading half a hundred books I was ripe for rebellion. Some of the books fell in with my restless mood. Wedekind's *Awakening of Spring* seemed to call to me; Artsybashev's *Breaking Point* was almost a warning that I might go mad in that prison of love. In any case, one morning when Will was presumably watching paramecia rub bellies in the biolog- ical laboratory at Columbia, I packed a small bundle, jumped upon my bicycle, rode to the ferry, crossed to the Battery, and pedaled through the traffic of I don't remember what streets, and then along the Boston Post Road until, somewhere in Connecticut, one of my tires gave out. I stood desolate as the traffic passed by, heedless of my thumb. Then a truck stopped, and the driver asked did I need help. "Yes," I answered; "could you take me and my bike into the next town, where I can get a puncture fixed?" He agreed, but "First," he said, "come with me and let's have some fun," and he tried to pull me into the roadside woods. I resisted so lustily and loudly that he retired to his truck and drove on. Soon a pass- ing motorist took me to a service station, and my tire was repaired. One bad man, one good man.

I rode on until my legs gave way. On the outskirts of a village I knocked at a door and asked for a night's lodging. I wore a divided skirt, and my hair was bobbed. The woman who answered my ring judged that I was just another disreputable vagrant; she closed the door in my face. At the next house I made sure to show my money, and I was given a room. On the following day I reached Boston, so tired that I almost collapsed on a park bench. I had the address of a Boston acquaintance, Dorothy Parrott, whom I had met in the birth control movement in New York, but I was in no condition to invade her rooms. A prim lady sat nearby; I feared that she was one of those Bostonians who spoke only to

God; but I broke some ice between us by talking with her child. I asked her just to let me into her home to wash up before presenting myself to Miss Parrott, who lived nearby at 33 Bellingham Place. She agreed, and presently I found, with Dorothy's help, a room and some new friends, including Michael Gold. Now, however, I began to long for Will, and to wonder how he had taken my leaving him without a word of explanation. I wired him, and he came at once; he took me in his arms, and sympathized with my wish to avoid further incarceration in New Dorp. Soon, he promised, he would get me some habitation nearer to the traffic and ideologies of Manhattan. I think he loved me a little more now; it seems easier to love a sinner than a saint.

But soon Will was absorbed again in his studies at Columbia or at home; or he was off to Labor Temple or elsewhere to earn a few dollars by lecturing; sometimes I was left alone in New Dorp till late at night. I was still only seventeen; my youthful energy craved outlet; my restless spirit longed for experience with the fascinating but now distant world. Was this to be the meaning of my life—to be isolated all winter in this summer colony and cold bungalow, with hardly a sound reaching me except of the ocean breaking furiously upon the shore? At times I thought that sea might be a solution to all my problems: why not pluck up my courage, walk out blindly into those breakers, and let them engulf me, ending it all?

Strange to say, a book that might have deepened that dark mood saved me from it. I came upon Alexander Berkman's *Prison Memoirs of an Anarchist;* I remembered him vividly from my Ferrer Center days; now I identified myself with his suffering strikers and his lonely incarceration. A mad idea formed in my head: I would run off to New York, get myself arrested, and find out at first hand just how the New York police treated their prisoners.

So, one day, when Will had gone off to Columbia, I walked to New Dorp Station, took the train and the ferry to Manhattan, and searched till I found a police station. I entered, and was surprised to see a quite amiable man behind the desk. "I want to be sentenced to jail," I told him. "What crime have you committed?" he asked. "None," I replied, "but I want to suffer with the many men and women the law has unjustly condemned." He smiled sympathetically. "Would you mind being examined first?" he asked. I assumed that this was standard procedure, and consented. An attendant led me to an ambulance, and soon I found myself in Bellevue Hospital.

So far as I can recall, no one came to examine me. I was put in with a motley group of women in various stages of insanity. A Dr. Gregory came, took a cursory look at me, and passed on. I began to worry that I would be kept there until I qualified as a bona fide lunatic. I demanded to be released, but no one took me seriously. Two days passed, and I became frantic. Dr. Gregory appeared again. I asked him when he proposed to examine me. "I don't have to," he replied; "I can see at a glance that you are suffering from . . ." The word he used was unintelligible to me. "Besides," he added, "you came here with your hair cut almost like a man's, a divided skirt, no stockings, and sandals instead of shoes." "So," I protested, "you judge a person insane just because he does not dress like everybody else!" He shrugged his shoulders. I begged him to let me write a letter to my husband. He seemed to feel that my notion that I had a husband was a delusion of grandeur, and further evidence of insanity, but he agreed to mail the letter. I wrote to Will and begged him to come and take me home.

He had set all my relatives and friends to hunting for me, but none of them had thought of inquiring at Bellevue. Soon he came, comforted me, and explained that he was to blame for having kept me too long in semi-isolation in New Dorp. I was released, and went back to that bungalow relieved and subdued. Will was all tenderness, and vowed again to find me a better home.

A pleasant event gave me a further reason for a change. When we realized that World War I had in effect interned my mother in Russia, Will appealed to his friend Alden Freeman to help us get her back to America. In August, 1915, a letter came from the State Department telling us that the U.S. consul in Odessa had arranged for Mrs. Kaufman's passage to the United States. She reached New York in December, and we went to meet her. When she saw the Statue of Liberty she forgot all her political heresies and, like so many others, said that she could kneel and kiss the ground. She went back to her stand, and I looked forward to living close to her again; for she, more than Will, understood me.

Among the many audiences that invited him to lecture was a group of prosperous Jews in the Bath Beach section of Brooklyn. His performance there won him two new friends who were to play a part in our lives. One was Louis Sturz, a certified accountant who was later the treasurer of the American Jewish Congress. We became very fond of him; Will called him *uomo d'ore*, or man of gold, and said Louis needed no degree since he already excelled in the two halves of philosophy—understanding and forgiveness. I was also attracted to his wife, Hattie, who, wherever she lived, opened her home to us with quiet but limitless hospitality. The firm of Louis Sturz and Company—now headed by his brilliant son Irwin—has handled our income tax reports from 1930 to this day.

Another friend made by that Bath Beach lecture was William J. Perlman, who lived unwillingly as an accountant, and yearned to become a successful dramatist. One day, visiting us in New Dorp, he told us that his house in Brooklyn was much too large for himself, his dentist wife Dr. Flora Perlman, and his son Norman; he proposed that we should sell our bungalow and move into the two rooms on his third floor, for a monthly rental that would include our meals. We agreed. We found a purchaser for the bungalow (we had by this time paid our debt to Ed White), and in the summer of 1916 we took up exalted quarters in the Perlman mansion at 2222 Bath Avenue, Brooklyn. It was not quite what I had hoped for, but Manhattan was now only five cents away.

In our new nest Will experienced temptation, and I encountered sickness. While he was alone in the house a woman acquaintance mounted the stairs, remarked on the heat, and opened her bodice to within a millimeter of her nipples. According to Will (uncorroborated) he returned her greeting with courtesy, and resumed his work; she retired.

My own affair was a respiratory ailment that bedded me for a week. Will celebrated my recovery by lapsing into poetry with

A Song to My Comrade

It is a joy to live in these full times,
when Life, at last grown conscious of its own
remolding purpose, turbulently flows
to its fulfillment. Happy those who feel
the swell and movement of the flow, whose hands
are busy with the work of time, and know
the fever of creative sculptury.

Comrade, 'tis good to know that you are here,
giving your own rich force to ends your own,
a string full drawn to vibrant melody,
all quivering to the subtlest touch of things—
O restless surge, insatiable will!

Grow strong, my comrade; take the willing wealth
of Life's tumultuous feast, that you may stand
unshaken when I fall; that I may know
the shattered fragments of my song will come
at last to finer melody in you;
that I may tell my heart that you begin
where passing I leave off, and fathom more.

Will agrees with me and everybody else that this was his worst metrical performance, saccharine in sentiment, juvenile in its braggadoccio mood of taking on the universe, and quite unwarrantably optimistic about my future performances. However, the third stanza served him as a pretty dedication of *The Story of Philosophy.*

CHAPTER V

Philosophy and Politics

1913–19

Will:

I entered Columbia University at an opportune time—September, 1913: it was then graced by a generation of notables second only to that which had just ended at Harvard with the passing of William James and Josiah Royce, and the flight of George Santayana to Europe. I had the good fortune to study biology under Thomas Hunt Morgan and J. H. McGregor, psychology under Robert Sessions Woodworth, and philosophy under Frederick Woodbridge, John Dewey, William P. Montague, and Felix Adler. Those were full and arduous days for me, since I was at that time lecturing to radical audiences twice a week, and would soon take on eighty more lectures per year at Labor Temple. But they were happy days, for a new world was opened to me by these men, and I bless their memory.

Ariel:

They were happy days for me too. I often accompanied Will to some of his classes, and we must have evoked some smiles as we walked across the campus hand in hand. In listening to Woodbridge and Dewey I could better understand Will's love of philosophy—especially for Plato and Spinoza. I parted from him to take courses in history under Vladimir Simkhovitch and James Harvey Robinson; I relished particularly the latter's course on "History of the Intellectual Classes in Europe," and I had the

67

pleasure of conveying to Will many a juicy item that had not yet come within his ken. I dropped into some biology lectures, and fell in love with Professor McGregor and Professor Morgan. I remember helping or impeding Morgan's famous aide, Hermann Muller (who, like Morgan, was a Nobel Prize winner), in caring for those free-loving *Drosophila*, or banana flies, whose genes and chromosomes were opening a new era in genetics. One day Professor Morgan invited me to his home; there I saw the genial giant getting down on all fours and carrying one after another of his children on his back. On another occasion he asked me where I was going that evening. After some hesitation I answered, "To hear Emma Goldman." Putting a finger to his lips, he whispered, "So am I." Yes, those were happy days!

Will:

I think it was my studies at Columbia University, as well as my slowly rising income, that diluted the wild radicalism of my 1914 letter to the New York *Call* into the mild liberalism of my pro-Wilson stand in 1916. The biology courses did most to sober me—though they merely expanded what I might have learned from Darwin's *Origin of Species* in 1905. They forced me to recognize the social and political implications of the inescapable, omnipresent struggle for existence. Now I saw that struggle not merely in plants and animals, but as well in the competition of man against man, of woman against woman, of class against class, of state against state, of religion against religion, of idea against idea; competition is the law of life. In this view the socialist call for a warless and classless society seemed doomed by the processes of nature and the resultant nature of man.

Moreover, the study of psychology indicated that variety and inequality are rooted in the needs and method of evolution as a survival of advantageous differences in the struggle for existence. Almost every organism differs from every other; two peas are never quite alike. All men are unequal, even at birth, in physical qualities and mental capacities; and congenital superiorities combine with environmental differences in developing acquired inequalities. In every society the majority of abilities lies in a minority of men; so, in every society, some concentration of wealth is natural, and grows with the complexity of the economy and the unequal value, to the community, of diverse talents in its individuals. In the light of these ABC's it became clear to my budding brain that the communist ideal of equal reward and a classless society was biologically impossible, and that socialism would have to reconcile itself to a considerable inequality of possessions and power. The natural concentration of wealth could be checked, now and then, by remedial legislation or disruptive revolution, but after every interruption it would soon be renewed.

I believed for a time that the anarchist saint, Peter Kropotkin, in his *Mutual Aid as a Factor in Evolution,* had provided an answer to Darwin and Spencer, and a biological basis for a socialist philosophy: cooperation had become increasingly important as a means to survival for individuals and groups, even among animals, as in ants and bees. But when I tried to think the matter out, I had to admit that cooperation is a tool, and disguised form, of competition; it disciplines and coordinates the economic, social, political, and military activity of individuals in order to strengthen their group in its actual or prospective struggle with other groups. The underlying reality is still competition, even to the contest of states in the final arbitrament of war.

The logical conclusion of this line of thought, in 1914–17, should have been to strengthen my socialism, for visibly, in those war years, the involved nations were being driven to control, even to regiment, not only their martial forces but, more and more, their natural resources, their industries, their transportation, and their banks. And since new inventions like the airplane and wireless, new weapons like long-range artillery and missiles, were reducing the distance between nations (and their immunity to external attack), internal cooperation was becoming ever more necessary to internal security; the freedom of the individual had to be sacrificed to the liberty of the group from alien domination. A kind of mathematical formula—internal freedom varies inversely as external danger—sounded the doom of Jeffersonian government, and made "creeping socialism" inevitable.

The relative liberalism of Woodrow Wilson's first administration (1912–16) led me to hope that the proximate aims of socialism might be realized sooner, and with less turmoil, if socialists should carry on their campaigns within the Democratic Party. As governor of New Jersey (1910–12), Wilson had broken a reactionary political machine, and had pushed through a reluctant legislature such modest but promising reforms as a corrupt-practices act, an employers'-liability law, and the direct primary. When, as president, he implemented the "New Freedom" by establishing the eight-hour day for railway employees, improving the working conditions of men in the American mercantile marine, providing easy loans for farmers' cooperatives, enfranchising women, advancing the direct popular election of senators, regulating the banks through the Federal Reserve System, and corporate industry through the Federal Trade Commission and the Clayton Anti-Trust Act—then the intellectual in me responded gratefully to the scholar in politics, and cherished the hope that this grim-faced professor might arrest the process by which the natural acquisitiveness of men was making a tragedy of the American dream. Should socialists stand intransigently aside from this drama of hard-won reforms, or should they join the Democratic Party, seek to mold it from within, and help to hold up the eloquent hero's hands?

I was not quite taken in by the Democratic campaign of 1916, which ran Wilson for a second term on a slogan of "Peace, Preparedness, and Prosperity." I suspected that the United States would not let its own position in the international struggle be weakened through the conquest of France and England by Germany, and that if such a turn of events should seem imminent every Anglo-Saxon in America would cry out against a triumph of the "Huns." But I saw that Wilson, resisting two years of clamor, had "kept us out of war," and that his opponent, Charles Evans Hughes, though apparently a man of exceptional ability and integrity, was being supported by Republicans who, like Theodore Roosevelt, urged our entry into the war.

So, in the fall of 1916, I announced to my Labor Temple audience that I would vote for Wilson. I have before me an undated clipping from the New York *World*, which reads in part:

> "Do we think it worth while for radicals to vote for Wilson and this year forget the Socialist candidate?"
>
> Spontaneous applause greeted this question last night when it was asked by Prof. William J. Durant in Labor Temple. . . . He had just completed an address in which he told in detail the achievements of President Wilson during the three years he has been in office. . . . Prof. Durant, in leading up to the question, announced that he himself is a socialist. He said he did not think Wilson would be elected unless a sufficient number of radicals voted for him. . . . "It is expected that 1,250,000 votes would be cast for the Socialist candidate. [Eugene Debs had received 901,000 in 1912.] The question is whether we are going to continue the progressive movement brought on by Wilson, or have eight years of inaction. . . . I think Woodrow Wilson has been the best president since Abraham Lincoln. . . . There has never been a president in the history of this country who has put through so much progressive legislation."

The Socialist New York *Call* greeted my apostasy with a stinging editorial entitled "We Know This Breed." I wish I had lost it, but here it is:

> The Socialist Party cannot be bought, sold, or delivered in any manner politically, either by those inside or outside, or those who hang on its fringes.
>
> But it is good capitalist policy to assume the opposite, and it is usually this third class of nondescripts, the anarchistic-progressive-super-radical and self-alleged ultra-revolutionary element, that is selected or featured to "deliver the goods."
>
> This accounts for the headlines of such news stories as the one published in yesterday's New York *World*, occupying fully two-thirds of a column and captioned: "Socialist Pleads with His Party to Vote for Wilson."
>
> The "Socialist" in question is one Durant, a hyper-radical, never a party member, who would not join the party even if he could—and that is doubtful. Mr. Durant is too "revolutionary." Hence his appeal to vote for Wilson.
>
> But the appeal was not made to Socialists. If Durant were a Socialist party member, and made such a plea, he would find himself on the outside looking in before he knew what had happened. . . .

As for the Durant type, it is well known. Loud and boastful in their assertion of their super-revolutionary character, ever trying to make Socialists appear as the rankest conservatives as compared to themselves, they nevertheless lose no opportunity for attempting to knife the Socialist party politically, when a political contest is under way. The real Socialist knows this type and regards it with contempt and disgust. . . .

That Durant is not and never was a Socialist, despite his assertions to the contrary, is well known. That he did not address a Socialist meeting composed of Socialists is equally attested by the fact that he got away with his drool without any comment from the audience.

This was fair fighting despite some unimportant errors of fact, mostly due to the assumption that, having taught in the Ferrer School, I had accepted the anarchist and "super-revolutionary" ideology. On the contrary, I had explicitly and repeatedly rejected that philosophy, so losing many friends in the Ferrer Association. I had been a Socialist Party member in Newark, but I had let my membership lapse. My audience was predominantly socialist, and several members opposed my plea.

I was rewarded for my politicking by an invitation from the New York Democratic headquarters to journey out to Long Branch, New Jersey, and hear President Wilson at close range. I was a bit disappointed by his address; it contained no pledge to keep us out of war, and the strained look on his face left me with the impression that he was not comfortable with the slogans that had been attached to his campaign. Nevertheless, when I was asked to join the "Wilson Volunteers" for a speech-making tour of New York State, I readily consented, convinced now that I was taking a hand in world-shaking events. The genial, skeptical, generous Amos Pinchot paid the expenses of the group. Its oratorical leader was Walter Lippmann—four years younger than myself, but far ahead of me in maturity and influence. He spoke in halls and theaters; I spoke to street-corner gatherings from the back of an open car. We continued our efforts almost to election eve.

That evening Ariel and I and her loyal brother Harry stayed up till midnight waiting for the returns. By 11 P.M. it was clear that Wilson had lost New York despite Lippmann's rational discourses and my passionate appeals; Hughes's election seemed so assured that he gave his wife a victory kiss and went to bed. Early the next morning Dr. Day, of Labor Temple, called to tell us that California had unexpectedly given its electoral vote to Wilson, and that this had sufficed to re-elect the President. Hughes unkissed his wife, and Wilson led us into the war.

Late in 1916, or early in 1917, we moved from Bath Beach to a three-room apartment on the fifth floor of a walk-up building at 854 East 175th Street, in the Bronx. There I wrote my first book, for the composition, publication, and defense of an original thesis was a prerequisite for the doctorate in philosophy. A corner of our bedroom became my study; a shelf of books by the window provided me with material for reference

71

and pilferage. I used a lamp-clasp from my bicycle to attach a removable drawing board to the right arm of a rocker. For each paragraph to be written I arranged notes and gleanings under cords running at my left from bottom to top of the board. That is essentially my machinery of study and writing to this day, except that the pilferable volumes now need more space. Ariel often peeked over my shoulder at the manuscript, and helped me with an *aperçu* or a pert line. "I want hammer phrases," she ordered, "sharp and pithy expressions that will concentrate an idea like a blow on the head."

I called the book *Philosophy and the Social Problem,* and armed it with a double-edged thesis: (1) Philosophy was ailing, and had forfeited public influence, because it had lost itself in the esoteric abstractions of logic and epistemology, and had turned, fainthearted, away from those problems of origin and destiny, nature and civilization, morality and government, religion and death, which had occupied Plato and Aristotle, Zeno and Epicurus, Thomas Aquinas and William of Occam, Bacon and Hobbes, Spinoza and Hume, Schopenhauer and Nietzsche; (2) the social problem—of narrowing the gap between our moral ideals of humanity and justice and the biological realities of human nature, economic greed, political corruption, and aggressive war—had elicited only superficial or impracticable proposals because it had been approached without a scientific study of needs and means, and without a philosophical grasp and reconciliation of desires and ends. The book began with a youthfully individualistic chapter on "The Present Significance of the Socratic Ethic," reducing virtue to intelligence—to action guided by considered foresight of probable results. It had a fervent chapter on Spinoza—who has managed to get into nearly all the Durant books—and a hair-raising chapter on Nietzsche, who had rocked our brains with the psalms of Zarathustra. My concluding panacea, disappointingly mild, was that the professional groups in each country—in science, medicine, economics, law, sociology, historiography, philosophy, religion, education, administration, and diplomacy—should appoint their finest minds to a "Society for Social Research," which should persistently study the living problems of economics, government, and morality, and periodically publish its results and its recommendations, to Congress and the people, for educational policy, communal action, and national legislation. I proposed no utopias, and now, like Clive, I marvel at my moderation.

The Macmillan Company agreed to issue my dual thesis as a book (of some 272 pages), on condition that I should guarantee the sale of a thousand copies. My undiscourageable angel, Alden Freeman, provided the guarantee. The little volume received a brief listing among Macmillan's spring publications for 1917; it appeared in all the glory and odor of print, and sold a hundred copies.

It was treated mercifully by the reviewers—even by my foes at the socialist New York *Call*. Henry Mencken, pleased to discover an appreciation of Nietzsche in a university product, wrote for the influential *Smart Set* a laud that turned my head. But M. C. Otto, brilliant professor at the University of Wisconsin, ridiculed the book as a "get-rich-quick philosophy"—though it had no such result in my case. And Felix Adler, who had led some of us students in a seminar on ethics, condemned the author as suffering from hypertrophy of the ego; "This young man," he told John Dewey, "thinks that he has discovered everything." More disturbing was a curt letter from my beloved *pater in spiritualibus*, Father Mooney. I had brashly sent him a copy of my masterpiece. His reply was brief: "Beautiful but bootless writing. The fool hath said in his heart, There is no God." I long brooded over that "bootless" and that "fool."

Macmillan, burdened with nine hundred unsold copies, appealed to me to come and take them away. I can't remember how we managed it, but Ariel and I finally carted those unappreciated volumes to our Bronx apartment, where we stacked them imposingly on a projecting cornice that ran around our living room. Remembering Thoreau's quip in a similar case, I wrote to some friends that I now had a library of a thousand books, nine hundred of which I had written myself.

I had another hurdle to surmount before getting my degree. I had to pass an examination in two foreign languages. For some silly reason I thought that French and Latin would be accepted; when I was informed that Latin was a dead, not a foreign, language, I had only nine days in which to become a German, a Spaniard, or an Italian. Unable to go to Germany and live there for two years as the only way to learn the language, I borrowed Gomperz' *Griechische Denker* from the university library. I set out to read it with a translation on my right and a German–English dictionary on my left. For nine days I struggled, helped by my recent study of Greek philosophy; then I presented myself to John Dewey for examination. Taking a volume from his shelves, he laid it before me, and bade me translate. Angels and ministers of grace!—it was Gomperz' *Griechische Denker*. I did well enough until I came to a sesquipedalian word in a proliferating sentence. I threw up my hands in failure and disgust. The kindly philosopher looked over my shoulder, puzzled a moment, and smiled. "I guess I'll have to pass you," he said, "for I can't make it out myself."

A final obstacle stood in the way of the desired degree: an oral examination in each of my chosen subjects. So, one May morning in 1917, I faced a cordon of professors from the departments of philosophy and psychology; Professors Morgan and McGregor, from biology, sent down word to pass me unheard. I made the mistake of differing with Professor Wendell Bush in interpreting a passage from one of the Greek philosophers; he frowned a bit over my self-assurance, but Professor Montague came to my rescue with a clarifying and appeasing word. By the grace of human kindness I became a Ph.D.

Soon thereafter I was appointed an instructor in the Extension Division at Columbia, and I began to prepare, for the fall session, courses on the history and problems of philosophy. Meanwhile the fame of my little thesis book had reached into the Middle West; Sam Schwartz, the enterprising educational director at Sinai Temple, Chicago, invited me to address his alert audience there; and an Iowa organization engaged me for six weeks to acquaint the farmers and tradesmen on its Chautauqua circuit with the philosophy and fate of Socrates. So I left Ariel with her sisters, and went off on the first of forty years of continental lecture tours. Both Ariel and I underestimated the strain that this long separation would place upon our union. I was so hurried and harried on that trip—orating on Socrates almost every day to tired men and women who had never heard of him, then traveling in hot coach trains, sometimes through half the night, to the next tent and trial—that I must have written too seldom, or too unfeelingly, to my deserted Ariadne. Then, amidtour, came a letter from a friend warning me that Ariel was so miserably lonely that only a heartless egoist would leave her husbandless any longer. I asked the Chautauqua bureau to release me; it did so with uncomplimentary promptness. I wired Ariel to meet me at Niagara Falls, and there, in August, 1917, we had another honeymoon.

In September I began my lectures as instructor at Columbia. As half the members of my classes were older than myself, I disguised my immaturity with a Vandyke beard. I soon betrayed my age by making some ungracious remark about Mary Baker Eddy's new revelation. A lady in my class happened to be a Christian Scientist; she complained to Dean Woodbridge of my irreverence; the dean summoned me to his office and gently reproved me. All administrators, he said, had to be stoics, and be harder than their sentiments; so I must forgive him for scolding me. Religion, he reminded me, is a precious consolation to many souls; to speak disrespectfully of it is a violation of good manners, and indeed of good sense. "You remind me of Max Eastman," he said; "like him you have an undisciplined mind." (Max had taught the psychology of poetry at Columbia; he was now editing a famous magazine.) I asked the dean had he ever read *The Masses*. "Them asses?" he queried; but I gathered from his smile that in the back of his heart he rather liked the brilliant Max.

That interview was a precious moment in my education. The word "undisciplined" shamed and worried me. What was an undisciplined mind? Vaguely I came to conceive it as a mind that let the wish father the thought; that let considerations of race, religion, party, class, status, or person affect the view; that stopped perception before it was adequate to the situation, and so leaped to judgment before the relevant facts were in; that failed to take a long view of the expectable results of an intended word or deed: all of which came close to my definition of virtue as foresightful intelligence. I began to realize how many adjustments the mind must make between abstract theory and complex situations, between our personal aims and ideas and a world throbbing with interests, opinions, and feelings different from our own. Would I ever have a disciplined mind?

America's entry into the war found me still a creature of emotion. I was a pacifist, and dreamed of governments that obeyed the Ten Commandments. I sympathized with young Americans, including myself, who were now called upon to register for conscript service in distant lands. Professor James McKeen Cattell, who had raised psychology to an independent department, wrote, under a Columbia letterhead, an appeal to a congressman from his district to vote against conscription, which threatened the life of his son. The university authorities dismissed him on the ground that he had misused its stationery. Professor Charles Beard, though supporting the war policy, resigned in protest against a summary dismissal which, he felt, violated professorial rights.

On October 10, 1917, I found myself on the steps of Columbia's Low Memorial Library in a crowd of students, most of them denouncing the dismissal of Professor Cattell and the acceptance of Professor Beard's resignation. Before I could clear my wits I was pushed forward to be the spokesman of the gathering. I walked out on the high concrete wall that abutted the library steps on the west, and I began to speak. The New York *Sun* of that evening reported some of my remarks: "We meet here to protest against the suppression of free speech. No matter how much we differ with Professor Beard, we must admire a man who has taken his whole career and offered it as a sacrifice for free speech. Woodrow Wilson, at the outset of the war, said he expected to be criticized, but nevertheless he continued his course." At this point a group of khaki-clad youths, apparently already in the service, formed a flying wedge, broke through my less martial listeners, and began to crowd me on the parapet. If they should press me further I would have no place to go but precipitately down, either to the hard steps six or more feet before me or to the ground ten feet behind me. Discretion got the better of valor: I proposed to the invaders that if they would allow me five minutes more I was sure that the audience, here to defend free speech, would listen to their leader. It was half agreed; I resumed my harangue, but I was never so brief again.

I am not certain that the administration took much notice of my hurried speech. When my one year as instructor neared its end I was called into the office of the university secretary, who quietly informed me that since volunteering and conscription had seriously reduced the expected registration for 1918–19, my classes, among many, would not be continued. Under the circumstances, he explained, it seemed fair that the teachers most recently hired should be the first to be let go. I could not complain, and soon resigned myself; I had been hard worked at Columbia, and my lectures at Labor Temple and elsewhere would keep me busy and sufficiently fed.

I must have been prospering, for in the spring of 1918 we bought our first car—a Willys-Knight Overland convertible coupé. It helped to reconcile my parents with their wayward son. When Ariel and I drove up before the old homestead at 524 Forest Street, Arlington, New Jersey, they opened their eyes; and when we offered to take them soon to see their aging relatives and childhood haunts in and around Champlain, they embraced us joyfully. That summer we overworked the frail chariot with the 320-mile drive; we arrived at our destination with some of the substructure dangling noisily on the pavement. But we were well repaid for that arduous trip, not only by the affection that Ariel won from my parents, but by our getting to know my father's sister, Tante Caroline, and her husband Mon Oncle Abram Lavalley, both in their seventies. Abram was a genial talker, but never effusive; with a minimum of education and a maximum of character, he was a believing and practicing Christian, taking no account of differences in creed. Indeed, he warmed up to Ariel much more than to me, holding her fondly on his knee while she babbled gaily, and taking her happily with him on his buggy rides from his farm to Champlain town; here was a new love affair flourishing while I was busy having the car repaired. I have never forgotten how, after supper and an hour of conversation and understanding silence on the porch, Abram rose with some creaking of chair and bones, went to his old wife, took her by the arm, and said to her, "*Viens, ma vieille, il faut se coucher*—Come, my old one, we must go to bed." The essence of life and wisdom shone out here: work and love.

As World War I progressed, and our conscripts were gracing their sacrifices with victories, my pacifism slowly changed into patriotism. I watched the bulletin boards anxiously to see what advance the colored pins would indicate for the Allies; by the time the armistice came (November 11, 1918) I was cheering for our side like the rest of America. But when Wilson was outmaneuvered by Clémenceau at Versailles (I varied an old limerick to read, "They came back from the ride with the professor inside, and the smile on the face of the 'Tiger' "); when the treaty put all the blame for the war upon Germany, and opened the door to Hitler by insisting on the abdication of the Kaiser—leading to the collapse of a relatively civilized, and municipally excellent, government; and when our Senate refused to sanction United States membership in the League of Nations—then my old doubts returned, and I became a pacifist again.

I was still a socialist, despite my vote for Wilson in 1916; I supported the Socialist Party candidacy of Morris Hillquit when he made a good run for the mayoralty of New York in 1917. When the Russians over-threw the czarist autocracy, and then the middle-class Duma, and de-creed "All land to the peasants, all power to the Soviets," I thrilled with the thought that utopia was getting born, however bloodily. When the United States sent its troops to join the British, the French, the Japanese, and the White Russians in an attempt to overthrow the "proletarian dic-tatorship," I dipped my pen in red, and wrote a fervent hymn to "Holy Russia," as if Dostoevski and Tolstoi, and not Lenin and Trotsky, had made the Revolution. Never again have any of my ebullitions been so mangled by history. It will excuse the reader from trusting any of my later judgments, but it belongs in this record of a mind's slow development.

Holy Russia,
There never was in history deed more beautiful and saintly than yours,
Nor in history deed more dastardly and unclean than the strangling of you by a
*   thousand wolves,—*
The strangling even of your women, who are the glory of the world,
And of your children, whose eyes have seen the portals of the kingdom.

Holy Russia,
We too are your sons, though you see us not.
Sons of your spirit, by the seeds that your geniuses and your saints have
*   scattered over the earth;*
The fire which you have kindled leaps across continents and oceans, and singes
*   our souls;*
We know that if you die we die,—all but the flesh and pelf of us;
We know that your blood is spilt for us, for your children and lovers
*   everywhere;*
And our shame is unspeakable that we are yet helpless to help you.
But not any victory of arms or wealth could match the glory you have won;
For now, because of you, we know that men can be boundlessly noble,
And that love can be limitless.

Holy Russia,
Forgive us that we have not yet come to you,
Or that we have not yet stayed the hands that would murder you;
Perhaps we shall be stronger soon, and not so carefully patient;
Perhaps we shall be brave enough to bear testimony that the truth is in you,
And that the future is the fruit of your blood and your loins;
Perhaps we shall at last scatter the thieves that cast lots for your raiment;
Perhaps—O God that it may be!—we shall take you down in time from your
*   cross,*
And heal your wounds with the love of the world,
O gentle Christ of the Nations.

Our own private lives were relatively peaceful in the years of the First World War. I escaped conscription because the armistice came just as the draft boards were beginning to take married men of my age and feebleness. At Labor Temple, in the 1917–18 season, I gave forty lectures on "Supermen: an Interpretation of History" (more Carlylean than Marxian), and forty on psychology. Sometime in 1918 Ariel (then twenty years old) shared the Labor Temple podium with me in a debate: "Which People, the Greeks or the Jews, Made the Greater Contributions to Civilization?" I took the side of the Greeks, and repeated the old story of Hellenic literature, philosophy, politics, science, and art; I knew little then of Byzantine culture; and the revival of Greek literature under Seferis and Kazantzakis had not yet come. Ariel, however, listed great Jews from Moses to Einstein. The audience of six hundred, of whom ninety percent were Jewish (I doubt if there was one Greek in the house), heard me with polite patience, but warmed to Ariel's fiery eulogy of her people; at the end I was fit to be buried. My lecture manager, smelling money and careless of my blood, arranged for a repetition of the debate at Park View Palace, at 110th Street and Fifth Avenue. It drew an audience of a thousand and more, nearly all Jewish; many eager listeners stood through the long program; some perched on windowsills, some on fire escapes. It was for me a double jeopardy and a second defeat. I had the consolation of pride in Ariel's capable performance, without experience or training in public speaking; obviously, if I should be snuffed out, or get myself jailed, she would be able to support herself.

For the present, however, it was my voice that had to turn air into gold. In June, 1918, I set out to lecture at the summer sessions of the University of Arkansas at Fayetteville, and the University of Oklahoma at Norman. I left Ariel with Romany Marie at a summer resort in Hunter in the Catskills. Repenting my past negligence, I wrote to her every day, sometimes twice a day. Her answers were usually brief and beautiful.

> I take as much pains with each letter as I would if I were creating a child. I take a fresh cold bath every morning, and intend never to miss a day. I am also taking exceptional care with my food and see that my system works well, sweetheart. Am I now the Ariel you would have me be? Please write me much on this point. Knowing just what I am capable of, accepting the necessary limitations, how would you like me to be? A true Hindu would answer, "Just what you are."
>
> Love me, sweetheart.

The simple tenderness of this letter so filled the solitude of my room that I wrote to Ariel on July 5:

> Your letter was wonderful, dear sweetheart, as natural as Nature herself. I received it . . . after returning from my long-anticipated swim, and it was a sweet reward for some loving thoughts that had been filling my head as I walked, or as I swam on my back, looking at your face in the sky. . . .

This afternoon, as I was reading in my room—my shirt stuck to my chair with the heat—a phonograph in a nearby room played "America." . . . I felt in the lines the suffering of many millions, and their eternal hope. I felt not so much their economic misery as their love-wrecks, their heart-breakings, their wholesale slaughter in wars which they never caused or willed. . . . Soon I found myself in a characteristically mushy state, almost tearful. I tried to laugh at myself, talked Nietzschean stuff to myself about the "herd," their worthlessness, etc. But it wouldn't do. . . . I kept right on thinking how we can help—even while the skeptic in me says, "It will all be unchanged a hundred or a thousand years hence. . . ."

Wednesday night I expounded Nietzsche, and scandalized my audience into speechlessness. . . .

Tonight ends my first week. I am counting the days till I see you; what a luxury it will be to sit beside you again, press down with a big toe, and send Beauty [our Willys-Knight Overland car] off to some shady spot where we can love in quiet, or to some brook where I can see your body sparkling with the wet. . . .

On July 20 I left Norman, Oklahoma, for St. Louis, and thence took the New York Central's *Southwestern Limited* to Cleveland, Buffalo, Albany, and Rhinebeck, where Ariel awaited me with Beauty. She reproved me for having allowed some ladies to drive me from my lectures to my room; I reproved her for letting a garage mechanic fall in love with her; we forgave each other, and moved happily toward the sixth year of our marriage, never dreaming that we had at least fifty more to go. On the way to New York we raced our little car up to forty-eight miles an hour, which, we were warned, was a devilishly dangerous and irresponsible speed. We were just like any other Americans, drunk with life.

We must have been restless youngsters, for early in August, 1918, we started out for Philadelphia, not with our car but on foot. On the first day we walked some thirty miles—from 175th Street in the Bronx down through Manhattan, across the ferry, through Jersey City, Elizabeth, and Cranford to Bound Brook, New Jersey. The next day we could hardly move, and it was torture for Ariel to get her swollen feet into her shoes. But we thought of Walt Whitman, and walked on in pride and pain. On the fifth day we reached Philadelphia. We had hardly entered the city when a policeman arrested us as vagrants, and myself as having violated the Mann Act. I protested that Ariel was my wife; he asked for our marriage license; I had none. Ariel informed him that I taught philosophy at Columbia University (she did not add that I had been fired); moreover, she said, "he has written a book on philosophy." The puzzled officer concluded that we were lunatics, who should be locked up for the safety of society. As we walked with him toward his police station I talked to him patiently, in my best but simple English. Suddenly he stopped, and looked at us doubtfully. "Well," he cried, "I'll be damned if I don't believe you. Go your way; you're free." We phoned our old friend Ed White; he came to guide us to his home, and soon we were enjoying Lena White's immaculate hospitality. We had to scrub ourselves lustily to be worthy of her clean and fragrant sheets.

When we had returned home (not on foot) Ariel and I held a summit conference on a subject that had peacefully divided us for years. Shouldn't we have a baby? I was thirty-two, and felt very old; Ariel was twenty, and wanted a few more years of untrammeled youth. I argued that I would soon be unfit to beget a child with properly equipped chromosomes. I shamefully added that a man with a pregnant wife would be longer deferred in the draft. Ariel yielded. We also agreed that a medical certificate of physical fitness and reasonable sanity should be a prerequisite to lawful parentage. So, on August 12, 1918, we went to Dr. William J. Robinson, author of many medical books, and had him examine us. He gave us carte blanche. Before that week was out Ethel (according to Catholic biology) had begun to be.

Sex and politics have one thing in common: once you have had some of it you never know when to stop. When World War I ended, and Wilson returned broken in spirit from the fiasco at Versailles, he took to his bed, and for the remainder of his second term it was his aides, not he, who exercised presidential powers. The patriotism of the people, raised to a religion by war and victory, sanctioned such a conservative and authoritarian reaction as a functioning Wilson (I felt) would never have allowed. I lost faith in the Democratic Party.

Early in 1919 a group of liberals—J. A. H. Hopkins, Allan McCurdy, George Record, Horace Liveright, McAlister Coleman, myself, and several others, began a series of meetings at 15 East Fortieth Street, New York, and formed a "Committee of Forty-eight" for the advancement of a humane democracy. They called upon me, as a man of words, to draw up a profession of principles. I have before me a faded copy of the resultant "Call to Americans" as published in *The New Republic* for March 22, 1919. It was signed by Allen T. Burns, George P. West, Robert W. Bruere, Lincoln Colcord, John Haynes Holmes, Otto Cullman, Will Durant, George Nasmyth, Gilbert E. Roe, Charles Zueblin, William P. Everts, Arthur G. Wray, Carl D. Thompson, Dudley Field Malone, Mary H. Ingham, Mary Pattison, Charlotte P. Gilman, and Mary K. Simkhovitch. Later signatures came from Herbert Croly, Percy Stickney Grant, Albert J. Nock, Amos Pinchot, Ordway Tead, Walter Weyl, and many more. In general the public response encouraged us, and we laid great plans for a convention that would meet in Chicago in August, 1920, to nominate Senator Robert La Follette for president. I was a kingmaker again.

I made no king, but I shared with Ariel, however modestly, in making Ethel. In the account which *Transition* gave of this enterprise Ariel bore the child, while I suffered all the agonies of paternal parturition. Now let the mother tell her side.

CHAPTER VI

A Child Is Born

1919–21

1 • GREENWICH VILLAGE

Ariel:

Our "seven fat years" from May, 1919, to May, 1926, opened and closed with our giving birth: myself to Ethel, and Will to *The Story of Philosophy*. These experiences concluded my physical, his intellectual, youth.

He did not realize, when he proposed parentage, that motherhood would require of me the ending of an infatuation that for a time had threatened our union. I had fallen in love with Greenwich Village. My husband, absorbed and consumed in his work, and always pregnant with literary embryos, took no notice of the fact that, only a few blocks from Labor Temple, a new culture was taking form, rich in colorful and initiative personalities, and destined to affect the mental and moral life of all nonrural America.

I had been prepared for this almost revolutionary atmosphere by the echoes that my mother had brought me from the Jewish prophets who were playing Amos and Isaiah to the East Side; and I had received a heavy dose of radical ideas from the Ferrer Center lectures and gatherings. But Greenwich Village was not merely a consortium of rebels. Yes, there were socialists and anarchists there; but more typical—in those apartments, tearooms, clubs, restaurants, saloons, lecture halls, and little theaters, all crowded within a space six blocks square—was the spirit of moral, political, sartorial, and verbal freedom, seasoned and lightened with sin and gaiety, with love of literature and sensitivity to art.

I came to Greenwich Village soon after my marriage, lured by my Ferrer Center friend Romany Marie. Her tearoom on Washington Square drew many celebrities, including Eugene O'Neill, Mary Garden, Muriel Draper . . . I believe it was there, in 1914, that I saw the aging Belgian violinist Eugène Ysaye, whom I had just heard in an exciting concert. He heard me gabbing about something or other, and beckoned to me: "Come here, you little philosopher." I can't recall what we talked about, but I remember that when we parted he kissed me paternally. He looked like a stouter Liszt. Like other women, I have always been more interested in musicians than in music; and the nonconformist in me responds to their alienation from bourgeois life.

Later (1926) I had my own tearoom in Greenwich Village, but at this time (1914–19) I was merely an onlooker, eager to take in almost any experience. I was happy to find my old friend Christine Ell Hovden presiding over the restaurant that George Cram Cook had opened on the second floor of the Provincetown Playhouse on Macdougal Street. I saw Eugene O'Neill there, but was too frightened by his gloomy visage to speak to him. A building on the same street housed a restaurant known as Polly's, managed by Polly Holladay; her chief cook, waiter, and lover was another Ferrer Center figure, Hippolyte Havel, who denounced nearly everybody, including Polly's customers, as "bourgeois pigs." It was probably he who defined Greenwich Village as "a state of mind; it has no boundaries."

I was in those years excluded from both the lowest and the highest levels of Village life. My indifference to liquor, and my fear of ruffians, kept me from the Hell Hole, a saloon at Fourth Street and Sixth Avenue; this was a favorite resort of the more bibulous mavericks of the vicinity. Will and I were still nobodies when Mabel Dodge gathered polite liberals in her "evenings" at 23 Fifth Avenue. I heard of them at secondhand: Carl Van Vechten, music critic; Jo Davidson, sculptor; Lincoln Steffens, reformer; Walter Lippmann, already a genius at twenty-five (in 1914); Hutchins Hapgood, a philosophical anarchist who told his hostess, "I consider it my first duty to undermine substantially the foundations of the community"; Max Eastman, Emma Goldman, Alexander Berkman, "Big Bill" Haywood, Frank Tannenbaum, Margaret Sanger, Edwin Arlington Robinson; and, last and most, John Reed, whose hectic free-love alliance with the great *salonnière* broke her spirit and ended the "evenings." These uncensored discussions were a powerful stimulus to the intelligentsia of New York in that exuberant and hopeful generation.

Other Village figures came more directly into my life. Lola Ridge, whom I had known and loved at the Ferrer Center, established her own salon in a basement on East Ninth Street; but this flourished just when motherhood was absorbing me. Maxwell Bodenheim amused me with his incalculable behavior and his whimsical verse. We knew Harry

Kemp, the "tramp poet," intimately; in *Transition* Will tells how, in the Western Union office in Arlington, New Jersey, "a tall, handsome lad, about twenty-one years of age, named Harvey Keap," had challenged God to prove himself real by striking him dead; Kemp mentions that office in *Tramping on Life.* We followed with more interest than admiration the running story of Harry's elopement with Upton Sinclair's wife. Will, like Upton, declared himself "an essential monogamist," and had little sympathy for any man who broke up another man's home.

There was a finer, subtler poet in the Greenwich Village of those days—Edna St. Vincent Millay, beautiful in mind and body; but she shone outside my ken. Closer to our world was Max Eastman, who was making *The Masses* a scorching fire under our fattening tycoons; we watched him rising like some spacecraft Apollo among the luminaries of his time; we liked everything about him but his languid and aristocratic air, which made me feel like an Untouchable. More to my taste was Art Young, whose drawings were almost as effective as Robert Minor's cartoons. Art was as radical as any, but he could not hate; his bald and round little head beamed upon everything about him. "At a guess," he wrote, "I am about 51 per cent sentiment."

Some other artists popular in the Village were known to me chiefly through the Ferrer Center: Robert Henri, George Bellows, Man Ray. I had posed in the nude for Man Ray; when he wrote his autobiography he thought of including this drawing among the illustrations, but (he told me later in Paris) he withdrew it for fear of offending me or Will. I don't think either of us would have been offended.

The Village was alive with art, drama, politics, and revolution. The Provincetown Players, established in 1915 at 133 Macdougal Street, were revolutionizing the American theater; *The Masses* was revolutionizing journalism; liberals like Percy Stickney Grant and Lincoln Steffens were organizing the Liberal Club; Arthur Garfield Hays was beginning his career as legal defender of liberals and radicals embroiled with the law; Sadikichi Hartman—child of a German father and a Japanese mother—was startling us with notions and dances that seemed outlandish even to Village Bohemians. I knew all of these rebels, and accepted them all with enthusiasm. I had a warm spot in my heart for Percy Stickney Grant, who preached liberalism from the pulpit of his Episcopalian Church of the Ascension at Fifth Avenue and Tenth Street; not only because of his long struggle to marry a dearly beloved but divorced woman, but because, in one of his sermons, he held aloft Will's *Philosophy and the Social Problem* and bade all his congregation to read it if they wished to be saved.

Most of the people whom I have named here as touching my life— artists, poets, actors, journalists—were highstrung, rootless spirits who were the last persons in the world to make a success of monogamy. Many of them lived in free unions or, like Max Eastman, changed lawful partners every few years. Edna St. Vincent Millay turned her kaleidoscopic bed into fluent verse:

> *What lips my lips have kissed, and where, and why,*
> *I have forgotten, and what arms have lain*
> *Under my head till morning; but the rain*
> *Is full of ghosts tonight.*

I confess that I was influenced by all this freedom, and that I mingled some wild ideas with my love for Will. When Robert Minor visited us in our New Dorp bungalow in 1914 I admired him so much for his art, his kindness, and his powerful figure that more than once I reached up and flung my arms around his neck. We put him up in a bed just a step away from the one in which I lay with Will. Slowly a desire crept over me for physical union with Robert—not (if I may trust my memory) for any erotic intimacy (for I have never been very sexual) but just to feel and share the warmth and strength of the virile body that housed so big a heart. Like a good wife, I asked my husband's permission: Might I get into bed with Bob for a little while? Will, who has never been bothered by the itch to possess, gave me his indulgent consent, as if understanding that it was the child, and not merely the woman, that was speaking. Suddenly Bob found me beside him. He smiled, offered me a paternal kiss, and sent me back to my proper bed. So far as I know, he was too much of a gentleman to tell this story to anyone, even when he sadly condemned us for expressing our disappointment with Soviet Russia in 1932. Will and I liked him to the end.

All in all, those Greenwich Village days made it hard for me to reconcile myself to motherhood. I thought of sexual love as a relation between two individuals, and only slowly came to see it as a prelude to parentage. And I had no very happy memories of family life. Will, on the contrary, remembered the generally happy relations between his parents, between them and their children, and among the children themselves. He has never stopped thinking of the family as the basic institution of social order, and as that which has most suffered from the Industrial Revolution. I agreed that he deserved at least one child, and I set out to give him one, even if I had to forget that alluring Greenwich Village for a year.

2 · MAY, 1919

When I felt a new human being stirring within me, I began to take pride and joy in being a woman fulfilled. I made no attempt to conceal my pregnancy; rather, I walked the streets of our neighborhood like one who was pleased to lend the Creator a hand. I left to Will the task of getting a good doctor; he consulted some medical friends, and finally brought to me one whom I shall mercifully call Doctor X. I followed instructions, but these (unless my memory deceives me) did not include any caution to go easy on meat and eggs.

I had been prepared for the usual discomforts, and took them without worry or complaint. But when my time approached I experienced not only the normal pains but convulsions that exhausted me and frightened Will. He called my doctor, who, refusing to disturb his night's rest, merely bade us call an ambulance from Fordham Hospital. Apparently I had consumed too much protein, and was suffering from albumin poisoning; our physician could have detected this had he bothered to examine my blood in the final months. He did not appear at the hospital.

There I had such severe convulsions—"eclampsia"—that the excellent physicians who took charge of me thought for a time of risking a Caesarean operation; but they succeeded in reducing the convulsions by bleeding me and giving me enemas, and they decided to await a normal delivery. Will has described these scenes in *painstaking* detail in *Transition*; he hardly slept from Saturday to Monday; he helped the doctors as well as he could, as by timing my pains; he tried to comfort me, and (I am told) begged me to forgive him for having asked for a child; but I no longer recognized him, and did not understand what he said. When at last Ethel was born (May 12, 1919), Will was almost as depleted of energy as I was.

The doctor drugged me to a restful sleep, and my good brother Harry took Will home for a rest. They returned soon after I had recovered consciousness. When Will was admitted to my side he was shocked to see my bloated face, and still more when he found that I was blind. I believe a day passed before I could see well enough to recognize him. Then the nurse brought the baby and put it on my breast. Now a new feeling came over me. I felt that this child was a part of me; I warmed it with my body, enveloped it with pride and love, and rejoiced as I felt it taking my milk. All my pains were forgotten. When Will bent over me and asked, "Will you ever forgive me?" I answered like any mother: "I'm glad she came. Isn't she sweet?" A hundred best books, all written by us, could not have filled our lives if Ethel Benvenuta (for so we named her) had not come.

During my ordeal Will had some troubles of his own. On May 13, 1919, one day after Ethel's birth, he addressed the Forum Association of Hoboken on "Japan and the Changing East." I would like to blame his parental agony for the uncalculated risk which he took in predicting (according to the *Hudson County Observer* of May 14) that there would be "no war between the United States and Japan for the next fifty years at least." It was not the last of his unlucky prophecies.

He had for four years past been lecturing for the New York City Board of Education to adult evening audiences in the high schools, and his ten-dollar fee per lecture had helped us to an average weekly income of ninety dollars. For these discourses he chose politically neutral subjects in history, literature, and art. Especially successful was a series given each Tuesday at Wadleigh High School at 114th Street and Seventh Avenue, where he regularly attracted a thousand auditors. Old Dr. Leipziger, supervisor of lectures, took a fancy to Will; but when age retired him he was succeeded by Wendell M. Thomas, who kept close tabs on the views of the speaker.

Thomas found no fault with Will's addresses for the Board, but he kept an ear open for Will's lectures at Labor Temple. In a course given there on sociology and economics Will did not conceal his faith in socialism, and even expressed some sympathy for the Russian Revolution. Word of this came to Thomas, who decided that such a firebrand had no place as a lecturer in the city's schools. He was stirred to action by the answer that Will gave to a question from the floor at one of his Wadleigh High School talks, "Were Lenin and Trotsky agents of the German government in 1917, or were they sincere idealists?" Will replied, "Probably they were sincere idealists." The reply was reported to Supervisor Thomas. On the morning of May 20 he sent Will a telegram canceling the lecture that had been scheduled for that evening, and informing him that the Board of Education would have no further use for his services. It was a real blow to us, for our expenses were running high in that eventful month.

Meanwhile Mr. Thomas had appointed a Hindu, Prince Sarath Ghosh, to take Will's place before the Wadleigh audience. In introducing the Prince the chairman announced that Dr. Durant would not be able to continue his course of lectures at the school. Saul Burns, one of the auditors, telephoned to our apartment and asked the cause of the change. Will read Thomas' telegram. Burns shouted out the news to the audience. According to the New York *World* of May 21, 1919,

> they booed and hooted and cat-called and jeered the Chairman and the Prince. . . . Men and women jumped to their chairs and swung threatening fists from a safe distance at the men on the platform. Others screeched their demands for Durant from the aisles. Hundreds jammed toward the platform to bawl their objections to the switch in the programme. In a few minutes the hall was a surging mass of flailing arms. . . . A lone policeman . . . ran in. He took one look . . . and ran out. When he came back the reserves were with him.
>
> It required half an hour to clear the hall. The audience appointed a committee of five men and five women to visit the Board of Education and demand that the professor's series on "The Philosophy of Art" be resumed.

It was not.

3 · WOODSTOCK, 1919

Facing new expenses and reduced income, we sold our Overland Beauty, and bought a baby carriage. Alden Freeman continued his seventy-five-dollars-a-month aid to us till 1926, and Leonard Abbott, though himself now burdened with parentage, sent us a check for twenty-five dollars. We felt ourselves exceptionally fortunate, and our evident happiness brought indulgent smiles from our neighbors. When we paraded through Crotona Park behind our prize baby, no one had the heart to question our evident assumption that she was the prettiest girl in town. Will, as he bumped that carriage up or down five flights of stairs to or from our apartment, thought it a blessed labor of love, and would have bristled if anyone had compared him to Sisyphus. When he carried our tot in his arms he hugged her so fondly that I felt jealous, but was soon squeezing her in turn.

We saved our dollars and decided to spare Ethel and her parents a hot summer by renting some cheap cottage in the Catskills. We found one in Woodstock, about 125 miles from New York: an old frame structure picturesquely called Mill Stream Studio. It had no toilet and no water, the outhouse was a favorite haunt of wasps and bees, but the water we drew from an outside pump was the best we have ever tasted in our lives; and just below us, hidden by shady trees and fragrant shrubs, ran a brook where we could have a cold bath any hour of any day.

In that natural arboretum Will placed a table and chair, and there, through many a morning, he sat writing a novel called *The Gentle Philosopher*. He had begun it in 1917, but the excitement of the war, and the multiplication of his lectures, had interrupted it; now, in what promised to be sylvan peace, he worked on it regularly, disturbed only by the occasional crying of our child, or by the mosquitoes and other insects that resented his intrusion and feasted on his blood.

I have the faded manuscript before me now—164 yellow, ragged sheets; he has proposed to destroy it as betraying his immaturity, but I have preserved it as a touching form of that sentimental, idealizing blend of love, philosophy, Christianity, and socialism which dominates his spiritual chemistry. It began with what I suspect was an imaginative reconstruction of Father Mooney's youth; he could never get that kindly but somber priest out of his memory, and he could not bear to believe that so good a man had been without some romance, however brief and tragic, in his life. Evidently the beginning was revised in terms of the present environment:

> Père Dubois, aged pastor of the little town of St. Pierre, was in the habit of reading his breviary, when the weather permitted, in the cool shade of the woods that lay between the parish house and the river. This morning, one of the rarest days in June, he had found his way, half unconsciously, along the path that led to a turn in the stream; and now, the sunlight on the water catching his eye, he closed the book, ended a prayer, and stood for a moment in restful enjoyment of the scene.
>
> Not enjoyment as much as reverie. The river had a painful fascination for him, above all at this season when spring was growing into summer, and

the stillness of the woods . . . [manuscript torn and blurred here] and the quiet lapping of the water. It was on just such a day as this, forty years since, that his betrothed had been drowned before his eyes, in another river beautiful as this, in far off southern France. He had lived through that scene countless times in memory; now he saw it again, acted it again, with twitching muscles and trembling frame; and knew once more part of the anguish of that morning when the body of his beloved lay before him, bloated and blue, and all the world seemed meaningless.

I don't believe that Will could ever have been a good novelist. He was too tied to his memories and feelings to develop interest in a variety of characters, or to describe vividly anyone but himself and those close to him, or to perceive and report those details, mannerisms, and nuances that can give fiction a captivating semblance of remembered scenes. These 164 pages are of interest only as a preparation for *Transition* (1927), which told our story with equal simplicity and better art.

I believe I know one of the reasons why Will failed with *The Gentle Philosopher*, though he succeeded in becoming one. Soon after our arrival in Woodstock our prize baby developed persistent colic, with a succession of painful boils, and her cries of pain made it impossible for him to "remember in tranquility" the events that he had experienced and the emotions he had felt. Our distress was multiplied when we discovered that we were to blame for Ethel's sufferings. Finding it difficult to get pasteurized milk in Woodstock, we yielded to the advice of the town doctor and fed her powdered and sugared milk. The powder produced constipation, the sugar produced boils. We tried enemas and palliatives, but the evils continued until Rose Abbott—Leonard's wife—recommended milk fresh from the cow, despite possible dangers from nonpasteurization. We took this advice, with some good results. I am ashamed that my own milk was judged inadequate; but I am more ashamed that Will and I were so inept in choosing doctors, and so ignorant of what even illiterate mothers now know about feeding an infant.

Will knew more about music than about children, and he seldom missed any of the Sunday-afternoon concerts given at the "Maverick"—a colony of innovative artists living a mile or so from Woodstock. When Ethel's health seemed restored he insisted on taking her with us to these performances, pushing her heavy carriage over a rough rural road amid a stream of automobiles. I mourned his foolishness, but joined in it.

When we returned to East 175th Street our child seemed to be literally in the pink of health. But one day a child specialist, Dr. Herman Sheffield, passing me as I carried Ethel up the stairs, noticed that she let her head fall to one side or the other. He asked pardon for the intrusion, and gently warned me that such head-turning in infants was a sign of rickets and vitamin deficiency. "You must give her plenty of orange juice," he advised. We did, and from that moment we put Ethel under his care. He refused payment for his services; he asked only that Will should read and correct some poems he had written. He was one of several scientific saints who have honored us with their friendship.

Our three-room apartment felt newly confining after our stay in that spacious Woodstock cottage, with a hundred trees within our sight, and a mountain stream bubbling audibly nearby. Will sharpened my discontent by going off for several weeks of barnstorming in the Middle West. He atoned by sending me the best of his poems—

Alone

When late I lay in distant loneliness,
Towered in gloom, in haunting darkness lost,
Fighting with evil powers that shook and tossed
Body and soul till life seemed less and less;
Love only held me, with her strong caress,
Faithful to earth and careless of her cost;
Redeeming nights, with ghastly horrors crossed,
Through her revealed and visioned loveliness.

As one might pierce the secret of a star,
I saw a woman framed in mist and foam,
And heard her whisper to a child afar:
"Sleep, little one; soon he will find his home."
My spirit rose and overleapt the gloom.
Oh, wait for me a while, dear hearts, I come!

After his return we asked ourselves: Can we bring up our child in a three-room apartment five flights up? He had enjoyed carrying her up the stairs, but the ecstasy of that union could not annul the risk of slipping or stumbling on those hundred concrete steps. Could we not now afford to buy a tiny home of our own? One day we saw an advertisement of a "dream house" for sale on Neck Road, Brooklyn, on the route to Sheepshead Bay. We were charmed by that word "dream"; obviously this was what we had visioned in our wishful fantasies. We drove out to see it; it was a two-story frame dwelling, proudly detached, separable from its present owners for six thousand dollars. Before the autumn of 1919 had turned the leaves we were settled there, and Will was pushing Ethel in her carriage along uncrowded streets, in still-unpolluted air, sometimes all the way to Coney Island.

4 • NEW FRIENDS, 1921

We continued to prosper financially. Besides his lectures at Labor Temple Will had plenty of engagements in 1921—twelve in Kansas City alone. All around us the rebels who had been ready to demolish capitalism were now earning a good living, and were developing the usual yearnings of the newly bourgeois. We were like them. We had money enough now to move into a seven-room house at 973 East Thirteenth Street, Flatbush, Brooklyn. One room occupied the only finished part of the third floor; having no use for it, we rented it to a jovial salesman who impressed us with his Pierce Arrow car. He paid his rent promptly, and took care of his room and bed. All went well until Will's mother, coming to bless our third home, noted a faint smell of alcohol at the foot of the third-floor stairs. During our roomer's absence we entered his quarters and found an apparatus for distilling alcohol. Prohibition had gone into effect on July 1, 1919; our tenant was one of thousands of "moonshiners" supplying the whiskey trade. We parted amiably; but later I wondered was not his final smile one of amusement at the simplicity of these young world-shakers who had taken so long to find him out.

We were quite well satisfied with ourselves. Our baby was flourishing, and our kindly neighbors looked up to Will as already a scholar and philosopher; about this time a young sculptor, Vladimir Glinsky, made a bust of him that turned him into Rodin's *Thinker*. He was brought back to earth by a bad attack of scabies. We had gone to spend a week at Camp Tamiment, a mountain resort maintained in the Pocono Mountains by the socialist Rand School. Some blankets there had been obtained from an army store; they were infested with itch-mites; we wrapped ourselves cozily in blankets, and when we came home we were burning with something like the medieval "Saint Anthony's Fire." My case was mild, but Will was soon scratching from chin to knees. It took several weeks of smelly sulfur applications to get the better of those mites.

Will:

The year 1920–21 was a hard one for Labor Temple. The problem of financing it without contributory parishioners became increasingly difficult. To meet these costs the Presbyterian Board of Home Missions leased the site for ninety-nine years to a corporation which proposed to replace the old church with an office building of which one-third would be a new Labor Temple with classrooms, club rooms, an auditorium seating six hundred, and an apartment for the family of the Reverend Edmund B. Chaffee, the devoted pacifist who had succeeded Dr. Jonathan Day as director. For an entire season I had to give my eighty lectures in neighboring halls. One series, on the history of art, required the help of my brother-in-law Michael, who handled the stereopticon machine and slides that gave my discourses some vitalizing illustration. I can still see his bright face alert for my cues.

Instead of succumbing to the task of keeping my audience despite several changes of meeting place, I rashly took on a larger commitment by proposing to Dr. Chaffee that I should use some rooms in the new building for various lecture courses to be given by diverse teachers under my management. An unexpected windfall helped to finance this project.

On a free afternoon in Chicago I decided to pay my respects to Clarence Darrow. I found him dressed in his loose and casual way, and could hardly make out, behind the lines of his somber face, the strange mixture of pessimism and benevolence that characterized his conduct and his philosophy. I apologized for polluting his room with the smell of my sulfur ointment; he assured me that I was giving forth a most delectable odor. I told him of my plans for a Labor Temple School, and asked him would he, on his next trip to New York, help raise funds for it by engaging me in a public debate. He agreed. How much would he charge us? He answered, "Nothing." A month or so later, in an East Side hall, we fought amiably over the question "Is Progress Real?" My old friend "Uncle Tim" Cairns served as chairman. I defended progress as well as I could. Darrow, with dry wit, picked out the fleas in my argument, and the audience shouted with delight. When it was all over Tim tried to console me: "Will, he just wins by sheer force of character." No, by force of intellect too. When I tried to guide the victor away from the sidewalk crowd, Darrow demurred. "Let me mingle with them for a while," he said. Ariel and I loved him.

The next problem was to secure, for the opening of the school in September, 1921, six or seven teachers competent in their subjects and capable of making them intelligible and rewarding to students with little schooling and little money. The students would pay twenty-five cents per lecture; the teacher would be paid only what his students brought in. It seemed unlikely that good teachers could be attracted by such an arrangement, but they came, out of pure goodwill; and professors like William Pepperel Montague from Columbia University and Harry Overstreet from City College gave at Labor Temple School the same courses which they were giving for far higher fees in their academies.

The most successful of our teachers was our friend Dr. Abraham Stone. We had met him in his work, with his wife, Dr. Hannah Stone, at the birth control clinic that Margaret Sanger had established despite religious and legal opposition. Both Abe and Hannah were first-rate doctors; we learned much from them; and Abe, a Polish Jew, polished his English by rubbing it against mine. Their lovable daughter Gloria became one of Ethel's closest friends. Dr. Abraham Stone undertook at Labor Temple a weekly class in the physiology and hygiene of marriage, and soon added to it a bureau of marriage counseling—perhaps the first of its kind in America.

Quite different from any of us, and yet soon dear to all three of us, was John Cowper Powys. He was one of the many gifts that Ariel brought me. One afternoon, passing by Percy Stickney Grant's Church of the

Ascension, she noted a number of people entering the building at an hour unlikely for religious services. She followed them to a small auditorium where, she was told, they would soon hear a lecture on Shelley. Presently a tall, bent, angular Briton entered, wearing the robe and cap of a Cambridge scholar; long legs and dangling, waving arms; a head of massive curly hair; a face of strong features and flashing eyes. He fumbled for words (Ariel reported), but he found them, yoked them, and made them form a picture so vivid and colorful that she was enthralled. Emerging, she ran to Labor Temple to tell me that she had just "seen Shelley plain" through a man descended from Donne and Cowper and combining their piety with the rebelliousness of Shelley and the sensitivity of Keats.

Some time later we visited him in his hemmed-in solitude at 4 Patchin Place—a dead-end alley at Tenth Street near Sixth Avenue. Of course my attention was caught first by his face, at once gauntly Welsh and proudly British, with features suggesting a long lineage of distinguished souls. I recall now the remark of his brother Llewelyn, who, like another brother, Theodore, wrote successful books: "Both I and Theodore have originality; John has genius." One look was enough to convince me of his genius. My second wonder was at a rosary hanging on the wall. There was something theatrical about John in those early days of our friendship; his wearing of his scholar's robe when he lectured may have been a stratagem to arouse a curiosity that would alert attention; that rosary may have been his way of declaring that he loved everything in Catholicism except its intolerance; he loved the ritual and the myths; and he loved his son who had become a Catholic priest.

Of course I asked him to teach at Labor Temple. It was an imposition to ask this volcano to come and erupt punctually at a stated hour each week for a few dollars. Learning that he was badly in need of three hundred dollars, I forced that sum upon him as an advance against the fees his class would give him. He agreed. We both improved our finances by arranging to debate each other, at Labor Temple and elsewhere; and these debates intensified our friendship. He would often warn the audience against me as "the crafty doctor," but privately he would refer to me (as in his *Autobiography*) as "the radical saint," which must have made the angels hilarious. He always asked me to speak first, confident that I would make so many mistakes, or utter so many platitudes, that they would give him, without any preparation, abundant material for his forty minutes.

Typical was our duel at Labor Temple over the question "Who Are the Ten Greatest Authors?" I began by listing the traditional names: Homer, Confucius, Euripides, etc. Secretly Powys admired these three; but when he rose he startled all of us by naming as his first choice one of whom probably no one there but himself had ever heard. It sounded like

"Whang!" and was reinforced by a powerful slap on the lectern; I was not sure whether it was a name or an expletive. It turned out to be Chuang-tzu, the Chinese idealist philosopher (b. 370 B.C.). Powys quoted from him a now famous story: "Once upon a time I . . . dreamt I was a butterfly. . . . Suddenly I awoke. . . . Now I do not know whether I was then dreaming that I was a butterfly or am now a butterfly dreaming that I am a man." This brought down the house, and made me wish I were a butterfly.

Soon thereafter we both went off on divergent lecture tours. I left Ariel with Ethel, Flora, and her son Louis, then four years old. From some unstated point I sent back a love letter with a poem in my most sentimental style:

Absence

My soul for yours (dear mother of our child)—
    Dauntless of space as any god above,
Swift overleaping the impeding wild—
    Searches, and finds, and nestles in your love.

Softly she sleeps, guileless and careless yet;
    And as the gentle moon, through clouds apart,
Bends from the sky to kiss her coverlet,
    We know again her beauty; and your art.

Safe in the tabernacle of your womb
    Through holy months you held her, scorning scorn;
Into the lonely shadow of the tomb
    You walked unfearful, that she might be born.

Oh, to be worthy such a sacrifice!
    Yet not long faith, though toiling endlessly,
Should win such love, nor Midas' gold suffice
    To laurel fitly such a victory.

How sweet, dear love, to watch her in her sleep.
    Here in the cradle is the gift you won.
Be now your life and hers my life; God keep
    Me servant of you both till life is done.

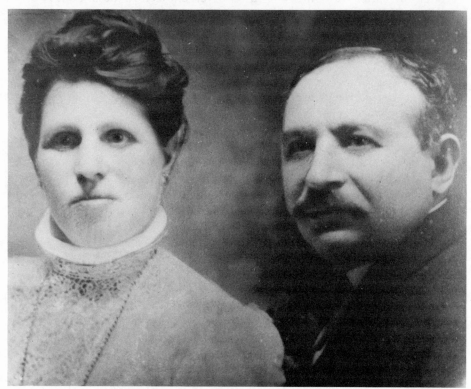

Ariel's parents: Ethel and Joseph Appel, 1903.

The Kaufman Family, 1902: from left, Mary, Harry, Maurice, Michael (infant), Mother, Father, Ariel, Flora. (Sarah was in a hospital.)

Ariel, Walter Groth, Christine Hovden, 1912.

Will's parents: Marie and Joseph Durant.

Lola Ridge, 1912.

Cora Stevenson and her class at the Francisco Ferrer School, 1913. Ariel, top center, wears a white ribbon in her hair.

Will and Ariel, 1915.

Alden Freeman, about 1912.

Leonard Dalton Abbott, 1912.

Emma Goldman and Alexander Beckman, 1917. UPI

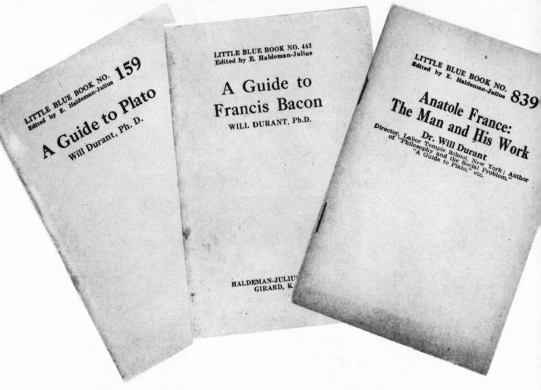

Little Blue Books, *sold at 5¢ a copy, formed the basis for* The Story of Philosophy. Plato, *published in 1923, was the first of Will's eleven essays to appear in the popular format from 1923–1925.*

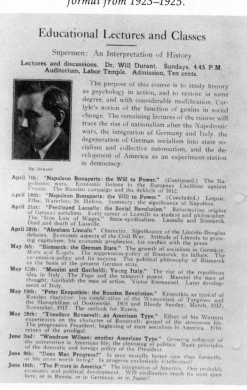

Spring Program Announcement, 1918, Labor Temple Lecture Series. GEORGE ARENTS
RESEARCH LIBRARY, SYRACUSE UNIVERSITY

Labor Temple

Winter
Announcement
1922

Corner Second Ave. and 14th St.
NEW YORK CITY.

Bust of Will Durant
by Vladimir Glinsky, 1921.

The Labor Temple, at the corner of Second Avenue at Fourteenth Street, New York City. Cover of Lecture Series Announcement. GEORGE ARENTS RESEARCH LIBRARY, SYRACUSE UNIVERSITY

A typical audience for The Open Forum held Sunday evenings at 8:15 in the Labor Temple. GEORGE ARENTS RESEARCH LIBRARY, SYRACUSE UNIVERSITY

Ethel Durant and her father, 1923.

Ethel Durant, 1924.

M. Lincoln Schuster and Ethel at Sea Clift, about 1930.

Will Durant, by George Hurrell, 1927.

Ariel, by George Hurrell, 1927.

Theodore Dreiser, 1944.

Upton Close, 1933. UPI

The Gypsy Tavern, 64 Washington Square South, about 1926. The Greenwich Village tearoom was housed in the small buildings beneath the Beech-Nut Gum advertisement.
NEW YORK UNIVERSITY ARCHIVES DIVISION

Will and Ariel returning from Europe, 1932. UPI

Ariel, Will,
John Cowper Powys,
M. Lincoln Schuster
at Phudd Bottom,
New York, 1931.

George Sokolsky, Ariel, Hu Shih,
and Will in Shanghai, 1930.

Mahatma Gandhi reading
The Case for India, *1931.*

Clarence Darrow, 1924. UPI

Bertrand Russell, 1935. UPI

Forward

מונטאג בּיולאַגע

זונטאג, דעצעמבער 30, 1934

SECTION

3

ּפיר פון די פּראמינענטע פּערזענליכקייטען ביי דער ערעפענונג פון דער לאיברערי פאר ביכער פון שרייבער וועמענס ווערק די
ּנאַציס האַבּען פארברענט אין דייטשלאַנד. פון רעכטס צו לינקס : פּראָפ. אַלבּערט איינשטיין, עדווין מאַרקהאַם, בּאַרימטער אמערי־
ּזאַנער פּאָעט ; וויל דוראַנט, שריפטשטעלער, און רעימאָנד אינגערסאָל פּאַרזיע פּרעזידענט פון בּרוקלין. די לאיברערי נעפינט זיך אין
„בּרוקלין ּדזשואיש סענטער."

Brooklyn Jewish Center, November 30, 1934.

51 Deepdale Drive, Great Neck, New York, 1934.

*Captain Louis R. Durant
returns from war, 1945.*

Lake Hill, New York,
Christmas, 1943.

The "Casa della Vista," east front, 1943.

At William Singer's home, 1946: from left, Italo Montemezzi, Thomas Mann, William Singer, Lion Feuchtwanger, and Will.

Will and M. Lincoln Schuster, 1963.

Will and Arnold Toynbee, 1963.

Will and granddaughter Monica at her graduation, 1969.

Will and Ariel upon publication of The Age of Napoleon.

Will receiving the Medal of Freedom from President Gerald Ford, January 10, 1977.
OFFICIAL WHITE HOUSE PHOTO

Ariel receiving the Medal of Freedom from President Gerald Ford, January 10, 1977.
OFFICIAL WHITE HOUSE PHOTO

CHAPTER VII

Accidents

1922–26

Ariel:

In 1922 I had my first contact with death. My father, then sixty-two, was keeping a newsstand at Forty-second Street under the Third Avenue "El." A truck, out of control, climbed upon the sidewalk and pinned him against a wall. He emerged with what seemed no more than a fright, but he had received some lasting injury to his heart. He was never well again, and the gloom that had shrouded his life and mind darkened with every exhausting day of standing on his feet or carrying heavy bundles. One morning we received an excited telephone call from my mother: "Come, please; Yussuf is dying." Will ran around the corner to the rented garage that housed our car; we drove hurriedly from Flatbush to our former home in Neck Road. My father's breathing and heartbeat had already stopped, and Will tried in vain to revive him. A rabbi came and directed the preparation of the body. The next day the family accompanied the corpse to the cemetery. I whispered to my mother, "I'm so glad it wasn't you." She silenced me with a stern look.

Will was busy that year organizing Labor Temple School, which soon had some six teachers besides himself. He continued, as usual, to give two courses through the scholastic year. He taught a smaller class for a shorter time at a Jewish Community Center in Brooklyn. A Brooklyn newspaper, on May 27, 1922, printed an interview in which Will bared his ego with unusual abandon.

> Dr. Durant's boyhood ambition has come true in the sense that he
> wanted to be a known writer, but it has not come true in the sense that he

94

wanted to become an internationally known writer. "Later, when I grew older," the young scientist said, "I felt that I would be satisfied with national fame. Still later my ambition would be satisfied with something smaller yet. It does not bother me now. I find pleasure in writing and studying."

It is his ambition . . . to lay aside enough money so that when he reaches the age of forty he may dispense with giving lectures, . . . and go on extended trips to France and England to engage in research work in preparation for a book that would show the interdependence, in history, of politics, economics, art, literature, and science. "These subjects," Dr. Durant said, "have been written up separately. My ambition is to write a complete [!] history of the world, showing all these factors working in harmony, and giving as a result the kind of world we know."

Obviously, at this stage, Will had no intention of writing a *Story of Philosophy;* indeed, such a book would be only another example of what he was to call "shredded history," treating a single strand of the complex web called civilization. A chain of trivial accidents overrode his intentions. I had known in Greenwich Village an impoverished, ambitious, book-loving youth called Emanuel Julius. In one of our meetings I told him about Will's lectures, and suggested that he drop in on one of them. He went west, married Marcet Haldeman, added her name and income to his, and set up at Girard, Kansas, a publishing firm which almost educated the United States with fragile but handy "Little Blue Books" at five cents a copy. In 1922, while passing Labor Temple one Sunday afternoon, he saw a sign announcing an imminent lecture on Plato by Will Durant. He entered, and was pleased with what he heard, but he had to hurry away without making himself known.

From Girard he wrote to Will proposing that the lecture on Plato should be written out and be published as a Blue Book. Will answered that his schedule was so crowded that he had no time to write anything. What a silly reply! If Emanuel had let the matter drop the whole course of our lives might have been changed. For Will's career from 1926 to 1957 was financed chiefly by the unexpected success of *The Story of Philosophy,* and that book would never have been written had not Emanuel sent another letter, enclosing a check for $150 in prepayment for the proposed booklet. Will was overcome by this act of faith. He made time for *Plato,* and before the year 1922 was out his essay was published as Little Blue Book No. 159.

We presumed that this concluded our affair with Mr. Haldeman-Julius. But that generous and enterprising spirit was fascinated by other subjects on Will's lecture course. He asked for a second booklet, and enclosed another check; Will sent him an essay on Aristotle. Emanuel found readers for it, and risked another check and another. So, at intervals from 1923 to 1925, appeared little nickelodeons on Bacon, Spinoza,

Voltaire, Kant, Schopenhauer, Spencer, Nietzsche, Bergson-Croce-Russell, James-Santayana-Dewey. And then it dawned upon both the publisher and the author that these eleven booklets, with some connective tissue added, could make *The Story of Philosophy*. Will's most famous baby, like so many, had been conceived by accident, and was to be born, in 1926, with fear, pain, and love.

In February, 1923, Will took a leave of absence from Labor Temple to help Dan Coombs set up the "Kansas City Academy" as hopefully a prelude to a university. I met Dan later, and his wife, Fern, both of them remarkable personalities: Dan for vision and enterprise persisting through a painful and incurable disease, Fern for unfailing competence and devotion through all difficulties and disappointments. In the thirty-four days between February 15 and March 20 Will gave forty lectures for the academy, on history, literature, philosophy, economics, and politics. On top of this, in Kansas City, he faced Clarence Darrow in another debate on "Is Life Worth Living?"

I was relieved to see him in good health and buoyant spirits when he returned to our Flatbush home. Soon afterward the Otto Sarony Company sent a man to take some pictures of my busy polymath. After several "shots" the photographer was about to leave when Ethel—now a plump and jolly girl of four—romped into the house from the street. Will caught her up in his arms and held her, cheek to cheek. "Hold it!" cried the photographer, and snapped them in a pose that still brightens our family picture gallery: Will with hair still black, beard Vandykely trimmed, big ears and big nose, eyes gleaming with proud love; Ethel chubby, disheveled, trustful, loving, lovable. Hardly a day passes without Will stealing a look at that photograph.

I think it was during that spring of 1923 that Darrow spoke at the Flatbush Jewish Center near our house. Of course we went to hear him. After he had completed his quiet speech, and had answered questions with his usual patience, candor, and simplicity, he accompanied us to our home. There, after some refreshments, he took up a book from my desk—A. E. Housman's *A Shropshire Lad*. "This," he said, "is one of my favorites." Seated on my bed, he began to read the verses aloud. I believe he read to us nearly all of that classic before he left for his hotel. It was one of the sweetest evenings in our lives. The spirit of Housman, and that of Thomas Hardy, had transmigrated into this Chicago lawyer, who had seen so many blighted lives that he had forgotten how to smile.

That summer we took Ethel for a week or two at Unity House, a delightful camp set up in the Pocono Mountains of eastern Pennsylvania by the International Ladies Garment Workers Union. Will paid for our room and board with a lecture or two. He swam and played tennis, took walks with us in the neighboring woods, and in the evenings he wrote that booklet on Spinoza which became a chapter in *The Story of Philosophy*. As he could not keep the light on while Ethel slept, he moved his chair and writing board into the bathroom, and proceeded with his work. All that week he was a Spinoza-intoxicated man, and he has never recovered. He interpreted Spinoza's God as the total of Nature in its structure and laws, and defined wisdom as acceptance of these laws as the guide to our reason and our striving. Now, remembering Mary's *Magnificat*, he composed a poem

On Reading Spinoza

My soul doth magnify the Law,
And my spirit is lifted to understanding.
For I was darkened, and it gave me light;
I was troubled with desiring, and it gave me bound and end;
I was driven by the storm, and it gave me port and home;
I was weary, and it gave me rest.

The stars keep their courses—and have I not heard their music?
Passion speaks for a day, but love ripens beyond utterance;
All things bide their time that flow to their fulfillment;
The rose is patient in the bud, and man is cradled in many years.

Behold, I was torn into pieces, and I am made one;
My strength was scattered into every wind, and it is gathered;
For now I know the Circle of the Law, and I shall not stray;
Within the Circle is my work, and within the work is my rejoicing.
My soul doth magnify the Law,
And my spirit is lifted up to peace.

I could not recall his being "darkened," or "driven by the storm," much less his hearing the music of the spheres; but now he tells me that he had deeply felt the loss of God, that he had been torn from me and his purpose by lecture tours, and that some insistent voice had for years been singing to him of a great work that he might accomplish if he would stay at home and keep his peace. I believe he was already dreaming of writing a history that would portray the past in its complex unity, and would consume the remainder of his life.

In 1923 we moved to 1979 Bedford Avenue, Brooklyn. A year later Ethel began to attend public school, and Will, usually stingy of his time, took pleasure in serving as her chaperon through the crowded streets; when a reporter asked him what were his recreations he answered, "Taking Ethel to school." Ethel was a good child, sound of body, quick of mind, good of heart. Seeing crates of chickens on their way to slaughter, she whispered to me, "Mother, don't you wish they didn't know it?"— and she was relieved to learn that probably they did not. I was jealous of

97

Will's love for her. In a notebook that I kept in 1924 I find some jottings that surprise me now. For example:

> It is more natural for a man to be a father than a husband. How easily a man gives way to the whim of a child jumping in upon him even in the midst of his most earnest reveries. How easily are met her solicitations to her daddy to leave all and play with her. How ungrudgingly he goes with her, descends on all fours when she does, and never pays the least notice of the clock ticking away the minutes into hours. But when his wife asks a question, . . . ah, how different!—indifferently he shakes his head, "Yes"; and in a moment is absorbed again in his work. It is not natural to have a wife, it is natural . . . to have a child. A woman, never capable of making a friend of another woman, how miserable is she when nature has robbed her even of husband-friend. Jane Welsh [wife of Carlyle] knew the truth of the above. Her story would have been even more pitiful if she and not Froude had told it. Even so, Froude knew what she suffered by having a genius and not a friend for a husband.

The entry under April 14, 1924, which will now for the first time be known to my mate, indicates a secret discontent occasionally hiding within the outward bliss of our marriage:

> An unrequited love forever smolders, and at the least provocation rekindles. "The thoughts of a woman whose husband is famous." Indeed, a statue hath fallen upon her. This, that, and the other thing she must not do. . . . Everyone who approaches her . . . merely uses friendship with the wife as an open sesame to the husband. . . .
>
> My husband is a romantic type who externally and in dress is very conservative. If he only would wear an orange tie and dishevel his hair a bit, his beautiful black hair, already tinging gray. Why does he sit away from me whenever we go to a lecture or a recital where there is a choice of seats? Is he so tired of me that my sitting near him would spoil his hearing or attention? * Yet he lends a willing ear to almost everybody who happens to sit near him. . . .
>
> April 16. Tomorrow I leave for a week at Loch Sheldrake. My heart is heavy. . . . I hate to leave him or have him leave me. . . . I wish he would come with me, but then I would be frustrating my purpose of giving him an opportunity to write in a week of peace. If only no one would come and bother away his time. I wish sometimes that we lived in the wilderness— he would accomplish so much more. Yet the crossroads and contacts are essential for character and vibrant thinking. . . . The woods of Nohant bored George Sand. . . .
>
> My husband—pretty much like a dog—lives by his sense of smell. . . . Every day he complains of smelling this and smelling that. Finally I had to leave his room—also my study—which I regret very much—and ask him to hire an office. He sends me crazy breaking out with a frown upon the different odors he supposes pass through this house. The smell of certain

---

* *Will:* I can't recall such occasions. We were notoriously glued to each other in public. But I was sometimes inattentive through absentmindedness.

foods makes him nauseous, and bodily odors make him faint with disgust—while I, nestling under his arm of an evening, am deliciously rapt with joy at the sweet human smell of his armpits.*

Apparently I had an admirer who offered me, *pro tem*, the romantic adoration that Will no longer gave me. A note in my diary looks like the confused draft of a letter that was never sent: "November 21, 1924.— Charlie—I am beaten. . . . I had to ask you not to call me up and not to come around. . . ." "Charlie" must have taken me at my word, for I reproached him in my diary under

> Wed. Nov. 26, 1924: Dear, I haven't seen or heard from you for a week and a half and my heart is full of uneasy premonitions—that you could be alive and yet not write to me or see me for so long—is that not enough cause for my sadness? You are sick, how I tried to get in touch with you. The number you gave me won't connect us. The letter I tried to write was discovered by Will [but] in time for me to tear it up and throw it into the wastebasket, a token of fidelity to him and treason to my heart.
>
> My kind sweet Will and my poor sick Charlie. My feeling towards each complements my feelings toward the other. If only they could understand the intricacy of a woman's heart.

I must have had a competitor for Charlie, for the next note addresses her:

> Here in this silence and solitude I can speak up and say that I have injured you, Miriam. You love him—your eyes say so, though your lips never, . . . and my monopoly of him keeps him, . . . yet for a while, from loving you, which is inevitable sooner or later, and the sooner as he comes really to know you. I say these things with the conviction of their truth, though I am sad at my knowledge of them.

Will:

Looking back now at this secret romance, I see that I had been neglecting my role as a lover to extend it as a provider. We had bought (and sold) our second house, we had a Buick car, and we enjoyed two months in the country every year, like other members of the lower bourgeoisie. But we had never tried to keep up with the Joneses. We dressed simply; Ariel seldom bought clothes, and never wore a ring; we rarely spent more than a dollar per person for a restaurant meal. Somehow we had saved thirty thousand dollars before *The Story of Philosophy* made us money glad in 1926.

So, by 1925 I had to become a financier, worrying how to invest our savings safely and profitably despite the vicissitudes of the economy and

---

* *Will:* This is all revelation to me. Why didn't she tell me? For years I hesitated to tell her how the odor of her armpits delighted me.

the skulduggery of men. I bought mortgages from the Bond and Mortgage Guarantee Company of Brooklyn, and lost a small part of our hoard in the collapse of that organization after 1929. Among our friends were two men each of whom was independently dealing in second mortgages. I knew that such mortgages were especially risky, but I so trusted Max Herzfeld and Abraham Eisenbud that I deposited eight thousand dollars with the one, and ten thousand with the other, to lend at their discretion. I was following the usual road from socialism to capitalism; my excuse was that socialism had not come, that hoarded money was daily losing value, and that I had a family to support and a financial cushion to build for our future. When the crash came I was saved from the penalty of my greed by the friendship and integrity of those two men; shortly before the mortgage market crumbled each of them returned my money, saying that he could no longer find a safe investment for it.

Early in 1925 we moved to half a house at 243 Ocean Avenue, opposite Prospect Park. Soon after settling down I left Ariel to go barnstorming in the East and the Middle West. I used myself up in almost nightly lectures and daytime and nighttime travel, for fees running from forty to a hundred dollars.

Under March 3, in my 1925 diary, I find this rash memo: "Send Alden [Freeman] outline of 4 vols. of Hy of Eur'n Culture in the 19th Cy." Here I was, not yet delivered of *The Story of Philosophy*, and already conceiving four volumes more. No one has invented a literary contraceptive; authors are always pregnant, and are naturally swelled up.

My letter of March 7 sang to Ariel a dithyramb about our new location:

> I like to think that you and I will be within half an hour of Labor Temple and Greenwich Village, . . . nevertheless Ethel will be brought up almost in the country. For in front of us, at least, it will be as if we were at Unity [House]—a real "Forest Park," with a real lake. In winter you will skate there, and I shall watch you and take you home; in spring, summer, and autumn we shall go boating, idling, reading, singing, on those waters. Perhaps some day I shall sing again.
>
> The cynic or skeptic in me (for the Lord knows I am always a sentimental romantic, and my skeptical and classical head is a necessary self-protection) writes a great ? against this picture, and tells me that after a month I will be so used to the park . . . that I will never see it, and seldom go to it. . . . But I am still young enough . . . to feel that now, though I shall be a little cramped in my room, I shall have mother nature (made more beautiful by human care) for company every day. Even in winter, I think, I shall do some of my studying in the Park. . . .

A few days later I was home, and resumed my semiweekly lectures at Labor Temple. We spent a pleasant summer at Camp Utopia, near Lackawaxen, Pennsylvania; its manager was our old friend Will Perlman; I paid for our board by giving two informal lectures per week. I had a hard time luring those lusty youths and lively girls away from the tennis courts and the lake. Ethel was already an expert swimmer, who laughed at my leisurely side stroke. On October 10, in New York, we celebrated the reopening of Labor Temple School with a festive dinner at which Powys, Joel Blau, Mrs. Charlotte Perkins Gilman, and I provided oratory.

About October, 1925, two publishing firms offered to publish my eleven booklets as a volume in "boards" and glue. After Haldeman-Julius had printed the last of my Blue Books he informed me that he intended to buy a large press and bindery, and to issue clothbound books of which one would be *The Story of Philosophy*, on which he would pay me the standard royalty. Later he abandoned the plan, and proposed that he and I should seek a publisher, and divide the royalty.

I took the booklets to the Macmillan Company at 60 Fifth Avenue, New York; there a kindly Mr. Latham accepted them. A day or two later I saw Haldeman-Julius on a street in Manhattan; he hurried me into a cab and told me that he had found a publisher. But, I protested, I too had found a publisher. And who were Simon and Schuster? I had heard of them, but only in connection with crossword-puzzle books. Why shouldn't I enjoy the prestigious imprint of the most highly regarded publishing firm in America, perhaps in the world? That, Emanuel countered, was just the rub: it was an old firm, grown cautious and stodgy; our book would be lost in the hundred or so volumes that Macmillan would issue in 1926. "Essandess," however, constituted a young and enterprising duo; our volume would be their first serious publication; their own fortune would in some measure be bound up with mine; they would push the book with a youthful initiative and energy that could not be expected of an established firm.

I believe it was the next day that I first heard Max Schuster's seductive voice. It came over the telephone. He explained that he had read those eleven booklets and loved them; he was anxious to turn them into an imposing volume. I promised to come and see him the following afternoon. Ariel went with me, and we at once fell under the charm of these two young men who were destined to revolutionize the publishing business in America. Max was then (in 1925) twenty-eight; his partner, Dick Simon, was twenty-six. Both were handsome—Max with a broad face alive with enterprise and interest under a full head of black hair, Dick with classically fine features under a forehead already pushing back his blond hair. Both were Jewish. All who came to know them learned to trust and honor them. Happy the day they came into our lives.

That same afternoon I went to Macmillan's, and easily persuaded Mr. Latham to release me from my agreement with him. I suspect he was relieved. In the next two weeks I wrote, and sent to Max, additional pages to serve as a frail bridge over some of the chasms between the booklets. Awful gaps remained—too little about Zeno and Epicurus, Epictetus and Marcus Aurelius, Abélard and Thomas Aquinas, Leibniz and Hegel, Fichte and Schelling, Hobbes and Locke, Berkeley and Hume.* The first line of the preface frankly warned the reader that he was being shortchanged: "This book is not a complete history of philosophy. It is an attempt to humanize knowledge by centering the story of speculative thought around certain dominant personalities." The word *Story* in the title promised an effort to present the ideas of the philosophers in non-technical terms, and to bring those ideas within the grasp and usage of the educated community in general, rather than leave them the jealous possession of a closed and esoteric minority; in this sense the book could be called popularization. It was not so if the term implies a skimping of scholarship, or a main reliance on secondary sources. I was happy when I read John Dewey's statement:

> Having had the privilege of reading an advance copy of Dr. Durant's *Story of Philosophy*, I am glad of the opportunity to commend such an admirable piece of intellectual work, as to its substance and its literary form. While the book is one of popularization, it is also much more than that as popularization is usually conceived. The work is thoroughly scholarly. Dr. Durant has gone to the original writings and not to second-hand sources. He has selected the thinkers who are expounded with good judgment; his expositions are accurate as well as clear; his personal comments are always intelligent and useful. He has shown remarkable skill in selecting quotations that are typical, that give the flavor of the author, and that are readable. In fine he has humanized rather than merely popularized the story of philosophy.

When *The Story of Philosophy* was published, in May, 1926, all four of us adventurers—Max and Dick, Ariel and I—hardly breathed while waiting for some sign of public acceptance. The first notice, by Henry James Forman in *The New York Times Book Review*, was so favorable that I wanted to dance—which, however, I had never learned to do. (This was a major defect, for Ariel danced *qual plum' in vento*—like a feather in the wind—and she had to depend upon better-equipped cavaliers.) "This review alone," Max predicted, "will sell a thousand copies of the book." And then, with his characteristic quickness of thought and generosity of motive, he conceived an idea that netted him nothing but brought me a long-awaited leisure.

"Will," he said, "our contract with Haldeman-Julius grants him half, and you half, of the twelve-and-a-half-percent royalty that we are to pay on this book. Why don't you offer him five hundred dollars for his share?" I would never have thought of this, and now hesitated to risk five hundred dollars. A few days earlier I had expressed the *expectation* that the *Story* would sell a thousand copies by Christmas, and the *hope*

---

* Most of these gaps were filled in *The Story of Civilization*, which includes a history of philosophy in all countries to 1815.

102

that it would sell fifteen hundred—at which point, Max calculated, the book would pay the cost of its publication. However, I took his advice, and sent the offer to Emanuel. He accepted it. It is to his credit that he never complained of this somewhat selfish transaction. On the contrary, he rejoiced in the success of a book which owed its existence to him, and he entertained me with fraternal hospitality when, a year later, my wandering lectures took me near his home in Girard, Kansas.

None of us had dreamed of the outburst of complimentary reviews that greeted *The Story of Philosophy*. I am sorely tempted to quote from them. But I must admit that there were hostile articles of considerable weight directed at us by Paul Weiss, Mortimer Adler, Morris Cohen, and others. Their criticisms were that the book had unforgivable omissions, that it paid too little attention to metaphysics and epistemology, and that its effect would be to make the reader think that he had now sufficient acquaintance with the philosophers. It was disgracefully and unforgivably popular. Professor Cohen was shocked at my dismissal of the Scholastics as mostly theologians rather than philosophers, since they assumed in advance the defined faith of the Catholic Church. The Paulist Father Gillis rejected the book because it had no chapter on Christ; the government publishing office of Soviet Russia rejected it because it had no chapter on Marx.*

Simon and Schuster verified Haldeman-Julius' prediction by entering upon an unprecedented campaign of advertising. They took full pages, sometimes a double-page spread, to quote Forman, Dewey, Van Loon, John Haynes Holmes, H. L. Mencken, Henry Hazlitt, Heywood Broun, and other benevolent souls. My book became a social necessity; every proper family felt obliged to display it on the table or the shelf. *Publishers' Weekly* reported in November, 1926, that the *Story* was heading best-seller lists of nonfiction throughout the country from Boston to Los Angeles. It maintained a place on such lists for over a year.

Our happiness at the success of *The Story of Philosophy* was extended by our growing friendship with Max Schuster and Dick Simon. We learned what creative publishing was: the unceasing search for new authors, the exploration of new subjects, the risking of great sums on editorial judgment and widespread advertisement, the active effort to find and

---

* Of course I had assumed that Christ belonged to the history of religion, Marx to the history of economics and politics, and the Scholastics to the history of theology. The brilliant "star" of the City College faculty probably thought that I had skirted the Scholastics because of unfamiliarity with them; he did not know that I had been fed great helpings of Scholastic "philosophy" during my years with the Jesuits and in the seminary. No critic pointed out a much more culpable omission: the *Story* said not a word about Chinese and Indian philosophy. As to the fear that the book would excuse or divert its readers from going to the originals, I received an unsolicited letter from the New York Public Library saying that the circulation of the philosophical classics had risen several hundred percent since the publication of the *Story*. Footnotes in the book directed the reader to the philosophers themselves, and specified the most significant and enduring sections of their works.

develop new markets for books, new techniques for distributing them. Ariel and I frequently referred to Max and Dick as our "publishers but friends," and to our relationship with them as another form of monogamy. In all the years from our meeting in 1925 to Dick's death (1960) and Max's retirement (1966) we never had a quarrel with them.

Ariel:

During the gestation of *The Story of Philosophy* Will was kept busy with his Sunday and Wednesday lectures, and with getting teachers and funds for Labor Temple School. In February, 1926, another public dinner raised a modest sum; and about that time he persuaded Dr. Frederick B. Keppel to have the Carnegie Foundation help the school with a gift of a thousand dollars. Then, in March, he went off to replenish our own coffers with some lectures in the Middle West. From that short trip one letter survives:

March 10, 1926

DEAR SWEETHEART:
This is my day of rest after a strenuous week. . . . Three vigorous lectures—Sunday, Monday, and Tuesday—have left me gasping for breath this morning. I am never tired until the day after. When the thing has to be done my nervous resolution lifts me up to it; but when the work is over I am limp for a day. . . .
    I am crazy with lonesomeness.

Lovingly,
WILL

Doubtless he loved me, but I wondered didn't he love his work more than me. When he was home he sat at his typewriter preparing his next lecture for Labor Temple, or he buried himself in correspondence, research, correcting proofs, or writing another book. I had not yet learned to share his studies or help in his research. I felt a bit neglected. I wandered back to Greenwich Village, and there, in the spring of 1926, I joined with Romany Marie in establishing the Gypsy Tavern, a tearoom and semi-restaurant at 64 Washington Square South. Both of us were positive and aggressive types, who could be friends, but only when not too closely associated; after a month or two Marie left to open her own restaurant, which became far more famous; for Marie had a color and verve that drew celebrities to her. For a time I was happy as the little *grande dame* of the Gypsy Tavern. I drew to my aid various pianists, violinists, singers, dancers, artists, and writers. Will came often, and sometimes gathered the customers together in an informal seminar. On one occasion he brought Theodore Dreiser to help him fete John Cowper Powys on John's fifty-fourth birthday.

Soon I fell into the habit of leaving our Brooklyn home every afternoon to officiate at the Tavern, for I found that when I did not keep an eye on the kitchen, the service, and the entertainment, a spreading carelessness threatened the enterprise with bankruptcy. Will complained that he hardly ever saw me at night; I answered that I hardly ever saw him during the day, for he was too absorbed in his work. On June 17, 1926, returning home about 1 A.M., I found on my desk this letter from my husband, who was asleep in the next room:

DEAR ARIEL:

I have spent a great part of the afternoon thinking over our problem. With all our talk we haven't agreed on any solution that will give you the social life you hunger for, and yet keep us from drifting apart. If we could only find a way in which each of us would enter more fully into the life of the other, our problem would be solved. I am willing to go out with you twice a week: once to a theater (or concert), and once to an after-lecture hour or two in a tearoom. In return you would agree to spend two evenings a week at home, and to be in on other nights by 1 A.M. . . .

I think you would enjoy helping me with the lectures, and entering into partnership in our literary firm. You could do much to recapture for me the hours I am here pledging to the night; not merely in typing notes, but in preparing some of the lectures. There are certain topics (e.g., the women novelists) which you could do entirely. . . . I suggest that you . . . either write a book, which I will help you to get published, or (which would be easier and wiser) write a substantial essay, of some 50 pages, which could be incorporated as a chapter, under your own name, in a book which I am planning on *The Mansions of Philosophy.* I will be glad to teach you the art of collecting and arranging material, and phrasing it in a style that shall have your vigor and my clarity.

Yours,
WILL

That dry "Yours" at the end chilled me. It seemed to me that he was asking me to abandon the Gypsy Tavern (where I was finding an outlet for my own active and social nature) and to accept an almost solitary confinement for several evenings in each week, relieved with a typewriter. Matters became worse when the *Story* made him famous; invitations called him to give lectures, write articles, debate notables, even to report a murder trial. Now we would be less together than before.

In July, 1926, he was seduced by an offer of a thousand dollars—from Roy Howard and the Scripps-Howard papers—for each of three articles on the approaching trial of Ruth Snyder and Judd Gray for allegedly murdering her husband. I suppose Will was attracted not only by the fee but by the promised spectacle of two human beings fighting for their lives in the labyrinths of the law. In any case he accepted the challenge, and prepared himself by visiting the scene of the crime. He wrote, in his first article:

> Come and see the home where the tragedy took place. It is 9327 222nd Street, Queens Village. What an address! Already one visions a little house lost in an endless row of similar dwellings, like the cells in a prison corridor . . . or a hospital. And it is almost so. The home of Arthur and Ruth Snyder differed only in minor details from the hundred homes that ran down the street on either side in long succession. What infernal "realtor" has deposited these houses upon the unoffending soil of Paumanok? Is it any wonder that this stupefying standardization drives men and women to desperate expedients in the gray prose of their monotonous lives?

Will attended several sittings of the trial, and sometimes squeezed me in beside him among half a hundred reporters in love with death by proxy. Then he hurried home and wrote his articles, each an unsteady mixture of realism and compassion; one critic called him the best of the "sob sisters." Roy Howard liked the product, and signed Will to attend and report the execution of Ruth Snyder at Sing Sing. The execution was postponed, and on the new date appointed for it Will had contracted to lecture in Denver. He proposed to release the Scripps-Howard papers from their agreement for a fourth article, but Roy refused, and asked Will to write about the execution, sight unseen. Seated in a Denver garden, Will composed from his imagination a more vivid description of the execution than if he had been present and hampered by the facts. He concluded with so strong an argument against capital punishment that Edmund Chaffee pinned it to the Labor Temple bulletin board. However, I wondered had Will lowered himself by accepting these lucrative assignments; and that was the general verdict of the literary world. So said a well-disposed critic in *Book Chat* for July, 1927:

> Dr. Durant had won his spurs with a gorgeous book on philosophy. And what spurs they were! The book has already gone over the 150,000 mark, and at $5.00 a throw. What Mr. Durant wrote about the trial is in my opinion the best writing that was done about it. But . . . I do not believe that it will add greatly to his reputation as a man of letters.

In the summer of 1926 our lease at 243 Ocean Avenue ran out. Max Schuster had by that time grown so fond of Will that he offered us, rent free, some unused rooms in the spacious "Mortgage Manor" that he had bought in Sea Cliff, Long Island. Will accepted, for he was warm with this new friendship, and he did not appreciate my warning that no single dwelling had ever been built large enough to house two families in peace. Max's parents and his gifted sister Muriel accepted all three of us bravely, and took very kindly to Ethel. We still have a fading photo of

Max standing with Ethel. Max—who, so far as we know, never had a child—would have made a most loving father.

In October, 1926, Will undertook his first transcontinental lecture tour. I was loath to remain almost alone in unfamiliar surroundings, but he persuaded me that we had better lay up a nest egg of savings while his fame lasted—which could not be long. So off he went, and he must have worked hard, for almost every town wanted him. In Hollywood (as he reported to me much later) he had a moment's spell of drunkenness. Invited to a dinner by a motion picture producer, he made the mistake of drinking on an empty stomach the glass of wine offered him in a welcoming toast. He was so untrained to alcohol that he became slightly dizzy, and this lasted through the lecture that he gave that evening in Rabbi Herman Lissauer's temple. After it was over the rabbi said, "It was a brilliant address, rich in risqué stories seldom heard from that platform."

While Will was working and frolicking in California I was fretting and freezing in Sea Cliff. Though Ethel was prospering in the fresh air and in a good school, I felt like an alien at Mrs. Schuster's table, and only Max's cheery return from Manhattan, faithfully every evening about seven, restored my spirits. Sometimes I stole off to Greenwich Village and the Gypsy Tavern. I wondered through how many more years Will would have to leave me for two or more months in the winter, how long it would be before the nest egg would be big enough to let us stay together the whole year through.

About this time—perhaps in November, 1926—I wrote the following rough and chaotic draft of a letter which shames me in my present content, but must find place in any honest record of our marriage:

DEAR WILL:

At last I cannot bear to hold up against you any longer. Your curt letter (three arrived at once, so you see how reliable the mails are) struck such a lightning blow that I marvel that I was not completely overcome, both by hurt pride and remorse. You see, this was my method of warfare for [your] getting along so completely . . . and happily without me in California. Don't protest; I read between the lines. Only you were still the methodical philosopher, so sold to the duty of a promise [to write daily?], and to the desire for domestic smoothness, that you even had time to write to me from there the few business lines, curt though roaming, that you did. But I have failed, and how!

You conquered, as always, and I surrender, a little wiser and a little older in the ways of the world. Should I hold out much longer I should be totally ruined, for who knows what justification would be trumped up? . . . Since I have watched you hold hands, and my imagination enhances the picture, I become too dazed to think.* . . .

* *Will:* One afternoon I entered a room where a private piano recital was about to begin. I sat down next to my handsome friend Maximilian Rose. The lady on his right was holding

Enough! Crazy as I am, . . . I love you. . . .

I am at mother's, where I tell all my trouble and heartaches, and get little sympathy in return. She adores you, and it is through her inspiration that I write and am made to swallow my pride. . . . I think and talk of nothing but you. You are my *dybuk* and shall leave me only when my soul melts into ether.

Last week I expounded *The Story of Philosophy* to Bob Chandler and six women who were with him in France and had never heard of it. Modesty forbids me telling you how they raved at my language, my lit-up happy face as I bore your *Philosophy* on the wings of love. You, you, you, when will you [cease to] be everything to my lonely, weeping, melancholy embodiment? Inconstant? I?—never did man so control and possess woman as every atom of me lives in and for you.

You see how sentimental this letter is. It's time for you to come home, lest I become a raving maniac. Now that you are coming back . . . I grow nervous and tremble and gray with fear. . . . Will I find the same Willieboy?—or spent and older or Hollywoodwisely younger? At any rate leave your perpetual bowel-talk* on the road, as well as the eternal accusation of extravagance and financial obsessions.

Ethel says she thanks God you are coming home. She is beginning to express herself, and is becoming more desirous and impatient for you every day. The last two weeks are the hardest and most hectic. So much thought spent on one person. . . .

When will we be equals?—and when so sure of each other that I can take a trip to Russia with impunity. For the little I mean to you and the little I get from you, how much do I have to stand? All my youth gone, no love, no companionship, no husband and no lover—always alone, mentally and bodily. Tell me, am I not the most envied of famous men's wives? And with it all, how I love you, or maybe only worship you. I don't know which, and must cease living when this ceases. For I have too poor an imagination to conceive the possibility of life without you.

What a letter, poor dear. I hardly know whether to send it or tear it up. But you can understand. Soon you will be back and we will muddle along. Life in the future holds nothing different for me than what it was in the past—and that hurts. . . . It is essential that we go away as students, just alone. . . . Is it absolutely impossible to go with you somewhere alone? . . . I love you always.

ARIEL

I did not send that letter. But I kept it as a secret repository of my doubts about our marriage. I think that what saved our marriage was

---

his hand, obviously hoping that he would warm to the current. I reminded her that Max was newly married, and that his wife might enter at any moment. Laughing, she released his hand and grasped mine. At that moment *my* wife came in and saw us. After forty-four years of effort I have not yet convinced her that I was just an innocent bysitter. But Ariel was right to keep me under a watchful eye.

* Keeping the bowels clean had become one of the refrains of Will's philosophy.

that when he returned from that long tour he felt that he had now, with our royalties, enough in the kitty to warrant his leaving his consuming schedule at Labor Temple and devoting nearly all his waking hours to what was to become *The Story of Civilization.* It was a task that would take the rest of his life. He asked for my cooperation, my help in organization, research, and ideas; I pledged them. Our love was renewed, and our lives became one.

CHAPTER VIII

Moneygrubbing

1927

Will:

Soon after the end-of-the-year holidays I prepared for a risky encounter—to debate Clarence Darrow on January 8, 1927, at Carnegie Hall on "Is Man a Machine?" On the way to the battle we visited Clarence in his room at the Belmont Hotel; no one could have told from our conversation that he and I were about to meet in combat. We could fill that time-honored auditorium the more easily because Darrow had recently (1924) won national fame by his brilliant plea for Nathan Leopold and Richard Loeb, the half-insane murderers of Bobby Franks.

I spoke first, and gave the usual arguments for a vitalistic view, borrowing heavily from Bergson. I ended with an explosion of sentimental poetry in which I finally identified myself with God. When Darrow's turn came he walked slowly to the podium, and began in his usual drawl, "That is the worst poem I have ever heard." Then, seeing me woefully deflated, and hurrying to heal my wound, he told the audience, "I am sorry if I hurt my friend. I would rather have written *The Story of Philosophy* than have done any of the things I have done in my life." It was an absurd exaggeration, but I readily forgave it, and long treasured it. He went on to argue that all human behavior can be interpreted by the laws of physics and chemistry; "the elements that compose a man can all be bought in a chemist's shop for approximately ninety-two cents." The audience gladly forgot my arguments in its enjoyment of

110

Darrow's dry humor. After two forgotten rebuttals we walked off the stage arm in arm.*

In February, 1927, I ended, except for an occasional talk, my lectures at Labor Temple, and resigned my post as director of Labor Temple School. After some thirteen years of mutually helpful association with some favorite students—Dr. Abraham Wolfson, Dr. A. L. Caesar, Abie Cohen, David DeWitt, Harry Grossman, Sam Nevins, Al Osterreicher, Abe Sarasohn, Joseph Slakin—I left them with only a temporary parting: we would all of us go on studying and learning; we would meet again. Many of them are still alive and active; some greet me now and then in the streets or at the Hollywood Bowl. They too were my teachers. Because of them I had to be clear in my exposition and arguments; and because they had to work for their food, I had to find a bridge between each of my topics and the problems of their current life. It was a boon to me that twice a week, during a dozen scholastic years, I had faced their eager and challenging minds. Without their patience, stimulation, and loyalty, *The Story of Civilization* could not have been. "My spirit to yours," O my Templars, wherever you are!

The picture that George Hurrell took of me in 1927 makes me look so angelically poetic that no one, looking at it, would imagine that this Shelley of the lecture circuit was on a money-making spree. *The Story of Philosophy* reached the 200,000 mark in 1927, and my royalty for half that year was $79,000; nevertheless, resolved to make hay while the sun shone, I undertook in 1927 the heaviest tour of my career. I took it for granted that the success of the *Story* had resulted from a series of accidents, and that I must not expect anything more from later books than some equivalent of the time and energy used in their composition. It seemed that my main source of future income would be from lectures, until the family treasure chest should offer sufficient security to let me give all my working time to my second *Story*.

So, on January 2, I began the new year 1927 by speaking at Labor Temple at 5 P.M., and at the Young Men's Hebrew Association the same evening. I continued with discourses in the Eastern states every day of that month except the first and tenth. On the twenty-ninth I presided over a fund-raising dinner for Labor Temple School. In February I peddled philosophy and history from New Hampshire to Missouri, twenty-three evenings out of twenty-eight; in March, chiefly in the Middle West, I performed every day except five, twice on the twelfth, the twentieth, and the twenty-first. The pace slackened in the spring, but in the fall I resumed my barnstorming with twelve lectures in October, twenty-one in November, and thirteen in the first half of December. These one-

* The debate was later published by Haldeman-Julius as a Little Blue Book. My contribution was polished into a chapter in *The Mansions* [later, *Pleasures*] *of Philosophy.*

111

night stands involved arduous traveling. It was not unusual for me to leave a lecture hall, sweating with eloquence, rush to a railway station, board a Pullman, discard my semiformal garb in the smoking room, wash off some of the perspiration, and try to sleep despite a head throbbing with the brilliant things I might have said. When I look back upon that 1927 schedule I wonder at the vanity, or the greed, that sustained me.

Some samples of a lecturer's life appear in the letters I sent to Ariel that spring. From Decatur, Illinois, March 1:

> Your letters are beautiful [but I was too self-centered and chaotic to preserve them as she preserved mine], and have brought me a touch of sunshine on a day made miserable by storm and illness. I am caught with the grippe, despite the most particular care that I have taken of myself. Apparently just to come out of a lecture hall after a strenuous hour and a half of work (which leaves me perspiring even in the coldest weather) is dangerous: the damp air of this mild but humid winter goes right through overcoat and everything to the blood beneath. So here I sit, after a five-hour ride from Chicago, uncomfortably accoutred in evening dress, . . . with my forehead feverish, my head aching, waiting for the man who is to drive me to the auditorium of Milliken University, where I shall discuss "psychoanalysis without sex." . . . Then I have to rush back to another train, untangle myself from my evening clothes, . . . and spend the night bumping back to Chicago, where I shall be expected at 7:05 A.M. At noon tomorrow I must address the Chicago Woman's Club, and in the evening I must talk again. It may be a reasonable thing to do, but only on condition that it saves me from doing it more than once again. [I continued doing it till 1957.] I hope I can get through with it all without going to a hospital. . . .
>
> Debated Powys last night. A draw. . . .
>
> May nature protect you till I come; then I will release her.

March 2, from Chicago:

> In the middle of my lecture [at Decatur] I grew confused, and for several seconds I did not know what I was saying. Then I swam up to the surface again, and got through with my job. I rushed to the train, and had to climb, dress suit and all, into an upper berth (they had no lowers). . . . I spent an awful night; the headache would not let me sleep. . . .

From Cincinnati, March 3:

> Your letters are so sweet that I, in my exhaustion, cannot rival their beauty or their tenderness. I begin to understand what this separation means to you. . . . I thought you would have a good time in my absence, and frolic about with your sisters; I bought you the new car that you could realize your desire to drive in to New York. . . .
>
> I know how long the days must be, and how uncannily silent the nights [at Sea Cliff]. My heart goes out to you. . . . Bear this for our common purpose, and I will come to you on April 9th like a good hunter, laden with

spoils. . . . We shall sit down and rest, and play and love and write. Perhaps we shall grow into real philosophers?

Be patient, my comrade!

From Erie, Pennsylvania, March 17:

. . . Between now and April 9th, when I [shall] see you, I shall have four nights in a bed and twenty-two nights on trains. You must expect me to come out of it a little dilapidated. . . .

It turns out that I had the "flu"—but as I never called in a doctor, I had to cure the thing without knowing its name. . . .

On the train from Dallas to St. Louis, March 31:

Ten days more.

Am on a long, dreary ride, midnight to 8 P.M., Denton to St. Louis, through a cold rain. . . .

I gave a poor lecture last night because I was tired and sleepy. . . . After the lecture I found myself, 11 P.M., at a little station so dimly lighted that I could not read, and deserted except for a . . . Mexican sleeping in a seat. I went out and walked up and down the platform for 45 minutes (the train came in at one minute after midnight) thinking of you and Ethel. . . . I was alone with space, the night, and the stars. I asked the earth what it meant with its life, movement, and death, but it moved on silently and patiently to its fulfillment and futility. Then I thought how many men had asked the earth that question, and gone away unanswered; perhaps I had lived before and wondered before, and I would live and wonder again. . . . Could you see me, across America, standing in the dark at the far end of the station platform, 2,000 miles from you, looking for Sea Cliff?

During that feverish trip—fifty-three lectures between February 6 and April 8, 1927—I had to run the gauntlet of some thirty interviews with reporters, the younger of whom were hoping to commit me to some hairraising pronouncement that would make the front page and earn a byline. I was still too immature to resist all such temptations. To one reporter I ventured the statement that "no one can love after thirty with the same ardor as before thirty." The editor shortened this to a novel headline: "Durant says, 'No one can love after thirty.' " Newspapers in a dozen other cities quoted this dictum; a syndicate sent it to a dozen notables, asking their opinion of this nonsense; for a month thereafter the replies kept pillorying me in the press. I asked the Associated Press to distribute a correction; it did, but the damning replies continued, and made good copy. The press can make you and it can destroy you.

Apparently these interviews, those fifty-three lectures, and the hectic scrambling from one town to another, on that 1927 tour, left me with time for more money-making. So, in hotel rooms or on trains, I wrote four articles for magazines. William Devereux, then of the *American Magazine*, had brought me the first tempting invitation: to discuss "The Ten

113

Greatest Thinkers" for its issue of December, 1926. He inquired what fee I wished. I coyly offered to let him name it. "Would one thousand dollars make you happy?" he asked. It did. The *American* asked for another article, and I responded with "One Hundred Best Books for an Education." The article was reprinted in various forms, and stirred some readers to an ambition that was rarely realized, for the list was outdated before anyone could complete it. However, I received, some time ago, a letter from a hero who informed me that he had just finished those hundred books—after forty years.

On April 11 the three Durants left New York by weary train for Miami—thirty-nine hours for what now takes three hours by plane; so time and space contract, force upon us a faster pace, and spend our nerves while saving our time. After twelve days of tennis, golf, swimming, and writing I set off again for three lectures in the Middle West; and not till the end of April was I back with Ariel and Ethel and Max in Sea Cliff. On May 7 I left by sleeper for Detroit, where, on the next evening, I was again to debate Clarence Darrow on "Is Man a Machine?"

I reached Detroit in time to spend some pleasant hours with my brother Sam, who was now a member of an architectural firm. His wonderful wife, Gene, had given him three daughters, and had resolved to keep on trying till she could satisfy his desire to have a son. That son anticipated my arrival by one day, and Sam was so happy that from a balcony, seeing me step out of a cab, he called, "Will, it's a stemwinder!" He came to the debate, and then rushed me off to an 11 P.M. sleeper for Cleveland. I never saw him again, for in July of that year 1927 he was shot, while playing golf, by a hunter's stray bullet from nearby woods. He died in the arms of his wife, telling her, with his last words, "I love you." He had lost his faith, but he had remained a Christian. His widow, with inspiring and uncomplaining courage, served thereafter as both father and mother to his children, and was rewarded by their development and their love.

I had hardly returned to Ariel when I succumbed to another temptation. The Cosmos Syndicate offered me five hundred dollars each for forty-eight weekly installments of a *Story of Civilization* designed for newspaper serialization. I signed, presuming that the notes of my Labor Temple lectures on history, literature, art, and philosophy would provide sufficient material to satisfy a popular audience. Meanwhile I had received an invitation from my old Maecenas, Alden Freeman, to visit him in Santa Barbara for the Christmas holidays. I was seeing through the press my third book, *Transition*. And I had promised Ariel and Ethel to take them with me on a Mediterranean tour that might help me prepare my future accounts of Egypt, the Near East, Judea, Greece, and Rome. I was a giant in those days, or I was a fool.

Toward the end of June Ariel turned her Gypsy Tavern over to her sisters Flora and Mary and her brother Michael. On July 4, 1927, Ariel, twenty-nine, Ethel, eight, and I, nearing forty-two, sailed on the cruise ship *California* on a Mediterranean tour. I spoiled the early part of the trip for Ethel by badgering her into practicing an hour every day on the piano, and beginning every day with a breakfast of bran.

In Egypt we made the usual trip to the Pyramids, and I began to appreciate Arabic art in Cairo's mosques, palaces, carpets, and lettering. In Jerusalem we were deeply moved by the sight of the Jews praying before the Wailing Wall, which they believed was part of their ancient Temple; all the more were we touched when one of their chants was translated for us:

> *Because of the Palace which is deserted, we sit alone and weep.*
> *Because of the Temple which is destroyed,*
> *Because of the walls which are broken down,*
> *Because of our greatness which is departed,*
> *Because of the precious stones of the Temple ground to powder,*
> *Because of our priests who have erred and gone astray,*
> *Because of our kings who have condemned God—*
> *We sit alone and weep.*
> *We beseech Thee, have mercy on Zion!*
> *And gather together the children of Jerusalem. . . .*
> *Let Zion be girded with beauty and with majesty. . . .*
> *Let the branch of Jerusalem put forth and bud.*

Ten years before our visit the British government, recognizing the services of the Jews in World War I, had announced through Lord Balfour that it "viewed with favor the establishment of a national home for the Jewish people; and will use" its "best endeavors to facilitate the achievement of this object." Israel in 1927 was as yet only a "home" for the Jews; not till 1948 would it be a recognized and sovereign state; but already the energy and skill of the immigrants had developed industry, new cities, and flourishing farms, so that in 1930 I could enthuse over a Tel-Aviv orange as "the noblest work of God."

In Greece—my second visit—I served as guide, and lectured my family, as a captive audience, on the history of the Parthenon and the story of Socrates; they rewarded me by taking a picture of me in the tomblike prison in which, we were assured, Socrates had so philosophically met death. While we were in Athens a cablegram came from my publishers announcing that my brother Sam had been killed in Pontiac, Michigan, and asking permission to send the widow three hundred dollars. I couldn't believe the news. "But," I cried, "I found him healthy and happy only a few weeks ago!" From that night, Ariel tells me, my hair began rapidly to turn white. I moved in a half-trance through the remainder of that tour.

We saw the gay poverty of Naples, the ruins of Pompeii, and the temples of pagan and Christian Rome. There we left the cruise, for I could not let Ariel and Ethel miss Florence and Venice. But I foolishly risked their lives by booking passage from Venice to Vienna in a single-motored four-passenger plane. We were time and again nearly capsized in the small motorboat that took us over the lagoon to the airport; and we thought, as we flew over the Alps, that the strong wind would sooner or later beat our wobbling plane to earth. After arrival at Vienna the pilot rode with us to town. I asked him could the plane have been upset by those gusts. He rejected the idea as mechanically impossible. "The same wind that lifts the right wing lifts the left wing equally, and corrects the roll. Our real danger," he added, "is in this car, which is being driven by a chauffeur who may be incompetent, or may have been drinking. It's here on earth that I feel unsafe." Nevertheless for an hour after that flight the whole world seemed to sway from side to side before our eyes.

In Vienna we ran into Henry Wadsworth Longfellow Dana, grandson of the poet and recently my host in Cambridge. Across a café table he read my fortune to me: "You will write many books, each more popular than its predecessor, and worse."

Shortly after our return to America we moved our belongings from Sea Cliff, much to the relief of Max's mother, and took an apartment at 5 West Sixty-ninth Street, Manhattan. Ethel went for a time to the Walden School, a few blocks away. It was operated on "progressive" principles, supposedly as suggested by John Dewey, and strongly colored by the libertarian doctrines that had enthralled me sixteen years before. From some visits to the school I received the impression that the Walden teachers, as I had done, allowed too much play and disorder, leaving their pupils without the steadiness of will and character that a measure of discipline might have instilled. In that way I had sinned as sentimentally as any teacher.

For me the great event of that fall was the publication of *Transition* (October, 1927). I had begun it soon after the appearance of *The Story of Philosophy*; one word leads to another. I was still shaking with my turbulent passage from intense Catholicism to eager doubt to violent socialism to cautious liberalism and proud parentage. It seemed to me that in the educated classes of Europe and America Christianity was undergoing a revolution more basic—liberating and searing—than the movement from capitalism to socialism; we were entering what Arnold Toynbee has called the "Post-Christian Age"; Darwin had cut more deeply than Marx. Hence my foreword to the

DEAR READER:

Perhaps this is your story as well as John Lemaire's. It tries to show the effect, upon one growing mind, of the profound transformation which modern science and research have brought in the faith of the Western world. In a lesser way it tries also to show the political experiments and

116

disillusionment of our time, and to trace the evolution of a fairly typical rebel from utopian aspiration through a cynical despondency to some measure of reconciliation and good cheer.

These changes have not been so impersonal as the abstract chronicle of history represents them; they have brought to sensitive individuals much suffering in mental transition and readjustments; they have broken up families and friendships; and they have unsettled the minds and morals of many generations by uprooting the customs and beliefs in which these generations grew. It is with this personal aspect of the Great Change that the story is concerned.

The book was subtitled "A Sentimental Story of One Mind and One Era." It was sentimental because I had felt those changes deeply, and had not the art to vivify the tale without describing the emotions; I forgot that many young men had made the same transition with less romantic perturbations. I gave the narrative the form of a novel, instead of an explicit autobiography, because so many of the protagonists were alive and sensitive, and because I recognized the absurdity of writing an autobiography when I was still in my intellectual youth. Having adopted the mantle of a storyteller, I felt free to insert some imaginary conversations (chiefly pages 306–11), and to picture myself as "blown up" by an anarchist bomb instead of being merely one auditor of the account given, by the sole survivor, of the bomb that killed Caron, Hansen, and Berg while they were preparing to dynamite with it the home of John D. Rockefeller. A dozen public corrections have failed to disassociate me from that explosion. Otherwise the story is of me and mine. — I had left the manuscript with Max Schuster before going off to Europe. I admitted to him that it was "a mental autobiography." He so described it on the jacket, and the limiting adjective was lost in the noun.

A hundred advance copies sent to pivotal personalities brought courteously favorable comments that misled me into thinking that I had laid another golden egg; soon the adjective was again lost in the noun. An intoxicating telegram came from Alden Freeman, whose story I had told in the book, renaming him Henry Alden. (He was a descendant of John Alden of the *Mayflower* and the legendary Priscilla.)

Many letters reproached me with having abandoned religion, and some pleaded with me to return to the faith; however, the Yale *Divinity News* called the book "one of the most vivid and absorbing human documents that have appeared in recent years." John Haynes Holmes gave the book some friendly praise but was disappointed by the concluding chapter:

> This is a thrilling story—in many ways a heroic one. Mr. Durant tells it with an *élan* which is contagious. I picked it up with groans on a night when I was sick in bed with a headache, sore throat, and 102 degrees fever, and finished it with shouts before the bed-lamp was extinguished.
>
> Yet now I find a lingering sadness in the memory of it. For is this the end

for those who struggle for the truth? Must all passionate battling for a better world lay down arms in a happy private home? Has Will Durant found "Utopia," or has he found "Nirvana"? I do not presume to say. But I must confess to a feeling of disquietude when a man forty-two years of age, in a world vexed with violence, injustice, and fear, indites his autobiography and calls his story done.

I felt deeply this reproach from a dear friend.

Most of the early reviews were comforting, but several were painful. My radical readers were shocked by my rejection of the mechanistic and supposedly scientific view of the world, and my idealization of family life; they felt that I had run out on them and had turned my back upon modern thought. After noting John Lemaire's participation in the intellectual and social conflicts of the time, and his subsidence into domestic bliss, Donald Ross complained that "this is not much of a solution to so intense a ferment, nor from so capable an analyst. The mountain has labored and brought forth a mouse. It is a nice mouse, but not very formidable." And Mark Van Doren, in *The Nation*, cut my throat without any anodyne: "*Transition* is a vulgar, barren, and simple-minded book. . . . It is a work of perfectly cool and commonplace conceit, . . . amusing for its badness when it is not shocking in its simplicity." Such honest lancing is good for a swelling author in the long run, but it took many a poultice of praise to heal that wound.

The excitement of the lecture platform, and of two debates with Bertrand Russell, kept me from brooding over my hurts. Our first encounter took place in Symphony Hall, Boston, on October 12, 1927, and "attracted the largest audience since the famous Butler–Borah debate." Judging from the five columns given to it in the morrow's *Herald*, our battle over "Is Democracy a Failure?" must have been the best sporting event of the year. Russell, of course, was the major attraction. He was already fifty-five years old, and could hardly have guessed that he had forty-two years still left to him. His hair was silvery white. His sharp nose and gleaming eyes promised an alert intellect and a pointed wit, a keenness and relish in debate. Luckily for me, I had dealt with him handsomely in *The Story of Philosophy*, so that we were friends even as our swords crossed. I need not summarize my share in the performance; I polished it up to form a chapter in *The Mansions of Philosophy*, where it still stands as proof that I can be as one-sided as a debate requires. The unusually full stenographic report in the *Herald* of October 13 did more justice to me than to Russell, for it could not convey the smile on his lips and the twinkle in his eyes.

The debate was repeated on October 22 in Mecca Temple, then the largest auditorium in New York. The reports in the *Times* and the *Tribune* indicate that neither speaker varied much from the arguments he had used in Boston. We had the honor of evoking editorial comment in some newspapers, and the *Times* whimsically remarked: "It certainly cannot be said of the participants that they . . . were swayed by personal prejudice. Mr. Russell is the author of a *Principia Mathematica* which has probably sold 120 copies. Mr. Durant has written a *Story of Philosophy* which is selling close to 200,000 copies. Yet Mr. Russell believes in the common people and Mr. Durant does not." (I believe in the equal right of common people to access to the education that may make them uncommonly fit for uncommon tasks.)

After the New York debate Mrs. Durant lured Russell to a more friendly bite with me in a nearby hotel. We made a bad choice, for the hotel orchestra disported itself in jazz music of a wild sonority that made conversation impossible; I was ashamed. We—or Russell—had a better time when, a week later, he had dinner in our apartment at 5 West Sixty-ninth Street. I was still at that time under the spell of the Little Corporal, and tried to convince Russell that Napoleon's defeat at Waterloo was a victory for reaction; I failed; I have yet to find an Englishman who can stomach Napoleon.

Our guest preferred Ariel. When he left she accepted his invitation to share with him the ride to his room in Eighty-fifth Street. He did not know that our car was driven by her brother Mike. After a few blocks the engaging Briton began to fondle Ariel's hand; after a few more he asked Michael to make a detour through Central Park. Michael sternly ignored the request and drove without delay to Eighty-fifth Street. When I consider that Russell was soon to publish his view that a man compelled by his business to be absent from his wife for more than three weeks should be allowed a temporary moratorium on monogamy, I tremble to think what might have happened in Central Park.

Each of the rivals now went off on a lecture tour. Between October 27 and December 10, I peddled my philosophic wares from New York to Reno, Nevada. Having accepted Alden Freeman's invitation to Santa Barbara, I was easily lured into making hay on the way. Ariel remained in New York for a while, having agreed to take part in a symposium on "The Revolt of the Modern Woman."

I believe it was on this tour, at Grand Rapids, Michigan, that I first met James W. Fifield, Jr. After my lecture we sat together on his porch, and began a friendship that has now lasted fifty years, surviving all the strain of ideological separation. He was a Christian conservative, I was a skeptical socialist. When he was given charge of the stately First Congregational Church in Los Angeles he repeatedly engaged me to address his congregation. He left date and subject to my choice, and allowed me such freedom of view and expression as no radical organization or forum would have tolerated. From his orthodox pulpit I expounded the heresies of Spinoza, Kant, Schopenhauer, and Nietzsche, and ardently defended the "creeping socialism" of Franklin Roosevelt.

After six weeks' travail, mitigated by such friendships, I reached Reno, where I spent three pleasant days with the faculty and students of the University of Nevada. My happy stay in the Nevada capital was clouded by a confusion of program with Alden Freeman. On December 7 he had sent me a telegram to the effect that his friends were "arranging an informal dinner of twenty of the choicest spirits, literary and artistic, of Santa Barbara, to meet the Durants on December 20th." I wired back that I could not get there by the twentieth and in a letter I explained: "Mrs. Durant is lecturing at the Brooklyn Academy of Music on December 18th, and cannot get started from New York until the 19th. I promised that I would meet her here at Reno. It will mean something to her to have me join her on the way, and I don't like to get to you separately and receive all the welcomes, so that none would be left when Mrs. Durant arrived." It was quite noble or prudent of me, but very troublesome for my old benefactor. Meanwhile I had set a novel precedent: a husband eagerly awaiting his wife in Reno.

Ariel:

In those days when Will was ogling the divorcees I was preparing fearfully for my joust with some other lively ladies—Fannie Hurst, "Texas" Guinan, Eva Le Gallienne, and Elizabeth Marbury—in a symposium on "The Modern Woman." I received a telegram from Will bidding me prepare well and then proceed with confidence, and assuring me that he was "tired and lonely, and longing for our honeymoon" in California. I bought railroad tickets for Ethel and myself to Chicago and thence on the Union Pacific to San Francisco, and had Will's assurance that he would board my train at Reno. Everything was well planned, except the symposium itself. The manager wrote: "As none of them [the other speakers] are married women, we should prefer to have you tackle the other side, of the wife." I, who had been a rebel all my life, who had been a friend of free-loving Emma Goldman, found myself casting about for arguments in defense of the respectable woman faithful to her husband and loving her home. It was good for me that I was now compelled to see the marriage problem from a conservative point of view. After all, I had by this time learned to be a dutiful wife and a fond mother, attending to all the chores of the household with (as yet) never a thought of engaging a maid.

So on December 18 I faced three very modern women (Miss Le Gallienne was too ill to come), and agreed to speak first, thereby giving many rounds of ammunition to my successors. As I proceeded my timidity yielded to the ardor of battle, and I spoke with a fire that must have alarmed—or amused—the cohorts of revolt. I accepted the emancipation of woman as a natural result of the continuing Industrial Revolution, replacing domestic drudgery with gadgets and cans. It was good that she was being freed from many of the cruel disabilities that had subjected her—in all but the higher classes—in all recorded centuries. But if emancipation meant a revolt against marriage, and an exaltation of career above motherhood, it would bring a regrettable masculinity in women and a corresponding effeminacy in men. "What will be the gain when women wear pants and men have soprano voices?. . . . What shall we say of the many abnormalities that have increased in . . . our age of transition? The progress of inversion, perversion, . . . a third sex? . . . Have we the right to say anything if men wistfully long for a home while women crowd tearooms, cafés, and cabarets—and give lectures?" (I had done all these things.) So I pleaded for moderation, for "a revolt against the excess of revolt."

I asked for a voluntary and educated motherhood; not because the world needed more babies but because complete and healthy womanhood included the functioning of the basic feminine instincts and physiology. I allowed for careers, but not if they were to replace motherhood. "The girls of the future will marry young, and . . . they will continue their education after marriage. . . . They will know the meaning and uses of birth control. And they will accept motherhood as the greatest gift and experience that nature has given them."

Miss Guinan spent her thirty minutes in jolly gossip about the characters she had met in her nightclub. Miss Hurst laughed at my fears that the revolt was going too far; most American women had not even heard of it.

> "You could stage a mass meeting of all the women in this country who are in revolt, in a telephone booth. All you've got to do is to travel across this country to see how difficult it is to get any new ideas into the heads of the millions of 'good old-fashioned' wives and mothers in the small towns and the farm houses between here and the Coast. I tell you, 'the good, old-fashioned' wife and mother is one of the biggest monkey-wrenches in the wheel of progress. And they think they are in revolt because they have come to call a limb a leg, because they have bobbed their hair and bared their knees. . . . Intellectually the great majority of modern women are still riding side saddles and wearing whalebone corsets." (New York *Sun*, December 19, 1927.)

I cannot resist quoting the same report as describing me as "a pretty little woman whose charm won her salvo after salvo of affectionate applause." In any case, I had held my own; and when, the next evening, Ethel and I entrained for Chicago, I felt that I could tell my husband that I too had met mighty warriors, and had emerged unharmed. When our train from Chicago reached Reno, 11:05 P.M., December 22, we saw our faithful breadwinner on the station platform; he clambered aboard, and almost into our berths. Then we sped together to San Francisco, and thence through a dozen lovely towns to Santa Barbara.

Alden received us graciously, despite his disappointment that we could not have come sooner. Ethel was then a blooming lass of eight and a half years, and her gaiety helped to open hearts and doors. It was our good luck that Alden had made friends with a neighbor and fellow philanthropist, Max Schott, soon to be founder and president of Climax Molybdenum Company. I took Max to my heart as soon as I looked into his almost childlike face, and again when I saw in his library hundreds of important volumes, including Spengler's *Der Untergang des Abendlandes*—which he had read in German. Here was a philosopher with money, and a Jew beloved of Christians; he had contributed substantially to restore the Santa Barbara Mission of the Franciscan friars. Moreover, his wife, Alice, had given him four daughters—Alice, Helen, Katy, and Mary Lou—all beautiful and bounding with life. They took Ethel into their sisterhood, and for the next week we hardly saw her. Father Augustin, head of the mission, came frequently to Max's home; he forgave Will's heresies when Will played and sang with him some traditional Catholic hymns—"O Salutaris Hostia" and "Tantum ergo"—which had been fondly retained in my philosopher's still-Catholic memory. It was a lovely gathering of three faiths (Protestant Alden, Jewish Max and me, Catholic Augustin) and one skeptic (Will, though really he is the most believing of us all) when we joined with Alice and her princesses in songs sacred and profane.

But a sad conflict developed. Alden had made appointments for his literary lion for every day of our stay till January 2, in many cases for both lunch and dinner, in some cases for breakfast too, in one case also for afternoon tea. Will was in the midst of his obligation to send to the Cosmos Syndicate, every week, another chapter in his first *Story of Civilization*. By coincidence he was struggling, in this Christmas season, with an account of the background, life, doctrine, and influence of Christ. As the week proceeded it became clear that he could not write a decent portrayal of Jesus if he kept all the engagements made for us by the man to whom he owed so much of his good fortune. At last he begged Alden to cancel some of our commitments for a day or two that would let Will hide himself and complete his task. Alden for a second time was deeply hurt, for these cancellations could not be made without displeasing his friends and humiliating him.

If I remember rightly, Alden stayed away from us on New Year's Day, and he merely sent a brief message of goodbye when Will left, early on January 2, to catch a train to Los Angeles. But almost at the last moment Alden came riding down from his hilltop, disheveled and in pajamas; he upbraided Will as an ingrate, and then embraced him. Will went off to give some lectures in Southern California. Ethel and I remained in the El Encanto bungalow hotel, near the Schotts, and waited for his return.

CHAPTER IX

The Wandering Scholar

1928

Ariel:

He was back with us for a few days in mid-January. He still carried the beard that he had cultivated as a Columbia University instructor in philosophy. A popular humorist of the time, O. O. McIntyre, who could never forgive him for shedding the Catholic faith, pulled this beard a bit in the Buffalo *Times* for January 22:

> I find myself unable to read the writings of two recent authors. Yet they have swept into amazing popularity, so don't mind me. I refer to Will Durant and John Erskine. Their efforts seem to me to be a lot of twaddle. I have the feeling that they try to be highbrow in a sort of patronizing manner when it isn't at all necessary. They try to tell us things most of us already know in simple "baby talk." However, I think I chiefly resent that little tuft of whiskers on Will Durant's chin. I have seen them too often on doctors, professors, and such, posing as something they were not.

And I believe that Franklin P. Adams, in his humorous column in the New York *World*, objected to Will's "flea-ladder." Soon thereafter, when that tuft began to turn white, Will cut it off.

Meanwhile he was laboring to convey the perspective of history to readers of his *Cosmos* articles, and the "dear delight" of philosophy to audiences on the lecture circuit. He kept me *au courant* with his travailogue:

A Dual Autobiography

Did you think I was unfaithful in not writing to you yesterday? Let me tell you how I spent the day.

I was awakened at 5 A.M. by the porter as the train . . . was approaching Albany, Oregon. I had gotten on it at 7 A.M. the day before; had spent all day writing "The Middle Ages" while children were crying and playing around me, and I had been finally forced to put ms. aside, at 8 P.M., from headache and mental exhaustion.

I landed at Albany at 6 A.M., in darkness, solitude, and rain. A car awaited me, and drove 14 miles through a pitch dark forest to this little town of Corvallis. Feeling a fever, I took a big dose of salts. After breakfast I sat down to work again, on an essay that should have been mailed two days before. . . . Continued till one; then had lunch with three professors and the editor of the local paper, who turned out to be an interesting old atheist. . . . At two they drove me to a great big auditorium, where I faced 3,000 people, of all ages, sexes, and species. . . .

After the lecture I rushed back to the hotel, and tried to finish the essay before the stenographer [typist] came. I couldn't; my head refused to work. When she arrived I had to dictate 5 pages out of my head; you can imagine how profound and polished they will be. We finished at 9:30 P.M. I sat up till 11 correcting errors, and then mailed the ms. and went to bed.—That is why I didn't write to you, sweetheart.

Today I feel better, but the specter of another [Cosmos Syndicate] essay to be planned, filled out with notes, written, and typed, all in five days, fills me with horror. . . .

Bellingham, Wash., 1-27-28

I am tempted not to write to you today, so that you may know in a small measure how worried and lonesome I am, not having a word from you since we parted.

So on January 30 I sent him a long letter from Santa Barbara, and assured him that I too was lonesome:

> . . . To show you how very lonesome I have been, I have had to bury my mind in reading, and finished almost a book a day. . . . I go to bed with Ethel, for she cannot sleep with the lights burning. As soon as . . . I hear her heavy and peaceful slumber I switch on the light and read till one, two, or three in the morning, and continue the minute she is off to school. In that way I read *Disraeli* by D. L. Murray, and the fascinating André Maurois' *Disraeli*. . . . What a mind, and in Victorian England. He worshiped Byron, and lived with him day and night, and was molded by him. . . .
> Happy at the thought of our approaching reunion.

That reunion was a strange conjunction. Will lectured at Salt Lake City on February 4; he reached Barstow, California, at 9:20 A.M. February 5; Ethel and I left Santa Barbara 6:35 A.M. that day, and changed at Los Angeles to a Santa Fe train that arrived at Barstow 4:50 P.M. There Will boarded our car, and we rode together to see the Grand Canyon. Thence to Denver, where Will made some newspaper noise by advocating a return to the dowry system to make early marriage possible and keep the boys out of brothels. From Denver we turned south to El Paso; at Tucumcari we had to wait several hours for a change of trains; Ethel made the time leap by teaching her bearded father the art and mathematics of hop, skip, and jump. We chaperoned him on his eight engagements in Texas, and then we moved on to Palm Beach, Florida, where he addressed the Current Events Club. On March 3 we reached home, but on March 8 our troubadour went off for seven talks around Detroit, which enabled him to visit and comfort his brother's widow, Gene, and half-orphaned children. He wrote from Akron, March 12:

> I saw Gene yesterday, and their gloom is terrible. The children seem fairly reconciled, and laugh occasionally, in no hearty way. Eva [the oldest daughter] never laughs, and has a far-away look in her eyes; and Gene breaks into tears every hour. . . . Gene has nothing of the actress about her, and never seems to be trying to arouse my sympathy; she cries more when she is alone in the kitchen than when I am looking at her. . . . You can see her hair getting grayer every week.
>
> Meanwhile the lawyer I put on her case gave up, and reported that the lad who killed Sam had full rights to go hunting at that season; that the boy shot into the air, and never saw Sam; and that the father cannot be held responsible. . . . I left a $50 bill with Gene, and came away weak with the sorrow I had seen. . . . It is a problem we must work out when I get home. . . . I was not wrong in making hay while the sun shines; with unfortunate relatives reasonably asking for help (though Gene has never asked), we're far from being out of the woods yet. . . .

The wandering scholar returned to us on March 17. On the twenty-fourth we drove up to Williamstown, Massachusetts, where on the twenty-fifth Will addressed the Students' Forum of Williams College.

On May 28, 1928, we moved to 44 North Drive, Great Neck, Long Island—a Colonial-style shingle house, with eight rooms and a spacious lawn that did not at once announce how much laborious mowing it would need. Here at last Will had a private study, on the second floor, away from the turmoil of the family. We were now enlarged by taking in with us my brother Michael, who drove the car, puttered about the building and the grounds, and brightened every day with his ready helpfulness and good cheer. My sister Flora came to live with us, and brought her eleven-year-old son, Louis. Her husband had proved intolerant and intolerable; we welcomed her, and, at her request, we gave Louis our name, and put him through Cornell; we have been rewarded a hundred times over by his development. For several weeks in that summer Gloria Stone, daughter of our dearest friends, came to be companion to Ethel in study and mischief.

Ethel was now a chubby lass of nine. Almost every schoolday, when he was home, Will walked her to the Great Neck public school, where she was happier than she had been in private school in Manhattan. Sometimes they were accompanied by Wolf, a mixture of police dog and collie, whom Will brought up on a vegetarian diet. The experiment seemed to succeed—Wolf never had to be wormed; but the diet proved too laxative for the good of our carpets, and perhaps had something to do with Wolf's excessive amiability: he proved useless as a watchdog. He must have inherited Will's sensitivity to music: he moaned almost continuously when Will played Chopin's Funeral March.

I wonder did my "constant lover" feel some sympathy with the cynic's view that the best way to overcome temptation is to yield to it often enough to dull its lure. In any case, hardly a week after establishing his now big family in a pleasant home, he accepted a proposal from the Scripps-Howard papers to write six one-column articles, at a thousand dollars each, about the 1928 political conventions. I suspect he liked to sniff the proximity of power. So he left on June 10 for the Republican convention in Kansas City. Let his letters tell the story.

Will:

DEAR SWEETHEART:

Unless I write to you here on the floor of the Convention I won't be able to write at all. It will be hard work, because my seat is right next to [below] the speaker, and delegates are climbing over my head to the platform every minute.

This is the most exciting day so far, and I shall probably stay here all day. . . . It's an interesting menagerie, and gives me a good chance to study the faces and character of the great statesmen who run the nation. Senator Moses, Senator Smoot, Senator Borah, Secretary Mellon, . . . Nicholas Murray Butler, and other philosophers are almost within touch, and as we pen-pushers (600 of us) are on a raised platform, I can study them at my leisure.

What strikes me most of all is the low level of intelligence here. I've seldom seen so pitifully incompetent and timid a chairman as Senator Fess. He has been replaced by Senator Moses, who talks like a bulldog. Chaos, noise, and cheap oratory. Smoot and Borah look like peasants—hair falling over the face, eyebrows as big as a beard, big bones, horny hands, slow-moving minds. Mellon looks like a scared weasel. Nicholas Murray Butler makes the best impression. . . . The most intelligent-looking people here, without comparison, are the reporters. However, the quick-action type of mind which these reporters show might be out of place in matters that require depth rather than brilliance.

The peak of the Convention just came when young Senator [Robert M.] La Follette [Jr.] came to the platform and read a minority platform which he offered as a substitute for the majority read by Smoot. The boy makes a picturesque appearance and a fiery speech. The platform he offers is a

126

dandy, moderate and sensible, yet full of passion and courage. The Convention wildly applauds his platform and then overwhelmingly defeats it. . . . Nothing could show more clearly that these delegates must vote as they are told, not as they feel. . . .

Kansas City, 6-16-28

Now it's all over, and I can sit down, the morning after, to send you this word. I'm still dazed with the fever of writing three articles in four days, so you mustn't expect either clarity or profundity from me. . . .

[Enclosure] "E" is a picture of Hoover on his graduation day, sent to justify my description of him as handsome—once upon a time. Now he looks as bad as Coolidge. "F" is the speech that nominated Hoover. . . . Will send you similar speech about Al Smith later.

In one of my articles on the Republican convention I expressed the feeling that Hoover would make a better president than Smith (the probable Democratic nominee). This was a drastic retreat from my youthful radicalism. I remained a socialist, but I had no faith in the coming of that system to the United States in my lifetime; meanwhile I would support those practical alternatives which pointed to the socialist goal. Smith had been a good governor of New York within the limits of his dependence upon the Democratic machine; but I thought that his problem with alcohol unfitted him for the presidency. Hoover impressed me as a new figure in politics: a man with few bonds and debts to politicians, but with a background in education, science, and engineering that seemed to promise something better than we had had under Harding and Coolidge. However, it was poor sportsmanship of me, as well as poor literary strategy, to announce my liking for Hoover before I had attended the Democratic convention.

Marysville, Mo., 6-18-28

I am reverting to type, traveling five hours on two little trains with but a single dingy coach on them out to Marysville, which has 2,000 students and a few citizens. Here I sit in a primitive hotel, musty, ancient, dimly lit; and tonight I must prove again that progress is real.

Pittsburg, Kan., 6-21-28

Mr. and Mrs. Haldeman-Julius drove down from Girard to see me, and inveigled me into driving back with them to their home . . . a twenty-minute ride. The wife is a simple and kindly woman. . . . Emanuel himself is also a simple person, bright and cheery. . . . To all intents and purposes he is loyal to his wife, and that is better than poems and philosophy with me. Nevertheless he recalls quite vividly his outings, or nightings, with you, and says that my suspicions of his conduct are well founded. I shall take my chances with the past, and take care not to find out too much. . . .

I played with the children and the dogs, gossiped about Clarence Darrow, Joseph McCabe, and Bertrand Russell; told how you discovered Clar-

127

ence in a Stutz at Geneva, and held hands, etc., with Russell in New York. Emanuel still likes you, and is sending you a pack of books, to contribute to your education. . . .

Houston, Texas, 6-24-28

I am again in . . . the Lamar Hotel, where you and I honeymooned in February. . . . I arrived here a day sooner than I had told [my prospective host, J. J.] Carroll to expect me; and rather than pop in on them 24 hours ahead of time, I'm spending a day in a hotel. . . . If there's anything a woman hates it is an early guest. The early bird not only catches the worm, he catches H--1. . . .

The delegates from Iowa, on whose train I came from Pittsburg, were an orderly bunch, but a lawyer with them recognized me from my whiskers, . . . and that put an end to my privacy and my comfort. . . . How can I loosen my pants, and the top button, when I am supposed to be a philosopher?

6-26-28

I am just back from the first session of the Democratic Convention. . . . Though it's a struggle to work up enthusiasm for "Al" Smith after announcing that I am for Hoover, I'm beginning to see my way towards imagining that I'm interested in the show here. . . . It's so hot here that I have not slept more than an hour the last two nights. . . . I shall be glad when I can sit again in the shade of our little pines.

6-27-28

MY SWEET DAUGHTER,—

Your letter has come to me, and though I am working like mad on my last article about the Democratic Convention, I am stopping everything to send you this little word. . . .

Be good to me when I get back, for I am as tired as never before. And be good to mother; nothing in the world makes me so happy as that.

Your loving DAD

In one of those articles I described in terms of rapt admiration the man who put Governor Smith, as "the happy warrior," in nomination for the presidency. Franklin Roosevelt had to be assisted to the convention podium; seven years before, at Campobello, he had suffered the crippling attack of infantile paralysis that had immobilized the lower half of his body; he had fought his way back to some control of his limbs, but he still could not stand except with supporting irons, and could not walk without aid. It was a pitiful sight to see this handsome American so dependent upon others for locomotion, and yet so clearly of fine mental and moral fiber. In one of the articles I sent from Houston I remarked that "the delegates would have been wise to nominate the nominator" instead of the nominee. Roosevelt had been assistant secretary of the

128

Navy under Wilson before suffering the stroke, but he had not yet proved himself in office, as he was to do as governor of New York (1928–32). However, the weekly *Literary Digest* reprinted my statement, and it won me Roosevelt's friendship, while my support made me *persona* moderately *grata* to Herbert Hoover. Like Cicero's friend Atticus, I had contributed to both parties.

After a reunion in Great Neck Ariel, Ethel, Flora, Louis, Michael, and I spent the summer in Woodstock. In October I accepted with hardly concealed pride a seven-hundred-dollar fee for an address in Iron Mountain, Michigan. While there I went down into a mine, and was so depressed by the conditions under which the miners worked that I wrote an indignant article under the title "Is Life Worth Living?" One paragraph especially displeased the mine owners:

> Today I went down into a mine: put on rough clothing, an old raincoat, boots, and a miner's cap fronted with a carbide lamp; saw the great pulleys hoist the cage, stepped into the iron trap, and dropped 1600 feet, in din and darkness, into the planet's crust. Long tunnels, dimly lit, paved with mud and splashing planks; underground rivers roaring and whirling at our feet; trolley wire two inches [?] above our hats, not to be touched on pain of "sitting down"; iron cars rumbling with iron ore, and crowding us against wet rocks; great beams at every yard, propping up a thousand tons of earth and metal above our heads; here, half seen in the perpetual dust of the catacomb, a miner protecting the passage from a fault; and there at last, at the tunnel's end, a group of men digging out the ore. Old men, middle-aged men, young men, and yet all of them old, cheerless, silent; not a word from any of them as they worked; only the click of the pick, the crunch of the hammer, the long scratching of the shovel, the weird throb of the drill. Big hands of a color with the earth, grim faces bespattered with black mud, cheeks pale with the dripping, sunless air, eyes as dull and silent as their tongues; minds resentful of pity, remembering the fate of entrapped friends, and counting long hours and pitiful gains; men de-animate and unsouled, outcast from the sun for uncommitted crimes, condemned to hell before their death. One of ten thousand mines—iron mines, coal mines, copper mines, zinc mines, lead mines, silver mines, gold mines, platinum mines, diamond mines; these are the roots of modern industry: dirty holes in the earth, swallowing men for every girder in the building, every rail in the track, every gun in the armory, every part of the motor, every rivet in the ship, every coin in the mint, every jewel in the brooch, every machine in every factory in a world of metal, steam, speed, power, prosperity, and wealth. Great God! I'd rather be a medieval serf under a murderous czar, and take my chance with death in the sun, than live half the hours of half my days in the wet filth of these guts of the earth.

My eloquence deeply moved some mine owners—to hot protest. The conditions I had described with such noble sentiment dissatisfied the proprietors as well as the workers; these difficulties, they urged, lay in the nature of the enterprise, and originated not in the miserliness of the owners but in the demand of consumers for rails, girders, engines, guns, jewels, and coins, and these had to be priced in competition with other producers. Had not a hundred costly improvements already been made to protect the lives and health of the workers? What did this ivory-tower poet want—a piano in every mine?

I thought I would never be invited to Michigan again—but I soon received a call to address eight convocations of the Michigan Education Association in the last two weeks of October. I stopped briefly with my widowed sister-in-law on October 18, and spent two days with her and her four children on October 27–28. From my letter of the twenty-eighth:

> I am still at Gene's, playing Santa Claus to an impoverished family. To keep me warm they had to take blankets from the other beds. I hear Eva [oldest of the three daughters], this minute, asking plaintively has she no other stockings than the worn ones she is wearing. . . . The noon meal is a soup and a glass of milk. Their trips to the movie are mostly confined to my visits. Every cent has to be counted.
>
> Sammy [two years old] is naughty but delightful, full of spirit and fun, rolling over the floor with the dog, quite conscious that he wears the only pants in the family, and dominating his sisters with the greatest efficiency. A strange instinctive thrill comes over me when I squeeze him in my arms; and yet I am not sorry that Gene refused our offer to adopt him. It would take so much time and patience and energy to form and educate him! [He has become an admirable American without my dangerously libertarian pedagogy.] . . .

After barnstorming through Michigan I found myself scheduled to address the last of the teachers' convocations, October 30, in the auditorium of the Battle Creek Sanitarium—the crown and throne of the man who, more than any other since Father Mooney, had influenced my life. The American Medical Association will be amused to hear me call Dr. John Harvey Kellogg a saint of science. Most physicians, until recently, thought him a quack, a money-making charlatan. On the contrary, he was a man dedicated to spreading knowledge and health. He lived with ascetic simplicity, treated many persons gratis, adopted and educated several children, and bore without bitterness a thousand taunts for being far ahead of his time. He not only healed the sick but told them how to live in such a way that they would seldom need a doctor again. He had lost a lung to some disease in youth, and had every personal motive for finding and maintaining a healthy regimen.

He believed that the best way to keep the doctors away was a combination of vegetarian diet (vegetables, whole-wheat products, fruits, nuts), regular elimination, vigorous exercise, and a daily bath. He thought that meat-eating was the chief cause of disease. He did not admit that meat was necessary for physical strength; consider the bull and the horse, and had not the vegetarian Milo of Crotona, six times victor in the Olympian games, been renowned for his strength? The good doctor called his system "biological living," because our simian ancestors had been vegetarians (with a taste for fleas). Human teeth, however, are obviously adapted to an omnivorous menu, and recall many millenniums of hunting and eating game.

In any case I was glad to receive an invitation from Dr. Kellogg to come and let him look at me. I found him lovable at first sight: a short, slightly stout man (he recommended "bulky" food as an aid to costive sedentaries), with kindly blue eyes. "I have read your *Story of Philosophy*," he said, "and I felt that here was a man worth saving." ("Something good," Rohan-Chabot had said of Voltaire, "might still come out of that head.") He was delighted to learn that I had been a vegetarian since the age of eighteen, barring my seminary days and incidental transgressions. He offered advice on almost every part of me, from my eyes (splash them gently with warm water twice a day) to my anus (cleanse it with warm water after every evacuation); he instructed me on the art of the enema, and warned me against the chicken-potatoes-peas-salad-ice-cream usually provided at lecture-consuming clubs. Long before the Americans heard of cholesterol he frowned upon the use of whole milk, and its derivatives, by adults. A hundred of his recommendations—whole-wheat products, vegetable proteins, physiotherapy, hydrotherapy—have won their way into our common life. He lived—on one lung—to the age of ninety-three.

Refreshed physically and mentally by my day at Battle Creek, I caught a night train to New York, and rejoined my family on October 31—our wedding anniversary. Ariel had sent out invitations to friends to come and celebrate our survival of fifteen years of marriage. We hardly dreamed that we would hold up for at least forty-eight years more.

CHAPTER X

Lovers' Quarrel

1929

Ariel:

Toward the end of 1928 Will went off on another lecture tour. I agreed with his purpose, but I suffered from lonesomeness during his absences. Louis was at a private school in Pawling, kept by Mrs. Scott Nearing; Ethel could be safely left with Michael and our excellent housekeeper, Gertrude. More and more frequently I drove off, in late afternoon, to join my sisters in managing the Gypsy Tavern on Washington Square.

Those nights in Greenwich Village redeemed my mateless days. I made many new friends, chiefly of the artist and Bohemian sort. I fed and protected, and in some measure financed, painters, singers, dancers, and musicians; and in return they gave the Tavern impromptu recitals, and left with me their minor paintings as security for loans which were rarely repaid. One of these pawns was an excellent copy of a Rogier van der Weyden; the twelve hundred dollars loaned for it never came back.

I was for a moment disturbed, during Will's absence, by a visitor who, seeing a picture of Will on the Tavern's walls, announced that he knew that man well. "I met him in San Francisco. He drinks heavily and carries in his pockets favorable reviews which he takes out and reads to you at every opportunity." I began to wonder was there some truth in this, but I was reassured as the braggart went on, "I know his wife, too, quite well." When a listener told him that the woman he was talking to was Mrs. Will Durant he paid his bill and hurried off. Will has rarely drunk liquor, and he had, to that moment, been in San Francisco only once, and then with me.

132

He was, however, on his way to California now. En route he stopped to revel again in the forms and colors of the Grand Canyon. He sent me some pictures of it, and added his own.

1-3-29

Though the high altitude (7,000 feet) made my wind short (usually I am longwinded), I went out alone for some walks, and saw some new vistas of the tremendous ditch. It grows on you with every added view, and now I am ready to confess that it is the supreme sight [yet known to me] in all Nature's catalogue. Imagine a chasm ten miles wide at the top, running along for 217 miles, and 6,000 feet deep . . . ; the abyss filled with a thousand Hindu temples of red sandstone, whose colors change with every movement of the sun; rocks carved as if by Brobdingnagian architects—you can hardly believe that they are the work of water wearing away hard stone. Once the river, they say, ran on the surface; slowly (thru millions of years) it eroded the sand and the rocks, until now the stream, tho a rushing and roaring rapid 300 feet wide, seems from the brink of the chasm to be a silent and motionless ribbon of toothpaste as wide as your finger. What a lesson in patience! . . .

1-9-29

Here in San Francisco again. I miss you most of all here, for when I took the ferry from Oakland I felt the emptiness of the boat that had once carried me with you and Ethel at my side.

Awaiting me here were four reporters and one gentleman—Rabbi [Louis] Newman, whom the Jews consider their greatest scholar in the West. Tall, thin, aristocratic, handsome, bright-eyed—I liked him at first sight. He is to debate with me on "Is Democracy a Failure?"—and I shall enjoy it. . . . I wish you could be with us [but] you would want to elope with him. . . .

1-11-29

Another job done. I met Charles Rowell, one of the largest and fattest politicians on the Pacific Coast, in debate on democracy last night. . . . Rabbi Newman was in the audience, . . . making notes on my speech. . . . I shall have great difficulty in keeping myself from a licking at his hands, as he is extremely popular here, and has a reputation as a splendid orator. . . . It will be almost a pleasure to be put in my place . . . by a scholar and a gentleman.

1-12-29

Today I played sightseer, and had a long ride with Rabbi Newman to Palo Alto. Fifty miles of beauty along the ocean, up and down hills like a roller-coaster, with every combination of sun and fog, in every shade of gold, red, and purple, making the mountains look like great big cones of lavender ice cream. . . . Then into an immaculate village, as quiet and pretty as Kent in Connecticut; up through a section of fine houses to a hill that commanded a view of half the Pacific; and there was the home of Herbert Hoover [then President-elect]. . . .

133

I am enclosing a caricature of your husband from today's paper. Rabbi Newman, you see, writes a column weekly in the San Francisco *Call*, and takes the opportunity to advertise our coming debate. . . . He writes well for a hurried man. Every man with brains pays the penalty of getting a thousand jobs to do. He took me into his synagogue en route to Palo Alto, and what a vast place it is! I remarked that surely the hundred threads that had to be kept together there must have enmeshed him in slavery; and he almost embraced me for stating his tragedy so completely. He is the Spinoza type of Jew, soft-eyed, sad, a scholar who has to be an administrator against his will. . . .

1-14-29

SWEETHEART,—

It was so pleasant to talk to you today. I won't tell you how much it cost—you'd murder me. But I could see you thru the telephone, taking care of your little girl and your big home. . . . I begin to understand your problem, how big it is—worse now in Great Neck than . . . in Manhattan. I shall try to be a better comrade when I get home, to make up for all this abandonment. More and more I agree with [Voltaire's] Scarmentado: "After traveling all over the world I have decided now to stay home with my wife. It is true that she probably deceives me, but I shall stay with her nevertheless."

1-15-29

I lived a week yesterday. As I told you, I was dragooned into the City Hall in the morning. . . . I got back to the hotel cubby-hole at eleven, and at 12:30 the League of Women Voters held a lunch in my "honor"—i.e. in the hope of getting a free lecture. I fooled them, and made no speech. . . .

Back in my room at 1:30; typed the revised Table of Contents of *Mansions*; bathed, packed, and off at 3:30 to Oakland to autograph books in a store at 4:30. At 5:30 another cubby-hole in another hotel. . . . At 8:30 . . . at the Oakland Auditorium. On the roof of the big building a vast electric sign, visible thruout the city—"Will Durant debate Monday." I thought Newman would destroy me, for I was tired to death, had a full stomach, and liked the Rabbi. . . I won by a mile. [Was this the rabbi's opinion, too?] The Rabbi . . . drove me back to San Francisco. . . . Up at 7 this morning to catch this 8 A.M. train. Such is a day. . . . Love and eternal troth.

1-19-29

This morning a young minister, Rudolph Erickson, . . . drove me to Monterey. [Edward A.] Filene had asked me to call up Lincoln Steffens and give him remembrances if I should pass here. I called him, and he drove over from Carmel, and spent the evening with us—a queer man, as traveled as Ulysses, and shorn of every faith. I wish you could have been with us, you so enjoy these strange ducks.

1-20-29

Where shall we go this summer? Why not set off in the Packard leisurely on a trip . . . to the Maine lakes . . . to Quebec, . . . and down the Adirondacks to Woodstock, and a good rest there? . . . I would spare no expense to make the trip comfortable for you, to find clean and pretty lodgings . . . and good food. And I will be free!!!—no weekly essays hanging over my head. You will teach me to be a comrade now. And I shall come to you, in February, healthier than ever, younger than I was five years ago, and very handsome in the dark.

I omit at this point an unhappy episode. Will replied despondently to a lost letter of mine in which, apparently, I told him I could no longer bear our long separation. I had agreed to this extended tour, for we had raised our expenditures by renting the Great Neck house, and by taking into the family, for various periods, Flora, Louis, Gloria, Michael, and Harry; and I knew that Will was laboring to build a nest egg for our security while he would write what he expected would be unpopular books. We had had a maid, but she missed her Manhattan friends and soon left us. Michael too was bored to gloom now that Will was not at hand to brighten the days. Nearly all the work and cares of the household fell upon me. On top of that I caught the flu, and took to my bed. I wrote to Will that I was at the breaking point. He replied by proposing to cancel the remainder of his engagements, at a cost of some five thousand dollars and a "black eye" with lecture bureaus and committees; I bade him carry on. The flu disappeared, and my courage returned. Meanwhile he worked his way north.

1-28-29

On the train, approaching Seattle. What a change! When I left Los Angeles it was overcoatless weather, and the sun shone bright; here everything is covered with snow, and more snow is falling. . . . At Portland, where we stopped for 35 minutes, I put on my rubbers . . . and went out for a walk in the snow. . . . Here was a pleasure I had not had for a long time. The South is warm, but its air is dull, as if the heat had killed the life in it; one breath here is worth a dozen there. And even in the matter of beauty these white woods we are flying thru are as magnificent as southern palms and dust. . . . Santa Barbara is beautiful; but Max Schott, after putting $100,000 into his house, confesses his opinion that health requires a climate with variations. . . .
Be patient for three weeks more and I shall never leave you again.

But enough of these letters for a while; I must not tire the reader with Will's travelogue, his ecstasies about the virgin snows of the Northwest, and his enthusiasm for vegetables, fruits, nuts, and enemas. So I pass over his missives from Tacoma, Spokane, Moscow (Idaho), Boulder, Tulsa, and Oklahoma City, but his letter from the Hotel Durant in Durant, Oklahoma, begins a story that I must not omit.

2-10-29

Everything is complete here except that I haven't a Durant car. The town and the hotel were named in my honor before I was born. It is a little group

135

of shacks on a miniature Broadway three blocks long; the hotel is a nice old-fashioned thing with rockers and 50-cent dinners. I like this simplicity; why should we just multiply the scale on which we live, and have, after all, no more health or happiness than these modest people, who "Sir" and "Thank you, come again" at every step? It is a relief to find a hotel without one flunky. . . .

I met yesterday the strange old man for whom the town was named—Mr. William A. Durant—son of a French Canadian father and an Indian mother; a simple fellow made rich by the discovery of oil on his land. The chief vegetation in Oklahoma is oil pumps. . . .

Tomorrow I must stay in this cubicle until I face 1,000 schoolteachers at 8 P.M. Then I come back to my hole in the wall and ease myself [!] with Spengler until two o'clock after midnight, when I go out . . . and catch the only train that will take me hence to Kansas City in time for my lecture there on the 12th.

Between this letter and the next Will had some wild adventures, which he reported from Kansas City.

2-13-29

SWEETHEART,—

Diary for Feb. 11-12, 1929:

10 P.M. I beg the clerk at the Durant hotel to wake me at 2 A.M. [He agrees.]

2 A.M. I sleep on. The villainous clerk sleeps on too.

4:30: He wakes up and calls me. I take down the receiver and say "Thank you." "Don't thank me," he says; "it's 4:30." "Oh, hell," says I.

4:35: phone to the railroads. No train to Kansas City in time for my lecture there at 8:15 P.M.

4:50—phone to Tulsa Aviation Field for a plane; nobody there.

7:00—phone to Robert Brewer, Tulsa friend; can he get me a plane?

9:00—phone from Brewer—"Yes, but it will cost you . . . $245. . . ." They'll arrive at Durant 11:15 A.M. . . .

1:05 P.M.—plane over town. . . . I buy fruit for the aviator's lunch. . . .

1:25—In the plane. . . .

3:05—land at Tulsa for gasoline. Why the - - - - didn't he do that before setting out? . . . Mechanic tunes up motor. Thirty minutes gone to nowhere.

5:30—Only 100 miles from Kansas City.

5:40–6:00—Wind turns against us.—Snow—Worse snow.

6:10—Pilot insists on landing. . . . Night falling; must find a landing spot before dark.

6:12—Bump, bump, bump, . . . on the earth; mud for miles. Far away a farm house. "Can you drive me to Kansas City?" "You're 80 miles away, and my car has no lights."

6:35—Bag-lugging again, into Greeley, Kansas; the main garage. . . . "Can you drive me to Kansas City?" "No, but I'll drive you to Garnett, and you can catch the Flyer to Kansas City." "Let's go." I pay the aviator $200. . . .

6:40—over deep ruts, mud, snow, ice, 14 miles in 20 minutes. . . .
7:00—Garnett, Mo.—Pac. Station. "Has the Flyer gone?"
"Yes." "Can I get a car to drive me to Kansas City?"
"Yes, but he can't make it before ten o'clock."

Will telephoned to Kansas City that he could not keep his engagement. The chairman fumed, and vowed never to engage him again.

We were at last reunited on Washington's Birthday. While we were there Ethel burst into our room and gaily announced, "Mother, did you know that you have given birth to another child?" She had heard Walter Winchell, in one of his breathless flashes, reveal over the radio that "Mrs. Will Durant, wife of the author of *The Story of Philosophy*, has just given birth to a son in a Washington hospital." This was news to us indeed, for at that moment I had been bustling about the room in full health of body and spirits. Walter had confused me with another woman of the Durant name. Will sent Winchell a jolly message: "You were half right; but it was I who gave birth. The child is called *The Mansions of Philosophy*. Both parent and child are doing well."

Will:

I too was inaccurate, for my fourth book was not formally published until May, 1929. In its original form it is now out of print, but in 1952 it was reprinted—with two or three chapters omitted—as *The Pleasures of Philosophy;* Max Schuster persuaded me to change the title on the ground that only a few readers would see in it an allusion to Christ's statement "In my Father's house are many mansions." I like the first title better, for I look upon philosophy as a garden (Plato's "dear delight") in which there are many pleasant groves. Three of the chapters had been debates; some others had appeared as magazine articles; fourteen of the twenty-five had been written for the book in the fever of lecture tours, even in the commotion of trains. Under the circumstances all I could do was a frank "popularization" of what seemed to me the living problems of philosophy, as in *The Story* I had tried to "humanize" its history. Even so, the analysis of our changing morals in 1929 stands up fairly well in 1977. The foreword, or "Invitation," ended with an ominous paragraph:

> Our culture is superficial today, and our knowledge is dangerous, because we are rich in mechanisms and poor in purposes. The balance of mind which once came of a warm religious faith is gone; science has taken from us the supernatural bases of our morality, and all the world seems consumed in a disorderly individualism that reflects the chaotic fragmentation of our character. We face again the problem that harassed Socrates: how shall we find a natural ethic to replace the supernatural sanctions that have ceased to influence the behavior of men? Without philosophy, without that total vision which unifies purposes and establishes the hierarchy of

desires, we fritter away our social heritage in cynical corruption on the one hand, and in revolutionary madness on the other; we abandon in a moment our pacific idealism and plunge into the co-operative suicide of war. . . . We move about the earth with unprecedented speed, but we do not know, and have not thought, where we are going, or whether we shall find any happiness there for our harassed souls. We are being destroyed by our knowledge, which has made us drunk with our power. And we shall not be saved without wisdom.

Nevertheless I had little faith in contemporary philosophy. Its academic practitioners seemed to have lost themselves in the labyrinths of epistemology and metaphysics; they wrote for one another in a kind of sacred and secret society, in an aloof and awesome dialect, in esoteric journals or professional brochures; and the world passed them by. I had said as much, too aggressively, in the first chapter of *Mansions*; but in the preface to a new edition of *The Story of Philosophy* I offered a palm branch, a bit prickly:

> These jealous ones who would guard their knowledge from the world have only themselves to blame if their exclusiveness and their barbarous terminology have led the world to seek in books, in lectures, and in adult education, the instruction which they themselves have failed to give. Let them be grateful that their halting efforts are aided by amateurs who love life enough to let it humanize their teaching. Perhaps each kind of teacher can be of aid to the other: the cautious scholar to check our enthusiasm with accuracy, and the enthusiast to pour warmth and blood into the fruits of scholarship. Between us we might build up an American audience fit to listen to geniuses, and therefore ready to produce them. We are all imperfect teachers, but we may be forgiven if we have advanced the matter a little, and have done our best.

But I was not really satisfied to be mere prologue. I longed for the leisure that would enable me to be scholarly as well as readable, to do the research that accuracy would require, and to mold the results into artistic form. I had taken advantage of my temporary fame, and had made myself "a motley to the view" on the lecture and dinner-club circuit; by 1929, aided by Ariel's economy, we had saved enough to deprive us of any excuse for further postponing our enterprise in "integral history."

I had expounded the idea in 1917 in a paper (now lost) "On the Writing of History," read before a meeting of the faculty and students in the department of philosophy at Columbia University. Its thesis: whereas economic life, politics, religion, morals and manners, science, philosophy, literature, and art had all moved contemporaneously, and in mutual influence, in each epoch of each civilization, historians had recorded each aspect in almost complete separation from the rest. I pictured Pericles going with his wife, Aspasia, and his friend Socrates to see a play by Euripides presented with chorus and music in a theater adorned with

138

pictures and statuary and dedicated to the god Dionysus; here, in one moment and action, a dozen elements of civilization—economics (there was an admission charge, in many cases paid by the state), politics, morals (Aspasia had been an hetaira), science (the mathematics, geology, and physics of building), philosophy, literature, drama, music, architecture, painting, sculpture, and religion—had come together in a unity and interplay rarely presented by historians. So I cried, "Hold, enough!" to what I later termed "shredded history," and called for an "integral history" in which all the phases of human activity would be presented in one complex narrative, in one developing, moving, picture. I did not, of course, propose a cloture on lineal and vertical history (tracing the course of one element in civilization), nor on brochure history (reporting original research on some limited subject or event), but I thought that these had been overdone, and that the education of mankind required a new type of historian—not quite like Gibbon, Macaulay, or Ranke, who had given nearly all their attention to politics, religion, and war, but rather like Voltaire, who, in his *Siècle de Louis XIV* and his *Essai sur les moeurs*, had occasionally left the court, the church, and the camp to consider and record morals, literature, philosophy, and art.

For years now I had been admiring myself as the destined practitioner of "integral" history; and only an accident (Haldeman-Julius' visit to Labor Temple) had deflected me into a book of "shredded" history—*The Story of Philosophy*. Far back in 1921, in one of our afterlecture gatherings, I had expounded to some "Durant addicts" my dream of writing a history of civilization on a collateral or horizontal plan. Several of them encouraged me; "If I were rich," said Abraham Sarasohn, "I would buy you the leisure to write such a history." Well, by 1929 Ariel and I felt that we had saved enough to live on our income, our risky royalties, a few lectures, and some possible magazine articles. (The Book-of-the-Month Club windfalls did not come into our lives till 1961.)

My courage failed at the outset. I was now forty-four years old; should I, at that age, undertake a history of all the civilizations, in all their aspects, from the cultures of Sumeria, Egypt, and India forty centuries before Christ down to our own times? The nineteenth century A.D. was itself so rich in interest and achievement—with its inventions and industries, its dramatic revolutions, its romantic poetry and massive novels, its creed-destroying, world-remaking sciences, its Darwinian biology and Marxian economics, its idealistic and materialistic philosophies, its emancipation of women from men and of sex from parentage, its soaring operas and resounding symphonies, its excited movements and theories in the arts—how could I do more in one lifetime than to record integrally that "wonderful century" from Napoleon and Beethoven to Edison and Freud? I was so fascinated by that potential panorama that I for a time planned to content myself with a single century.

Then, on further rumination, I felt ashamed of quaking before half a dozen millenniums; after all, a large perspective was the soul of my creed. Tentatively I began to study the ancient Near East. That region, through Ionia and Crete, had mothered Greek civilization, which, with the Judaic, had come down to us through pagan and Christian Rome; our civilization began as our Oriental heritage; it rose, like the sun, in the East. Why should I not face this fact and begin at the beginnings (with writing and the wheel) and work through to the end of the nineteenth century? If I had been told that the enterprise would take eleven volumes and forty-six years (1929–75), and would then stop a century short of its goal, I might have turned and fled. Innocence and Ariel drew me on. Moreover, as the Romans said, *initium dimidium facti*—the beginning is half the deed. We began.

We knew that Volume I would be the hardest for us—so much of Asia was virgin soil to our studies as well as to our feet. We realized that our first task was to study the Near East at first hand, and to *feel* Egypt, Palestine, Asia Minor, Syria, Iraq, Iran, India, Burma, China, and Japan; these were dangerously weak spots in our geographical background. As if for our convenience, the Cunard Company arranged a round-the-world tour on the S.S. *Franconia* leaving New York January 11, 1930. We laid out some eighteen thousand dollars for two staterooms—one for Ethel, one for Ariel and me and two hundred books on the history and civilization of Asia. Then, vowing to raise some of that eighteen thousand dollars, I committed myself to another lecture tour in the fall.

Perhaps my decision to go troubadouring again, and Ariel's continuing devotion to the Gypsy Tavern, brought on the most lasting quarrel we have ever had. Her side of the argument has not been preserved; so far as we can recapture it across forty years, it concerned her doubts of my marital fidelity on my wanderings, and my reciprocal wonder what personal attachments led her so constantly to the Tavern, and to such generous "loans" to irresponsible geniuses. Ariel explained that her nightly presence there was necessary to the tearoom's solvency; and no reassurances of mine would ease her doubts about the sirens who lay in wait for me on my tours. All the sadness of a fading romance, and all the irritations of travel and finance, of ever new trains to catch and new audiences to face, speak in the letters which a punitive fate has preserved to shame me. I can hardly believe that our marriage was so near to shipwreck, or that I had ever sunk to such weak self-pity. These letters clamor for concealment, but here they are, with some irrelevant trivia omitted.

The first is dated October 21, 1929, and was apparently written at Huntington, West Virginia:

To My Former Sweetheart,—

I am sorry I spoke so frankly yesterday. Not that it was wrong or unwise to let these specters out into the light, so that we might know just where we were going; but that I had hoped to keep our tragedy a secret between us, leaving Ethel as far as possible untouched by it. But even that consolation was denied us.

I sat up all last night, almost, sleepless and dreary, and found sleep only at 3 P.M. today.

Good-bye.

WILL

From the same city, a day later:

Yes, you are still dear to me, and always will be, for these sixteen years together—which will be completed [October 31] when we are both physically and spiritually so far apart—have made you part of me; and you are quite right when you say that in leaving you I shall tear myself to pieces, and never know happiness again. How well your mother foresaw that after our good fortune would come misery. Our sin was what the Greeks call *Hybris*—arrogance in prosperity.

I am to blame, for it is my addiction to libertarian ways that has ruined me. I wanted to give you freedom—or, rather, not to take it from you. I dreamed . . . that you could handle that freedom like a philosopher. A woman cannot give herself promiscuously (even in spiritual promiscuity) to many men and yet maintain that unique and complete devotion which is love. It is the story of *Strange Interlude*—we are not content with one lover, and in the end we lose them all. The choice of the promiscuous life leaves us alien to each other, and even aliens in our own houses; the home too requires devotion and fidelity to it before it will give us peace.

The trees everywhere are beautiful, and if it weren't that the rain is cold I would lie down among them and let myself rot into the earth.

How Byronic! But probably even Byron never made so unfair an argument. For though Ariel had been forming friendships in Greenwich Village, I had been indulging in some "spiritual promiscuity" in the friendships I had made particularly on the West Coast—with women as well as men; and I had let fragrant women buzz around me with bewitching compliments in almost every port. I had thought of myself as a Galahad immune to seduction, but I had enjoyed its proximity.

At the Auditorium Hotel, Chicago, October 26, I reached the bottom of bathos:

By the repetitiveness of history I find myself again in this old hotel, in the same room, facing the same fog-invisible lake, sitting in the same chair, writing to—a different Ariel. As I stepped off the train I saw a young wife run to her husband [I presumed], clasp him around the neck, and kiss him many times. She has not yet found the charms of many superior to the fidelity of one. Perhaps there are no tea rooms where she lives. . . .

In the dining car today I found myself in the first stages of insanity—aphasia. I tried to order pumpkin pie, and said "pumpkin kie." I tried three times with the same result. The waiter smiled. . . .

141

Your praise of Ethel consoles me, in my isolation here, with the thought that perhaps, after all, I have not spoiled her, and that the method of libertarian lenience has made her a tender and loving daughter, as well as a splendid mind. . . .

Thank you for being a mother again.

I did not go insane, and did not rot in the earth. I gave signs of recovery.

Chicago, 10-28-29

I went this morning to Kroch's bookstore to pay my annual respects to the best bookseller in America; and found that he had bound in leather several copies of *Mansions*. He let me have one for the very reasonable price of $10, and I am sending it, inscribed to you. . . .

I have just heard that the stock market has crashed again. I shall lose perhaps $15,000—not on my own investments but merely on the $5,000 which I gave Will Perlman on account; it seems that he bought with this not merely $5,000 worth but several times that, buying "on margin." . . . In short, I have fallen into a nice mess. Your own losses will be much less. . . . Forget about it, sell nothing, buy no more stocks or bonds of any kind; and let us hope that now that we are poorer we shall be happier.

I have written a paean of praise of [Powys'] *The Meaning of Culture;* I wanted to send you a copy of my piece, but Kroch wishes to tack it up in his store.

Since we now regularly summered in Woodstock, New York, Ariel recommended buying a house there as a wiser expenditure than a world cruise. So I wrote from Shreveport, Louisiana:

11-16-29

Ah, how happy I would be to have a "permanent home in Woodstock"! But do you really think that you would be content there, where Greenwich Village comes for only a few months per year? . . .

As to the Round the World tour, it is the only thing I have asked for myself in many years of work. I feel more and more the need of deepening myself with a vaster perspective. I have won time-perspective through the study of history; I need space-perspective now through travel. . . .

Another accident brought a partial solution to our differences. A friend told us of what seemed a bargain in Lake Hill, five miles west of Woodstock: a twenty-year-old eight-room frame house, with seventeen acres of good land around it. Ariel, Ethel, and I motored up to see it. We were pleased with its sturdy structure and pleasant design, and especially with the broad covered porch that curved around it, front and side; we liked the pretty bungalow that adjoined, and the separate garage, itself as big as a house. On January 2, 1930, we bought the property for fifteen thousand dollars. Ariel was happy, and agreed to go round the world.

On January 10 some six hundred friends, students, and acquaintances gathered in the Aldine Club in New York to give us a sendoff dinner. We had a noble roster of speakers: John Dewey, Rabbi Stephen Wise, John Haynes Holmes, and Hendrik Willem van Loon; the persistent cordiality of these men, despite my mounting blunders, left us always in their debt. In mid-dinner a lady came to the dais and introduced herself as Nan Britten, and her daughter as the late President Harding's private production. I was amused, but Dewey, sitting at my right, was uncomfortable. Matters went further awry when Augustin Duncan, brother of Isadora, came up and announced that he had been commissioned by my old benefactor, Alden Freeman, to crown me "the Molière of our time." I had never dreamed that I resembled Molière; later I found that Alden had asked Augustin to crown me the *Voltaire* of our time. Drunken Duncan got the message confused, and insisted on pressing the wreath upon my unwilling head; I removed it (the wreath) with confused modesty. *The New Yorker* gave a satirical but accurate account of my coronation.

I did not recover from that dinner until, on January 11, 1930, Ariel, Ethel, and I set out to see the world.

CHAPTER XI

Around the World

1930

Ariel:

I let Will's story of our quarrel stand. He could never feel the depth of my loneliness when he was away, or the bitterness of my doubts as to the ability of his erotic and romantic nature to resist the charms of women after a week or two away from his wife. And perhaps I did some flirting myself with those Greenwich Village ready-to-wear lovers whose lawless spirit awoke in me some memories of my rebel ways. It took me time to simmer down into a bourgeois matron.

Once we sailed off on the *Franconia* we rediscovered each other, and those cold and querulous letters were burned away in the warmth of our embraces. The *Franconia*, however, was not made for love; it was hardly out of sight of New York Harbor when Will's stomach and ears began to swim with the rolling and pitching of the ship. He was incapacitated for two days. Gradually he learned that the only way to overcome seasickness is to yield to it, to give up the attempt to have and to hold, and to begin with a clean slate and stomach after each surrender.

By that time the cruise director, Ross Skinner—a man of uncanny tact, patience, and good humor—had noticed how our two hundred volumes were almost crowding us out of our stateroom. He offered William an extra room for his books and his writing, and when Will had settled down in this luxury, Skinner gently suggested a Durant discourse to the floating congregation. The staff already included an official lecturer, Mr. Batchelder, who was scheduled to speak on each of the countries to be

144

visited; and a Protestant clergyman, Ralph Sockman, who would speak on general subjects; it might have embarrassed them to have a third voice break in, but they took Will's intrusion quite amiably. He thought to pay his debt with his lightest piece, "The Ten Greatest Thinkers," but before the cruise was completed he had also expounded "Chinese Philosophy," "Chinese Poetry," "Democracy," and "Marriage." He made a few enemies, but also some precious friends.

First was Kasimir Zurawski, a Polish physician from Chicago. He specialized in dermatology because, he said, a dermatologist's patients rarely get cured and rarely die of their disease; in any case his clean, pink complexion at age sixty spoke well for his competence. Will, a romantic soul struggling for classic calm, relished the doctor's keen, clear mind, which discarded all ideologies and penetrated every pretense, while never forgetting courtesy. I learned to appreciate Kasimir's quiet way of puncturing my exaggerations with raised eyebrows and diluting my dogmas with a smile. He rewarded my unusual docility by serving as my escort when Will stayed on board to write *Our Oriental Heritage* while most of us took every chance to sample strange shores.

The three of us found a unique and distinguished friend in the ship's doctor, George Jameson Carr. He was, to begin with, the handsomest man on board, the best dancer, the most alluring bachelor; maidens looked at him lovingly, and matrons exaggerated their ailments to get him out of his office into their rooms. But he had had an unhappy marriage, and had gone through the abrasions of divorce; he was always gracious to women, but he knew their frailties; even a lovely mouth could scold. He was now about forty years old, and had some twenty years of worldwide adventure behind him, often skirting death. Will became his patient by taking into his blood an undiscourageable fungus. Dr. Carr not only brought this "epidermophytosis" under control; he could keep pace with Will in philosophy and history; so could Zurawski; and in the evening quiet of Carr's rooms the four of us had many an exciting exchange of ideas and memories, calmed now and then by the doctor's well-chosen phonograph records. In these conversations I learned that candor can live with courtesy. I complained a bit when the Three Musketeers, as I called them, left me for expeditions too tiring for my feet; and I wondered whether it was my mind they feared to tire, or my morals they feared to offend. However, they assured me that on these unisexual forays they never talked of sex.

Will kept close to Ethel and me on shore trips, for we had the probably mistaken notion that the streets of foreign cities were less safe than New York's. We slid together down Madeira's roads of smooth little stones; mounted the cliffs of Gibraltar, explored the aromatic alleys and open shops of the Kasbah in Algiers, rode La Grande Corniche from Nice to Menton, and gamboled in Monte Carlo. Will had his third, Ethel and I our second, view of Naples and Pompeii. Then through "Scylla and Charybdis"—between Italy and Sicily—back into the full radiance of the Mediterranean and on to its eastern ports. We were frightened into silence by the waves that buffeted our little boats as they rose and plunged between the rocks in the sprayful passage from the *Franconia* to the docks at Haifa. There we enlisted for an optional tour by car through Nazareth, Tiberias, Cana, and Nablus to Jerusalem. Will washed away some of his sins by swimming in the Sea of Galilee. Part of his old piety seemed to return to him, and I am sure that he had visions of Christ walking on the waves. I was disturbed to find only a handful of Jews in a Tiberias swarming with Arabs; not till we sighted the towers of Jerusalem did I feel that this Land was Holy to me too, as the native soil of my scattered and afflicted people.

After three days in Palestine we passed by train through the Sinai Desert to Cairo. I was a bit uncomfortable there, feeling the incipient strife between Arab and Jew, but Will, who is a man for all nations, was soon darting around enthusiastically gathering material for the chapter on Egypt in *Our Oriental Heritage*. On our visit to the Pyramids Ethel and I had an hour of cruel merriment to see our philosopher seasick on a camel, and almost lost on a camel; for at one stage his "ship of the desert" evaded both his and the guide's control and ambled off at a speed, both horizontal and vertical, that had Will clinging to the hump before him as the only accessible security in a swaying world.

A day later he and Drs. Carr and Zurawski joined an optional tour up the Nile to see the marvels of Pharaonic architecture in Luxor and Karnak. When they returned Will astonished us by telling how he had stood on Rameses II's ear. This organ, he explained, was three and a half feet long, and was part of a statue fifty-six feet long, lying broken and desolate in the sands; this was the Ozymandias whom Shelley had commemorated in a perfect sonnet mourning the brevity of grandeur. Will, of course, fell in love, despite the distance, with Rameses' great queen Hatshepsut, and then with Ikhnaton's pretty wife with the slender neck, Nofretete. He quoted Ikhnaton's favorite form of royal oath: "As my heart is happy in the Queen and her children," leaving me to understand that he felt that way about me and Ethel; but when he added that the poet-ruler spoke of his wife as "Mistress of his Happiness, at hearing whose voice the King rejoices," I began to doubt.

Egypt impressed us with the size and splendor of its monuments, but India appealed to us as the victim of foreign conquerors, tribal and class divisions, native superstitions, uncontrolled fertility, and enervating heat. How could so handicapped a nation raise itself to all the zest and risk of freedom? Will approached that steaming, teeming semi-continent in a mood of wonder and humility; so I gather from the first paragraph of the report he sent to a syndicate in 1930:

Tomorrow I shall see India. Sitting alone on the promenade deck, I watch the tip of the mast picking its way slowly among the stars; and I ask myself why I have come so far to see so alien a land. Not because it is almost as large as my own—"size is not development"; nor because it is nearly three times as populous as my own—God knows that the multiplication of mouths is a problem and not an achievement. I want to see India because it is alien to me; because its civilization, its literature, its philosophy, its religions, its manners, its morals, its arts are so utterly different from those that I have known. Surely I shall be plowed up to some effect, the earth about my roots will be turned up and freshened, by new faces and ways and strange points of view. Perhaps if I can learn to understand so uncongenial a culture I shall be a little broader and deeper, a little less provincial and prejudiced, than before.

We had sent a letter to Mahatma Gandhi, then living at Ahmedabad in Bombay province, telling him that our ship would stop at Bombay February 14 to 22, and asking might we come up to see him. We waited for a reply till February 20; none came. We set out to Fatehpur Sikri, Agra, Jaipur, Delhi, Benares, and down to Madras, Madura, and Ceylon. When we rejoined the ship there we found a cordial invitation from Gandhi, too late to be used. We missed the great apostle, but Will gathered reams of data that went to warm and color the chapters on India in *Our Oriental Heritage*.

Of course our dominating impression of India in 1930 was of its dearth of food and its profusion of mouths. Perhaps Will exaggerated the poverty in his travel report:

> Everybody exploits them [the peasants of India], even their own countrymen: the British, . . . the Hindu money lenders, . . . tourists (including the writer) haggling them down to a few coins for the product of many months' patient work and art. . . . In the end the peasant exploits himself: he knows no birth control, and longs for many sons to work and pray for him and carry on his name; thus all the profit from such sanitation and peace as he has is swallowed up by a mounting torrent of hungry mouths. "When goods are increased," said Malthus Ecclesiastes, "they are increased that eat them, and what is the good thereof?"

We were almost as depressed by the religions of India as by its poverty. The sight of thousands of men and women crowding the roads to Benares to pray on the "bathing ghats" or wash away their sins in the Ganges did not offend us; physical symbols for spiritual renewal appear in many cults, and may serve a good purpose. But we found it hard to bear the sight of young as well as old "saints," naked but covered with ashes, squatting on worn rumps and crossed legs, staring into the face of the sun, willing to become blind if thereby some vision of Brahma, the World-Spirit, might be attained, or if they might be excused from rebirth. Had the inescapable heat of central and southern India brought on

this surrender of life to death? Will included in his now forgotten travelogue a touching paragraph:

> Another saint is a boy, blonde and handsome, scion, surely, of the Aryan
> race. He sits quietly and modestly, dressed only in a string of beads. I try to
> get his attention, but he has fixed his eyes steadfastly across the river,
> hoping to see divinity. How gladly would I sit beside him, share his mode
> of life for a while, and talk with him soul to soul! What is he thinking?—or
> does he despise thought as a superficial thing, not to be compared with the
> direct inward perception of the flow of reality? The books tell us that these
> saints fast and pray for Nirvana—to be freed from all . . . desire, all sepa-
> rate delusive personality; to be one with Brahma, the great impersonal
> God; to be washed, by suffering, so clean of sin as to merit the greatest gift
> of all—never to be born again. . . . Can this be what my young saint feels,
> so soon in his years? Could there be any bitterer condemnation of life? . . .
> We of the West love our egos so dearly that we cannot reconcile ourselves
> to mortality; these ["holy"] men of the East despise their passing, suffering
> selves, and beg for nothingness. . . .
>   I long for a Malthus to come and teach these poor people that education
> is frustrated when reproduction is unrestrained; and still more for a Vol-
> taire to come and laugh to death this disheartening theology and these
> ridiculous gods. [But if Voltaire could not change the climate?]

Buddhism, which was to Will's taste, has almost disappeared from
India. It survives in Ceylon, but we were shocked to see its transformation in a Buddhist monastery overlooking Kandy, the ancient capital.
The walls were frescoed with paintings illustrating the weird theology
that had here replaced Buddha's gentle and agnostic religion; some lurid
scenes show Buddha himself inflicting horrible punishments upon the
damned in hell. Will, who had learned to think of Buddha as the last
person in history who would hurt anyone, asked a monk to explain the
disharmony between these pictures and Gautama's doctrine and spirit.
The monk replied, "A religion without a punishing god would not check
the crimes and sins of this unruly people. They are not ready for reason;
they must be ruled by fear." Will hoped that education would someday
replace fear as the basis of morality and social order, but it seemed to me
that the Ceylonese were breeding and dying faster than you could edu-
cate them.

We liked Burma. In Rangoon we stood in awe before the overpower-
ing, gold-leaf-covered Shwe Dagon pagoda, which claimed to contain the
ashes of Buddha himself. Here too was a priest-ruled country, where
supernatural fears and hopes controlled the populace and provided theological insurance for the government, and a steady income for the
priests. But the heat seemed less oppressive than in India, and the people seemed stronger and more cheerful; there were not so many appli-
cants for Nirvana.

We had quite a dose of Southeast Asia. Our ship sailed south from Rangoon along the Malay Peninsula to Singapore, where Will was pleasantly surprised to receive a request for a newspaper interview; apparently someone had dropped a *Story of Philosophy* there. Then around the great port and north to Siam (now Thailand) and its capital, Bangkok. We enjoyed meeting Noël Coward there, and received useful advice for the uncomfortable overland trip we were planning from Bangkok to Saigon.

While the *Franconia* (with Ethel) sailed south and around Cambodia to Cap Saint-Jacques, Will and I and Dr. Zurawski went by car into the land of the medieval Khmers to view the amazing temples at Angkor. We climbed the tallest one, and found the descent more difficult than the ascent, since gravity doubled the impetus of every step; for the most part we came down on our bellies. Then on to Pnom-Penh, the populous capital of Cambodia; but we found a hundred lizards for every inhabitant. We noted the silent efficiency of our Japanese driver, who informed us, "This country is very poorly managed. Things will run better when my country gets control here." We thought this to be chauvinist boasting, but ten years later the Japanese seized not only all Indochina but most of the coastal provinces of China.

We drove across the Mekong River and through what is now Vietnam until, weary and dirty, we reached Saigon. In 1930 it was a beautiful capital, where both the French and the Oriental aesthetic senses came together in a splendor of fine buildings, wide avenues, brilliant temples, fragrant plants, and little women dressed like walking flowers. We were too innocent and provincial to appreciate the hunger of these charming people for their own independent state.

At Cap Saint-Jacques, the port of Saigon, we rejoined the *Franconia* and Ethel, and sailed south to Java (now Indonesia), where we thought the Dutch were behaving like relatively decent imperialists. We were too tired to take the optional trip to Bali; for some time thereafter Will had to take Bali on trust and fancy, idealizing those uncorseted nipples, until Charlie Chaplin ended the mystery by showing us the motion pictures he had taken in the enchanted isle.

From Java our ship zigzagged through the Malay Archipelago to Macassar on the island of Celebes, and then to Zamboanga and Manila, where one newspaper thought Will's arrival (March 28) worthy of the front page. We visited the American governor general in Malacanan Palace, and there Will succumbed to an invitation to address a gathering of the American colony.

On March 31 we had our first sight of China. Will sent in a picture-card report:

> In the harbor of Hong Kong a thousand sampans rise—a thousand
> bouncing boats flat and broad and short, propelled by long oars at the rear,

and covered in the center with a vaulted shelter under which a Chinese family increases and multiplies. For it is cheaper to buy a sampan than to rent a house, cheaper to have children than to hire slaves; there are no landlords on these waves, and no schools. As the *Franconia* moves carefully among them to her dock at Kowloon the awkward boats rock and splash about us, and their human flotsam offers us a foretaste of Hong Kong's million wares.

Oranges and pajamas, wicker chairs and embroideries, suitcases and Mandarin coats, candy and silks, canes and cloisonné, porcelain and ivory, joss-sticks and jade, firecrackers and gods—here they are, almost flung up at us from the cordon of sampans. We can hardly see these articles, for their salesmen are too interesting. . . . They do not speak English to us, for they know that we should understand their English as little as that of a London Bobby; they *sing* Chinese, and rely upon the tune of their sentences . . . to break through the barriers of our ignorance. How strange we must seem to them, with our alien speech so lacking in melody, with our complex and irksome garb, . . . with our . . . habit of writing from left to right in characters that make no pictures for the mind, . . . with our infinite capacity for buying antiques that are among the chief products of contemporary Oriental art. Some of us have the feeling . . . that our new hosts are sightseeing as well as we; and that they have shown their ancient wisdom, Mahomet-like, by letting the nations of the earth come round to them. Like good marines, it costs them nothing to see the world.

Will:

We landed at the Kowloon docks, and rode to our hotel in rickshas. I was (for a moment) ashamed

to be carried along by these poor coolies, running barefoot over rough macadam and sharp stones. . . . But they themselves feel apparently no humiliation; they compete fiercely for every fare; they are happy to be among the called and chosen. Privately they console themselves with their varied superiority to us, who do not know Chinese. Nature has eased every lot with egotism; there is no worker so lowly, nor any swain so homely, but some delusion of grandeur will come to comfort and sustain him. . . . If we could see ourselves as eternity sees us we should hang ourselves on the nearest tree. A short perspective is the secret of happiness.

After some days' shopping and gazing in Hong Kong we were transported by a special train to Canton, the capital of South China. This was one of the unforgettable sights of our tour. Canton, I reported to my syndicate,

is the Chinese Manhattan; it is as crowded on every street as Broadway is at noon, or the East Side at night. What a litter of humanity, what a riot of 'rickshas, what . . . a sky-full of colored banners waving from the stores, and crying out, so much more gayly than our gigantic electric signs, the hundred thousand items that Canton has to sell! . . .

150

Shall we ever forget that last alley, where we had to . . . trust to our feet on narrow paths bordered by ditches running with liquid and solid filth? Privies are expensive in Canton; the streets will do—and the earth is so grateful for nitrogen! Next to us is a group of coolies carrying, on bamboo poles slung over their shoulders, buckets of human waste. . . . Placidly the procession moves along, the buckets dangling near meat, fish, and vegetables exposed for sale on alley stands. No one is offended; no one but our alien and provincial selves notices; all the rest gossip, laugh, and sing, as if China were the happiest country on earth. How can these people ever be subdued, when they are so satisfied with simplicity, and scorn almost equally the victors and the victims in war?

All in all, I liked the Chinese of 1930. I felt in them a clearness of intelligence and a sturdiness of character formed by at least four thousand years of government, religion, philosophy, literature, and art.

They are as clever in trade as any pious Yankee, and probably far profounder in their understanding of men. They are superstitious, but not priest-ridden; they pay scant attention to the bonzes that tend their temples, and they are so terrestrial and secular that the missionaries call them atheists despite their thousand gods. . . . They are the most conservative of all peoples, and they have made the completest of revolutions.

Peking in those days was desolate, having lost its power and revenues; but Shanghai was thriving with Chinese coolies working for foreign millionaires. We were met at the dock by George Sokolsky, soon to win fame as a columnist in the United States, and by Hu Shih, then professor of philosophy at Kuang Hun University, and later Chinese ambassador to the United States. They took us, at George's expense, to the city's most famous restaurant, which served us a twelve-course dinner composed of various parts of duck, from bill to coo; when I asked for Chinese vegetables the waiter frowned upon me as an unappreciative yokel from barbarous America. On this occasion I had another surprise, for George had invited some singsong girls to entertain us with music; they came, frail, pretty, and babbling; but their charm was diluted by the hot-water bags they wore over their stomachs. I asked Hu Shih to inquire the reason; they answered that they had to dress lightly to please their guests, but they had to wear the bags to keep warm. My imagination was chilled.

We liked Korea, and still more Japan, where we had eight days to study the charm of the women, the subtlety of the men, the disciplined splendor of the scenery, the aesthetic refinement of princes and paupers alike; everyone seemed to love flowers more than food; and a geisha girl in all the flow and color of her raiment was a glory to behold. But at Osaka we could see Japanese industry conquering world markets with assimilative genius and cheap labor; and in the shipyards and docks of Kobe and Yokohama we might have seen the enterprising spread of Japanese commerce over all seas and into every port. We were surprised to find that Tokyo had not only the most inviting bordellos but also eleven universities and colleges. All went well until our friend Dr. Zurawski started out on an evening visit to a "tearoom." Ariel took it for granted that she might accompany him as usual. The doctor explained, as delicately as possible, that tea was but hors-d'oeuvre in an adventure where two women could be worse than one. "I understand, my dear Doctor," said Ariel; "I will stay with the tea while you disappear, and I will await your return." So it befell.

The Pacific lived up to its name on our quiet crossing from Yokohama to Honolulu. Like a hundred million other visitors we were delighted to find that there Jupiter Pluvius and Old King Sol had reached a gentleman's agreement to provide a harmonious mixture of moisture and sunshine, of morning coolness and noon warmth, almost every day in the year. We swam at Waikiki Beach, and sat in awe on the crater edge of the burning volcano Kalauea on the island of Hawaii. On May 11, in mid-Pacific, the *Franconia* dedicated its luncheon as "Birthday Greeting to Mrs Will, and Miss Ethel B., Durant," who had been born on May 10 and 12. On May 13 we had a day to greet our friends in Los Angeles. Then we sailed south and through the Panama Canal and the Spanish Main to Havana. A provocative contrast was forming there between the poverty of the people and the wealth of foreign visitors; we subsiding socialists found ourselves classed among "malefactors of great wealth."

On May 29, after an absence of four and a half months, we docked at New York, sated with sights, glutted with gleanings, and ready to begin writing Volume I of *The Story of Civilization.*

By the time our ship reached New York I had a little book, *The Case for India*, ready for my publishers. Max Schuster and Dick Simon heartily agreed with me that India deserved at least the same home rule that Canada then enjoyed; they rushed the book through the press; soon it was in the stores, and was making some noise. Not all the noise was pleasant; one reviewer suggested that the tenderness of my heart was associated with softness of my head; and another, perhaps justly, warned me that I had no idea of the chaos that would follow a British withdrawal from India. I was consoled by receiving from Rabindranath Tagore a review he had written of the book.

> Will Durant [it said] has taken trouble in this book . . . trouble to know. The miserable conditions of the country he has seen with his own eyes, but, what is rare with most tourists, he has explored the history of our misfortune. Will Durant treated us with the respect due to human beings. . . . I noticed in his book a poignant note of pain at the suffering and indignity of the people who are not his kindred, an indignant desire to be just to the defeated race. . . . I know that the author will have small chance

to reward in popularity from his readers, . . . but he, I am sure, has his noble compensation in upholding the best tradition of the West in its championship of freedom and fair play. I am especially thankful to him for the service he has rendered to the English nation by largely quoting from its own members the condemnation of British policy. . . . I sadly need confirmation of the faith I still wish to maintain in the rare magnanimity of soul of those who are the true representatives of this great race.

Evidently copies of the little book had been smuggled into India; a friend sent me a picture of Mahatma Gandhi reading it; Nehru's sister wrote me that she was taking a copy to her brother Jawaharlal, then in a British jail.

In June, 1930, we began our first summer at Lake Hill in the Catskills. We were happy to have a large house, however quaintly old-fashioned, for we were a large family, including Ethel, Louis, Flora, Mike, often Mary, sometimes Harry, and usually my father and mother, who made themselves loved by everyone. And I had now a full-time secretary, who helped us to coordinate the boxes of notes, pictures, and other material that had been gathered for *The Story of Civilization.*

This was to be something quite different from the weekly articles which I had sent to the Cosmos Syndicate in 1927; those had been hastily written amid a whirlwind of travels, lectures, and family cares; they had been designed for a newspaper audience, and were frankly "popular"; they deserved no great credit for either scholarship or style. I put them away, and made no further use of them. Now I was embarking upon something more pretentious: a five-volume history of civilization from its oldest known forms to our own times. My favorite bookseller, Adolph Kroch of Chicago, tried to dissuade me from the task: only a handful of people, he argued, would buy five volumes on anything; my public was expecting a one-volume history of civilization, in the style and scope of *The Story of Philosophy;* if I would compress the tale he would guarantee the sale of a hundred thousand copies. His suggestion was financially tempting, but it left me cold. I wanted to write something substantial and adequate, readable but scholarly. I could not cover in one volume all those phases of human life—social organization, government, agriculture, industry, commerce, finance, law, religion, morals, manners, science, philosophy, literature, music, and art—which in my view constituted civilization, and would have to be creditably presented in an integral history. So now, with Ariel always helping, and with an intelligent secretary at our side, I set to work.

The work was interrupted on August 13, 1930, by a telegram: "The President and Mrs. Hoover would like to have you spend the week-end with them at their Rapidan camp, leaving here at three o'clock Friday afternoon. Please advise whether you can come. Lawrence Richey, Secretary to the President." I wondered why Ariel had not been included; but she bade me go and enlarge my view of the decision-making process in the United States.

I arrived at the White House a bit ahead of time, but the President did not keep me long waiting. Adolph Ochs, who was making the New York *Times* the world's most complete and trustworthy newspaper, joined us, and the three of us began the three-hour drive to Camp Rapidan, a hundred miles away in the Blue Ridge Mountains of Virginia. Ochs was already seventy-two, and moved with the weight of his years; but in the next two days he thawed, and a week later he ushered me through the sancta of the *Times* editorial rooms; I found there a score of men whose range of information humbled me.

After a day in the camp I reported to Ariel:

August 17, 1930

. . . It's been a thrilling experience to me to talk with the President not for a few minutes, as I had hoped, but for hours. His range of information is by far the widest I've ever met with. He knows more about India than I do (he lived five years in Mysore), more about China, by a hundred times (he lived there for several years), and of course he is a mine of knowledge about Europe. I have heard him talk with members of his cabinet, and with the chairman of one of his expert boards; and it was clear in a minute that he knew more about their own fields than they did. . . .

And Mrs. Hoover is in her own way just as fine. Sixty and beautiful; hair that shines like silver; simple dresses, simple manners, and yet always with a jolly twinkle in her eyes. She makes Queen Marie of Romania look like— but I just recall that I've never seen Marie. When I was playing Lindbergh for the ping pong championship of the camp, and he was ahead four games to two, I heard Mrs. Hoover encouraging me—"I'm betting on you," she said. I braced up and took the set—though God knows what may happen if we play again.

Lindbergh is thinner than I thought; the aviation leaders here call him "Slim". . . . He is even more modest than the papers say; never speaks unless asked to; and in his own line he seems to have the most knowledge and the clearest head of all.

Lovingly, WILL

Obviously I was overwhelmed; I was not accustomed to presidents. I put on whatever charm I had, and luckily found Hoover interested in philosophy. A reporter in the 1932 campaign wrote that Hoover was "as much at home talking philosophy with Will Durant" as in talking economics with businessmen. (I rely on my memory here.) It took me a month to recover perspective and modesty.

CHAPTER XII

Love and Friendship

1931

Ariel:

The first item in Will's diary for 1931 is: "Ethel should ask Pa's blessing."
It was a lovely custom among Catholics for the children to come to the
father every January 1, kneel before him, and, with bowed head, recite
the carefully prepared request *"Mon père, voulez vous me donner votre
bénédiction, s'il vous plâit?*—My father, will you please give me your
blessing?" We coached Ethel carefully in the formula, and after we had
driven out to Arlington, New Jersey, for the regular New Year's Day
reunion of the Durant family (children, sons-in-law, daughters-in-law,
grandchildren, great-grandchildren), and Will had received his blessing,
she knelt, bowed her curls, and began her prepared speech; but, confused by the crowd around us, she forgot the big word *bénédiction.* Pa
Durant, then a benign patriarch of seventy-six, eased the crisis by making the sign of the cross upon Ethel's head and reciting his blessing at
once. To this day Ethel warmly recalls her stumbling, and Pa's sympathetic understanding. We all loved him. None of us can remember him
ever saying an unkind word. No wonder Will ranks him beside Father
Mooney as among the noblest men he has met.

Meanwhile the Great Depression spread. We did not jump from a hotel
window, but our income had a bad fall. Our mortgage investments were
shaky, our royalties were slenderizing, the magazines had lowered their
fees. However, contrary to Will's fears, his lecture engagements continued to be numerous and helpful, and I had to let my guide, philosopher,

and husband go off again, on January 8, for two months of breadwinning. I promised to watch my pennies, my waistline, and my Greenwich Village patronage of needy poets and artists. As usual, Will wrote to me nearly every day, and I can let his letters tell our history during this winter of discontent. He praised my letters, but he did not preserve them, and no one can tell how wrong he was. From Lexington, Kentucky, he wrote,

1-11-31

Write me long letters. You write like a genius. My own letters won't be as long as I would like yours to be, for I'm finding the task of revising *Adventures in Genius* a much more difficult task than I had banked on; there's much nonsense that has to be circumcised. I am buried in the manuscript every day, and drowned in the glare of the footlights every night. . . .

He told me later how much he had enjoyed, on January 12, 1931, the spotless home and wholesome food of President and Mrs. Frank McVey at the University of Kentucky. I presume they have long left this planet, but I wish we could tell them what a warm memory their simple kindliness left with Will, so that the old term "Southern hospitality" took on flesh and blood in his use of it.

His next letter was apparently designed to make me rejoice in my loneliness; it gave, almost hour by hour, his schedule for January 8–16: a daily turmoil of alarm clocks, taxis, porters, trains, hotels, autograph sessions at bookstores, radio talks to drum up an audience, dinners, seventy-five-minute lectures, question periods, enemas, baths.

I bear up . . . by keeping myself in health so far as I can . . . If I can get through two months of this without smashing, I shall just creep up to you as I did after that canoe trip down the Hudson, go to sleep at your feet, and marry you all over again.

Another troubled billet-doux came from Pittsburgh:

1-15-31

. . . I am still only half through preparing the ms. of *Adventures in Genius*, which was due on January 5th. . . . Meanwhile I worry and worry—when shall I at last have all the books read, all the data gathered, all the material classified, for the first volume of *The Story of Civilization?* Every reporter, and every bookstore, asks me about the book, and I give them alluring descriptions of the enterprise, and how the whole Durant family is busy on it, three slaves building their little pyramid; but soon the world will lose faith in me, and classify me . . . as a good salesman but a poor creator. . . .

I'm happy to learn that you are trying to reduce, both of you plump sweethearts. Next to your love, the best reward that could come to me, after this most absurd of all lecture-trips, would be to find you and Ethel physically beautiful again, victors in the great war with appetite. I don't want you to be thin; even as you are I love you; I just want to walk proudly beside you, and have all eyes envying my good fortune. . . . Already I am longing to be back with you, . . . and to hear you both prattling about the house.

A letter from Chicago revealed him still a socialist despite his fees:

1-19-31

Snowing; streets full of city slush, wet, slippery, mucky. Everybody coughing, and leaking at the nose. . . .

In the bleak wet dawn I saw women cleaning the windows of cars in the railroad yards, and thought how fortunate my ladies are that they may sleep in comfy beds and rise always later than the sun. The other day I saw a sight which, as now addicted to Pullmans, I have not seen for years—a coach full of passengers too poor to afford Pullman berths, and riding all night in a coach—slouched, hatless, collarless, shoeless—in their seats, sleeping, . . . with faces swollen. . . . They must wake sore in every muscle, dirty in every pore, with one soapless, towel-less wash-basin for thirty people. How shamelessly lucky we are. . . . At the hotel, yesterday, the maid begged me to let her come in and clean my room so that she might go home at last—4 P.M. Sunday. My heart goes out to all these people, and I almost feel like standing at the gates, Amos-like, and starting a new religion, calling upon our masters to put an end to their greed and their wars, and joining hands to teach birth-control, to replace all menial labor with machinery, and to help, not oppress, the ignorant and the weak. Instead I strictly control all my altruistic impulses, and go forth to make as much money as I can for those dearest to me. So this is the [thin] line between love and selfishness.

Chicago, 1-24-31

. . . Rode all day to Marshalltown, Iowa, arriving at 5:36 P.M. At 6:30 a dinner, with ministers, politicians, schoolmasters, etc.; at eight a lecture. At 9:30 the audience asked questions, and the first was: "Do you believe in personal immortality?" I knew it was a Fundamentalist audience, but I couldn't resist the evil temptation to speak the truth. I said "No," and tried to soothe them by saying how glad I should be to believe with them, and asked them to bear with my unbelief patiently. Whereupon a minister from a suburb called out: "We'll *have* to bear with you; we can't do anything else now." I lost half my temper and told him that if this was to be the spirit of the discussion I could not go on; that I was open to information and reason, but would not tolerate discourtesy of this sort. The audience surprised me by long applause, and said minister rose and apologized.

Marvel to relate, when it was all over an old Irish Catholic priest came up, applauded me for my sincer-r-r-ity, said he had read all three of my books to date, and liked me despite the error of my ways. Then the Congregationalist minister, in whose church I had lectured, came up and gave me his absolution too. It all ended by the old priest taking us off—Protestant, skeptic, and a few others—to his rectory, where, while waiting for my train, we discoursed, as the Scholastics said, *de omnibus rebus, et quibusdam aliis*—"on all things, and a few others." At 11:52 P.M. I climbed up into another sleeper. . . .

157

I arrived here 7:30 this morning. . . . To Kroch's bookstore to examine his books on Japan . . . To the Art Institute; . . . wandered among its Japanese and Chinese collections till my legs broke under me; then retired to the Ryerson Library, where the attendant . . . brought me loads of books and prints of, by, and about Hokusai, Hiroshige, etc. Tomorrow at 10:30 I shall go to Kroch's home and examine his collection of Japanese prints and netsukes (fobs). . . . At 1 P.M. I eat with Dr. Zurawski; at 3, if we can get in, we shall go and hear Yehudi Menuhin. . . . Meanwhile the stenographer downstairs is working away copying extracts for me. . . .

Wayne, Neb., 1-28-31

BELOVED DAUGHTER,—

I wish you and mother could be with me here on this sunny day. Below my open window move the cheery workingmen of the Middle West— husky, jolly, kindly fellows, not itching for gold, not rushing feverishly from place to place, but doing with bluff comradeship the simple work of the day. The farther inland I go from the big cities, the healthier, handsomer, kinder, and happier the people seem to be. Our cities are tumors on the face of the globe, sucking all the blood of the country to them, and then poisoning that blood with bad air and shut-in work. Happy girl, to be preserved from the noise and filth and rush and subways of New York— and yet close enough to it to enjoy all that it has to give you in music, drama, sights, and friends.

This was the most arduous, though the most remunerative, of Will's lecture tours. Typical were the one-night stands between February 4 at Butte and February 14 at Cedar City, Utah. A letter from Pullman, Washington, helped me to bear my uneventful days at Great Neck.

2-7-31

This has been the toughest day of all . . . After a two-hour lecture on India last night at Tacoma, I had to sit in a lonely station till 11:40 P.M., take a . . . train to Auburn, change there at 12:40 A.M. to another train, with a sleeper; at 6:35 A.M. I had to change to a coach and ride from 7 A.M. to 10, breakfastless. At Pasco I changed to an automobile, which drove me 49 miles in 67 minutes thru mountains and valleys . . . to Walla Walla, where I transferred to another Pullmanless train, and rode from 11:25 A.M. to 3:55 P.M.; then I had to carry my heavy grip . . . to another train half a block away; rode on that till 5:05 P.M., shaved, dressed, and gave my Progress reel to the college boys here. I am tired and headachy, but I expect to be all right in the morning.

I tried to make the weary trip unconscious by sorting my Japan slips. This is my fifth day given to that job; will finish it tomorrow, en route to Seattle. The conductor on one of the trains was curious to know what all my slips meant, and, observing one section on Japanese philosophy, asked had I read Durant's *Story of Philosophy.* I said, "No, but I wrote it." It took him five minutes to believe it, I looked so harmless; then he went all over the car telling everybody, in whispers, what a monster of learning was among them. . . .

I pass over some minor letters, and come to a very stirring message received by Will in Los Angeles February 17, 1931:

DEAR SIR:

Are you aware that the world is soon to go thru one of the darkest periods it has ever known. Are you aware that that terrible day of indignation is being brought upon the people because of its leaders. Are you aware it is such ignorant harlots as yourself that is causing the people to err. A whore in Gods eyes is them who sell a lie for gain. You in Gods eyes are just as low as the lowest of whores. . . . At the present time you are exalted and magnified in your own heart, but in a score of years Will C. Durant the anti-Christ, foolish, ignorant, philosopher, . . . will be known as a foolish harlot who sold lies for bread and glory.

Will solaced himself with sunshine and Einstein.

2-17-31

[Rabbi Herman] Lissauer was waiting for me at Los Angeles, and gave me a warm greeting. . . . I spoke twice in the same Ebell Theater yesterday where you were greeted as Ariel in January 1928 . . . As my reward Lissauer took me to the Ambassador Hotel, . . . and, hiding in a little room we found Herr Doktor Einstein. . . . One of the finest faces I've seen— utterly guileless, and almost free of egotism. A crowd gathered round him, each pushing himself forward. I thought it a little silly, and left.

From Tucson Will pictured for me a sunrise in Arizona. I suspect he had not forgotten that marvelous passage in *Salammbô* where Flaubert traced the transit of the rising sun over the roofs of Carthage.

2-21-31

I went to bed early last night, and waking before dawn, saw the sun make the rim of the barren hills turn first pale orange, then blue and green and gold, then peering over the ridge and scattering handfuls of light with shining fingers everywhere. These sandy deserts and mountain ranges are beautiful only in the kaleidoscope of the sun, which plays études and nocturnes of shadows upon them at twilight and dawn; at noon they reveal their sterile nakedness, and you almost pray for rain. . . .

All of us, including our vegetarian dog Wolf, gave him hugs and kisses when, on March 10, after the longest of our separations, he reached home. On March 16 he was off again for lectures in South Bend, Indiana, and Lorain, Ohio, and a debate in Cleveland with Randolph Churchill on "Should India Be Freed from British Rule?" I have a lovely picture from the Cleveland *Plain Dealer* (?) of March 20, showing Will, Randolph, and his mother, Mrs. Winston Churchill. Randolph was then only twenty years old, but his good looks, his charming manners, and his aura of ancestry were obstacles that Will must have found hard to overcome.

This encounter came amid our final preparations for the publication of *Adventures in Genius*. On April 4 we sailed with Ethel, Drs. Abraham and

Hannah Stone, and their daughter Gloria, to spend a few days in Bermuda. On May 28, 1931, *Adventures* was born, and a letter reached us from John Haynes Holmes:

> I rejoice to report that I am reviewing the book for the *Herald-Tribune* literary supplement, and I am going to be able, with a good conscience, to give it an enthusiastic endorsement. I am telling every reader of "The Story of Philosophy" to get this book and renew the great experience of a few years ago. May I say on my own account that I think your two essays on Spengler and Keyserling are among the greatest things you ever did.

Adventures in Genius, except for the essays on Flaubert and Anatole France, was a gathering of magazine articles, but some of them, like the fifty-four pages on Spengler and the eighty-three on Keyserling, were honest and substantial essays. They had been written for a new magazine, *The Thinker;* either Will's mammoth contributions or the magazine's name scared readers away, and *The Thinker* soon collapsed. The review of Bertrand Russell's *Marriage and Morals* had been hastily composed for *The Dial.* It contained a shameful error in the first paragraph, which spoke of Shelley's first wife as having drowned herself in the Thames; of course Harriet Westbrook had chosen as her grave the Serpentine in Hyde Park; and thirty-six years later we tried to atone by making a pilgrimage to that tragic spot.

Now that our beloved John Powys has been freed from his pains I can say, without hurting him, that I found Will's essay on him, in *Adventures in Genius,* excessively worshipful. However, I, who had discovered Powys, and had led Will to him, thrilled to the description of our friend as he strode the public platform:

> . . . tall, thin, ungainly, angular; . . . long arachnid legs, long simian arms, long, restless, pseudopodian fingers, the Word made not flesh but bone and naked nerves; the stooping carriage of a solicitous giant. . . . the trembling mouth of the poet, . . . the eyes startled and piercing, hunted and hunting, tossed and pulled about with things vividly seen, haunted with mystery and frightened with understanding. . . .
>
> And what speech! . . . At first hearing a medley of amazing phrases and epithets, meaning nothing to the dull; then an unfurled cloth of gold, sparkling and shimmering with beauty, and blinding the mind to the body of meaning whose gorgeous raiment it is, . . . the Oriental mosaic and music of a philosophy as profound as Spinoza's and as kindly as Christ's.

Well, well, my lover, can all this be true? I begin to suspect that there has always been a twitch of the homosexual in you. Was there ever such a love of one writer and speaker for another? There's not a jealous molecule in Will's constitution, except for some momentary worries about my Greenwich Village nights. I've never heard him utter a derogatory word about any of his rivals; I've never seen him relish a hostile review of a rival's book. With Powys he skirted idolatry, and often I led or followed him. I too fell for that magnificent curly head, those darting, searching eyes that seemed to be looking for Plato's heaven of ideas, or trying to catch Shelley's west wind.

May I abuse chronology and bring together the disjointed story of our relations with John Powys from the time in 1921 when we went to visit him and his bride, Phyllis Playter, at 4 Patchin Place in New York to the year 1934, when they left America for England? I have before me a dozen incomparable letters from John to us, but as they bear no date but the day of the week, I can't vouch for their chronological order.

Sometime in 1928 John finished his novel *Wolf Solent*. Will read its fifteen hundred typed pages, and sent them to Simon and Schuster with an assurance that this was a work worthy of Thomas Hardy, written in prose worthy of Walter Pater. Max shuddered a bit at the length of the story, and feared that the leisurely, meandering style would cut the sale. Will promised to write a "rave review" for the *Times* or the *Herald-Tribune;* Max said let the book be printed—gave it, literally, his imprimatur.

When publication neared we planned to celebrate with a modest dinner at the Gypsy Tavern. There some twenty of John's admirers came together on May 18, 1929. Theodore Dreiser, Hendrik van Loon, Dr. Abraham Stone, and Will made informal speeches, John responded with charming confusion, and Beethoven contributed two sonatas for violin and piano, played by our old Brooklyn friends Maximilian Rose and David Schapiro. Powys sent us a grateful word on

May 19, 1929

Dear William

I was too bewildered and excited last night to be able to convey to you a tithe of what I felt . . . about all you said in that curiously felicitous speech. I shall never forget that aphorism of yours [after remarking on the rosary hanging on John's wall] "To believe in nothing and worship everything." That was really an aphorism worthy of Kwang [Chuang-tzu] himself and it sank into my mind and doubtless will suddenly leak out like a fish when I'm lecturing somewhere. Aye! but it was an evening. Never to my dying day shall I forget it, and all due to the care and tact of that dear little lady of yours. . . . It was sweet of her to take so much trouble.

With love from us both to both of you,

John

Will's enthusiastic review of *Wolf Solent* hailed it as a unique contribution to English literature. The book was a complete success with the critics, and a reasonable success with the public; John could now eat without counting pennies. We wondered why he should continue to incarcerate himself and Phyllis in one room in a noisy quarter of Manhattan. Will proposed that he should visit us in Great Neck, spend some days with us, and look around for some picturesque cottage where he could invite his soul in clear air among flowers and trees, where the night would fall without hurt and the day would break without noise. John opened his heart in a letter characteristically running from southwest to northeast, with marginal addenda from pole to pole.

> *4 Patchin Pl*
> *New York,*
> *Sept. 6 (1929)*

DEAR DURANT

It's hard to tell you how touched I am by this incredibly generous and kind letter of yours. . . . This noble invitation of yours demands, as the least return I can make, the frankest statement of why it is impossible for me to accept it.

The truth of the matter is I've been living now with a lady friend Phyllis Playter, whose parents [the Franklin Playters of Galena, Kansas] are old friends of mine, for the last five or six years,* and we've got a room in this alley to which we've become very attached. We do both of us often pine for the country, but our situation as Mr. and Miss has always made it difficult to risk a country cottage even if I could afford such a thing. . . . Neither Miss Playter nor myself want to cause any shock to my priest-son or his mother in England; and as long as we remain in this country no such shock is necessary. But we have to pay the price of this dislike of agitation and of upsetting things, by having to live in extreme retirement! We hope all the same that some day we may find some little place in the country where we should be allowed to live unmolested by startled neighbors; but hitherto we haven't had the funds or the spirit for so daring a move. . . .

Listen now! Won't you and your wife (and Ethel too, perhaps) fix a day soon when you can come to tea with us here. I've long wished Miss Playter to meet you. With best salutations to you all,

> Affectionately,
> J.C.P.

He compromised by accepting our invitation to come and spend a few days with us in Great Neck. He brought Phyllis with him, and it was almost as inspiring to us to watch her modesty and solicitude as to keep pace breathlessly with the brilliance and hesitating depth of John's conversation. Like John Dewey he stopped now and then amidsentence for *le mot juste* to come to him out of his heritage (Cowper was one of his forebears), and usually it came, bringing light. He enjoyed our vegetarian menus. He fell in love with Ethel, and agreed that our wills should name him (with Dr. Stone) as one of her guardians; henceforth he referred to her as "my ward." He and Will took rambles in the less traveled lanes of that once quiet town, and no weather stayed them. Indeed John, as an Englishman, especially enjoyed walking in, or just after, rain; he

---

* Powys had long been separated from his wife, but she refused to give him a divorce.

sniffed with delight the moisture of the air, and carefully, with his cane or fingers, moved the drenched earthworms from the pavement (where other feet might crush them) to the safety of the grass. He might have been a Buddhist mystic, feeling no gap between himself and any form of life. I have met many ardent spirits who in their youth practiced this "reverence of life" before Schweitzer named it; nearly all of them soon left that religion behind them as the world molded them in its eat-or-be-eaten image; John and Will are exceptions, who, through all their years as known to me, never hurt any sensitive thing.

I believe it was in 1930 that John and Phyllis took a cottage at what he called Phudd Bottom in a farming community in Hillsdale, New York. On August 28 he sent us a troubled letter telling us how they were playing host to his brother Llewelyn—whom he called Lulu—and wife, Alyse Gregory.

> It is a bit of a crowd for this tiny place, but we are an affectionate *à quatre,* and are happy as far as we can be under rather agitating circumstances, for Lulu's lungs are shaky, he's got a temperature, dreads of course a hemorrhage, and is at the moment very worried over his affairs.* . . .
>
> Well, good luck, old friend, and our united loves to your wife, and your little daughter—my dear ward in God—and to your next book [*The Case for India*] even if it upset the Empire!
>
> Yours as ever,
JOHN

Will dropped in upon Powys' retreat en route from Lake Hill to New York with Drs. Abraham and Hannah Stone. An undated letter contained an irresistible invitation:

> DEAR WILL:
>
> We did enjoy seeing you, but . . . aye: 'twas so tantalizing, so short, and we did miss having Ariel. . . . Listen! Couldn't Michael and that new car bring you and Ariel and Ethel over here before you go back to your [Long] Island home? If you could get here by one o'clock we would take you all to a mid-day dinner at a neighboring farm house where the widow-mother of the young boy-farmer has become a passionate admirer of yours (as we have lent her *The Story of Philosophy* and also *Transition*). It would be a Day of Days to this pastoral family.

We went, taking Max Schuster with us, and I have treasured a photograph that Phyllis took of four of us lolling on the lawn.

When *Adventures in Genius* appeared, reprinting Will's tribute to Powys, John returned the flattery with compound interest:

> *June 5th, 1931*
>
> I must thank you, my friend for the most generous essay on me in your book. God! you beat me, Master, here at my own game, with "Welsh"

* Llewelyn died of tuberculosis in 1939 at the age of fifty-five.

imagination, or Gallic and magical adjectives and serpentine interpretations! I am as proud as Punch to be the subject of such writing, and to find myself in such company. . . .

No, but seriously, William, your pattern of magnanimity—I'll never catch you up there; for those Jesuits, or their God, squeezed a drop of the real saint into you, for all your rogueries. I do feel grateful to all you've done for me in enabling me to live like this in peace and quiet by my pen and avoid going on the Road. You were the "fons et origo" of my initial escape from the Tread Mill—and I tell you I don't forget it! . . .

You've got some fine things, my friend, in this green book—aye! but you have a real Voltairian-Fontenelle touch now and again—very subtle, light, and deft.

Will:

So much for this friendship, which ran like a song through the middle third of our lives. A still older friendship fared badly in 1931. Alden Freeman, Maecenas of my youth, was ruined in the stock market collapse of those years, chiefly through the carelessness of those who had managed his investments; and now, from Santa Barbara, where he had built a bizarre mansion that no one cared to buy, came an appeal for five hundred dollars. We sent it at once, and received a strange telegram in reply, July 18, 1931:

> You have saved my life and restored my faith in human nature. . . . I shall have a grand comeback through my architecture landscaping and the Charles Bolton chain of hotels [which Alden had proposed to finance]. Mother Church has been very gentle and kind to my misfortunes. Through my dear mother I was convent bred, and Father Augustine led me by the hand in my illness. The new rector [of the Franciscan mission] is giving me instructions, and on St. Francis' day, August 2nd, I am to be received into the fold as Francis Alden Alexander, and later taken into the third order of St. Francis. I have traveled a long weary road, and found a haven and heaven at last. I hope you received my letter about how to stop bootlegging with the aid of my telescope, and restore light wines and beer. . . . Heartfelt gratitude and love to all.

Alden, in a condition of harmless feeblemindedness, was taken to Florida, where we shall find him in his later years.

Ariel:

That summer, at Lake Hill, Will joined me in a shameful extravagance. One intoxicatingly beautiful day Alex Ferguson, car salesman from Kingston, drove into our driveway in a tremendous twelve-cylinder Cadillac. He showed us the immaculate motor and explained its miraculous operations; we pretended to understand, while we marveled at the splendor of the design and the elegance of the interior. Alex to Will: "Don't you want to buy this for your lady?" Will to me: "Would you like to have it?" I can't recall my answer, but I'm sure I smiled. Will lost his mind. "It's yours," he said. We surrendered our old car. A few days later we drove down to Woodstock to shop. A young radical scowled at us. "Spinoza in a Cadillac twelve," he snorted. Will felt the sting; I wilted; we hurried home.

In a mad effort to recoup the losses we had incurred in the stock market collapse, Will set forth again, in mid-October, 1931, on an arduous tour, at fees considerably reduced from pre-crash seasons. "Good news is bad news," he wrote from Cleveland: "sixteen lectures in fifteen days, October 18th to November 2nd. . . . I'd better make hay while this October sun shines, and be grateful that I have, temporarily, a crowded schedule."

Chicago, 10-23-31

Here I am again, like a *déjà vu*, back in my old room no. 516 at the Auditorium Hotel. . . .

From Fort Wayne . . . I took [a train] to Chicago at 4:18 P.M., and walked right into Clarence Darrow. He was coming off the car as I was trying to get in. He had been killing God in Harrisburg, and was now looking for a minute's walk on the platform. I invited him to have dinner with me on the train at six; he agreed, and then I went to my seat hoping to get in a little work, but Clarence soon ambled and shambled along and asked me to come to his seat and "chew the rag."

He is a figure out of primitive American legend—ungainly, disheveled, and unpressed. His hair, scattered in stray locks over his ears, sticks out in tufts—gray turning to white. He is weak, but still loves an audience. His little eyes are afire with irony and kindliness and bitterness. He called Hoover every hard name he could think of. He expects a Democratic landslide in 1932, and believes that Newton Baker will be the next president. That would suit me, . . . if I can't get Darrow himself as president; but I suspect that Franklin Roosevelt will walk away with the Democratic nomination.

Will reached New York on November 4, and at the Gypsy Tavern we celebrated his forty-sixth birthday. After a night in Great Neck with the children, we drove to Stamford for a lecture there, and on November 6 to New Haven for a lecture at two-thirty, and then to Bridgeport for another in the evening. On the seventh I helped to get him home. I was surprised that he was not a physical or mental wreck. On November 8 he was at work on *Our Oriental Heritage.*

CHAPTER XIII

To Russia

1932

Will:

I suspect that the excitement of facing an audience, and the enjoyment of applause for even a mediocre discourse, had something to do with my accepting so many lecture engagements. Doubtless I was moved also by the desire to add to the family hoard; and there must have been in me a bit of the money lust that agitates, in America, all but a few hereditarily rich and a few comfortably poor. I was seventy-two years old before I had the spirit to swear off making money, and even then my virtue was prompted by a hypertension spell.

I ended my oratorical fast on January 3 by addressing Stephen Wise's Reformed Jewish congregation in Carnegie Hall. The rabbi and I had long been friends; he had often helped me to raise funds for Labor Temple School; and I had looked up to him as not only the most eloquent speaker in America but a man of massive energy and daily devotion. Ariel and I felt honored to join him and his dedicated wife at their table that Sunday noon. We had a precious common friend in Louis Sturz, who was among the rabbi's most selfless supporters in the work of the American Jewish Congress.

On February 9 we heard Winston Churchill speak in Carnegie Hall. I must be a poor judge of men, for I remember that I was only moderately impressed by the future hero, who was then fifty-eight years old; I was not well acquainted with his early record as statesman and author; perhaps I compared his careful and leisurely speech with my impetuous and world-shaking oratory, and found him wanting. Not till "blood, sweat, and tears" rang across the seas did I realize that I had listened to one of the enduring figures in British history.

Early in February, 1932, because the owner had decided to occupy his property, we moved from 44 North Drive to a simpler residence at 2 Henry Street, Great Neck. The rent there was only half of what we had been paying, and the house was within a few blocks of the high school where both Ethel and Louis were to be enrolled.

Our amiable bitch Wolf soon won us fame in our new neighborhood by falling in heat so powerfully that all the male dogs in the vicinity gathered around our house to serenade her with desire. Yielding to the puritan ethic that surrounded us, we guarded Wolf's virginity, but she escaped our vigilance, and was soon engaged in an ancient fertility rite— right on our lawn. I ran to her rescue, and to her wonder, by emptying a pail of cold water upon her suitor, who looked at me with the pitiful eyes of a lover caught in the clutches of love. In any case I had come too late, for some weeks later Wolf could hardly walk.

When her time came she chose for her lying-in a wind-protected nook under the porch of our new home. One day I found her laboring there, with one puppy already born. I took it up and carried it into the house and down to the cellar, while Wolf followed me, growling. I made a bed of old clothing near the warm oil burner, settled the mother in comfort, and watched while, at intervals, she propelled one pup after another into the world. I was fascinated as I saw how zealously she licked the head of each as it emerged; how she consumed the placenta; how she cut the umbilical cord with her teeth, ate it to the pup's belly, and licked the navel feverishly. Eleven pups came, and all received the antisepsis of her tongue, especially at those points—eyes, mouth, navel, and genitals— which were most open to infection; I was amazed to see how much medical science had been hidden in my bitch's genes. I helped some of her babies to find her teats; others, though still blind, reached the founts without my help; soon six or eight mouths were feeding at one time, while the mother lay exhausted but content as her milk was drained. I steeled myself to drowning three of the pups lest all of them be half fed. I was astonished to see with what silent wisdom Wolf had played her part in the chain of life. I was happy that she had let me handle her offspring, though she growled when other people came near. I felt like some genie who had assisted at the Creation.

In this state of exaltation I sallied forth to peddle philosophy at one-night stands in Florida and points west. Ariel has mercilessly preserved the letters I sent her on this trip. I find nothing immortal in them, but here and there some items may fill in the picture of a modern Sophist, or the record of an evolving soul.

A Dual Autobiography

I have just come back, all sweating, from a six-mile walk. . . . I started off half dead, with bent and aching back from eight hours poring over slips; but the last hour of sunshine restored me, and after the first mile I was enjoying it. . . . I trudged for three miles, . . . and found myself face to face with our old [Great Neck] neighbor, Eddie Cantor—on a billboard in front of a little local theater. . . .

Walking back in the early evening, I could see many families taking their ease on their porches. I felt very lonely then—no home to go to but only a hotel. I perceive that with all its irritations and conflicts, all its hot collisions of stars, a home is still the last refuge of the soul; that a man wants above all not sex, not even food, but a woman and some children to greet him on his return from work, to put up with him, pamper him, tuck him in, and give him that affection which he never quite deserves. . . .

Give my totally abandoned love to Ethel and Louis and you, and trust me to be always faithful to you in every way, more and more.

Emporia, Kan., 3-8-32

. . . Next morning I set sail for Emporia in 3 degrees above zero, and found William Allen White, most famous editor in America, waiting on the platform for me, his coattails flying in the wind. He whisked me off to his home, and in the evening gave a great dinner with half the brains of Kansas [at his table]. . . . A fine old fellow, full of vivid reminiscences of everybody in public life in the last 20 years. More of him and his fine wife when I see you . . . on the 13th.

Soon after my return home I had to prepare for publication (in September, 1932) a little book *On the Meaning of Life*. Ever since my loss of religious faith I had brooded over this problem, and at times (as described in the "Nadir" chapter of *Transition*) I had sunk into a mood of despondency akin to the *angst* or *angoisse* contemporaneously expressed by German and French existentialists. The problem was forced upon me when, as I was raking leaves at Lake Hill in 1930, a decently dressed stranger walked up to me, said quietly that he was thinking of killing himself, and challenged me to give one good reason why he shouldn't. I bade him get a job—but he had one; to eat a good meal—but he was not hungry; he left visibly unmoved by my arguments. I do not know what happened to him. In that same year I received several letters announcing suicide; I put them aside as probably disguised appeals for money. I learned later that there had been 284,142 suicides in the United States between 1905 and 1930.

In 1931 Ray Long, the genial, enterprising, skeptical editor of *Cosmopolitan* magazine (who killed himself in 1935), asked me for an article. I proposed to sound out various notables on the meaning of life, to print their answers, and to add my own. He agreed, and I sent out on June 8, 1931, a letter which may have worried Ray Long a bit if he ever read it:

To Russia

Dear ——

Will you interrupt your busy life for a moment, and play the game of philosophy with me?

I am attempting to face, in my next book, a question that our generation, perhaps more than most, seems always ready to ask, and never able to answer—What is the meaning or worth of human life? Heretofore this question has been dealt with chiefly by theorists, from Ikhnaton and Lao-tse to Bergson and Spengler. The result has been a species of intellectual suicide: thought, by its very development, seems to have destroyed the value and significance of life. The growth and spread of knowledge, for which so many reformers and idealists prayed, appears to bring to its devotees—and, by contagion, to many others—a disillusionment which has almost broken the spirit of our race.

Astronomers have told us that human affairs constitute but a moment in the trajectory of a star; geologists have told us that civilization is a precarious interlude between ice ages; biologists have told us that all life is war, a struggle for existence among individuals, groups, nations, alliances, and species; historians have told us that "progress" is a delusion, whose glory ends in inevitable decay; psychologists have told us that the will and the self are the helpless instruments of heredity and environment, and that the once incorruptible soul is only a transient incandescence of the brain. The Industrial Revolution has destroyed the home, and the discovery of contraceptives is destroying the family, the old morality, and perhaps (through the sterility of the intelligent) the race. Love is analyzed into a physical congestion, and marriage becomes a temporary physiological convenience slightly superior to promiscuity. Democracy has degenerated into such corruption as only Milo's Rome knew; and our youthful dreams of a socialist utopia disappear as we see, day after day, the inexhaustible acquisitiveness of men. Every invention strengthens the strong and weakens the weak; every new mechanism displaces men, and multiplies the horrors of war. God, who was once the consolation of our brief life, and our refuge in bereavement and suffering, has apparently vanished from the scene; no telescope, no microscope, discovers him. Life has become, in that perspective which is philosophy, a fitful pullulation of human insects on the earth, a planetary eczema that may soon be cured; nothing is certain in it except defeat and death—a sleep from which, it seems, there is no awakening.

We are driven to conclude that the greatest mistake in human history was the discovery of "truth." It has not made us free, except from delusions that comforted us, and restraints that preserved us; it has not made us happy, for truth is not beautiful, and did not deserve to be so passionately chased. As we look upon it now we wonder why we hurried so to find it. For it appears to have taken from us every reason for existing, except for the moment's pleasure and tomorrow's trivial hope.

This is the pass to which science and philosophy have brought us. I, who have loved philosophy for many years, turn from it now back to life itself, and ask you, as one who has lived as well as thought, to help me understand. Perhaps the verdict of those who have lived is different from that of those who have merely thought. Spare me a moment to tell me what meaning life has for you, what help—if any—religion gives you, what keeps you going, what are the sources of your inspiration and your energy, what is the goal or motive force of your toil; where you find your consolations and your happiness, where in the last resort your treasure lies. Write briefly if you must; write at leisure if you possibly can; for every word from you will be precious to me.

Sincerely,
WILL DURANT

P.S. The purpose in view is purely philosophical. I trust, however, that there will be no objection to my quoting from the replies in my forthcoming book.

There may have been many absurdities in that letter, but the absurdity of the postscript was beyond doubt and beyond belief. I was so ignorant of human nature as to think that statesmen would be willing to bare their thoughts on life and death, or that authors would be willing to formulate their philosophy to swell a rival's royalties. Naturally some of the notables made no reply; others answered briefly and vaguely. George Bernard Shaw found a postcard sufficient to expound his views on the meaning of life: "How the devil do I know? Has the question itself any meaning?" Bertrand Russell excused himself lazily:

20th June, 1931

DEAR MR. DURANT,

I am sorry to say that at the moment I am so busy as to be convinced that life has no meaning whatever, and that being so, I do not see how I can answer your questions intelligently.

I do not see that we can judge what would be the result of the discovery of truth, since none has hitherto been discovered.

Yours sincerely,
BERTRAND RUSSELL

But, O lordly shade! that was a poor way to dismiss a fellow Sophist who had so often met you in friendly debate; and if life has no meaning, why be so busy?—and how could you be so sure that no truth has hitherto been discovered unless you already possessed some truth to serve as standard and test? Count Keyserling, who never doubted that he had the truth, was more bluntly honest: "It is absolutely impossible to answer such questions as you ask, in any seriousness in the frame of a letter. Besides, when stating my ideas, I prefer using my own setting to providing material for the book of another author." More mannerly than these inheritors of grace was our own dour O'Neill:

Thank you for the copy of the letter. Frankly, I have nothing to contribute that would be worth your while. I feel I have found no answer to your questions of the slightest importance to anyone but me personally—except those which are expressed or implied in my work. So I'm afraid you must pass me up.

I hope the trilogy [*Mourning Becomes Electra*] will interest you. It answers most of your questions to its author.

Sincerely,
EUGENE O'NEILL

Nicest of the refusals was from Senator Borah:

6-23-31

MY DEAR MR. DURANT:

I am in receipt of your recent letter, which I have read with mingled feelings of indignation and appreciation.

In your letter you say: "I take it for granted that my name will be unfamiliar to you."

Mr. Durant, I think I have read everything you have ever written. I doubt if anyone has read what you have written with more pleasure. Now, to have you say that your name is unfamiliar! But I have always understood that modesty is characteristic of great authors.

I am deeply interested in your letter. I do not know that I can be of service to you, possibly I may. I shall be happy to think the matter over, and, if I feel an "inspiration," I will certainly give you the benefit of it.

At any rate I shall certainly read your book when it is out.

Very sincerely,
WM. E. BORAH

Substantial replies came from Theodore Dreiser, H. L. Mencken, Sinclair Lewis, John Erskine, Charles Beard, John Cowper Powys, Edwin Arlington Robinson, André Maurois, Will Rogers, Dr. Charles Mayo, Ossip Gabrilówitsch, Vilhjalmur Stefansson, Havelock Ellis, Carl Laemmle, Ernest M. Hopkins (president of Dartmouth College), Adolph Ochs, Jawaharlal Nehru, Mohandas Gandhi, John Haynes Holmes, Ernest Dimnet, Gina Lombrosa, and tennis champion Helen Wills Moody. Looking over those replies today across nearly forty years, I like best those of Beard, Powys, and Maurois. The most touching letter came from Convict 79206, serving a life sentence in Sing Sing prison.

When it came my turn to face up to my questions I could only say that life's meaning is that it is the theater and instrument of development, the possibility of growth and fulfillment, individual and communal. "The secret of significance and content is to have a task which consumes all one's energies, lifts the individual out of himself, and makes human life a little richer than before."

As for myself, . . . the meaning of life lies perhaps too narrowly in my family and my work; I wish I could boast of consecration to a larger cause. The sources of my energy are egotism and a selfish altruism—the greed for applause, and a mad devotion to those dependent upon me. . . .

Where, in the last resort, does my treasure lie?—In . . . Nature herself.

And, in a last frail lure to the pessimist who contemplated suicide:

> Come and spend an hour with me, and I will show you a path through the woods which will better dissuade you . . . than all the arguments of my books. Come and tell me what a childish optimist I am; lay about you freely, and damn this middling world as you will; I shall agree with everything but your conclusion. Then we shall eat the bread of peace together, and let the prattle of the children restore our youth.

It was a bit superficial, and the little book was justly condemned to drop silently into an ocean of ink. I do not believe that it reduced the rate of suicide in America.

Still strong in hope, Ariel and I set out, in July, 1932, to see what the Russian Revolution had done for Russia or mankind. We were not quite deserting Ethel, who was now a blushing thirteen; she was to spend the summer at a girls' camp near Ausable Forks, New York. Our two houses were left with brother Michael and sister Flora, with instructions and funds for giving my parents a long vacation at Lake Hill.

We were well disposed toward the Russian experiment; in those years of the Great Depression millions of Americans felt that capitalism was facing collapse, and that it might be saved by an infusion of socialism— governmental control of the economy, and mitigation of poverty; this was very nearly what Franklin Roosevelt would attempt a few months later. However, resolved to get an objective view, we planned to avoid Russian guides as far as possible, and arranged to enter European Russia unobtrusively from its Siberian rear. I studied Russian desperately, and mastered some forty words before we reached Harbin. Hoping to reduce our travel difficulties, we bought in New York, from Intourist, the official Soviet agency, all our railroad tickets for the trip.

We left New York on July 3, spent July 4 in Chicago with Dr. Zurawski and Lorrian Cook—a loyal and accomplished friend from my Chautauqua days of 1917. That night we boarded the Burlington Railroad's *Empire Builder* for the three-day ride to Seattle. Anatole France might have had such a train in mind when, in *Penguin Isle,* he satirized our American transcontinental expresses; it had a dining car, a lounge car, a barbershop and shower bath for men, a beauty parlor and shower bath for women, a soda fountain, a radio, a sun room, and a valet.

On July 9 we sailed from Seattle on the S.S. *Cleveland* for the long voyage across the North Pacific. We reached Yokohama July 22, Kobe July 23; then by train to Shimonoseki; by overnight boat to Fusan; thence by rail two days and nights through Korea and Manchuria to Harbin. From Kobe to Harbin we were under the Japanese government; at every stop we had to show our passports to suspicious Japanese officials, who resented America's refusal to recognize the Japanese conquest of Manchuria. We almost forgave their hostility when the courteous attendants bathed our sweating faces with hot towels. We liked the Koreans, who, under their basket hats, patiently and competently tramped the rice paddies or tilled the fields. We found Harbin dominated by "White Russians" still faithful to the czars, and as prosperous as ever; they had "cornered" the fur trade in Manchuria. Some of them gave us little parcels of food to eke out the meals on the Russian trains, and wondered what insane ignorance was leading us through the cold chaos of Siberia to the enthusiastic chaos of Moscow.

From Harbin we rode on the Chinese Eastern Railway twenty-one hours through Manchuria to the Russian border at Manchuli. There, trying to board the Trans-Siberian Express, we met our first impasse: the "commandant," or head conductor, refused to honor the tickets we had bought from Intourist for fare and *wagon-lit* to Moscow. We were faced with the ukase that we must buy new tickets at the Manchuli station, and would have to pay for them in rubles. Scared by repeated warnings against buying or selling rubles at any but the official rate, we had bought our rubles at two for a dollar; now we found that their purchasing power was two cents. An English-speaking Russian officer came to our rescue by persuading the commandant to accept our tickets. After the usual delays the train began its serpentine crawl across Siberia.

Nearly all the other compartments in our *wagon-lit* were occupied by officers of the Russian Army or government, or by Chinese emissaries to Russia. We made friends of them by joining in singing "The International"—the hymn of the world revolution. At each stop we were appalled by the poverty of the people who had come to the station to sell articles of food or clothing to the passengers; we presumed that their destitution was a result of the climate or the civil war of 1918–21, and that it would soon be remedied by a humanitarian state. At Krasnoyarsk, in midsummer—July 30—we shivered with cold in our berths.

Three days out from Manchuli we took advantage of our stopover tickets, and alighted at Omsk, resolved to sample, unguided, the life of a Siberian city. I did not recall that Omsk had been the headquarters of Kolchak's White Army in his attempt to overthrow the Soviets, and that it had in consequence borne the brunt of the civil war; unconsciously I judged what I saw by comparing it with the America of 1932 (sad as that was) instead of with the Siberia of the czars. So Ariel and I were shocked, on entering the station, by the ragged dress and frightened faces of a hundred men, women, and children who covered every bit of seat or floor. We were told that they were waiting—some had waited for days—to get a train out of Omsk, clinging to the hope that elsewhere there would be more food or better shelter. Later we found that nearly every railway depot in Russia was crowded, day after day, with homeless, desperate people like these.

173

We fought our way through the melee to seek a cab; we located one, but the driver made plain, with his fingers, that he would charge us 120 rubles to take us to the Metropole Hotel. In terms of what our rubles had cost us this meant sixty dollars (in dollars of 1970, $180). Nevertheless we climbed into the open carriage and proceeded on mutual faith. At the hotel we learned that an almost bare room would cost us thirty-six rubles per day. We asked for a restaurant; we were told that a nearby café would serve us a filling dinner for ten rubles each. We calculated that at this rate we would soon be bankrupt. We were rescued by Joseph Popick, a member of the secret police; he unrolled a wad of rubles, paid our driver and the landlady, and sent out for food. We offered him American money; he refused it, and explained that he knew where rubles were printed.

That evening we walked through mud and puddles to visit a scholar whose address had been given us in New York. With doors locked behind us he told us that as a Jew and a liberal (not a Communist) he and his like lived in hardship and fear. The next day I boarded a bus to the station, and presented to the stationmaster the sleeping-car tickets Intourist had sold us for passage from Omsk to Moscow on the train due Friday. He shrugged his shoulders helplessly; the space bought for us had been commandeered by Russian officers; no other space was available; perhaps he would have space for us on the next train to Moscow, due three days later; he would not know till Monday morning.

I looked up friend Popick and begged him to help us. On Monday he accompanied us to the station, persuaded the stationmaster to assign us space on the expected train, and remained with us till the train arrived, several hours late, and our tickets were honored. When we parted I again offered him American money; again he refused, but secretly whispered, "Try to get me into America." He gave us the address of his mother in Seattle, and begged us to tell her that he was alive and well. We did.

Another three days, and we reached Moscow (August 4, 1932). Things were bustling there; the air was noisy and dusty with construction; the trains were crowded like New York subways; and American tourists and students filled the hotel lobby. One of them, reasoning from experience, presented a roll of toilet paper to us. Maurice Hindus, who defended Soviet Russia as long as he could, helped us and we helped him: he explained that the poverty and authoritarianism were the natural result of revolution, civil war, and individualistic lawlessness; he was flush with royalties (earned by his books in Russia) which he could spend only there, and we shared moderately in that operation. Walter Duranty was of no help; when I asked him why he was sending such optimistic reports to the New York *Times* about conditions in Russia, when they seemed so discouraging, he answered gaily, "You don't take these matters seriously, do you?" He was handsome and knew Russian; half the girls in the hotel were wooing him, and he had no reason for pessimism. However, 1932, according to Stalin's daughter, was "the frightful year of hunger, . . . of enforced collectivization"; it was the year when Stalin's wife, aged thirty-one, killed herself, "driven to despair by a profound disillusionment, and the impossibility of changing anything."

Our sightseeing, fact-seeking tours in and near Moscow were chaperoned by girl guides charmingly faithful to the Communist cause, and resolved that we should see only the most presentable aspects of the Soviet scene. Sometimes their precautions were inadequate, as when one took us to a model collective farm and we arrived when nearly all the work force was in church, observing a holyday despite the instructions of the Communist catechism. We saw the muzhiks filing back to their tasks, and rarely had we seen so dismal a group of men—backs bent, eyes downcast and lifeless, spirits broken; for the spirit of the peasant is hunger to own the land that he tills. Ariel wanted to visit her relatives in Proskurov; Intourist offered to sell us one-way, but not return, tickets, which was a gentle way of warning us that if we went we would have to walk back.

We became increasingly uncomfortable during our twenty-four days in Moscow. The inhabitants were glum in the vise of the Man of Steel; voices were hushed in fear of omnipresent spies; all publications were censored, elections were fixed, every air wave proclaimed the virtues of the state. Revolutionary ardor was gone. The new system, taking surplus value out of all producers to finance the government, the army, and industry, was building an oligarchic authoritarian state.

So we, who had come to Russia singing hymns to the great experiment, were glad to leave the scene of shattered hopes and broken men. Again we had to fight for the berths we had paid for in New York; they had been sold to others as well as to us, and every space in the appointed train to Warsaw was occupied. We wore down the commandant with our protests, for we had learned that the best way to proceed in such cases was to make a noise. Finally he allowed us to use his own cramped compartment while he slept on a seat in the corridor. Miserable and happy, we fled from paradise.

At Warsaw our capitalistic stomachs rejoiced in the good food and abundant fruit available, for a price, in the station and the hotel. We passed on to Berlin, and lived for a week in a pension kept by a simple family that won our hearts with good cooking and cleanliness; but we found it living in secret terror of the approaching Hitler regime. We met our close friends Abraham and Hannah Stone in Berlin; they were shocked to find that our brief visit to Russia had disillusioned us of Soviet Communism, which seemed to them the hope of the world; but our friendship survived, to the end of their lives, the strain of our diverse views. Together we boarded the S.S. *Europa* at Bremerhaven on

September 1. On that spacious and comfortably stable boat we found a vulgar extravagance, a spendthrift display of luxury, jewelry, and aimless expensive leisure, which almost overcame our distaste for Communism, and made us judge it more leniently.

On our return to New York (September 7) our first endeavor was not to disenchant Ariel's mother, whose trust in Communism had helped to sustain her through hardships of every kind. But we could not lie often enough to conceal our skepticism from our friends. Besides, with my propensity for analyzing every experience and judging every event, I had written, *currente calamo*, several articles about our trip. My literary agent, the genial and enterprising George Bye, tried to dispose of these to *Harper's Magazine* and *The Atlantic Monthly*; both of these rejected them on the ground that they would alienate too many readers; for Russia, in our Depression years, seemed to millions of Americans the last best hope of men; liberal editors were just as straitened by their partisan attachments as the conservative weeklies and the daily press. *The Saturday Evening Post* offered $1,500 each for the four pieces, and I was too mercenary— and too resentful of the two refusals—to resist. The articles frankly called the Soviet system a dictatorship *over* the proletariat, and described without glamour or prejudice—but perhaps with insufficient knowledge and understanding—the achievements and failures of Communist Russia in economics, morals, manners, religion, and government. I was warned, by a well-informed editor at Simon and Schuster, that the printing of these discourses in book form would further alienate the literary fraternity, and especially the reviewers, who were sympathetic with Russia; but pride overcame caution, and I had the material issued as *The Tragedy of Russia* (1933), a book long since out of print.

Despite our criticisms, we urged the American government to recognize the new state. (Editor George Lorimer appended to this recommendation a note of protest, but Franklin Roosevelt overruled him.) And I predicted that increasing freedom of intercourse between Russia and the United States would lead to a profitable mutual influence and exchange:

> As water in communicating vessels finds a common level, so two economic systems trading with each other will approximate through mutual imitation of their most successful elements. Peaceful intercourse between Russia and America will accelerate that gradual approximation of socialism and capitalism which is now going on in socialist and capitalist countries alike.

The little book concluded with my usual flourish of hope:

> Russia's plan for destroying the strong and enthroning the weak has had to fail, for there is no mechanism in nature by which the weak may control the strong; but it was an heroic undertaking, out of which many gifts will come to the human race. We too have failed; the individualism which made

176

us rich now makes us poor, and we flounder about for some escape from suicide by revolution. Perhaps out of the trial and error of a suffering Russia and a bankrupt world we may find at last a synthesis which may provide some conscience for our ability, some unity for our powers, some distribution for our production, some education for our leadership, and some order for our freedom.

My lectures in the fall of 1932 were predominantly on Russia; they won me large audiences and many enemies.

On October 18 Ariel joined me in Chicago, and together we addressed a dinner club on our experiences in Russia. I let her speak first, but it was a mistake; she gave so spirited and yet humorous an account that when my turn came I could only go through the same tribulations and disappointments with less verve and wit. I wish Ariel could have accompanied me more often, not only as wife and mother (for she takes care of me as of a child), but to share the platform; we would have made quite an oratorical team in the heyday and autumn of our energy.

CHAPTER XIV

Among the Stars

1933

Ariel:

I will not take that compliment seriously. My passion and *élan* could serve for one discourse or two, but Will carried with him such a fund of experience, reading, and thought that he could have lectured on a different subject—or a different phase of a subject—a dozen successive nights without running out of matter or interest.

And, at the risk of making this book a barter of compliments, I must protest against Will's repeated self-accusation of egotism and moneylust. Some little touches of vanity I detected in him now and then—his eau de cologne, his finicky cleanliness in dress; but I have seldom known him to violate what he preached to us: "Judge others leniently, yourself severely." That he was mercenary, or eager for money, is the last thing I would ever think of. I have never known him to bargain about the fee for his lectures or his articles. If he continued to lecture and write articles it was not only to add to our future security but because his royalties were now (1933) quite modest and could not keep us in the comfort which he loved us to have. He spent very little upon himself, but we had to check his propensity to give to everyone who asked. He paid for our travels and researches by writing about them.

Wherever he went, in these years, he continued to prepare *The Story of Civilization*. I did not take part in providing material for the early volumes, but, so far as my duties and my few amusements allowed, I shared gladly in classifying the heaps of notes that Will had been gathering for *Our Oriental Heritage* and *The Life of Greece*. I gave up my Green-wich Village diversions and obligations; Flora, Mary, and Michael took over full responsibility for the Gypsy Tavern. I learned to love my home and my work.

It took me some time to realize how important a role was played in a book by the organization of the material, and how the same contents less wisely arranged might have led to repetition, confusion, and failure. The mere organization (as distinct from the gathering) of the material was the most back-breaking part of the total operation. Will undertook the initial part. As he explained it to me, he divided the book into chapters, gen-erally following the geographical order (Near East, India, China, Japan), and, within each region, mediating between chronological sequence and topical unity (economics, government, religion, language, literature, phi-losophy, etc.). Then he marked with a Roman numeral each of the ap-proximately thirty thousand slips that had been gathered for Volume I, according to the chapter to which it belonged. Much of this weary job he performed on his lecture tours.

At home he prepared and typed, for each chapter in turn, an outline consisting of several hundred headings, consecutively numbered with Arabic numerals. Then he presented to the family and his other aides the slips that he had assigned to Chapter I, together with the chapter outline; and our task was to read each slip and to number it according to the heading under which we judged it to belong. We estimate that an aver-age chapter of the *Story* used some fifteen hundred slips, or about thirty thousand per volume; our attic rooms are bulging with the boxes of used slips. After numerically arranging the classified slips for a chapter in one or more shoeboxes, we handed them over to "the Master," and bade him turn them into a book. All in all, the gathering of the material for Volume I (ignoring the gleanings made before 1929) took two years; the classifica-tion, one year; the writing and rewriting (in longhand), and the typing, two years; the printing, proofreading, and illustration, one year.

Our Oriental Heritage presented special problems of order and treat-ment. First, should there be an introductory chapter on the nature and constituents of civilization?—for why write a history of something that had not been defined and described? The challenge fascinated my trou-badour; the historian in him was never separated from the philosopher; he became absorbed in the introduction, and gave it five chapters in-stead of one. His publishers liked those ninety pages so much ("Your prose," said Dick Simon, "cries out to be read out loud") that they de-cided to issue them as a separate book, *The Foundations of Civilization* (1935).

This, and Volume I, began with a summary definition: "Civilization is social order promoting cultural creation." I objected that the definition should include freedom—of movement and thought and expression—as a necessary element in civilization; but Will answered that there could be order and cultural creation under authoritarian rule, and that our politics should not color our definitions. I yielded. Looking again at those first four pages, I like them best of all the 999. How relevant to our time are some of the factors listed on page 4 as contributing to the decline of a civilization:

> Mental or moral decay from the strains, stimuli, and contacts of urban life, from the breakdown of traditional sources of social discipline and the inability to replace them; the weakening of the stock by a disorderly sexual life; . . . the decay of leadership through the infertility of the able, and the relative smallness of the families that might bequeath most fully the cultural inheritance of the race; a pathological concentration of wealth, leading to class wars, disruptive revolutions, and financial exhaustion: these are some of the ways in which a civilization may die. For civilization is not something inborn or imperishable; it must be acquired anew by every generation, and any serious interruption in its financing or its transmission may bring it to an end. Man differs from the beast only by education, which may be defined as the technique of transmitting civilization.

And I am struck by the continuity of thought between the last paragraph of Chapter I—

> Civilizations are the generations of the racial soul. As family rearing, and then writing, bound the generations together, handing down the lore of the dying to the young, so print and commerce and a thousand ways of communication may bind the civilizations together, and preserve for future cultures all that is of value for them in our own. Let us, before we die, gather up our heritage and offer it to our children—

and, thirty-three years later, the last lines of *The Lessons of History:*

> If a man is fortunate he will, before he dies, gather up as much as he can of his civilized heritage and transmit it to his children. And to his final breath he will be grateful for this inexhaustible legacy, knowing that it is our nourishing mother and our lasting life.

The love and care of that heritage have been Will's religion; the accumulation of it has seemed the main fruit and meaning of history; the recording of it has seemed to him the basic task of the historian.

The second problem in organizing *Our Oriental Heritage* was whether the Sumerian, or some other Mesopotamian, civilization was older or younger than the Egyptian, and should precede or follow it in the narrative; Will gave priority to the Sumerian, and thereby offended our greatest American Egyptologist, James H. Breasted. The third problem: how to mold into rational sequence and logical unity the many civilizations of the Orient—Sumerian, Babylonian, Assyrian, Hittite, Phrygian, Lydian, Phoenician, Arabic, Judean, Persian, Central Asian, Indian, Malaysian, Chinese, Korean, and Japanese? The difficulty was compounded by

Will's decision to carry the account of Indian, Chinese, and Japanese civilization to "our own times" (1930)—on the ground that they had little cultural interaction with the West before the eighteenth century— whereas he had to interrupt his history of the Near East at Alexander's conquests, since its later development was subject to Greek influence and Roman power. These problems of order were not quite overcome, but I can attest that much thought and time were given them.

I suspect that he found it as easy to work on his book in hotel privacy as amid the many interests and obligations of home. In any case he accepted engagements in Ann Arbor and Detroit (where he became friends with Frank Murphy), and then joined me for a few days in Miami (January 14–30, 1933). There, in Temple Israel, he spoke to an audience that had not forgotten, in its precarious affluence, its days of poverty. We visited Alden Freeman, now living peacefully in Florida, his mind reduced to a childlike innocence. On January 21 Will left for a heavy schedule of one-night stands reaching to Seattle and Los Angeles. Some lines from his letters:

Seattle, 2-1-33

I had a touching reunion last night with the mother of Joseph Popick who helped us so much in Omsk. She came to my hotel with her two sons, and broke into tears and hugged me when I told her how fine, vigorous, and generous a fellow Popick was. . . . She is only 60 or so, but looks like 90. . . . I brought them to my lecture, got them seats among the 150 extra customers who sat on the stage, and then told my story to an audience of almost 2,000 people. When it was all over we had another few minutes together, and the old lady just burned me up with a sort of sad gratitude. . . .

Tacoma, 2-4-33

Everything is busy, and so far successful, at this end; vast audiences (1800, 3900, 1600, etc.)—and many turned away; so many turned away at Portland, after 1800 had been squeezed into a hall seating 1500, that the Portland *Oregonian* . . . is financing a repetition of my lecture [on Russia] there tomorrow. . . .

Portland, 2-5-33

I am here . . . to repeat tonight the lecture I gave here, in the same hall, Tuesday. . . . I am touched by the eagerness with which they come, and the simplicity of their trust in me. . . . I begin with an impish delight in portraying the collapse of our own system, and end with the argument for recognition of Soviet Russia. At Seattle a great balalaika orchestra played, and a Russian *danseuse* danced, before my lecture; they were supposed to do the same at Tacoma, last night, but refused because I had advocated recognition. Both parties shoot at me. At Vancouver the communists in the gallery refused to let me speak; howled "liar," "crook," and other delicacies

181

at me. I waited patiently and silently until they exhausted themselves; then, when they saw that I was trying to be fair, they listened without interruption. Then I invited one of them to come to the stage; he came, and gave the conservatives Hell for labor conditions in Canada. It was a lively night.

About this time I (Ariel) gave three lectures under the title "Women of the Great Salons" to small audiences at the Gypsy Tavern, in an effort to help Flora and Mary to attract new customers. On February 14, 1933, I spoke on "Ninon de l'Enclos to Madame du Châtelet and Voltaire"; February 21 on "Madame de Staël and Madame Roland"; and February 28 on "George Sand to Madame de Caillavet and Anatole France." Meanwhile Will was "going Hollywood"—i.e., he was enjoying mental intoxication by association with movieland celebrities.

2-19-33

Now you'll read me with jealousy, for I fell in love last night with one of the most charming and gracious beings on earth—Charlie Chaplin. After dinner with Stuart Chase I went with his local manager (and mine) to hear his lecture. Into the box behind ours came Charlie. . . . At the close of the lecture he extended his hand without waiting for anyone to introduce us. He explained why he had not answered my long letter on the meaning of life; he puzzled over it for weeks, and concluded that he could add nothing to the letter. . . . A villainously handsome fellow. Perfect complexion, blue dancing eyes, fine features, and curly gray-and-black hair . . .

Stuart Chase, Palmer (the manager), and Herman Lissauer . . . joined us, and Chaplin suggested that we go to some Gypsy Tavern in Hollywood. What a car the villain has! An enormous cowl, concealing, I suppose, half a hundred cylinders; . . . enormous long doors, . . . just one on each side . . . but opening upon both front and rear seats. . . . I sat in back with him and a tid-bit of a girl who is courting him in the latest fashion—with modesty and timid quietness. . . . In a moment we were lost in philosophy, economics, and everything. . . . He remembered every part of "On the Meaning of Life," and laughed as he recalled Keyserling's blunt refusal to create royalties for me.

Arrived at our destination, we found a highly modernistic restaurant designed in steel and glass, with the entrance so queer that Charlie could not distinguish it from the wall; so he pushed the wall, found it immovable, until the manager . . . came out and said, "This way, Mr. Chaplin." We entered through the strange revolving door, and I remembered how long Charlie had been learning how to get thru such doors.

After a while Stuart Chase, Palmer, Lissauer, Mrs. Palmer, and Lissauer's new bride joined us, and Charlie exposed to us his plan for solving the economic crisis: to have the government own all natural resources, including the land, and to have the government buy food directly from the farmer, and sell it at cost to the consumer. [Very much like the Soviet system, except for the "at cost."] We tried to punch holes in the little nostrum, for each of us had a different nostrum up his sleeve . . . ; but he defended himself with considerable knowledge of economics.

We talked about everything—from 10 P.M. to 1:30 A.M. . . . He has invited me to have dinner with him at his home Tuesday. With dinner with Will Rogers on Thursday, . . . I shall have my fill of celebrities for a while. I know how you would have enjoyed meeting these really good-hearted and generous fellows, quite unspoiled by their fame.

2-22-33

I visited Charlie Chaplin last night, and found him again . . . an astonishing personality and intelligence. My [depressed] mood got the better of me, and instead of an evening of wit and brilliance we had an evening of pretty serious philosophical browsing. He had read "On the Meaning of Life," and I asked him for his answer to the question. He replied at once, and quite without conceit, I think—"The meaning of life for me is Charlie Chaplin"; that is, the meaning is self-development, the realization of all our potentialities and capacities. He talked most revealingly of his attitude to life. He is a great student of Schoepenhauer, but cheerful and optimistic nevertheless. When I told him how two things above all had made me a little less jolly than before—namely the killing of Sam and the bitter disillusionment in Russia—he recounted his own little tragedies (he has felt keenly the terrific publicity given to his family affairs), told of the awful poverty of his early days, when he was brought up in a poorhouse, and said that he had always faced trouble by reminding himself that it could not last. He has some inkling of the situation in Russia, and applies his formula to it: It can't last; it must change soon. . . .

I can't begin to tell you what a charming youth of 45 he is; how alert mentally, how unassuming and considerate. We talked from 7:15 to 11:30 and I thought it was not yet 10 P.M. I have persuaded Will Rogers to invite him to our dinner tomorrow night, so that I shall have the pleasure of seeing him again. They are both coming to my lecture at Santa Monica.

2-25-33

Thursday Will Rogers sent a nifty Cadillac Roadster for me, and after a 50-minute ride I found myself in his immense ranch—an expanse of farm land, grazing pasture, polo field, golf links, bridle paths, barns, garages, and a rustic home. He was in the stables when I arrived, and greeted me, out of overalls, boots, leather jacket, bronze wrinkled face, and tousled gray hair, with the broadest, wholesomest grin in the world. He looks like a cowboy, but has the nerves and mental activity of an artist. He introduced me to his beloved horses, and warmed up to me when I told him that next to a racing horse and a Jaffa orange a beautiful woman was the noblest work of God. He had eaten Jaffa oranges, and had flown over Jerusalem from Baghdad to Cairo. . . . He has flown a hundred times, has had one crash, was badly shaken up, but kept . . . the story out of the papers lest it should hurt aviation.

He has three children—a boy of 24 who rivals him in polo; a girl of 19 who is in college; and a girl of 16 who is in some academy. His wife is a simple and kindly woman, to whom Will has been notoriously faithful through all his climb to wealth. She had recently been operated upon for appendicitis, and was in bed; but she asked me to come up and chat with her, and told us how both she and Will treasured Ethel's letter of a year or so ago.

Charlie Chaplin and . . . Paulette Goddard came to join us for dinner, and Charlie made my head swim with the economics of finance; these millionaire boys know so much more about the mechanics of money than a poor thousandaire like me. . . . Will Rogers told us of the moving picture he was making; at once Charlie added a hundred valuable suggestions, and the story took on subtler and ampler form as he rose and, impromptu, acted possible scenes. I felt that I was in at the birth of a movie.

The four of us then drove off to my Santa Monica lecture. . . . In the vestibule of the auditorium crowds gathered about Charlie, Will, and Will; but I noticed that neither of these two most beloved Americans was spoiled by, or even conscious of, the silent adulation. Charlie refused to let me squeeze him in ticketless; bought tickets, and took seats in the front row. The chairman asked Will Rogers to . . . introduce me, and Will did it in . . . a speech which was one of the most amazing pieces of extemporization that I have ever heard—every line a witticism, until the house was convulsed. Imagine my job, keeping up the pace so set.

I lectured for my usual brief two hours, and practically everyone stayed for a half-hour of questions. Then Rogers insisted that I spend the night at the ranch; Chaplin and his lass came up the hill with us, and we chewed the cud of economics, politics, and philosophy till 1:30 A.M. Then Charlie and bride went home, and I fell asleep in Will Rogers' gigantic pajamas. When we parted at ten the next morning his last word was "Remember me to that fine little girl of yours."

Well, that's that. I like those two men immensely, and I can't believe, as I look into Chaplin's almost innocent blue eyes, that he could ever have been unjust to anyone. He smiled appreciatively when I told him that Russia made no provision for [lady] gold-diggers. His lady asked me, as we parted, would I like Charlie to send Ethel a postal. I said that Ethel would jump over the moon if she got such a card. . . .

Well, that's all the gossip for a while. I'm dreary with longing for home, even with stars shining so close to my head. Give my love to Michael and Harry, Flora and Mary, Baba [Grandmother] and all. And to Louis. And to Ethel. And to you.

While Will was far away from me the bank crash came; President Roosevelt ordered the banks closed, with the freezing of all accounts. Will anticipated my trepidation.

Cincinnati, 3-6-33

I hasten to send you a little note of reassurance. First of all I have some $800 in cash, which I have had the brains to collect en route. . . . I like Roosevelt's inaugural address, and his fine spirit . . . No difficulty which falls upon all of us alike can destroy my spirit; I am willing to take my share

184

of the blow, . . . and I find myself strangely apathetic and unmoved at the thought of losing money. I should say of a lost fortune what the Chinaman said when reproached for breaking a promise—"Well, I go make another one." . . . We shall muddle thru.

Lansing, Michigan, 3-8-33

Tomorrow morning I leave here, stop for supper in Detroit to give Gene a word of good cheer, and then into a sleeper for Cleveland. . . . Saturday morning I get to you. Sunday, perhaps, we ought to go out to Arlington and see to it that ma and pa are not starving. . . . Alden has written that he too is in need, and has asked me for a modest $10. I sent him a $20 money order—my poor check being worthless now. . . .

Worry not. . . . Be of good cheer, work busily, love everybody, especially me, and prepare to talk, eat, and sleep with

WILL

So on March 11, our battered philosopher reached home. On the thirteenth he and I drove to New Paltz, New York, thence to Boston and Exeter, and back to Great Neck. A request from Senator Smoot to send the Finance Committee of the Senate his ideas on the "American crisis" brought a ready response from Will, as I gather from the following letter from the publisher of the New York *Times*:

April 15, 1933

MY DEAR MR. DURANT:—

. . . I have read with much interest your observations to the Finance Committee of the U. S. Senate on the causes of our economic depression and outline for possible remedies. You cover the field admirably, and I am sure it will be an acceptable contribution in the deliberations of the Finance Committee. You touch upon a great many controversial questions and you present your view very clearly and succinctly. . . .

I hope this finds you well. Drop in and see me some time. Would be glad to have you come in and take luncheon with us almost any time.

Yours faithfully,
ADOLPH S. OCHS

The big event of our 1933 summer in Lake Hill was our vegetable garden. Our guide in this project was the Great Neck florist, Émile Fardel, saintly disciple of Rousseau, who went up with Will and Michael aforetime to plow and weed and plant. Local farmers smiled at these city yokels, and warned against sowing before the full moon came; we ignored their advice, and we grew a wonderful crop of vegetables, including barrels of tomatoes, and the sweetest corn we ever ate. Will, who uses nuts instead of meat, insisted on planting peanuts—in the Catskills! They grew, but with such small kernels that only a fanatic could give the time to peel them. Soon we had a big family with us: Harry, Flora, Ethel,

185

Louis, Michael and his wife Vera, occasionally my mother, usually Will's mother and father, whom we all loved; and for a month Will's brother Joseph, and his brother-in-law Maurice, stayed with us to paint the house, the cottage, and the barn.

To finance all this Will went off, in midsummer, for lectures in the Midwest. On his tours this year and the next he wrote several articles, chiefly for *The Saturday Evening Post*. Its aging editor, George Lorimer, liked Will and published such sermons and heterodox essays as "The Crisis in Christianity" and "What Education Is of Most Worth?" Anticipating the theology of the 1960s, the 1933 article proposed that Christian churches should cease to require acceptance of the Christian theology, and should concentrate on the ethics of Christ; all persons should be welcomed into church membership who accept the ethics of Christ as the goal—even if not the actuality—of their conduct. Some clergymen wrote to Will that they would gladly follow such a policy but the most influential (presumably the older) members of the congregation would not allow it. Lorimer suggested an article on "My Views Reviewed," in which the wildcat of Bayonne would tell how his opinions of 1914 had changed over twenty years. Will excused himself very much as the editors of *Harper's* and the *Atlantic* had backed away from his "Dictatorship over the Proletariat"—such an article would lose him what liberal friends he still retained. "Ah, you see," said Lorimer, "you are as hampered by your associations as we editors are." He had been criticized for printing Will's fourth article on Russia, but the criticism subsided when the circulation rose.

CHAPTER XV

On Trial

1934–35

Ariel:

So we moved into 1934; and so, in the spring of that year, we moved from 2 Henry Street to 51 Deepdale Drive, still in Great Neck. This time, tired of paying rent and courting landlords, we bought the property. To amortize the mortgage each of us sallied forth on lecture tours: Will across the continent, I to stints at Sheboygan, Michigan, January 16, and Rockford, Illinois, January 23. Will, foraging ahead, cleared my way:

> *Auditorium Hotel, Chicago, 1-7-34*
>
> Here I am in the old meeting place of the Durant clan. I have already secured a good room for you and your husband, after what Geneva would call protracted negotiations. . . . You will find this room—No. 606—reserved for you when you arrive on the 14th; and at 1 P.M. that day . . . Dr. Zurawski will meet you here . . . and take you out to dinner. Harold Bauer and Gabrilowitsch will play, in your honor, a two-piano recital that same afternoon . . . at Orchestra Hall, . . . three blocks from your hotel. A week later, in the same hall, Horowitz will play for you, and on January 18th the Chicago Symphony Orchestra will play a program of Mozart and Wagner—i.e., wine and cheese.

There followed travel instructions for Sheboygan, and, on

> *1-11-34*
>
> . . . Perhaps you should fortify yourself with an enema bag. . . . Traveling means sitting upon the intestines; and though you may not like the

187

idea that a lady has intestines, you will find that yours are just as resentful of being sat upon as any pupil in school.

On January 13 I left Great Neck and New York, and on the fourteenth I found everything arranged for me in Chicago. Dr. Zurawski soon showed up, and lavished upon me all his Old-World courtesy. On the sixteenth I took the train to Sheboygan and discoursed on the French salons. I returned to Chicago late that evening; and the next morning I found my husband at my bedside. I brightened him with an account of my triumph, and with a letter from Arde Bulova (January 11, 1934) complimenting him on "the profound mind" at play in *The Mansions of Philosophy,* adding, "I beg the privilege of visiting you some day," and sending watches for three of us. Will hurried off the same day for Toledo and south; on the twenty-third I rode off to Rockford and addressed the Women's Club on "Experiences in Russia." We were reunited at home on January 28.

Now Will sat down to the job of typing, with untaught six fingers, the manuscript of Volume I. I find in his Memo Book for January 30: "To type pages 1–860 of OOH by June 23 I must type 7 ms. pp. daily." So was made the third draft of *Our Oriental Heritage;* the first and second had been made in his minute longhand in massive bookkeeping ledgers. A substantial part of the typescript was delivered to Simon and Schuster on July 18. We lived in semi-suspended animation until, six days later, two enthusiastic notes arrived from our publishers:

July 23, 1934

DEAR WILL:

Every day since the manuscript came I have been reading a few pages, and I am now up to page fifty. If it keeps up as it has begun, this will be the greatest piece of work with which Essandess have ever been associated. I used to marvel at your ability to make things clear, and at your prose. Now I marvel even more at your tremendous knowledge and scholarship. . . .

Ever yours,
DICK

July 23, 1934

DEAR WILL:

On landing from Italy the most exciting personal news I received was Dick's engagement to Andrea; and the most exciting publishing news was Dick's report about "The Story of Civilization." I can hardly wait until I get the manuscript myself. Naturally Dick will be reading it first, since he will soon be on his way to Hawaii. . . . I almost literally found Dick's hair on fire—what with his forthcoming nuptials and this *maximum opus* of yours. . . .

M L S

Dick's "fire" cooled as the days and pages proceeded; he, like me, must have found it hard to get excited about the ancient empires of Mesopotamia.

On November 4 Will rode south for a week of lectures. As usual, he sent us a letter every day, mingling love and laxatives. On November 12: "How anxious I am to get back to you, and the cozy home you make for me, and the healthy food, and the strength that passes from you to me in every hug!" When he returned, and had received his strengthening, we drove together for his engagements in Montclair, New Jersey, and West Point; and on the way we stopped to see his parents in Arlington. On November 29 he shared with Albert Einstein, Edwin Markham, and others in celebrating, at the Brooklyn Jewish Center, the opening of the "American Library of Nazi-Burned Books." I hope my old clipping from the *Jewish Daily Forward* of November 30, 1934, can be reproduced, for though Will spoiled it by an unusual pose of boredom and pride, the pictures of Einstein and Markham are delightful.

On January 1, 1935, we went out to Arlington to get the patriarchal blessing, and to meet the Durant clan, now some thirty strong. Mother Durant and her daughter Leah had done all the cooking, and now fed the tribe. It was at this or a similar gathering that Will's mother, with her arm around Pa Durant's neck, said fervently, "I thank God for having given me this good man to take care of me these fifty years." Will often recalled those words, and I looked forward to the time when I might say them about him. (It came.) Will is a Catholic when it comes to marriage: when a man is once stuck with a bride he should cleave to her till death, barring adultery or insanity in his mate; and I believe he would overlook even these deviations. The alternative, he thinks, is chaos.

The day after that feast he set out on the most arduous of his tours, taking him from the Northeast to the Northwest to the Southwest to the Southeast. I will quote very sparingly from his letters, for I know that they cannot be as interesting to others as they still are to me. But I must quote the first one almost in full, as my final picture of a talking trouper's life.

En route to Chicago, 1-5-35

I am back at the same grind. . . . I felt a case of the flu coming upon me . . . as I neared Boston Wednesday night. At Boston I had to taxi for half an hour through traffic and ice-covered streets to another station, and there took a local train to a Puritan suburb, Wakefield. The only hotel I could find was an old colonial home, with one bathroom for twenty people. I got thru my lecture well enough. . . . Then I scandalized the old bonneted ladies in the little hotel by carrying my enema bag half a mile from room to bath. . . . The ladies guessed I was under the weather, and asked if they could help. I suggested a lemon toddy, but they had no lemons, no brandy or wine. I made them squeeze three oranges into a bowl of hot water, and drank it all. Then they asked for three autographs. . . .

Felt better the next morning; headache gone, but catch in the throat. Long ride all day in a hot train, thru snow blizzards, to Detroit. There, yesterday morning, I spoke to a big audience. . . . Gene and Eva were there, and were my guests at the luncheon which the Town Hall Club gave me—with a big cake bearing in frosted letters, "Detroit welcomes Will Durant." Probably 1 out of 500 in Detroit knew that I was in town.

Then a long distance call from Bay City (115 miles away), saying they couldn't come and get me as agreed; would I please take the bus. A lady, seeing my heavy bags, volunteered to drive me to Flint if Bay City would volunteer to meet me there, half way. So I trusted my young life to a woman driver, who turned out to be an excellent one; and after two hours on snowy and icy roads we reached Flint. There a Cadillac Twelve . . . was waiting for me; . . . an hour and a half more and I was in Bay City, 7 P.M. At eight Mrs. Anneke, the impresario, came for me, and suddenly, as I spoke to her, I found that I had almost completely lost my voice. She was dismayed, for all the élite of Bay City, in evening dress, were crowding the big ballroom of the hotel to hear me salvage civilization. I managed to make them hear me for an hour; but then my voice was finished; nothing but a hoarse whisper remained. I thought with anxiety of the 50 lectures remaining to be given. . . . The good ladies called a doctor, who nearly suffocated me by sticking far down my throat sticks of cotton soaked in Argyrol. Then to bed.

This morning I am en route to Chicago. . . . I am gargling with Hexylresorcinol, and the voice seems slowly improving. . . .

Warn Louis and Ethel again to . . . prepare for the midyear examinations. And take care of your health, all of you, my precious ones.

I joined him for five days in and around Chicago, and then he faced west. From Iowa City he wrote:

1-23-35

The weather is the severest I've ever had on a lecture tour. Below zero nearly everywhere. Had to change cars at 5:40 A.M. this morning at Burlington, Iowa, at 8 below zero, then ride in a poorly heated day coach to West Liberty, then in an automobile for 18 miles to Iowa City, just in time to face—unshaved and breakfastless—Prof. Shambaugh's class in philosophy. He has a class of 200, who use both the *Story* and *Mansions* as textbooks. He was reading from *On the Meaning of Life* when I entered his classroom. . . .

You will see from the enclosed . . . 40 below zero in Duluth, where I must be day after tomorrow, and 20 below in Minneapolis, where I speak tomorrow. . . .

We had arranged that I should join him in San Francisco on February 16. The house was to be closed for a month; Louis was to stay with his mother, Flora; and Ethel, completing her final year at Great Neck High School, was to be cared for by Émile Fardel (florist philosopher) and his wife and daughters.

When Will reached San Francisco on February 16 he found me awaiting him at the Mark Hopkins Hotel. On the seventeenth we had dinner with Joseph Strauss, the modest engineering genius who built the majestic Golden Gate Bridge; Will often named this as an example of how science can become an art, and mathematics a poem. On the eighteenth Will and I rode north to the lovely town of Santa Rosa, where he celebrated "The Ten Greatest Thinkers" before a high-school assembly. On the nineteenth we invaded Sacramento; on the twentieth, Stockton; on the twenty-first Mrs. Herbert Hoover showed us through her home in Palo Alto; on the twenty-fourth a lecture in Fresno; then a midnight train to Los Angeles, where, on the twenty-fifth, in Philharmonic Auditorium, Will met John Strachey in debate on "America: The Way Out." Will Rogers commemorated the battle in his little column of February 26. Chaplin took us to a restaurant afterward, and I soon perceived that Will had not exaggerated the verve and meat of Charlie's conversation. Rogers wrote in the Washington *Herald* of March 10:

> I was telling you all away back days ago about our going with Charlie Chaplin to hear a debate between Will Durant, that wrote the wonderful book, *The Story of Philosophy*. He is just one of the finest fellows you ever met. He made the same trip across Siberia into Russia that I made. He was debating an Englishman named Starchey [*sic*]. This Starchey was a Bolshevik, but he was very fair in his talk, and it was a brilliant thing to hear. Debates don't settle nothing, but they are entertaining.

I now sampled the wild program that Will had to follow: on February 26 at Santa Ana; on the twenty-seventh at the University of Southern California; on the twenty-eighth at Long Beach. On March 1 we took a sleeper to Grand Canyon, spent three hours marveling at the colorful ditch, and then rode on to Santa Fe and by bus to Taos, where we explored the relics of D. H. Lawrence and his loves; and then by weary and oratorical stages to Arlington (Texas), Nacogdoches (Texas), and Tuscaloosa (Alabama), to three restful days in St. Petersburg (Florida). On March 15 we reached home. After three days of final preparation, Will delivered to "S and S" the terminal pages of *Our Oriental Heritage*. On the eighteenth he was off again for lectures in Buffalo, Detroit, and Millersville, Pennsylvania. Finally, on March 25, he was really home, after three months that might have permanently broken his health had he not been sustained by nightly doses of applause. Now he buried himself in correcting the proofs for the thousand-page book upon which his whole career seemed to depend.

Tireless and reckless, he had committed himself to teach two courses on philosophy in the summer session of 1935 at the University of California at Los Angeles. Perhaps this new chore was designed in part to give the family a reason for seeing America. So we turned over our old manse at Lake Hill to relatives and friends, closed our Great Neck house, and sallied forth, on June 9, on our first motor crossing of the continent. My sister Mary accompanied us, and we picked up Dr. Zurawski in Chicago. Arrived in Westwood (western Los Angeles), we found a spacious home at the Kappa Kappa Gamma sorority house at 734 Hilgard Avenue. Will had contracted for it some months before, when it was gay with pretty coeds; he had ambitiously proposed to take the house "and all its present contents"; but now those fascinating girls had vanished, and he had to make do with his wife and Mary and, after July 1, daughter Ethel, who had remained in Great Neck to graduate from high school on June 24. In July we were joined by Drs. Abe and Hannah Stone.

We were enthusiastic about the climate, the ever dependable but seldom oppressive sunshine. We admired the Moorish architecture of Royce Hall and the UCLA Library. I found time to attend some of Will's classes, which had begun on June 24.

In addition to these fifty-six lectures in thirty-nine days my indefatigable sophist addressed large general audiences in Royce Hall on July 1, 8, and 15. It was a strenuous summer. When his schedule, and his obligations as paterfamilias, allowed, he played golf on the Bel Air course with Dean Gordon Watkins. The dean headed the list of the many new friends we made at UCLA, whose keen minds, good hearts, and fine manners raised our estimate of man. Their wives were womanhood at its best— loveliness, modesty, solicitude. I remember especially a little party on the lawn of the Watkins' home; enough coeds were present to agitate my "constant" lover; and when he was called upon to make his contribution to the evening he surprised us all by singing, unaccompanied, and seated on the grass, "My Love Is Like a Red Red Rose." He had some trouble reaching the high notes, but he managed to convey the idea that he proposed to be faithful to his troth till all the rivers of the world ran dry. I was comforted.

We had some extracurricular friends. Charlie Chaplin and Paulette Goddard took us for a two-day outing (July 6–7) on his boat across the tumbling waters from San Pedro to Catalina. Will became seasick, Paulette retired early, and I had Charlie to myself for several hours. I was again impressed by the range of his knowledge and the activity of his mind. On the island, as we approached the little "zoo," we were startled to hear a caged bird cry out, "Hello, Charlie."

My excitable gallant fell in love with Norma Shearer when he saw her on the screen as Marie Antoinette. He sent her a telegram of praise; she responded warmly, and invited us to a dinner she was planning for her Santa Monica home. We begged off, for we had asked Lewis Browne to come and dine with us that same evening. She suggested that we bring him with us; we did, and Lewis stole the party away from Douglas Fairbanks, Sr., Moss Hart, and my professor by telling some of his rollicking stories.

On Trial

On August 1 we gave a little party in our sorority house, with Charlie, Paulette, Aldous Huxley, and the Drs. Stone as our nonacademic guests, plus some professors and their wives. Charlie was in fine form. He acted out almost every idea he uttered. When he told of the histrionic elephant who ad-libbed with liquid ease (Will's phrase, of course) while performing a role on the stage of a London music hall, Charlie accompanied the story by rising from the dinner table and raising his leg against the fireplace.

The next day we left Westwood: Will, Ethel, Mary, and I in our car, the Drs. Stone and their two friends in another. We spent the night at Sequoia Lodge amid the big trees; then on to San Francisco, Portland, and Seattle. There we parted for a while, as Will had to go to Vancouver to deliver his discourse on Russia. I cannot recall accompanying him, and I must here rely upon Will's account. Robert Cromie welcomed him, and served as chairman; but a bevy of Bolsheviks had filled the gallery of the theater, and they refused to let Will speak. He managed to convey to them a proposal that if they would let him speak for half an hour he would then offer the rostrum to their spokesman. They subsided; Will proceeded in fear and trembling, and ended in safe time. The Communist orator took the floor, and Will and Cromie listened humbly for a while. But then the bourgeoisie on the main floor began to walk out by the score. In the confusion Will and Cromie escaped, and Will caught the night boat for Seattle. From that city we and the rolling Stones went on through majestic scenery to Spokane. There the two families parted again, to go by different routes and reunite in Chicago. We arrived in Great Neck on August 22, just in time to be in at what threatened to be the death of Volume I.

The big book (1,049 pages) was published on July 10, 1935, dedicated "To Ariel." The jacket entitled it *The Story of Civilization: Our Oriental Heritage;* most of the reviewers referred to the volume by the series title, causing some confusion. On rereading the preface today I note that the plan called for five volumes: one for Asia, one for ancient Greece and Rome, one for the Middle Ages and the Renaissance, one for Europe 1517 to 1789, and one for "Our Modern Heritage"—from the French Revolution "to our own time." The humor of history decreed that the first four of these parts should take ten volumes, and that the fifth should remain a dream unrealized. Even so the plan was ungratefully incomplete: no mention was made, in this prospectus, of the Americas. But in scope the proposal was recklessly inclusive. Said the preface:

> I have tried in this book to accomplish the first part of a pleasant assignment which I rashly laid upon myself some twenty [sixteen?] years ago to write a history of civilization. I wish to tell as much as I can, in as little space as I can, of the contributions that genius and labor have made to the cultural heritage of mankind—to chronicle and contemplate, in their causes, character, and effects, the advances of invention, the varieties of

economic organization, the experiments of government, the aspirations of religion, the mutations of morals and manners, the masterpieces of literature, the development of science, the speculations of philosophy, and the achievements of art. I do not need to be told how absurd this enterprise is, nor how immodest is its very conception; for many years of effort have brought it to but a fifth of its completion, and have made it clear that no one mind, and no single lifetime, can adequately compass this task. Nevertheless I have dreamed that despite the many errors inevitable in this undertaking, it may be of some use to those upon whom the passion for philosophy has laid the compulsion to try to see things whole, to seek perspective, unity, and understanding through history in time, as well as through science in space.

Here was Will's disclaimer that he was abandoning philosophy; history as he saw it was a part of philosophy; it provided data toward the understanding of man, as science provided data for the understanding of nature; here, as in the old adage, history was to be philosophy teaching by example. That large historical perspective could be achieved only by making history a record not primarily of politics and war but of all those facets of man's activity which constitute his cultural as well as his civic life; civilization is their totality and their interaction; and the highest aim of history should be to present those elements in their united movement through time. So the preface declared for *integral history*:

I have long felt that our usual method of writing history in separate longitudinal sections—economic history, political history, religious history, the history of philosophy, the history of literature, the history of science, the history of music, the history of art—does injustice to the unity of human life; that history should be written collaterally as well as linearly, synthetically as well as analytically; and that the ideal historiography would seek to portray in each period the total complex of a nation's culture, institutions, adventures, and ways. But the accumulation of knowledge has divided history, like science, into a thousand isolated specialties; and prudent scholars have refrained from attempting any view of the whole— whether of the material universe, or of the living past of our race. For the probability of error increases with the scope of the undertaking, and any man who sells his soul to synthesis will be a tragic target for a myriad merry darts of specialist critique. "Consider," said Ptah-hotep five thousand years ago, "how thou mayest be opposed by an expert in council. It is foolish to speak on every kind of work." A history of civilization shares the presumptuousness of every philosophical enterprise: it offers the ridiculous spectacle of a fragment expounding the whole. Like a philosophy, such a venture has no rational excuse, and is at best but a brave stupidity; but let us hope that, like philosophy, it will always lure some rash spirits into its fatal depth.

The "merry darts of specialist critique" came on the heels of the book's publication, in the July 13, 1935, issue of *The Saturday Review of Litera-*

ture, in a ten-column review of *Our Oriental Heritage* by Dr. James Henry Breasted, director of the Oriental Institute of Chicago. This dean of American Egyptologists felt that "the elaborate effort to include so much detail has involved the author in disastrous difficulties." He specified many alleged errors, and thought that these were due to a wrong choice of secondary sources. "If these had always been wisely chosen, and the author's charming and genial comments had therefore been more successfully documented, his book would have been a safer record of the state of knowledge of early man." Although Breasted leavened his criticism with many kind words, the general effect seemed to me and others devastating. Max Schuster called it "distressing," and urged Will to send an early reply to *The Saturday Review of Literature*.

Will at that time was sipping the adulation of motion picture celebrities for his two courses at UCLA; Breasted's barrage brought him down to earth. Then, as he considered carefully each of the alleged errors, he recovered his courage, and sent to *The Saturday Review* a reply which it printed in its issue of August 3, 1935. He examined twelve points of the indictment, refuted, in his own judgment, eight of them, and concluded with a most unmannerly pun: "with these exceptions I should say that the Doctor's stricture is well deserved."

For the rest the reviews were highly favorable, and turned Will from despair to quiet acceptance of salutary chastisement. But two friendly critics spoke of Will's book as aimed at a popular audience, and as based on secondary sources. I asked him to clear up these points. He replied:

> I write to be understood by educated people. Of course I do not write for specialists; I depend upon their work. In that sense I am, or would like to be, a popularizer. If popularization means skimping on studying and scholarship, or sparing the reader the rough passages of the road, I should not call myself a popularizer. As to seeking the largest possible sale—not guilty. Remember Kroch's warning that to write a history in five or ten volumes would ruin the sale, but that if I could compress it all into one volume he would guarantee a sale of 100,000 copies? Now would a man seeking a large sale let his book run to 900 pages? On the contrary we were reconciled to a small sale, and modest royalties. As to secondary sources the answer again requires a distinction. In *The Story of Philosophy*, which was aimed at a lower common denominator than *The Story of Civilization*, almost all the material came from primary sources, as Dewey pointed out— i.e., from the philosophers themselves. In planning *The Story of Civilization* it was out of the question to go chiefly to primary and contemporary sources for every aspect of the history of a score of nations through 6,000 years. I tried a middle course. I relied on secondary sources in political and economic history, which had been repeatedly presented, as in Bury's *History of Greece* or Mommsen's *Rome*; there would have been no sense in spending half my life making a first-hand study of all the written or lapidary sources in those fields, which would merely have duplicated work

already well done. So I covered the political and economic aspects of each civilization primarily as background for the cultural history, which has been my main interest and purpose; and there—in religion, literature, philosophy, science, and art—you may bear witness that I—we—went to the original sources. We studied the poets and philosophers directly, the poets usually in their own language—Greek, Latin, Italian, French, German. We visited a hundred churches and monasteries, and one of us spent many months in a seminary, reading Catholic theology. We spared no expense of money or energy to see with our own eyes the art that our books were to describe. Remember that weary, bumpy ride over hundreds of miles and thousands of lizards from Bangkok to Saigon to see and feel the temples of Angkor Wat?

I remembered.

So much for the cons and pros of the reviewers concerning Volume I; Will was already immersed in Volume II. Meanwhile we had to eat. Royalties for the six months ending September 30, 1935, were only $900.53. We faced new, however welcome, expenses for sending Ethel to Bryn Mawr and Louis to Cornell. Will returned to the lecture platform.

After many years under the management of the Alber-Wicks Bureau, he was now under the management of W. Colston Leigh, with whom he remained until his hypertension reached a crisis in 1957 and compelled him to stop "peddling philosophy." He began in October, 1935, with lectures in or near New York; then to Joliet and St. Louis; home on November 5 to confront his fiftieth birthday. Of his nine engagements in December the most interesting was on the sixteenth in Passaic, New Jersey, where his boyhood teacher, Sister Celeste, now old and blind, invited us to her nunnery, passed her seeing hands fondly over his face, and—episcopal excommunication notwithstanding—invited us to join the nuns in their evening meal. "This," she told them, "was my most difficult pupil in St. Cecilia's, but he is the one I loved most."

And then Christmas, and that trying year 1935 melted away.

CHAPTER XVI

To Greece

1936–39

Will:

Meanwhile I had passed from admiration for Herbert Hoover to love for Franklin Roosevelt. When I saw with what bold initiatives and inspiring confidence the new President faced the spreading chaos and trepidation that came with the failure of our banking system, I felt that here was another Solon who, though himself a member of the upper classes, would ease the burdens of the commonalty, and achieve a partial and peaceful redistribution of our concentrated wealth. Governmental regulation of the banks; governmental support of the labor unions to bring the bargaining power of employees nearer to parity with that of employers and financiers; temporary governmental employment of the unemployed in enterprises of social worth; governmental support of insurance against accident, unemployment, and old age; governmental funds for education and recreation . . . My heart went out to this man, so hated by those whom he was saving from the breakdown of capitalism; so respondent to the pleas of a poverty that he had never experienced; and fighting the battle against his own class while fighting a crippling disease that might have broken the spirit of a lesser man. I was one of hundreds of thousands who wrote to him in gratitude and support.

Perhaps he remembered that I had told his party to nominate him in 1928. His secretary sent word that the President would see me on January 13, 1936. I took Ariel with me, but the aide in charge of admissions asked me to leave her in his anteroom. Roosevelt turned our conversation to the writing of history, and suggested that when my present literary plans had been effected I should write a history of the presidency in terms of its class basis and support; I was not quite enthusiastic. When it came time to free him for more pressing matters I told him that I had left my wife just beyond the door, and that she would be very unhappy if, being so near, she had never been allowed to give him in person a word of gratitude and allegiance. "Of course you must bring her in," he said. I brought Ariel to him, and I shall always remember his blushing apology to her: "You know, Mrs. Durant, that I can't rise." The heavy irons that supported him when he stood were regularly removed when he imprisoned himself behind his desk. With such men, molded by our crises, I can never lose faith in America.

Nevertheless I knew that there was much incompetence in our government, much malfeasance and venality. One of the pet ideas that I had been expounding since 1917 was that our universities should give as much attention to forming governmental administrators as to preparing men for the practice of medicine or law; and that a U.S. Civil Academy should be set up in or near Washington to give further and more practical training in government and diplomacy. On January 14, 1936, Representative Wesley Disney, a member of the House Committee on Ways and Means, wrote to me that he would introduce a bill for the organization of such an academy. His proposal dropped dead. Meanwhile several universities established schools of government.

I continued, during that winter, to peddle my diagnoses and prescriptions from pillar to post. Ariel has preserved some of my letters, but these deserve little recording. I was happy that spring at home, with trees and flowers flourishing around us; but Ariel had hardly taught me their names when I sold myself to an arduous undertaking. William Barber, head of a tourist bureau in Wellesley, Massachusetts, snared my ego by naming the venture "Will Durant Leads a Tour in the Wake of History." My sole responsibility would be to give informal talks to the group about the historical background of the Mediterranean spots to be visited. A business director (Alfred Carlson) would take care of traveling arrangements; and I would be allowed to take Ariel and Ethel with me. We would all leave New York by tourist class on the S.S. *Rex* of the Italian Line. There would be six days in Egypt, four in Palestine, one each in Damascus, Baalbek, Beirut, Tripoli, Cyprus, Rhodes, Smyrna, Istanbul, Mycenae, Tiryns, and Crete, nine days in Greece, one in Paestum, one in Naples and Pompeii, six in Rome, one in Genoa, one in Cannes, and so by the S.S. *Roma* to reach New York on August 27, 1936. I accepted because I was planning books on Greece and Rome, and had intended to go there in any case to refresh my memories of classic art and historic sites, and because it would give Ariel and Ethel a stimulating vacation from Great Neck and Bryn Mawr—and might compel them to hear my lectures.

The *Palestine Post* of July 12, 1936, greeted the group's arrival in Jerusalem with a true story:

> Twenty-five meek Palestinian donkeys waited outside the railway station yesterday morning, just before the arrival of the morning train. Twenty-five American tourists, belonging to a party led by Dr. Will Durant, the famous American philosopher, mounted the donkeys, and rode to the Fast Hotel. They had been told that there were no cabs in the city owing to a "general strike."

Jewish cabdrivers had not joined the strike, but Arabs had threatened to fire upon any taxi driven during the strike. When Rabbi Judah L. Magnes invited us to visit the Hebrew University, then on Mount Scopus, Ariel proposed to hire a Jewish driver and risk the strikers' bullets, and she ordered me to remain in the hotel. I quoted the Book of Ruth to her: "Whither thou goest I will go," and accompanied her. No shots were fired at us, and we had an inspiring hour with a fine gentleman.

Back in the Hotel Fast, Ariel learned that some Moslem muftis were conferring there with representatives of Hitler, and she made out from the conversation of these emissaries that they planned to win Arab support for Germany against England and the Jews. She asked the editor of the *Palestine Post* to investigate; he did, and her suspicions were sufficiently confirmed to lead to a warning article in the paper.

On July 17 we had our second view of the classic temples at Baalbek; their grandeur and perfect form even in their ruin deepened my feeling that the Roman Empire was the greatest achievement in the history of government. At Mycenae, Tiryns, and Cnossus I had my first chance to study the relics of pre-Homeric Greece and Crete. At Epidaurus we marveled at the preservation of the 2,400-year-old amphitheater. At Athens I lectured on Greek art to an audience seated on the steps of the Parthenon. At the foot of the Acropolis I spoke (without amplifier) on the Greek drama from the "orchestra" (the "dancing place" of the chorus) in the Theater of Dionysus; my auditors scattered themselves over the vast structure; some took seats in the uppermost and most distant tier; later they told me that they had understood my every word. We motored to Delphi, and explored the haunts of the Eleusinian mysteries; amid those ruins I held forth on Greek religion and philosophy. We continued over nerveracking, stomach-wrecking roads to Olympia, where I expounded Greek athletics and shocked the museum curator by stroking the legs of Praxiteles' *Hermes*.

We took a pleasant cruise through the Corinth Canal to Patras, and thence across the Adriatic past Odysseus' Ithaca to Brindisi. Trains that tried our eyes and hearts with dust and heat bore us through southern Italy to Paestum, where, among the ancient Greek temples, I dilated on the Greek colonization of Italy as one step in the transmission of Hellenic culture to Rome and Western Europe. Amid the ruins of Pompeii and the

Roman Forum we discussed the history and art of classic Rome. On the S.S. *Roma,* homeward bound, I closed antiquity and our tour with a talk on "The Triumph of Christianity."

I had hardly settled back into the routine of family life when I plunged quite needlessly into the campaign for re-electing Franklin Roosevelt. I knew that the tycoons of America "hated his guts" as a "rabble-rouser" and "traitor to his class"; and I wrongly assumed that all the wealth of the country would be mobilized against him. I wrote to the New York *Times* eulogizing the President. My lectures in the fall of 1936 were anything but nonpartisan. The President was on the road, too, and sometimes my schedule enabled me to watch how a seasoned campaigner, without legs, can conquer thousands of moneyed bipeds. So I wrote from Detroit,

10-15-36

Ex-mayor of Detroit Frank Murphy, meeting me here yesterday, placed me on the Detroit Reception Committee to welcome the President . . . tonight, and invited me to join his group and go to the City Hall and have a place near the President when he speaks from the steps there at 8:30 this evening. . . . I don't think poor over-worked Roosevelt will be able to say much that he has not said before, but it will be interesting to watch an old-time political demonstration. He is getting crowds unprecedented in political history. Wednesday noon 30,000 turned out at Grand Rapids to see and hear Landon; Thursday morning (today) 150,000 turned out to see and hear Roosevelt.

I'm off to join the big fracas. . . .

Akron, Ohio, 10-17-36

I was within a few feet of him [Roosevelt] on the 15th, seated with women relatives of . . . Murphy, who is running for Governor of Michigan. . . . I saw with these old eyes 300,000 waiting patiently and happily . . . in the great plaza before the City Hall [of Detroit]. After ten days of uninterrupted travel, five talks a day, thirty conferences a day with state and city leaders, . . . he stepped out of his car young, clean, fresh, handsomer than his pictures, leaner than when we saw him. . . . So worry not, sweetheart, your F.D.R. is as good as re-elected. . . . The rich have overplayed their hand by taking sides too definitely.

When I read today (1970) this ecstatic description of Roosevelt in 1936 I think of the worn-out President I saw in 1944—drawn face, bags under the eyes, skin sagging and bloodless, but still a picture of resolution, of grim confidence in the victory that he was never to see.

It turned out that F.D.R. would have been elected without my help; he won all but two states. By 1937 the New Deal was in full ardor, and the "welfare state" in America began to catch up with the Beveridge plan in Britain. I believe that the enlightened legislation of 1937–41 saved the

American system of free enterprise by financing consumption (as the bankers had financed production), and thereby setting the wheels of the economy turning again.

For our family 1937 was an uneventful year: no triumphs, no tragedies, many lectures, steady progress on Volume II. On January 6 I began a heavy tour across the country. Ariel and her sister Mary met me in San Francisco. We had a lively week in Los Angeles. On February 19 Charlie Chaplin and Paulette Goddard came to the Biltmore Hotel to have dinner with us; on the twenty-second Norma Shearer fed us in her Santa Monica home; on the twenty-third Jim Fifield turned over to me the pulpit of his First Congregational Church; and on the twenty-fourth we had a stimulating evening in Chaplin's home.

We ruined our last day together on this trip (February 24), with a shameful quarrel over expenditures. The details are too sordid for public display; I leave them unquoted in the correspondence that we are bequeathing to a university for general scrutiny after our death.

That strenuous trip ended on March 20. We recovered our health in Lake Hill, and on September 28 I took to the road again. A letter from Indianapolis noted a visit from my nemesis—high blood pressure:

10-22-37

. . . At ten A.M. I was facing a wild crowd of college boys and girls in the gymnasium of the State Teachers' College, Indiana, Pa.

In the midst of my speech I had a slight dizzy spell. I had become too eloquent, and probably my face was getting red with unwarranted seriousness. For a "split second" the audience swam before me, as if in a great swing dance; my sense of balance gave way, and I saved myself from an ignominious collapse by grasping the table in front of me. Then the spell passed, I cooled down, and went on. . . .

From Lincoln, Nebraska,

10-28-37

Just got your sweet letter, vowing to me that which is the dearest thing in the world to me—your love. Then Ethel comes, then Louis, then those funny yellow pages I am writing.

I've done precious little on *The Story of Civilization* on this trip. I have had more day-time travel than usual, and the trains shake too much for writing. . . . I hope to finish Chapter VI . . . before I get home. Then, after getting a little "strenk" from you, I'll rewrite it and try to pour some style into it.

Wallace may come on Nov. 4th, and in that case I'll help him classify.*
. . . Take my head in your lap.

---

* Wallace Brockway, through all these years, was giving us the benefit of his varied erudition.

1938 was the year in which Ariel and I conquered Hawaii, and renewed our love affair with UCLA. I had received from David Crawford, president of the University of Hawaii, an offer of fifteen hundred dollars for five lectures, February 10–20. The fee would do little more than cover our expenses, but the trip would allow us to have another honeymoon without harm to Ethel and Louis, who would be in college at the time; and some engagements en route would help to balance our budget. So on January 5 Ariel and I left by train for stops at Norfolk, Columbus (Georgia), and New Orleans, and reached Los Angeles on January 16. We renewed our friendships with Douglas Fairbanks, Jr., and Lewis Browne; I introduced "The Ten Greatest Thinkers" to the young ladies of the junior college at Pasadena; I solved "The World Crisis" at the Ebell Club, the First Congregational Church, and the Polytechnic High School in Long Beach; and on February 5 we sailed on the *Lurline* for Honolulu. On that voyage we began a warm friendship with Allan Lehman, of the famous banking firm; we were surprised to find the soul of a poet in this modest financier.

It was a rough trip, but I did not let my rolling stomach keep me from making progress with the second draft of *The Life of Greece*. Generally I wrote at home the first draft of the ten volumes constituting *The Story of Civilization;* for there I could spread my data slips and garnered clippings across my drawing board, keep a dozen reference books and dictionaries within reach, and have increasingly the help and inspiration of Ariel. Parts of this initial manuscript were taken on my lecture tours, risking many adventures (like the mishap at Durant, Oklahoma); and on trains and planes, and between interviews, dinners, and orations, I anodyned my loneliness by rewriting every paragraph before sending the pages to faithful and competent "Sally" (actually Regina) Sands—and later to our equally competent daughter, Ethel—to be typed. Max Schuster used to display these typescripts as models to revisionist authors.

We reached Honolulu on February 10, and were ritually lassoed with leis by buxom Hawaiian belles. We were so overcome by this pretty custom, by the welcome so universally offered us, and by the blue skies and open-air life, that when I reached the office of President Crawford I could not resist telling him, "I feel as if I had entered Paradise, and you must be God." If David Crawford was not a deity he was a wise and kindly man, whose spirit had not been hardened by administrative and disciplinary chores. We had a choice of a room at the Halekulani Hotel for eighteen dollars a day or two simple rooms in a student dormitory at two dollars a day. We chose the latter, and ate in the college cafeteria at fifty cents a meal. We felt as if we were students again.

However, this insatiable student had to lecture as agreed. Never have I faced a more generous audience. Many dignitaries of the island, and their ladies, joined the faculty to hear the timid rash intellectual tell them just how to run the world. Men who led the industries, plantations, and government of the territory took all this calmly, and invited us to their palaces; one of them offered us a home, and the use of a car, if we would move to Honolulu. The newspapers gave the lectures prominent and favorable reports. But one columnist did not like me; he wrote a powerful indictment of me as a crypto-Bolshevik, condemned the lectures as superficial, and wondered why so much fuss had been made over us. Ariel neglected to preserve this item, but her comment on it made the rounds of the Honolulu intelligentsia: "This must be Paradise, for we have found a snake in the grass."

We left Honolulu on February 26, and reached San Francisco on March 3, 1938. On our way across the United States we had to stop at Omaha for one more exposition of "The World Conflict"; this was catching up on me, for Hitler was making martial moves. The *City of San Francisco* streamliner deposited us at Omaha at 3:45 A.M. on March 7. That night Ariel, sitting at the speakers' table, slept throughout my discourse, to the amusement and envy of my audience. The next morning, at 1:35, we caught a train to Chicago for another visit with Dr. Zurawski. On March 12 we reached home.

Ethel and Louis came for the Easter holidays. Louis, arriving, spent no time on greetings; he threw his hat in the air, rushed to the phonograph, and placed upon the turntable a record that he had brought from Cornell for the special gratification of my classical tastes. It was an explosive farrago called "Tiger Rag," whose wild cacophony seemed to his unspoiled barbarism the music of the spheres. That done, he embraced us. He was making the grade at Cornell despite inadequate preparation in high school, and he could be indulged in a merry prank.

Ethel's problem was more complex. On her weekends home she developed an affection for David Easton, a handsome law student who gave every sign of being a gentleman and becoming a breadwinner. But this new ecstasy made the Bryn Mawr curriculum quite savorless. Ethel lost interest in her studies, and pleaded with us to let her exchange college for marriage. "David is my major subject," she argued. Privately I sympathized with Ethel's feeling that a college education was not the best way to prepare a young woman for marriage. But we counseled delay.

Soon spring slipped by, and I faced another commitment: to repeat at UCLA the two courses I had given there in 1936. The idea occurred to me that Louis and Ethel might take courses in the summer session, and get credit for them at Cornell and Bryn Mawr. They liked the notion, perhaps because it promised to let them motor across the United States and back; each of them was and is a good driver. So on June 12 we set out in two cars: Ethel, Mary, I, and some baggage in one, Ariel, Flora, Louis, and Mike in the other. We stopped at three points en route to pay with lectures the cost of our jaunt. We arrived at Los Angeles June 26, tired, sunburned, and happy. I had engaged the Phi Beta Phi sorority house at 700 Hilgard Avenue, Westwood; the twelve rooms and four baths were just the arrangement that our troupe required. The next morning I began my courses, and Ethel and Louis attended other classes. Ethel flirted with a handsome young doctor, but found time to type the chapters on art and science for *The Life of Greece*.

There were some alert young actresses among my students. One of them, Sally Eilers, spread the news of my lectures around the studios, and Ariel and I were invited to meet celebrities. I was introduced to John Barrymore, who was as handsome as ever; but he seemed half asleep, and could not act more than a line at a time; it was pitiful to see the wreck of the man whose face and charm had almost swept us off our feet as he danced his partner into a bedroom in *Reunion in Vienna*. Mrs. Carmel Myers Blum arranged a party for us, where we had a chance to see some stars and starlets at close range; we found them not very good-looking but very likable, and more modest than we had expected. After dinner we played a game called "In the Manner of the Word": one of them went out of the room while the rest agreed on a word—usually an adverb—which, when he returned, he was to guess from the way each of us acted the word. When "amorously" was chosen, and it came my turn to act, I took the opportunity to embrace the lady next to me, much to Ariel's displeasure at my crudity; at least I showed that seduction was not my forte. The adverb was best acted by Luise Rainer, who fondled a Chinese vase so lovingly and yet delicately that the word was soon guessed.

Later on that starlit evening, we sat on the floor, and I became the victim of a little game secretly arranged by Josef von Sternberg, who prompted Constance Collier to ask me, "Is there a God?" This was a strange question to put to a man who had eaten too much, had drunk some unaccustomed wine, and was absorbed in contemplating a circle of famous legs spread out within arm's reach before him. Luise Rainer raised her clasped hands to me pleadingly: "Please say yes." I answered, stumblingly, that there were many conceptions of the Supreme Being, from that of the child imaging a bearded patriarch sitting on a sunbeam to that of the philosopher thinking of God as the creative force in nature, in the combinations of atoms, in the growth of a plant or a child, in the reproductive power of a woman's body, in the wisdom of the sage or the benevolence of the saint—but here I suspect that I am embellishing my memory. I concluded that all these conceptions were legitimate in their place, and had served a function in the development of the individual or the community. I don't believe that anyone was satisfied, but Sternberg took me aside, confessed his trick, and thought I had done well enough for a man half intoxicated with wine, women, and food.

On July 26 Will Rogers gave a party at his ranch for Amelia Earhart, who was planning what proved to be her fatal flight. Ariel and Ethel and I were among some thirty guests. I half humorously proposed that Amelia should take me along; she patiently explained that her plane had no room for excess baggage. That afternoon was the last time we saw Rogers; soon afterward he flew to Alaska with Wiley Post; both were killed in a crash near Point Barrow.

My service at UCLA ended on August 5, and on the seventh we began to motor to the East. We stopped at Lake Tahoe to pick up Mary, who had gone there to establish residence for a divorce; during her stay she grew lonesome for her husband, Max Schwartz; when we reached New York she returned to him, and she has been a good wife ever since; they are still near and dear to us. Meanwhile Ethel had been gaining weight, and she asked us to let her off at Danville, New York, where she would spend a few weeks at Bernarr Macfadden's Physical Culture Hotel. I decided to stay the first week with her, and left Michael and Louis to handle the cars for the remainder of the drive to Great Neck.

I reached home on August 25. Ethel stayed in Danville till September 19, when she transferred her studies from Bryn Mawr to Sarah Lawrence College, while still making David Easton her major subject. Louis went back to Cornell. I buried myself in work on *The Life of Greece*.

We got off to a flying start in 1939: I left on January 11 for fifteen lectures in the Midwest, ending at Miami. Ariel undertook, "over my dead body," to drive down there with sister Mary in our new LaSalle— the most reliable, least troublesome car we have ever had. (A General Motors man in Chicago told me they had to discontinue it because too many buyers were preferring it to the Cadillac.) Even so it was an arduous enterprise, for most of the roads between New York and Florida, which were what we would now call second class, ran through crowded business centers. But Ariel managed it, as I judge from my letter from Lincoln, Nebraska.

1-15-39

You villain! You got off to a late start on the 11th, and nevertheless made Miami Beach on the 14th—four days for 1400 miles; 350 miles a day; and only you . . . to drive. What a man you'd be if your skirts and your husband didn't get in your way! But I'm glad you're not a man. . . .

Kansas City, 1-19-39

I am conscience-stricken when I think that I let you face that long trip to Miami with no one to help you drive or to face the difficulties that always punctuate an automobile tour. The thought of you driving in the rain all the way to Daytona Beach appalls. . . .

Everything well, except that a toilet seat fell on the most precious part of me and nearly broke it off. Every part of me joins in sending you love.

Apparently I received, en route, forwarded from Great Neck, the following letter from the liveliest, honestest mayor New York ever had:

January 17, 1939

DEAR MR. DURANT:

It was indeed a great pleasure to receive your very heartening letter of December 28th. I regret that at this time it is impossible for me to consider Mr. Lewis, whom you recommended for appointment to the Bench. . . . I think very highly of Mr. Lewis, and hope that some time his name will be reached for appointment.

Very truly yours,
F. L. LaGUARDIA

(P.S.) Do you recall the Sunday lectures at Labor Temple, some 25–30 years ago? I used to attend regularly, and learned a lot from you there.

F. L. G.

Husband and wife were reunited on February 15, and had twenty-four days in Miami Beach. Then we motored north to Cincinnati for four lectures in Ohio, and reached home on March 18. Soon thereafter I submitted the final pages of *The Life of Greece* to Simon and Schuster, and I could pay attention to what I at last realized was imminent war.

I was against it. I had no Anglo-Saxon blood in me, so that I could see some validity in the argument that Britain's control of the seas warranted the swelling industries of Germany and Austria in seeking some export outlet—and some sources of fuels and new materials—by breaking open a land route to the East. (I had as yet no conception of Hitler's resolve to exterminate the Jews of Germany by deliberate massacre.) So I defended Neville Chamberlain's Munich agreement with Hitler (September, 1938). If Hitler had his eye on the Ukraine as the political breadbasket of an industrial Germany, and was anxious to push through Czechoslovakia into Russia, why not let the two dictators—each of them irreconcilably hostile to the West—fight it out to a common exhaustion? Hitler's army, though now the strongest in Europe, might, like Napoleon's, be smothered in the "mattress" of Russian space; and even if victorious, German arms and money would be consumed for at least a decade in occupying and controlling a never-quite-conquered country. During that war and occupation France, England, and the United States would have time to arm themselves, to accumulate military material, to make more secure the allegiance of their dependencies and allies. (Such was my argument as given by the Chattanooga *Times* of July 7, 1939, in reporting my lecture there on July 6.) It was all nicely thought out, and worthy of Machiavelli, except that Hitler decided to march through Poland, and Poland and Great Britain had pledged themselves to mutual aid in case of attack. Britain kept her pledge, and World War II was on (August, 1939).

Amid the turmoil *The Life of Greece* came to a quiet birth (September

30, 1939). The preface began with a majestic declaration of method and intent. (Here, I suspect, I felt the influence of Macaulay's proud proem to his *History of England.*)

> My purpose is to record and contemplate the origin, growth, maturity, and decline of Greek civilization from the oldest remains of Crete and Troy to the conquest of Greece by Rome. I wish to see and feel this complex culture not only in the subtle and impersonal rhythm of its rise and fall, but in the rich variety of its vital elements: its way of drawing a living from the land, and organizing industry and trade; its experiments with monarchy, aristocracy, democracy, dictatorship, and revolution; its manners and morals, its religious practices and beliefs; its education of children, and its regulation of the sexes and the family; its homes and temples, markets and theaters and athletic fields; its poetry and drama, its painting, sculpture, architecture, and music; its sciences and inventions; its superstitions and philosophies. I wish to see and feel these elements not in their theoretical and scholastic isolation, but in their living interplay as the simultaneous movements of one great cultural organism, with a hundred organs and a hundred million cells, but one body and soul.

By conceiving the volume as the biography of a civilization, I was able to give it unity and continuity through a semicircular structure of rise and fall from birth to death. From the viewpoint of organization it is the best of my books.

I had not expected any great success for Volume II, for who would be interested in ancient history when present affairs were so exciting and so weighted with results for half the world? The reviews were nearly all favorable, but not enthusiastic; in any case the book surprised the author and the publishers by forging its way into the best-seller list till December, 1940. The most pleasant of several friendly comments came from Maurice Maeterlinck (as printed in the New York *Times* of December 17, 1940):

> DEAR SIR:
> I know not how to tell you with what interest and pleasure I have read your admirable *Life of Greece.*
> Like so many others, I thought that I knew Greece. But for the first time, in your book, I have found a united view, which embraced in one perspective all Hellas, gathered everything into its proper place, and incidentally taught me a great deal.
> To succeed in such an enterprise one needs an encyclopedic spirit, a universal erudition. And the miracle is that your learning is so profound, so natural, that it never encumbers the text. Everything flows from its source, as in the pages of Xenophon, and as if you had lived in the time of Pericles.
> In all the fields that you cover—whether it be literature, or science, or architecture, or politics, or sociology, or philosophy, or astronomy, etc.— you dominate your subject, or maintain the same high level, without ap-

parent effort. For example, your surveys of the dramas of Aeschylus, Sophocles, and Euripides have a clearness, a sureness, and an elevation that are admirable.

I have read this book with ever rising passionate interest, as if it were a novel. It is a masterpiece, and I salute in you the indefatigable worker, the great savant, the great critic whose critique palpitates with life, the great writer whose taste never errs.

With kindest remembrances and many thanks,

MAETERLINCK

Only a great and generous soul could have written such a letter.

Ethel was married to David Easton on November 18, 1939, at the Riverside Church, New York. The ceremony was performed by John Haynes Holmes, then at the peak of his career as the preacher of a living Christianity. David was a graduate of Dartmouth College and Columbia University Law School; a youth of good mind and character. We helped the couple with a substantial dowry, and found a home for them in walking distance of ours. I began to look forward to being a grandfather.

But my own future was now clouded by the growth and spread of arthritis in a score of my joints. A friendly doctor in Great Neck had, about 1936, argued me into abandoning my vegetarianism for a diet that took its proteins from meat. Whether my arthritis had any connection with this return to the hunting stage, I cannot say. I consulted various physicians, including Dr. Cecil, who had written on arthritis a volume as hefty as any of mine; he gave me an anti-gout regimen, and recommended golf; he interrupted one prescription by taking a golf club from a closet in his office and demonstrating a stance and grasp that might mend my weakened wrists. After a month without improvement I tried another specialist, who used diathermy and poisoned me with various injections; I grew worse. I decided to go back to my vegetarian diet, and to put myself in the hands of my old mentor, Dr. John Harvey Kellogg, who had opened a new Battle Creek in Miami Springs, Florida.

Ariel and I drove down together in December, 1940, taking Flora and Mary with us. A preliminary examination showed that almost every joint in my body was affected; and the dynamometer, measuring the strength of my pulls with arms and legs, neck and feet, showed me shamefully weak. I confessed my bloody sins; the good doctor forgave me and comforted me: "We have had many cases of arthritis here; we have cured some, we have benefited all." He showed me the knuckles of his right hand. "I had it myself," he said, "but nothing remains of it but a slight elevation of some knuckles." Evidently vegetarians were not immune.

I settled down under the complex drugless treatment that he prescribed: a big glass of orange juice three times a day; a vegetarian diet low in starches and sweets (I believe our addiction to sweets is a main cause of arthritis); a daily hour of sweat-producing exercise; a vigorous massage; an electric steam bath; a shower bath alternately hot and cold; an hour in the men's solarium, naked under the sun; and a nightly enema. I could stay only three weeks, but in that time sixty percent of the arthritis disappeared; my neck was still stiff, but my wrists and ankles were strong again; and I set out on a lecture tour carrying my bags without pain. Every day on that tour I took a long and vigorous walk, followed by a hot and cold shower; I stuck to my vegetarian diet through all tempting banquets (but still indulged my sweet tooth); I laid in a supply of nuts to replace meat. By the end of that tour only twenty percent of the arthritis remained. A bit of it still persists: now and then in the "pinkies," some in the neck. Every night Ariel and I go through calisthenics to keep that devil—and others—away.

For all his guidance Dr. Kellogg refused to take a penny. My dear friend Dr. Stone called him a quack; I repeat that he was a saint.

CHAPTER XVII

To Rome

1940–43

Ariel:

Will hands the pen to me here, but really these years are all his story; he carried our fate in his health and in his head—which was now throbbing with the history of Rome. While he made his way through one audience after another, Flora, Mary, and I took an apartment in Miami Beach, and daily waited for his letters. Nearly always they ended with a word of love, not altogether spiritual. So from Springfield, Massachusetts, January 8, he concluded: "What I remember above all is our last kisses; their sweetness lingers in my memory, almost on my lips. I am already lonesome and hungry for you. Look for me under your pillow on the 20th. . . . " From Bartlesville, Oklahoma, came a real love letter:

1-25-40

DEAREST:

You can't know how much your letters mean to me. . . . Cooped up here now in a little town far from anyone I know, your letter, full of you and love, . . . has brought me such pleasure that reading it I sat quiet for several minutes, "smiling all over," as when I hear fine music. Write me some more!

Knowing how jealous I was of the pretty, outflowing women whom he met on his lecture tours, he sent me assurances of fidelity—too frequently for belief. Apparently these ladies were too kaleidoscopic, for on January 29 he sent me a long telegram asking me to join him in California. So on February 6 I set out with Mary (Flora returning to New York to be near Louis, now a graduate engineer), and began the long trek to Los Angeles—not by train, as he had advised, but by car.

Our memorandum book for 1940 has disappeared, and I can only guess that we spent some ten days in or near Hollywood. I note a letter from Douglas Fairbanks, Jr., March 13, telling us that "both Mary Lee and myself are so delighted with your visit to our house." Apparently we drove east together as far as Livingston, Kentucky, and I continued with my sister to New York while our breadwinner filled some engagements in the Middle West. We were rather reckless in those days, crossing and recrossing the country by car when all America was debating whether the United States should enter the war. Will argued for abstention, as witness his letter of June 13, 1940, to the New York *Times*:

To the Editor:
Sir:

I think I have felt as deeply as any other American, excepting our President, the tragedy of the news that your magnificent reporting has brought us from Europe in the last ten months. I detest despotism, and have always fought on the side of freedom; I owe everything that I am or have to the opportunities and the tolerance afforded me by our American institutions and ways. I have denounced the despicable treatment of minorities in Germany, and long ago I signed—and have since tried to carry out—the boycott against German goods. I have in a hundred public addresses, since September 1st, urged unstinted material aid to the Allies. The triumph of the Fascist philosophy in the war would be a major disaster for democracy and liberalism everywhere; it would promote religious and racial divisions, and would inflate to unbearable proportions the amateur dictators that lurk amongst us, waiting for their day. I say nothing of potential victories for German trade; for I do not suppose that any humane American would want to shed the blood of our youth for foreign markets so long as there are 30,000,000 Americans whose pitiably low standard of life creates a challenge to our economic genius, and a possible market, here within our doors, for all the goods that our inventive industry can produce.

But I can understand how a great number of my fellow-citizens, seeing the terrible plight and ordeal of the French and British peoples, could be so deeply moved that they see cowardice in every caution and feel that every American youth should enlist in a war to preserve the beauty that is France and the freedom that is England. Though born in Massachusetts, French was my native tongue; I know what it means to love France; and I am horrified at the spectacle of her gracious soil overrun by her ancient enemies, and at the prospect of the fairest city on earth being shattered into ruins by a million guns and bombs. I know that the Government of Great Britain has created, and that her empire has disseminated, liberty more bravely and abundantly than any other nation in history. I recognize the quiet heroism of the British, their willingness to die without rhetoric, their unequaled success in reconciling freedom with order, and power with

211

courtesy. When Americans of French or British descent cry out to us to send our conscripted manhood to the rescue of their mother countries—mother of the best in our institutions—I sympathize so strongly with their call that I would never utter one word against it if I were not haunted by the faces of young men.

Like millions of other Americans I have been distracted during the day, and kept awake at night, by the awful question, What should we do? . . .

My own answer, submitted with the diffidence of one who has often been wrong, is that we should offer the Allies, with no financial profit to ourselves, all the aid of our resources and our credit; but that under no circumstances should we engage in war outside this continent and our own possessions, or compel any American family to sacrifice its sons on a foreign battlefield. Half the meaning of America has been that it should be a haven of refuge from the wars and hates of Europe; to let ourselves be lured into them again would be to surrender forever the American dream. For my part I shall refuse to hate anyone. . . .

I would not despair of England and France. If they are right they cannot be defeated long; sooner or later the consciousness of right will give them the strength to overcome in their turn an enemy weakened by the pride and sloth of victory, and the dissensions born of wealth. Nor do I despair of civilization; it has survived many crises in the past and will survive this one. Democracy can be destroyed only by its own incompetence, extravagance, disorder, and dishonesty; Christianity can be destroyed only by forgetting the simplicity and sincerity of its Founder; great civilizations and states must break down from within before they can be conquered from without. If we do not deserve to die, we shall live.

WILL DURANT

I trust that Maurice Maeterlinck and Jules Romains had not seen that letter when (October 3, 1940) they met Will as participants in a symposium at a reception given by the Walt Whitman Society at the Cherry Valley Club of Long Island "to distinguished French and Belgian Guests." Those leaders of French literature were among the refugees from fallen France, and they were naturally hoping that the United States would soon go to her rescue. Maeterlinck spoke in French, Romains in English, Will in American, and Countess Renée Maeterlinck sang in French Whitman's poem "O Star of France." Will avoided the question of America's entry, and spoke of his great debt to French culture. Maeterlinck expressed a desire to meet him again.

So we arranged a dinner party at our home on October 27. The Belgian poet-philosopher came with his wife and an interpreter, Romains came with an interpreter, Charlie Chaplin came with Tim Durant, Max Schott brought his wife, Alice, Max Schuster came with Dick Simon, and our family completed the cast. The language barrier threatened to obstruct the flow of genius, but Chaplin saved the evening by explaining to Max Schott the evils of capitalism. Charlie spoke with his customary vivacity;

the president of Climax Molybdenum Corporation listened smiling, questioning the actor's competence in economics, but admiring his verve. That party was my severest trial as a hostess, but Will assured me that I had performed well.

Soon thereafter he was off on another campaign. From the Stevens (now the Conrad Hilton) Hotel in Chicago he sent a billet-doux as sensual as ever:

11-3-40

Hello, sweetheart, sweet body, sweet soul! . . . I took a long walk on the lake front today, and missed you; when last I promenaded here you were waiting in the hotel, and I could *feel* you at every step. I passed the spot where you and I awaited the car for the Minneapolis plane on October 9th; now I looked around for you, but you were far away. I get to miss you more and more with each trip, and I wish you could join me at least once a week wherever I go. . . . And—don't be shocked—I miss you more because my love for you is more complete than ever—shamelessly physical as well as spiritually so enslaving that I can't think without thinking of you. . . .

Make yourself beautiful for [our reunion on] November 9th. I shall then want to celebrate my birthday with you, but with no other gift asked of you except *yourself*.

Why don't you fly to me?

Mad about you,
WILL

He was with me for a while in November; then away again. He returned to New York 6 P.M. December 13, just in time to address the National Association of Manufacturers at its annual dinner. He had written out his speech, which was published by *The Saturday Evening Post* (January 18, 1941) under the title "Self-Discipline or Slavery." Reading it now, I find in it the first expression of Will's feeling that we Americans were carrying freedom to an excess where it threatened social order and moral character. Some paragraphs of that lecture show Will in stern reaction against his youth.

Every truth is tempted to expand until it becomes a falsehood. Every virtue is made a vice through excess, and nothing fails like excess. In all the realms of our democratic life liberty has run its course from stimulus to disorder, from beneficence to disintegration.

Freedom of thought, speech and press melted down old basic stabilizing customs, traditions and beliefs. Science, subsidized and hypnotized by its own mechanisms, turned biology into physics and chemistry, and could see nothing else in the world except machines. Philosophy, divorced from the growth and miracle of the soil, capitulated to an enervating skepticism, a hopeless cynicism that found in completed rebellion the same absurdities and tyrannies, and in science the same incredibilities, as in the rules and faiths of older days.

Education, above all in America, surrendered to the student. For the most part he chose his teachers and his courses, discountenanced discipline, avoided tasks that required concentration, and helped a superannuated curriculum to transform school and college days into an enfeebling isolation from the realities and responsibilities of life. Pedagogy gave up the training of character, and devoted itself to equipping the unmoral intellect with all the armory of science. Now the intellect is an individualist; when it discovers the tricks of thought and reason it uses them for the aggrandizement of the individual self; only late in life does it discover the necessity and needs of the group, without whose co-operation and survival the civilized individual could not be. . . .

Whatever the newly emancipated intellect could not understand was rejected as false, and ideas were venerated in inverse proportion to their age. Ancient faiths began to lose their hold on the mind, and their moral influence on urban life. Every lad of eighteen sat in judgment upon institutions of society, and codes of conduct, that represented the experience of a thousand generations of men; if he could not understand in one adolescence what had been learned in a millennium, he was free to trust his powerful eighteen-year-old reason, and to reject the family as tyranny, marriage as bondage, religion as opium, government as exploitation, and property as theft. Every restraint aroused resentment; standards faded from conduct—even, here and there, from memory. Individualism flourished in morals, especially among those who denounced it in industry. A thousand brave experiments were made in the relations of the sexes, a million lives were ruined, a million marriages and families were broken up. The stoicism that had cleared the wilderness and made a civilization passed, in many men and some women, into the epicureanism that reveled through night after night, exhausting the body and emptying the soul. . . .

Let us begin at the beginning and proclaim, with all the humility of a repentant prodigal, the return of discipline to our homes. Libertarian education was a mistake, a pleasant indulgence of parental love, a week inability on our own part to command because we had never learned to obey. The result is an adolescence without responsibility, a maturity without character; and the maturity of our children will not thank us for the liberty of their youth. To exact nothing of a child that its intellect cannot understand and approve is the depth of the nonsense to which some of us dedicated ourselves in the days of our dreams. Parents must learn again to command, to assign duties and see to it that they are performed; they must not be ashamed to require—and must fit themselves to deserve—filial respect, quiet obedience, and such courtesy as may comport with the vigor and exhilaration of growth.

It was predominantly the reaction of a fifty-five-year-old man to the unprecedented speed of social change; but near the end Will told the most conservative audience in the United States that it must learn to live with the Roosevelt revolution:

In general the reforms of the last three administrations should be amended rather than rejected; essentially—if an inexpert opinion may be allowed—they are sound, and may peaceably mitigate that natural concentration of wealth which periodically disturbs every vital society. They will help our economic system to meet the challenge of thirty million Americans living on the edge of destitution and forming for our production a potential market as precious as any for which we may wage a costly war. The spread of profit sharing would give the worker a stake in the stability of the firm and industry for which he works. We must put a bit of America under every American.

Now that Ethel was making her own home, and Louis had found work in the West, we were free to go south and spend the Christmas holidays at the "Miami Battle Creek." After two weeks in this paradise, Will flew north for his semiannual bout with audiences, dinners, and storms.

On January 19, 1941, suffering from a headache, a cold, and a running nose, he hurried from an afternoon engagement at Newton, Massachusetts, to catch a plane from Boston to New York, and there another to Miami. On his arrival there at five-forty the next morning he was met at the airport by a masseur from the sanitarium, who, when he saw Will's condition, invited him to come at once into the treatment room "and be cured." "Cured of a cold?" Will asked. "I thought there was no cure?" But he agreed, and after surprising me in bed, and explaining why he must not kiss me, he changed his clothes and disappeared. When I saw him again, two hours later, his cold was gone. He summarized the miracle:

"First, they gave me two enemas. Then a massage. Then a steam bath till I was reeking with sweat. Then a hot and cold shower, which I was sure would turn my cold into pneumonia; then, with a hose, they played strong jets of alternately hot and cold water upon every part of my body except my head and genitals; then a vigorous rubdown; then banishment to the solarium, where for almost an hour I let the sun warm my naked flesh. The cold had gone. Now I'm ready to jump at the next audience I see."

I could hardly believe that he had had so bad a cold as described, but I have never yet caught him in a lie—perhaps because he has a good memory.

On January 31 he was off again into the Middle West. As Colston Leigh had dated him for February 15 with the Knife and Fork Club of Mexico City, Will drew up a travel schedule by which I could precede him to the Mexican capital, and could visit Havana on the way.

I arrived in Havana just when Batista was preparing to overthrow the Machado government; the coup was effected during the night without disturbing my sleep. Nobody seemed to pay much attention to the event; revolutions in Latin America are sometimes more peaceful and orderly than a presidential election in the United States. I did not let this changing of the guard upset my determination to see all the sights, especially the forbidden ones. A German transient offered to chaperon me if I would pay all expenses; I agreed. We visited some nightclubs, where I enjoyed the lusty-sentimental music, and saw the rhumba, the samba, and other dances that were soon to become popular in the States; we sampled the red-light district along the waterfront, and risked a drink in the "Shooting the Horse" tavern.

On the following day I foolishly allowed my cicerone to row me about the bay. When I saw him pulling out to the open sea I took fright, and bade him turn back to the shore. He refused, and I began to have visions of being thrown overboard in one more "American tragedy." Another boat came within hailing distance; I appealed to the men for help; they drew alongside and helped me to step from one boat to the other; the German cursed me as a coward.

Safe on shore, but fearful that some harm might come to me from the vengeful Teuton. I resolved to leave Cuba as soon as possible. However, the steamer which Will's *Railway Guide* described as plying between Havana and Vera Cruz had suspended service; I could get no space on any scheduled flight; and in a flurry of fright I paid three hundred dollars to a private aviator to fly me to Mérida.

There I found myself within a day's reach of Chichén Itzá, site of some famous remains of the Mayan-Toltec culture that had flourished in Yucatán hundreds of years before the Spanish conquest of Mexico. I mused that Will would want to cover that period in *The Story of Civilization;* perhaps I could save him a difficult trip by visiting the ruins myself and gathering firsthand impressions and details. I was told that no bus or train service reached Chichén Itzá; that I would have to walk many miles through the rude hamlets of the vestigial Mayan population, and that I would find no safe shelter, no trustworthy food or drink. Before setting out I wrote a solemn letter to Will, telling him of my plan, and assuring him that I would be happy to die in his service, and that my last thoughts would be of him and Ethel. I was drunk with drama.

The next day I rode for hours on a ramshackle bus along a corrugated road, and then for hours I marched through the scattered settlements of the poorest people I had ever seen, who nevertheless were sternly proud of their Mayan blood. At Chichén Itzá I found a village of some twenty families, living in huts around the slowly disintegrating temple and pyramids of a lordly past. I climbed, on my hands and knees, up the broken steps of the massive mound that served as pedestal for a fortresslike "castello" one hundred feet high. I surveyed my surroundings, took notes for Will, and then began the dangerous descent; which I managed by slipping down, step by step, on my hands and knees and belly. That night, though the natives offered me the hospitality of their huts, I slept on a hammock with all my clothes on; I was still not sure that in some orgy of piety I woud not be sacrificed, as a presumptive virgin, to an Aztec god. I woke up prosaically safe, and walked and bounced back for what seemed to be a hundred miles to Mérida. There I caught a scheduled flight to Mexico City (February 6).

I did not like the Ritz Hotel, where a room had been reserved for us; I found the Hotel Geneva quieter. On the fifteenth Will flew in from Corpus Christi, delivered his lecture, and then relaxed for ten days of sightseeing and high blood pressure; one day, as he sat reading, his nose began to bleed. Nevertheless we managed to see Chapultepec, Xochimilco, Oaxaca, Guadalupe, and Taxco, and the curator of antiquities guided us through some of the most recent excavations of pre-Columbian remains. Meanwhile we came to love the Mexican people—their songs, their passion, their laughter, their somber tradition of a colorful civilization slain by superior guns. The government encouraged our studies by giving us a pass for all the railways of Mexico.

On February 25 we left by train for Juárez. We had recently learned that Kevin Lynch—Will's victorious classmate at St. Peter's College—was now among the most honored physicians of El Paso. On reaching the border I called him up; in half an hour he was with us, hardly changed (Will assured him) from the time of their graduation thirty-four years before; he was still handsome, kindly, athletic. He guided us smoothly through the customs barriers, and drove us to his suburban home, where his wife, Florence, had prepared a breakfast that gave us ballast for all that flighty day. She had, at brief notice, brought together some of her literary friends, and she prevailed upon both Will and me to make brief speeches. Will was so moved with affection for Kevin that he soared aloft into a philosophical discourse on friendship as surmounting all differences of race or creed. Then Kevin rushed us to the airport, where we caught a plane that enabled Will to keep a lecture appointment in San Francisco. Already in those days a lecturer's itinerary relied largely on planes, though most contracts held him financially responsible for engagements broken by plane delays. I accompanied my troubadour through nearly all the remainder of his schedule. We did not reach home till April 10.

We found there a letter from a man unreasonably accused, in the public memory, of responsibility for the Depression of 1929–33:

March 13, 1941

MY DEAR MR. DURANT:

I hear that you are going around the country saying kind things about me. I want you to know that anyone, taking as many brickbats as I am at the moment, is most grateful for those [comments?] that are helpful.

Yours faithfully,
HERBERT HOOVER

At Lake Hill that summer Will worked ten hours a day on *Caesar and Christ*, and one vigorous hour a day in the garden that helped to keep him in health. We interrupted our stay in the mountains to go to New York in July to attend the funeral of our friend Dr. Hannah Stone, one of the heroines of the birth control movement in America. When we tried to console her husband, Abe said quietly, "We were very close." We have rarely heard deep feeling so simply but strongly expressed. Back in the Catskills we had the comfort of many new friends—Jack Greenberg and Charles Bensley (both of the New York Board of Education), Drs. Frank Teller and Edward Lear, and others; we came together once a week in a discussion club that was a model of civilized debate. When the trees began to don their autumn gold Will set off again to add to what he called our "Civilization Kitty." He was now fifty-six, but his letters were as sensual as ever. In one of them (February 5, 1944) he gave a novel apology for his sensual wooing:

> Instead of deriving spiritual love from physical desire (which may be biologically true), I find physical desire deriving from spiritual love; you could not be so sweet to me if you were not so dear. But the sensual De Maupassant stole my lightning when he wrote: *"Dans le véritable amour c'est l'âme qui enveloppe le corps*—in real love it is the soul" (of one) "that embraces the body" (of the other).

Some of his letters were disturbed with worry about Ethel, who, like her mother twenty-two years earlier, was having a troubled pregnancy. Will begged her doctor to keep meat out of her diet in the final months, but the doctor refused.

From Janesville, Wisconsin, November 24, 1941, Will wrote: "I am sure that Ethel and her baby would have cleaner blood if she took a [high-colonic] twice a week, taking care to keep the pressure of the water down to say one half of the usual amount." And from Chicago on November 28: "I think of you, and of Ethel, every waking hour. Please ask the doctor again shouldn't Ethel avoid meat, fish, and eggs, for the remainder of her pregnancy." On November 30, suffering much pain, Ethel was taken to a hospital in New York. The physicians there decided upon a Caesarean operation for December 2. We expected Will to arrive that day, but he did not. Let him explain.

Will:

On December 1, at Kansas City, I received a telegram about Ethel's condition. I had to give two lectures that day. I managed to get a seat on a plane early the next morning; but we were grounded at Pittsburg by stormy weather, and had to change to a crawling train. I wired Ariel that I could not reach the hospital till late that night. As I rode through a heavy rain that afternoon I could not take my thoughts from the danger of losing a daughter who was very dear to both her parents; and I denounced myself for being so far from her as she faced her trial. Then the sun came out in the shape of a conductor who handed me a telegram from Ariel: "Ethel has given birth to a boy. Both are well." I was so overcome with gratitude to everyone from God to Western Union that I felt on the verge of disturbing the whole car with my cries of relief. I went into the smoking room, locked myself in the toilet, and let my tears flow freely, while I repeated, again and again, "Thank God! My dear Ethel! Thank God!" When I reached her bedside at 11 P.M. she had just regained consciousness. She held out her arms to me. And my grandson Jim, washed and simian, looked unspeakably beautiful. Three days later my father, eighty-seven years old, came alone from Arlington, New Jersey, to embrace his granddaughter, and to welcome Jimmy as one more great-grandchild. So, through all the woes and joys of the human comedy, the race stumbles on.

December 7, 1941, was a bright Sunday in Great Neck, with a foot of snow on the ground, and the sun beaming in anticipation of his solstice victory over the forces of darkness. I went out for a long walk with two neighbors—Joe Eaton and Art Young (our second friend of that name). We discussed the war in Europe, and the negotiations then proceeding in Washington with emissaries from Japan. Would Japan, then allied with the fascist powers, attack the United States if no accord was reached? "No," I assured my friends; "the Japanese will never attack us as long as we stay out of the war; they have too much sense." When our walk ended at the Eaton home, the radio was announcing that a Japanese fleet and air force had that day attacked United States vessels in Pearl Harbor, had destroyed or fatally damaged nearly all of them, and had escaped unharmed. I discarded my robes as a seer, and joined ninety percent of the American people in ardent support of President Roosevelt's summons to war.

Ariel:

We had not yet heard the most revolting aspects of Hitler's genocidal massacre, but I had heard enough to rejoice at Will's conversion to Roosevelt's view that America could not tolerate a Hitler victory. Like Flora, to whom Louis was now the sustaining solace and pride, we worried that our collective son would almost certainly be drafted, but none of us—Louis least of all—did anything to prevent it. He was now twenty-five years old; he was working in Salt Lake City; and when Will spoke there in February he spent some pleasant hours with the young engineer.

2-22-42

In the evening [February 21] Louis came, took me out to dinner in the pretty "coffee shop" . . . [Today] Louis came at one; we had lunch, and are now in my room, cheated out of the long walk we had planned because a thick wet snow is falling, and Louis has a cold. So we read till 3, then lay down on the bed, "side by each," and took a nap. Lou is still snoozing as I write. It's good to be with him; he's completely healthy (despite his cold) in body, mind, and character; and we can all be happy in his fine develop-ment. . . .

In the evening [February 22] . . . Louis took me to his apartment, . . . which he shares with another engineer. He speaks in high terms of this roommate, and indeed of all the men who are associated with him at the Remington Arms plant; one of the finest qualities in him is that he very seldom speaks ill of anyone, and is continually telling me what a "fine fellow" so-and-so is. . . . He showed me your last letter to him; it was full of characteristic tenderness. He said, "Yes, I think Ariel loves me." The thought that you and I [as well as his mother] have so high a regard and profound an affection for him serves as a kind of strong basis for his life, and keeps him cheerful amid minor difficulties and possibly lonely wanderings.

After spending an hour in his cozy rooms I braved the tempest like King Lear, and tho it was still snowing rather heavily I turned up my pants, put on my rubbers, buttoned up my neck, and set out thru the snow for the two-mile walk from his place to the hotel. It was a pleasure to buck the storm, to spit the snow out of my mouth, to shake it out of my diminutive mustache; and when I reached my room I had the unusual thrill of one who has at last proved to himself that he is a man. I cleaned up under a hot and cold shower and slept the sleep of a virtuous boy.

I believe it was at Lake Hill, that summer, that Will wrote, for *The Saturday Evening Post*, a threnody on "Freedom of Worship," as one of four essays, by different authors, to accompany the remarkable paintings Norman Rockwell made to illustrate the "Four Freedoms" which, in the President's view, America was fighting to protect. Rockwell's picture showed seven faces, six of them in prayer, but one of them with the sad, quizzical wonder of a skeptic in and around his eyes. Will felt that he was hardly the man to write acceptably on religion, but he softened his doubts with sympathetic understanding of the villagers who attended services in the little church down the road from our Lake Hill home.

An echo of the Nazi fury reached our doors in the person of Naoum Aronson and his accomplished wife, Hélène. He was one of France's greatest living sculptors, but because he and his wife were Jews they had to flee from the fascist occupation of Paris, and after a thousand tribula-tions they found their way to a cottage in Woodstock, New York. I am no judge of art, and perhaps Will is not, either; but we marveled at the photographs of Naoum's works, then secreted in France. We became very fond of him and Hélène, and did what we could to help and console them. He repaid us many times over by making a flattering pastel of me, which hangs in Will's study as a memento of that friendship.

When we returned to Great Neck Will responded to an appeal from the

U.S. Treasury to speak at meetings for the sale of war bonds; and we bought many of them ourselves, not minding that "history is inflationary." In October the revived patriot went off again on the lecture circuit, competing with the government, the Army, and the Navy for trains and planes. He continued to send me risqué bouquets. At Kansas City he was met by Louis, who was now a sergeant. The *Star* caught them in a fine pose of father and son, and Will, perhaps for the first time, had Louis as a captive in his audience. Soon thereafter Louis was accepted by the Air Force, and was sent south for training.

Ethel, in January, 1943, moved to Washington, where Justice Frank Murphy had secured a place for her husband, David, in the National Labor Relations Board. We went to Ethel's Great Neck home to help her prepare her belongings for transport; still thinking of himself as an athlete, Will carried many heavy parcels from house to car, and so severely sprained his back that it took months to recover.

I left for Los Angeles, and Will set out for more lectures. He had to, for most of our savings were tied up in war bonds, and his royalties had sunk below a thousand dollars a year; *The Story of Civilization* was not then a money-maker. While he was losing his tonsils for the second time, at Battle Creek, Michigan, I lost forty-two pounds in California. On reaching Los Angeles (January 21, 1943), I found myself harassed with gall bladder pains. With Esther Talbot, a friend, I went to Murietta Springs and adopted, on my own responsibility, a reckless diet which I hoped would cleanse my internal organs as well as clear my skin, and would bring me back to a presentable form; for four weeks I lived on buttermilk as my only food—two glasses three times a day. I grew so weak that I had to give up bicycling and any but short walks, but I persisted. When Esther and others warned me that I was carrying my fad to foolish excess, I pretended that I was acting on the doctor's advice and under his care. In any case the gall bladder pains disappeared, and my skin cleared.

On February 17 I returned to Los Angeles, took an apartment at 848 South Oxford Street, and prepared for Will's arrival the next day. He came an hour before I had expected him, and found me lying naked under the ministrations of a masseuse. He could hardly recognize me, for I had reduced from 158 pounds to 116; and perhaps he was not sure that he had not entered the wrong apartment. When I held out my arms to him he cried out that he had found a young wife.

We entered upon a week as happy as could be in a land at war. We renewed old friendships with George Brown and Upton Close; through George we met Mario and Ruth Chamlee (former stars of the Metropolitan Opera), whom we came to love; and through Upton we met Fred Blickfeld, who was to be our guide and mentor in Hollywood. Soon we formed new friendships with Ruth Conrad, David and Geraldine Kroll,

Signor Italo Montemezzi and his wife Katherine, Richard and Eleanor Hageman, Harry and Lilian Kaufman, Richard and Mildred Crooks, Wayne and Elinor Griffin, Marie and Eric Scudder, John Anson Ford, Theodore Dreiser, Lion Feuchtwanger, Sian-Mae and Hsin-hai Chang, and many others. Upton took us to meet Walt Disney, who showed us his staff in the process of animating their famous figures; however, we did not meet the man who had filmed *The Vanishing Desert*—one of the most realistic and Darwinistic pictures ever put upon the screen.

Indeed, we had so many friends in or near Los Angeles that we now asked ourselves why should we not make this city of brief sunny winters and cool summer nights our home—and if Will had to cross the continent once or twice a year to earn a living, why not cross it from west to east and back rather than from east to west and back to east? Will was fond of snow, but I worried when, though approaching his sixtieth year, he insisted on cleaning the snow from our Great Neck driveway and pathway with his own big shovel and minuscule muscle; I had heard of heart attacks from such displays. We kept our eyes open for a tempting new home, but our tastes and our pocketbooks seemed never to jibe.

On February 28 Will once more occupied the pulpit of his old friend James W. Fifield, at the First Congregational Church in Los Angeles. He took for his subject "A Philosophy of Life for our Times," in which, among other ventures, he expressed a pantheism that must have disturbed that audience a bit; God, he told it, is the creative power in nature—in the growth and flowering of plants, the physical and mental development of children, the stirrings of love and genius. Jim, who might have winced at such a dilution of Jehovah, took it as poetic license, and offered to help the poet find a landing place in Los Angeles. He obtained from his bank a list of the properties it had for sale, and steered Will to what is now our home.

They found it in discouraging disrepair, with windows broken, a wall and floor ruined by rain, and, covering the surrounding two acres, weeds four feet tall. However, the house itself was sturdily and handsomely built, it had thirteen rooms, and it stood on a hill overlooking Hollywood and with a view through Beverly Hills even to Santa Monica and the sunlit Pacific. Will was so unwilling to burden me with the task of rehabilitating this "Casa della Vista" (as its builder had christened it) that he returned the keys to the bank. But when he described the property to me I insisted on seeing it. That evening we climbed over the concrete wall that surrounded the property, waded through the weeds, stood on the front terrace, and marveled at a city sparkling below us with a hundred million lights. I urged Will to get those keys the next morning; he did, we examined those thirteen rooms, and agreed that they could safely (barring an earthquake or two) shelter ourselves, Ethel, David, Jimmy, Louis—if we could meet the price asked. Negotiations were begun, but we had to return east before an agreement could be reached.

On March 9 I went with Will to San Francisco, where he had to address the Town Hall in the Curran Theater. While we were in that lovely but chilly city word came to us that Will's father had passed away. We struggled all day to get airplane passage to New York, but all seats for the next three days had been taken by military or governmental personnel. Will's habitual gaiety was now subdued, but he consoled himself with the thought that his father's death had been the natural end of a full and beautiful life.

We spent the summer at Lake Hill, and there in August, 1943, we received notice that our revised offer for the Hollywood house had been accepted. We returned to Great Neck, and began to prepare our furniture and our three thousand books for shipment across the country at a time when all railroad schedules were confused by war. In October we pulled up some deep roots, bade goodbye to a lovely house in Great Neck, and submitted cheerfully to the predictions of our neighboring friends that we would soon regret our departure from the centers of intellectual and political affairs in the East. They gave us a farewell party, and chanted a song beginning with "California, here we come," and ending with "Manhattan, here we come." We helped arrange that David should be soon transferred from Washington to the Department of Justice in Los Angeles, and sent word to Louis, then in Florida, that we had a new address—Hollywood, California. In October Will and I, with Dr. Stone, began another drive across the United States.

We arrived before our furniture, and while we waited for it Ruth Conrad put us up generously. It came on October 23; we suffered the usual tribulations of lost or damaged goods; and Will caught a cold helping the movers on an unusually cold day. Our beds and tables were set up, but our books were piled up on the floor of an upstairs room while a carpenter began to build shelves for them on all available walls. On November 7, while matters were still in disarray, Will took off for two weeks of lectures, and I was left undisputed mistress of chaos. He went all the way to Tampa in hope of seeing Louis before our young hero was sent overseas; but Louis had been transferred before his foster father came.

Plagued by the problems of wartime travel, Will made his way toilsomely through a dozen cities and back to his new home. Now, in a quiet, window-rimmed, semicircular study on the second floor rear, he spread out his slips again and wrote the concluding chapters of *Caesar and Christ: A History of Roman Civilization and of Christianity from Their Beginnings to A.D. 325.* Before moving west he had left most of the manuscript with Wallace Brockway for editorial scrutiny. When all of it reached the publishers, Max Schuster warmed us with an enthusiastic letter, and Dick Simon added a gracious note: "I can't help pausing, in the Day's Occupation, to tell you how wonderful it is to think that for all these seventeen years we have been publishing your books, Will, and to wish both of you a Merry Xmas out there where men are men."

Ten years later, in the preface to *The Reformation,* Will wrote:

> A tardy acknowledgment is due to my publishers. In my long association with them I have found them ideal. They have given me every consideration, have shared with me the expenses of research, and have never let considerations of profit or loss determine our relations. . . . We have been together now for twenty-seven years; and it has been for me a fortunate and happy union.

That union continued till Dick's death and Max's retirement. It continues with their successor, Leon Shimkin. They and I were and are the lucky partners of an undiscourageable monogamist.

CHAPTER XVIII

An Election and a Book

1944

Will:

Ariel took her time learning to love her new home; she could not forget the New York in which she had grown up; and for a while it seemed as if we would have to return to Great Neck. I think it was Fred Blickfeld who did most to help us fall in with our novel environment. This famous voice teacher to cinema stars had transformed into an Eden the hilly slopes around his own home; now he proposed to transfigure likewise the weedy, rocky soil of our Casa della Vista. He went with us to buy seeds, fertilizer, saplings, and tools; he led the way in brutally cutting off the prickly arms of cactus plants, in digging holes for a dozen palm trees, a dozen fruit trees, half a dozen nut trees. I nearly re-ruined my recently healed back in trying to emulate his energy; I wheeled so many barrows of fertilizer that Ariel called me "the Napoleon of the manure pile."

But she too fell in with the game. She was the only one among us who ever won an argument with our lovable dictator as to where and which trees should be planted; and meanwhile she fed us meals that were seasoned with her affection and our fatigue. When Fred prematurely passed away (1954) Ariel revised most of his work, and planted thirty trees and flowering shrubs, so that most of the place today, inside and out, is her work. Gradually, as chaos yielded to order, and old friends to new, she forgot New York, and came to love her hilltop home. Now we are resolved to abide there till the Reaper finds our door.

Someone had to pay for all this moving of matter from one place to another, and a hundred audiences chipped in with fees for my oracular prescriptions. So I was off again, on January 20, 1944, to Bakersfield and sundry stops . . . , to New York. I broke bread with old friends, then turned back in my tracks, and recaptured Ariel on February 29. Her sister Flora, and Ethel with baby Jim, came to spend part of the summer with us. In July and August we took our first season of "Symphonies under the Stars" at the Hollywood Bowl, just twelve minutes' ride from our home.

On August 16, 1944, we visited Lion Feuchtwanger and his wife in Pacific Palisades. He was the most peculiar European I had ever seen: so short that he made me feel proudly tall; his face seared with the dangers, anxieties, and humiliations of his flight from Hitler's Germany in 1933, his arrest in France, his escape into Spain; his penetrating eyes darkened by *Judenschmerz* (the pain of the Jews) but lighted by a wry humor that knew history, and a memory that had the best literature of the world in its stores. With the help of the United States government, he had had his priceless library transported from country to country until it reached him in California. It must have contained some five thousand volumes when I saw it, hundreds of them rare, ancient, precious to scholars and biblio-philes alike.* No wonder that each of his powerful novels was a work of meticulous research as well as of literary art.

He had two rivals in the Los Angeles of 1944: Theodore Dreiser and Thomas Mann. On August 20 Dreiser received us, among others, into his home and garden at 1015 North King's Road. Burly but genial, he growled with scorn of the human race, but smiled upon everyone except tycoons. He had come to the conclusion that with whatever faults and crimes it had been tarnished, Russian Communism had shown the way for man's escape from brutality and greed. Fortunately, he was among the 200 million Americans who had not read my *Tragedy of Russia;* our common admiration for John Powys and Franklin Roosevelt united us across our ideologies. Some time later he visited us at a soiree that we held at our home. I still recall his comment on entering: "It's all right; it's all right"; we were relieved that he had not blasted us as shamefully bourgeois. Theodore drank away his inhibitions that night. Suddenly he stood up and interrupted some irrelevant discussion. "Isn't it beautiful, what Russia is doing?" he asked; and tears of happiness came to his eyes. He died before hearing what Khrushchev revealed about those years in Russia. We liked him nevertheless, glad that faith had come to comfort him.

On September 24 we met another lion; not so frightening, but with a longer reach. Thomas Mann, the disputed hero of German literature, had abandoned his Munich home after Hitler's rise to power, and had come

---

* After his death in 1958 his widow donated the library to the University of California at Los Angeles.

to live in America, where, after a stay in Princeton, he had joined the company of other distinguished refugees in Pacific Palisades. Soon after his settling there he accepted the invitation of Mrs. Cortland Fitzimmons to attend a meeting of the PEN Club at her home in Los Angeles. I did not take to him as readily as I had done to Dreiser; he was always the aristocrat, and his tall, slender figure, stooping when he spoke, emphasized his aloofness and reserve. When he asked me what I was writing, I answered, with silly bravado, "I'm beginning a history of medieval civilization, and I propose to write so impartially about its competing cultures that the reader will be unable to tell whether I am a Christian, a Mohammedan, or a Jew." "Then," said Mann, "you must be an atheist." I did not consider the conclusion inevitable, but it was not a tempting time to expound my sentimental pantheism. In any case that sharp reply chilled me, and I thought a potential friendship had been blighted. However, he responded handsomely when, in 1945, I asked him to help the "Declaration of Interdependence" with which Meyer David and I were planning to make all men behave like brothers.

The presidential compaign of 1944 might have brought us more closely together, for Mann too was an enthusiastic supporter of Franklin Roosevelt's unprecedented plan for a fourth term. When I reached New York, October 20, on my fall lecture tour, I found all my Eastern friends working ardently for the President. Ariel came in from Los Angeles, and joined Max Schott and myself in an audience of two thousand that greeted Roosevelt when—after riding in a cold rain and an open car through Manhattan and the Bronx to check rumors that he was too ill to serve another term—he came to address the Foreign Policy Association. We were stirred with sympathy as this wounded warrior entered the hall, and approached the speaker's table, not on foot but in a wheelchair; he humbly explained that the day's campaigning had left him too tired to bear the heavy irons that would enable him to walk. He talked to us seated, not like a teacher or a magistrate, but as a humble petitioner for permission to lead his country into peace, as he had so long waited for its permission to lead it into war. I was so moved that I sent to the press a fervent avowal:

> Despite a sincere respect for the ability, record, and promise of his opponent [Thomas E. Dewey], I shall vote for Franklin Roosevelt because he has saved American democracy by one of the most statesmanlike peaceful revolutions in history; because, undeterred and unembittered by reckless and ruinous abuse, he has defended the weak against the strong, and restored a healthy balance to our economic life; because he has revealed to American industry its unsuspected powers of production and prosperity; because he has risked his popularity, and given all his strength of body and soul, to lift his country to the heroism of a supreme sacrifice for a supreme cause; and because we need his patient humanity, his informed and undiscourageable

leadership, in the perilous transition from war to peace, and from international barbarism to a free, secure, and happier world.

My "publisher but friend," Max Schuster, sent a clipping of this effusion to the President, with a copy of *Ceasar and Christ*. He (or an aide) replied,

October 31, 1944

DEAR DR. DURANT:

I am deeply grateful for that copy of your new work, *Caesar and Christ*, and I shall look forward with keen anticipation to an opportunity to read it. I am sure you have written luminously on that significant period of history. Not only do I appreciate the warmth of the personal inscription, but I am also grateful for the faith and confidence expressed in your generous statement to *PM*.

Sincerely yours,
FRANKLIN D. ROOSEVELT

I had some trouble realizing that the election of November 7, 1944, was a bit more important than the publication, two weeks earlier, of Volume III. I had worked so obstinately on it, often amid travel distractions doubled by the turmoil and exigencies of war, that I probably exaggerated its worth. Yet, when I reread its recklessly ambitious preface, I see that I was in some measure conscious of its pervading defect: I had taken too large a subject—Rome and her complex empire from the Euphrates to the Atlantic, from the Sahara to Scotland, from its triumphant government to its lowliest arts and ways, from 776 B.C. to A.D. 325—to achieve the meticulous accuracy demanded of and by specialist, analytical, historians who confined themselves to one aspect or period of the tale. I begged for mercy in the second paragraph:

The method of these volumes is synthetic history,* which studies all the major phases of a people's life, work, and culture in their simultaneous operation. Analytic history, which is equally necessary and a scholarly prerequisite, studies some separate phase of man's activity—politics, economics, morals, religion, science, philosophy, literature, art—in one civilization or in all. The defect of the analytic method is the distorting isolation of a part from the whole; the weakness of the synthetic method lies in the impossibility of one mind speaking with firsthand knowledge on every aspect of a complex civilization spanning a thousand years. Errors of detail are inevitable; but only in this way can a mind enchanted by philosophy—the quest for understanding through perspective—content itself with delving into the past. We may seek perspective through science by studying the relations of things in space, or through history by studying the relations of events in time. We shall learn more of the nature of man by watching his behavior through sixty centuries than by reading Plato, Spinoza, and Kant. "All philosophy," said Nietzsche, "has now fallen forfeit to history."

* "Synthetic" suggested artificial, and was soon changed to "integral."

Professor John Day, of Barnard College, considered my enterprise with what seemed an open mind, and rejected *Caesar and Christ* as a failure.

> This is a very ambitious undertaking [he wrote in the New York *Times* of December 10, 1944], for it includes accounts of religion, philosophy, literature, sculpture, painting, architecture, education, law, science, and still other aspects of Roman life.
>
> The professional scholar would undertake such a comprehensive work only after many years of preparation. But Dr. Durant has undertaken even more through this volume, which is the third in a five-volume account of world history. He describes his method as "synthetic," and admits that there will inevitably be errors in detail. An accomplished professional historian of Rome has recently taken somewhat the same position, saying in effect that as long as the history is portrayed "as an organic whole" (to use the words of Polybius), some errors and some omissions of the latest results of research are permissible.
>
> However, it must be admitted, if such errors and omissions mount above a certain minimum, the work as a whole loses value and authority. It is the reviewer's opinion that this minimum has been exceeded in "Caesar and Christ." In the bibliography it would be easy to point out a very considerable number of serious deficiencies. Moreover, much of the literary criticism and a number of the biographies of literary men are unsatisfactory.

The critic went on to praise the "readable style," and to say that the book "possesses positive merits," but those lines seemed to be words of mercy, and they did not soften the blow. I could understand Professor Day's dissatisfaction with my bibliographies; several late monographs in the professional journals had escaped me. My experience with such scholarly excursions was that they made minor corrections of no vital value to a general study, or that they replaced earlier views with suggestions and theories that in many cases were replaced in their turn, in a game that was of interest only to an esoteric few. I could not give the time to keep abreast of these controversies. The professor did not specify the errors that he had found in the text, so that I hardly knew how to defend myself. I began to wonder should I go on with my enterprise, or whether my book had values that outweighed its faults. I came crying to Ariel in a letter from Buffalo,

10-31-44

> The president of the Ad-Club handed me the enclosed review. . . . It has nearly broken my heart and consumed my courage. Each reviewer, it seems, asks not have I written a good history of Roman civilization, but have I written a diatribe promoting his own cause. Joseph Freeman was sorry I hadn't gone into more detail about early Christianity (he's been making a special study of this period)—forgetting that Christianity was merely one of a hundred aspects of Roman civilization in the last *quarter* of its history. . . . Harry Hansen . . . was sore because I had written with

"objectivity" instead of attacking Christianity as a symphony of nonsense; and Francis Hackett . . . complains that I have not denounced Caesar as a symbol of state power, and have not sufficiently raised up Christianity against him as a symbol of goodness. But I think it is a serious misunderstanding of the historian's function to ask of him a partisan argument instead of an impartial revelation of the facts. The historian should tell what happened; he ought to leave the reader to form his own opinion. . . . The reviewers will be simply horrified by the objectivity and impartiality of *The Age of Faith.*

The Catholic *Tablet* (December 9, 1944) shed some humor over the situation by complaining that I had not recognized the divinity of Christ and the supernatural elements in his miracles. Nearly all other reviews were favorable.* The most surprising acclaim appeared on October 22 in a now extinct newspaper, *PM,* from the pen of Joseph Freeman, a Communist; surprising because the Communist rule of literary criticism was to praise every book favorable to the cause, and to condemn any book by an author who had written against Communism or the Soviets. A university professor, Albert Guérard, himself an historian, came to my defense in the New York *Herald-Tribune* of November 5—a welcome morsel for my fifty-ninth birthday.

Illogically, the bouquets that best restored my ego were sent by friends whose verdict would hardly have stayed the academic guillotine. John Haynes Holmes assured me (in a letter of November 17, 1944) that my new volume was "incomparably the finest thing you have ever done—a superb piece of literature"—but John was prejudiced by our long comradeship in liberal causes. H. L. Mencken, who did not enthuse over those causes, enthused over me, even crediting me with common sense (letter of May 14, 1945):

> I have just finished "Caesar and Christ." What a book! It is not only the best thing you have ever done yourself; it is the best piece of historical synthesis ever done by an American. I can imagine no improvement in it. It is perfectly designed, it is clearly and beautifully written, and it shows a hard common sense in every line. I have never read any book which left me better contented.

Thomas Mann spoke a word of praise for Volume III at our "Declaration of Interdependence" dinner in April, 1945. Best of all was a veritable shower of bouquets from Maurice Maeterlinck in a letter of

October 24, 1944

> It is a magnificent success. Your book is worthy of the greatest histories of mankind. It is as complete as an encyclopedia; but instead of being the moth-eaten labor of an obscure compiler, it is written by a great writer and

---

* E.g., New York *Times,* October 28; New York *World-Telegram,* October 24; Chicago *Sun* and Philadelphia *Inquirer,* October 22; Kansas City *Times,* November 17.

a great artist, and each of its pages is a page from an anthology. The work
has a tremendous flow; it is luminous and without blemish. It has none of
the defects of an American "best seller." . . . You are never guilty of a
platitude; and when we think for a moment that we are on the point of
meeting one it is spontaneously transformed, before we have time to suspect it, into a gem.

One would imagine that the book had first been written in French by a
great French man of letters, and then translated into excellent English by a
translator who knew both languages completely.

Your pen seems to clarify, to light up, to simplify everything that it
touches. At times one would believe that he is listening to Montesquieu,
the Montesquieu of *La Grandeur et la décadence des romains*—but a Montesquieu who has not reached out for effect. . . .

Nothing escapes you; you explore all the most secret corners of the life of
the people; you know everything because you have had the courage to
learn everything. Such a book, if the electorate knew how to read, would
establish you in a high political career, where now only the blind are
placed.

Has one author—already a classic—ever been so kind to another? I
should have asked, on reading this, what the pretty maiden asked after
hearing her lover's ecstatic compliments: "But tell me, dear one, can all
this be true?" And I, who had made so many foolish predictions—I, who
could manage a phrase but not a family—my friends know that I would
have collapsed after a week of trying to manage men.

Anyway, these friendly encomiums raised my spirits, and I resolved to
go on. Moreover, the book had a good reception in the stores; I hope
Maeterlinck was not shocked when it appeared on the best-seller list. In
the course of this rarity the publishers ran out of paper, having exhausted their allotment; the stores ran out of stock, and *Caesar and Christ*
became a casualty of the Second World War. I shed a tear, and buried
myself in *The Age of Faith*.

On November 7 Ariel and I left for Washington, where we spent some
pleasant days with Ethel, David, and Jim. On the tenth we headed for
Los Angeles, encountering four lecture audiences on the way, and not
reaching home till the nineteenth. There I received a cordial invitation
from Professor William Ernest Hocking to come and teach either philosophy or history at Harvard, as I chose; but I was too much in love with
California, and trapped in Volume IV, to accept this disarming dignity.
Instead we busied ourselves with furnishing our new nest, while the old
year ran out its bloody course.

CHAPTER XIX

Interdependence

1945

Will:

The year 1945 was to be an eventful one for both hemispheres: the death of a great President, the development of atomic energy, the bombing of Hiroshima, the suicide of Hitler, the advent of peace, and the efforts of the victors to build an international order despite the provincialism of patriotism, the individualism of states, and the disruptive contradictions, in the United Nations, between the egalitarian theories of democracy and the persistent inequalities of power.

Ariel:

For us it was an ordinary year: lecturing, studying, washing dishes, planting trees, piling up—and classifying—mountains of facts and ideas for the hardest volume of the ten. Will left on January 17 for a thirty-five-hour trip by train to Eugene, Oregon. His first letter spoke of what was then darkening our thoughts: Louis had been ordered overseas.

1-19-45

SWEETHEART:

We're both lonely now: I here in the first of fifty foxholes, you in a twelve-room house, mourning our mutual separation, and Louis' departure to an unknown destination and destiny. I know how hard it must have been for you to part with him. Only after my train pulled away did I face the blank [bleak?] possibility that I might never see him again. I wished

232

then I had embraced him, but I hesitated to make him feel that I looked upon the situation as tragical, or that I was not confident of seeing him again. I have just sent him an affectionate letter to try to make up for that restrained good-bye.

And you, the mistress of so many empty rooms, I can see you lying awake in bed at night, wondering at the meaning of each little noise in the contracting woodwork or in the streets outside. I still think you should close everything up and go to New York.

He liked to eat one or two of his meals each day in his hotel room on fruit, nuts, and raw vegetables; this was his way of making up for what he called the poison of a dinner-club meal. So he wrote on January 20: "Just opened box of nuts and dates; what a picnic you put up for me!" And from Corvallis, Oregon:

I've given two of the forty lectures I must sell on this trip, and they have been well received. I have lived all day on fruit and nuts and those neat pumpernickel sandwiches you made, and I feel fine. . . .

I have made a list of important Arab or [other] Moslem works which have been translated into English or French; I am sending the list to Max Schuster with a request that he get in touch with some Islamic society in New York with a view to getting these books for me. . . . I am also writing to Arthur Upham Pope asking for help in getting books on Islamic Persia. The field is rich, but the proper books are so hard to get. . . .

The Age of Faith has now caught hold of me, body and soul, with no rival but you. When I return I shall be half Moslem, but still monogamous.

He was worrying more about Louis than was Louis (who, before embarking for Armaggedon, was doubling jeopardy by marrying):

Salem, Oregon, 1-22-45

The thought of Louis is so much in my head that I have written him again today. I've asked him . . . not to seek danger, but not to shirk any duty laid upon him. I've told him that wherever he goes I'll be with him. . . .

What a pity it is that such fine lads must, even one out of twenty of them, be consumed in war. There must be fine lads like Louis on the other side, too.

Perhaps we'll be spared another year of this bloody test; those marvelous Russians may sweep everything German before them, and compel that surrender which we have not been strong enough yet to win. I am glad that the Russians are shaming my suspicions that they might stop at the German frontier; apparently they are invading Germany itself; and some German foresight of their advance helped our soldiers to turn Rundstedt eastward again. . . . Meanwhile the Germans multiply and improve their V-1 and V-2 weapons, and apparently a hundred of these fall upon England every day . . .

I get farther from you, and nearer to you, every day.

His oratorical triumphs were paid for with some pains.

Seattle, 1-27-45

. . . The trip is getting tough. Only one station in four has red caps, and even then they are hard to corral. I've had to carry my own bags almost since I left you. The fingers swell up, but I soak them patiently in hot water every night, even in crowded Pullman wash rooms, and they subside.

The weather has turned cold, cloudy, damp, and I've already contracted, and come out of, a mild case of flu. Running nose, headache, constipation, malaise, backache—you know the combination. The Yakima apples helped my enema bag, and gargling zonite, to cure it: I'm 95% O.K. now.

Today I began reading Helen Waddell's *Peter Abélard.* It's indescribably beautiful. When I finish it I'll send it to you; lose yourself in it. . . . The half-dead poet in me longs to tell this story in my own way. . . . If I don't write a good chapter on Abélard never let me kiss your breasts again. . . . Ach! I'm so lonesome for them!

Louis, about to be shipped to Armageddon, called me from Greens-boro, North Carolina, seeking my consent, and Will's, to his marrying Mollie van Ameringen. We had never heard of Mollie, and had no fore-sight of what a wonderful wife and mother she was to make. I told Louis to call Will at Great Falls, Montana; I would abide by Will's decision. Will reported to me on

2-5-45

Last night I . . . called Louis, and argued with him. . . . He said he would gladly defer marriage if it were not that he might be sent off any day now, and he wanted to get this girl as his wife before going. I warned him that his blood rather than his brain was speaking; that his marriage would lay upon both the girl and himself an obligation to chastity which it would be difficult to maintain; that he might come back a cripple and she would not be willing to remain his nurse forever, etc. . . . It was clear that the boy had set his mind upon marriage before war, and that no opposition would stop him. I can remember that mood clearly enough. So I told him, "If you insist, Louis, you have the right to go ahead." He wasn't satisfied; asked me to consent; I did, assuming that you and Flora had done so. . . .

So there. Each generation must go through the same fanfare—youth aflame, parents fighting fire with vain prohibitions. And we shall never know who was right, except that we know *our* parents were wrong.

Well, we now know who was right: Louis. And it was good, when he found himself in Paris with girl-hunting GI's around him, to feel that cord of marriage around his neck, keeping him clean for his bride. Soon after the wedding he was shipped to Europe, with now two families praying for him. The next we heard from him he was in a Belgian hospital suffering from what he called "crotch crickets"—bugs with a passion for genitals. By the time he was cured the war on the western front was slowing to its end. Louis returned as a captain, proud and handsome, and became a good husband to a good wife.

On February 12 I shared in a symposium at the Hollywood Women's Chamber of Commerce. A complimentary letter from its president, Mrs. Leland Atherton Irish, opened a new friendship. Meanwhile Will was fighting one storm after another to get to his engagements. He sent an unusually gloomy letter from Helena, Montana,

2-8-45

. . . Feeling pretty low. Had the flu in [the state of] Washington; caught bronchitis up here; kept lecturing every night till ten, and coughing the rest of the night; I'm just getting over it. . . .

At Butte I met in my audience Mr. Sennett, brother of Florence Lynch; he confirmed Kevin's death—of heart stroke; a lesson to me. He says Florence has hardly gone out of the house since this happened last June; that she lives as if in a dull trance. What a blow. At college Kevin was the envied ideal of proud health.

A breezy letter from Waterloo, Iowa, contained one of Will's most elongated puns:

2-12-45

I was met at the Winnetka station by the philosophy class of Lake Forest College; a delightful group of alert and wholesome boys. They use *The Story of Philosophy* as their text. . . . They took me to my lecture at New Trier High School, where I was introduced to an audience of 2,000 by Mr. Gaffney, principal of that school, and formerly principal at Great Neck. Most of his introduction was about Ethel—what an intelligent girl she was. . . .

Tonight another audience, then another sleeper. Tomorrow I face the faculty at Michigan State College . . . from which you and I flew, some 2,000 years ago, when we spent a hectic emetic day: Lansing Michigan, Wheeling West Virginia, and Flushing Long Island.

Will's letter of February 21, too long to quote, gave me an exciting account of his fight for places in plane, bus, and train to get to his rendezvous with Ethel, David, and Jimmy in Washington, and then (having "let Jimmy tear me apart for two hours") to New York, where he had two engagements with lecture audiences, and twenty with his friends. Then he returned to the road, invaded the South, and enthused:

Meridian, Miss., 2-23-45

. . . Twelve city fathers were awaiting me at luncheon; the home economics class at the lovely high school here (as fine as Great Neck's) had cooked a meal for me. . . .

I am astonished at the change that has come over these Southern cities since you and I "did" them in 1940. The Negroes still live in shacks for the most part, but a considerable number run around in fine clothes and good shoes, with their heads held high; and the whites are correspondingly prosperous. Good schools, colleges, roads; great office buildings, majestic post offices, stores crowded with shoppers and goods; even books are selling. The war has lifted the South visibly to economic wealth that peace could have brought only after a generation. The reaction after the war may be tragical, but these splendid schools and this spread of new comforts must remain a great stimulus to all who have known them.

About the end of February Ethel arrived from Washington with Jimmy for a long stay, and on March 1 Will sent her a letter of varied advice: ". . . persuade mother to get a maid, for I don't relish reducing my wife and my daughter to being my servants. Until a maid is secured . . . divide the chores. . . . I'll help with the cleaning. . . . Kiss Jimmy's eyes for me, and kiss mother for me."

From Ogden, Utah, he sent me his own *De Senectute,* and the periodical assurance of his perambulatory chastity:

3-5-45

> Your talk about growing old amuses me. . . . Why not grow old? If we increase in stability, wisdom and patience, old age has no terrors, and much attractiveness. . . . I too am aging; this trip, I think, has taken a year out of me. But we're not licked yet! We're going stronger than ever. One night together, and our youth will be restored. . . .
>
> P.S. I have just reread your letter of Feb. 26th. It is beautiful. Don't worry about my everlasting fidelity to you. I have been, and will always be, altogether yours.

A quarter century has passed since that letter. He still talks that way about old age, and I have begun to believe in his fidelity.

We were hardly a month together when we received news that my mother had suffered a severe paralytic stroke. I left at once for New York, anxious to share the problems of this crisis with the rest of the family. I arrived on April 12, the day Franklin Roosevelt died. My mother had lost the use of her limbs, but her voice remained, and she lived for six years more. Will could not accompany me on that trip, for he was now involved in an affair called the "Declaration of Interdependence." But that is a complicated subject, and I leave it to him to explain his sudden relapse into public affairs.

Will:

One day, I believe in April, 1944, a Jew, Meyer (now Michael) David, and a Christian, Dr. Christian Richard, came to me with an unusual request: to suggest some constructive enterprise that could give their social ardor some work and wings. I proposed that they do something to mitigate racial and religious animosity in America. Just as *independence* had been the motto of states and individuals since 1750, so the motto of the coming generations should be *interdependence*. And just as no state can now survive by its own unaided power, so no democracy can long endure without recognizing and encouraging the interdependence of the racial and religious groups composing it; we need a Declaration of *Interdependence*.

On April 15, 1944, Meyer and Christian issued the following

Introductory Statement
to a
DECLARATION OF INTERDEPENDENCE

Dr. Will Durant, at his Hollywood home, recently, in a conference with Dr. Christian Richard and Mr. Meyer I. David, suggested the desirability of an organized stand for human tolerance. "Write a declaration of interdependence," said Dr. Durant, "and I will sign it."

This idea appealed to them. They worked at it, and presented a draft. . . . The Declaration needed a finishing touch, and Will Durant gave it its final form.

This final form seemed to us a document worthy of Thomas Jefferson himself:

Human progress having reached a high level through respect for the liberty and dignity of men, it has become desirable to re-affirm these evident truths:

That differences of race, color and creed are natural, and that diverse groups, institutions, and ideas are stimulating factors in the development of men;

That to promote harmony in diversity is a responsible task of religion and statesmanship;

That since no individual can express the whole truth, it is essential to treat with understanding and good will those whose views differ from our own;

That by the testimony of history intolerance is the door to violence, brutality, and dictatorship; and

That the realization of human interdependence and solidarity is the best guard of civilization.

Therefore, we solemnly resolve, and invite everyone to join in united action,

To uphold and promote human fellowship through mutual consideration and respect;

To champion human dignity and decency, and to safeguard these without distinction of race or color or creed;

To strive in concert with others to discourage all animosities arising from these differences, and to unite all groups in the fair play of civilized life.

Rooted in freedom, children of the same Divine Father, sharing everywhere a common human blood, we declare again that all men are brothers, and that mutual tolerance is the price of liberty.

The form as we had originally finished it concluded: "Rooted in freedom, bonded in the fellowship of danger," etc. Dr. Everett Clinchy, then president of the National Conference of Christians and Jews, suggested that this should be changed to "Rooted in freedom, children of the same Divine Father . . ." His proposal was submitted to an "executive committee" composed of Mr. David, Dr. Richard, Dr. Stewart P. MacLennan (a prominent clergyman), John Anson Ford (of the Board of Supervisors governing Los Angeles County), Eric Scudder (a leading attorney), Mrs. Althea Warren (county librarian), and nine others, including myself. The proposal was accepted, and the Declaration was sent out over America, with a request for signatures and contributions. We received signatures from Curtis Bok, Theodore Dreiser, Arthur Garfield Hays, Herbert Hoover, Thomas Mann, Rabbis Edgar Magnin and Max Nussbaum, my former teachers Robert S. Woodworth and William Pepperill Montague, Princess Laura Orsini, Professors Edward A. Ross and Pitirim Sorokin, M. Lincoln (Max) Schuster, David O. Selznick, Upton Sinclair, Senator Elbert Thomas, John Haynes Holmes, and many more.

Emboldened by the response, we engaged the ballroom of the Hollywood Roosevelt Hotel for an "inaugural dinner," and Thomas Mann, Theodore Dreiser, and Miss Bette Davis agreed to address the gathering. My letters from Los Angeles to Ariel (in New York) noted the progress of our preparation.

4-17-45

. . . On Saturday a lady called up and protested at our having Dreiser on the program, on the ground that he (she said) is an extreme Communist, and that he had attacked Roosevelt bitterly . . . for getting us into the war. She vowed that she'd never step into the same room with Theodore. A few minutes later Mrs. Dreiser called up, and said Theodore had learned that Herbert Hoover was a member of our organization, and that he was unwilling to have anything to do with a movement in which Hoover was in any way involved. I told Dreiser that Hoover had signed, and that I had invited Hoover to speak for us; but I talked Dreiser out of quitting on us. This human comedy is funny indeed.

11-20-45

It's a big blow to me that you can't be by my side at the dinner day after tomorrow . . . ; we have 100 reservations beyond what we can place. . . . The hotel has agreed to squeeze 425 diners into its California Room, though it contracted only for 400. Ethel and many others have been working heroically to prepare everything.

On April 22 the first dinner of "The Declaration of Interdependence" went off well enough, with a hitch now and then. Thomas Mann delivered in his quiet way a philosophical discourse—on the struggle between liberty and equality—which went to the roots of our conflicting ideologies, American and Russian. Bette Davis not only spoke with her usual incisiveness, but took over from my bungling hands the unpleasant task of appealing for funds. The result encouraged us, and we rashly threw ourselves into an exciting campaign to capture all Los Angeles for brotherhood by staging a complex program in the Hollywood Bowl for the afternoon of July Fourth.

Ethel had to return now to her husband in Washington. Ariel returned to her husband in Los Angeles, and was soon absorbed in our make-or-break enterprise. I was diverted for a day (May 3) into a debate for a *Town Meeting of the Air* in Philharmonic Auditorium on "Is War Impairing Our Moral Standards?" A prominent clergyman, J. Herbert Smith, and an alluring actress, Irene Dunne, took the affirmative. Eddie Cantor answered them with an astonishing display of good nature and extempore wit. My own discourse amplified a now commonplace idea: "We are not losing our moral standards. We are merely adjusting them to the changed conditions of an industrial society. Our moral code changed when we passed from the hunting stage to agriculture, involving a change, for example, from polygamy to monogamy. We must expect some similar adjustment in passing from agriculture to industry," etc. I think now that the courteous clergyman and the fair Irene had the better of the argument: it seems undeniable that war did impair even our basic moral standards in America. It is continuing to do so at this moment (1970), for war abrogates morals, and does not restore them when peace comes to soldiers trained to kill and to civilians hardened to casualties and blood. Three months after our amiable debate some of our bravest Americans, following orders, killed, at Hiroshima, 130,000 men, women, and children with one bomb.

While various members of our Declaration committee proceeded to make arrangements for the big affair at the Bowl, I was assigned the task of getting speakers. Risking a good part of our funds, I wired Frank Murphy, Associate Justice of the Supreme Court, offering him a thousand dollars and expenses if he would make the principal address for us on the Fourth. He wired back: "I will come, and for nothing." Here was another saving remnant in Gomorrha.

With the most prominent lay Catholic in America as our star, I went to another Catholic, Federal Judge J. F. T. O'Connor, a leading jurist in Los Angeles, and persuaded him to ask Archbishop John J. Cantwell to offer the invocation. Fortunately that genial prelate had never heard of me; he consented. Judge O'Connor brought me to Mayor Fletcher Bowron, who agreed to contribute an address of welcome—if I would write it for him. Then one of our most distinguished members, John Anson Ford, arranged for the participation of the Los Angeles Symphonic Band. I conceived the idea of getting a Catholic, a Protestant, a Jewish, and a Negro choir to provide choral music, first separately and then, symbolically, together. This involved a month of running around, coaxing, bribing; finally they were all organized and committed.

Justice Murphy arrived on July 2; our board of directors went to Union Station to meet his train, and my head grew as I saw that he had a copy of *Caesar and Christ* in his hand. He was full of questions about the book, and proposed to thrash them out with me at the first opportunity. Ariel had arranged a reception for him at our home for that afternoon. Ethel, who had just come back to visit us with Jimmy, helped with mind and will to meet one problem after another. Looking back upon that affair, I can hardly understand how we found room for the 150 guests that the press calculated as having been present. We made matters worse by scattering half a hundred chairs over the lawn; as most of the people preferred to move about, the chairs proved to be a hindrance. One group gathered around Leopold Stokowski, who fascinated us with his white mane and fluid hands. Then most of us crowded into the house, for Justice Murphy responded to persistent requests by making an extempore speech, using our kitchen sink as a podium.

We continued to the end the fight to get a good crowd into the Bowl. Ariel asked Chet Huntley to allow her a few minutes on his daily newscast over local radio station KNX; he welcomed her (July 3), and she explained our purposes and plans to the satisfaction of at least one auditor, for Chet added his warm appeal in support. The next morning, July Fourth, I made the main address at a meeting of the prestigious Breakfast Club, and may have won an additional customer for our event.

When Ariel, Ethel, and I reached the Bowl that afternoon I was near the end of my physiological rope, but the sight of those eighteen thousand people—Catholics, Protestants, Jews, agnostics, Negroes, Mexican-Americans—each with a copy of our Declaration in his hands, restored me. The program was complicated, but it went off well. A unique musical prelude was provided by the Jewish choir under the lead of Cantor Leib Glantz, the Catholic choir under Roger Wagner (who was just beginning a generation of high service to music in Los Angeles), the Protestant choir under Halsted McCormack, and the Negro choir directed by Lavenia Nash. John Burton introduced Archbishop Cantwell and then Mayor Bowron. Judge O'Connor presented Justice Murphy, and we heard a stirring address on the horrors of racial hostility in Nazi Germany and the need of guarding ourselves from similar savagery here by developing racial and religious amity. When the applause subsided I asked the audience to recite the Declaration of Interdependence with me, sentence by sentence, as a solemn pledge taken before a justice of the Supreme Court. It was done, and many persons who had not attended told me later how moved they had been by hearing those words thundering over the air. Then Rabbi Magnin spoke eloquently for his people, Señora Consuelo de Bonza for the Mexican Community, Dr. Harold

Kingsley for the blacks. Robert Young recited well a one-act play, which described the fellowship of Catholic, Protestant, Negro, and Jewish American soldiers in danger and death. The four choirs united symbolically to sing "America the Beautiful." Choirs and audience together sang a stanza of "America." Dr. E. C. Farnham, executive secretary of the (Protestant) Church Federation of Los Angeles, gave the parting benediction. I thanked the speakers, thanked and dismissed the audience, and marched, with the rest, from the stage, uttering a Te Deum "to the unknown god" who might have heard with benevolent doubt our announcement that all men are brothers.

We had recklessly promised our friends in or near Lake Hill to spend some summers there and help carry on our discussion club. So we entrained on July 12 for Chicago, dined there with Dr. Zurawski, renewed old acquaintances in New York, and motored up to our mountain home.

Ariel's mother and sisters were already there; Mary was classifying material for *The Age of Faith*. Soon Ethel came with Jim, and Ethel became my favorite typist and stern editor. Jim, aged four, astonished me with theology. One day that summer, as I rocked on the porch, holding him close on my knees, face to face, and perhaps because he felt me press him fondly, he said, solemnly, "Popsy, even when you're dead you'll remember how much you loved me." So this precious Lord of Misrule, as I called him, was already learned in eschatology. His remark, soon noted and now faithfully quoted, set all of us wondering; none of us could remember talking to Jim about death, much less about life after death. In other respects Jim was not so abnormally learned. Ariel used to lull him to sleep with stories that she invented on the spur of the moment about an adventurous character whom she named "Woe-is-me." Four years later, recalling those bright inventions, Jim asked Ariel, "Was Woe-is-me real?"

After two happy months with loved ones who spoiled me more than I spoiled Jim, I set out in two and a half months and forty-seven lectures to replenish the exchequer. One letter will suffice for this tour:

Omaha, 11-19-45

> I've been leading the pace that kills. For example, I spoke on the radio at 1:30 P.M. yesterday in Chicago; dined with Dr. Zurawski at 2:30; took a train at 5:15 to Winnetka; suffered a reception at 6 P.M. in the home of the town banker; lectured at eight; got to bed at eleven. . . .
>
> I reached Chicago 8 A.M., fought for a taxi, rushed ten miles to the airport, and was told that the flight was postponed by bad weather. Picture me waiting and fretting till noon; surrounded by sweating, dripping people whose planes were also grounded; and wondering whether I would ever get to Omaha. At last the skies cleared; then our plane developed engine trouble; . . . finally we sailed off and up at 12:15 into and over the

clouds into blinding sunshine. A smooth flight, and a happy landing here at 3 P.M. . . . At 6:15 I was facing another audience.

I begin to agree with you that I must give this nerveracking business up. As I lay in bed this afternoon I noted my heart missed a beat now and then, and I felt a slight pain at the same time. I've been straining the poor muscle too much. And I'm horrified to note that my hand trembles a bit when I . . . carry food to my mouth. I shall no longer have reason to smile at Dr. Zurawski's shaky voracity.

Now my evening task is done, and I soothe my post-oratory excitement by writing to you. A love-note from you would have been a soothing ointment. . . . I hope that you have taken some of the trips you planned—Acapulco, for example—and that when I arrive you will be a happy bird, ready to let me bill and coo around you amorously. . . . But I'm forgetting that heart beat.

Meanwhile Ariel was having similar tribulations. Trying to fly from New York to Mexico, she was grounded at Atlanta by the sudden sickness of her plane. Ever resourceful, she pulled strings, until the president of the Coca-Cola Company secured a place for her to Brownsville, Texas. From there the Braniff Airlines took her to Mexico City. For two weeks she was free to roam about the lofty capital—until I joined her on November 28. I talked to the Knife and Fork Club, and on December 5 we began a series of flights that got us to Los Angeles on December 8.

I believe it was in that month that we had an exciting evening with Charlie Chaplin, Noel Coward, Clare Boothe Luce, and Clemence Dane in the Pacific Palisades home of Douglas Fairbanks, Jr., and his wife, Mary Lee—who looked then, and looks now (1970), like a rose that will never fade. Just before dinner Mrs. Luce suddenly challenged me: "Mr. Durant, when are you coming back to the Church?" I was rather startled, as I hadn't thought of that in the last thirty-four years. I could hardly enter into a theological disquisition at that moment, but Chaplin took charge. Leaping from his seat, and standing directly in front of Mrs. Luce, he overwhelmed her with a vehement declaraction, of which I remember only these words: "Your Christianity has done more harm than good in history." The lady was near fainting when Clemence Dane calmed the storm by explaining that Charlie did not quite mean all that he said. As we went in to dinner, Mrs. Luce walked beside me and tried again: "Don't you think you're suffering from intellectual pride?" I confused her by answering, "Yes." I knew that she had been upset by the death of her daughter in a traffic accident, and that a religious faith had become for her a precious consolation. Life had not yet so tested my philosophy.

Dreiser died on December 28, 1945. Ariel and I attended the funeral. I sent a brief word about this to H. L. Mencken, whose enthusiastic reviews had helped Theodore to fame. He replied from Baltimore,

Interdependence

January 9, 1946

If you ever feel like it, I wish you would send me a more or less particular account of the Dreiser funeral. I'd like to know, for example, what sort of religious service, if any, was held, and where the poor old boy is buried. You speak of the ceremony as "weary," so I assume that some gentleman of God had a hand in it. Were there any speeches?

My apologies for bothering you, but I am curious to know more about the last act in what to me was an almost lifelong drama.

Sincerely yours,
H. L. MENCKEN

I replied on

January 21, 1946

DEAR MENCKEN:

Your letter of the 9th has just reached me here in Spokane, where I am peddling philosophy.

I knew Dreiser only in the last two years of his life. He lived in comfort, and usually, so far as I could see, in good spirits. His new wife took fond care of him; he had many friends; and his childlike faith in Russia as the realization of the brotherhood of man held him up in the face of the imperfections of our life. I had him in my home on several occasions, and found him a friendly old bear, whose gruff ways never succeeded in concealing his almost sentimental tenderness.

He was buried in Forest Lawn Cemetery, Los Angeles, on the afternoon of January third, after services in the Chapel of the Recession there. The body had lain in state that morning, but no attempt had been made to secure a procession of sightseers. Some 200 persons attended, and some fifty of those followed him to the grave. The services were conducted by a Rev. Hunter, a Congregational minister and friend of the Dreisers. He introduced John Howard Lawson, also a friend of Dreiser's, who spoke with a quiet elequence for some thirty minutes, chiefly in praise of Dreiser's recent enlistment in the Communist Party. He was followed by Charles Chaplin, who read with his usual skill the poem "Drums" from Dreiser's book called *Moods*. Then the clergyman spoke for perhaps half an hour; not theologically, but chiefly in reminiscence of Dreiser's career, and . . . suggesting with polite vagueness that, after all, Dreiser had been an essentially religious soul, a creative fragment of some Great Spirit.

The spectators then filed past the coffin. Dreiser looked handsomer in death than in life; his face expressed a repose and an acceptance which his pugnacious idealism had seldom permitted him before. The pallbearers (Dudley Nichols, Chaplin, myself, and five others, whose names have escaped me—chiefly Dreiser's relatives and friends) carried the coffin to the hearse. Some twenty cars followed this to almost the highest hill in the picturesque cemetery, overlooking many miles of Los Angeles. We carried the body from hearse to grave, and stood aside while the minister read the usual funeral services of the Congregational Church. . . . As we walked

243

back down the hill the body was lowered into the grave, and the covering earth was completely overlaid with flowers.

You, who helped him to recognition, should have been the one to pronounce his final eulogy. We missed you keenly.

Mencken answered,

DEAR DURANT:

Thanks very much for your letter, and my apologies for putting you to so much trouble. It is dreadful to think of Dreiser being bumped off by a Congregational minister and a Communist propagandist. I am only glad that the agents of Holy Church did not sneak upon him at the last moment and drag him back to grace.

I am in the midst of your first volume, and enjoying it immensely. Like *Caesar and Christ,* it is a really first-rate piece of work. As soon as I finish it I'll tackle No. 2.

My best thanks again.   —

CHAPTER XX

Toil and Trouble

1946–47

Ariel:

Will has left to me the assignment of describing a friend who was as maverick as myself; and one maverick can seldom understand another. Almost forgotten today, Upton Close, in 1943–48, was an influential radio commentator, holding a national audience of ardent supporters and fervent foes. His real name was Josef Washington Hall, but this had been superseded, even among his intimates, by his pen name—Upton Close— as a war correspondent in the Far East; we never came closer to the origin of this pseudonym than "up and close to the battlefront." We had known him through his books on China and Japan; but in 1943 we began to meet him intimately at the home of Fred Blickfeld, maestro of voice culture and arboriculture, and father-in-law of our trees and shrubs.

Upton had been a liberal, but he had come to look upon that amiable tribe as weak-kneed and weak-minded; he admired the men of action who made decisions and fortunes, and who saw no sin in taking and enjoying the fruits of superior courage and skill. The world and mastery belonged naturally and inevitably to the able minority through the survival of the fittest in the selective competition of life. So Upton laughed at Will's persisting socialism, ascribed all progress to individual inventiveness and initiative, and opposed Franklin Roosevelt with the intestinal fever of a suffering tycoon. He predicted, with tragic accuracy and ready resignation, "Roosevelt has an embolism, and will collapse soon."

We found Upton's politics hard to take, but we were stimulated by his criticism of our surviving liberalism. Will advised him not to commit himself so completely to the political Right, lest all liberals should cease to listen to him, and conservatives should fall away as already knowing and accepting his views; he would then lose value to the conservatives, who would soon withdraw their financial support. This prediction came true.

On January 12 Will went on the road again for nine lectures in the Pacific Northwest. He was suffering at the time from oak poisoning, caught while working in our private jungle; his letters of this period record his itching with it on trains and planes, in bed and on the podium. Amid these woes he borrowed a radio to hear a distant friend perform:

Spokane, 1-20-46

> Just heard Harry Kaufman play Rachmaninoff's Concerto No. 2 on a program with the Los Angeles Symphony Orchestra, from Claremont, Calif. It is a magnificent composition, full of a wild sweep of melody and harmony; and Harry played it with delicacy, tenderness, and fire. You will remember that from the first time I heard him play I felt that he was among our greatest pianists. I am happy that he is at last coming into his own. The applause at the end was tremendous, almost passionate; I'll bet Harry is still on that platform, taking bows. Congratulate him and [his wife] Lilian for me.

This was hardly necessary, for he sent Harry a telegram of unlimited praise.

He had taken a heavy package of books with him, for he was now—indeed, he had been since 1943—giving his days, wherever he was, to preparing *The Age of Faith*. So he wrote from Spokane:

> Have finished ten books since I left you, and am taking them to the Chamber of Commerce to be packed and mailed to Miss De Witt. . . .
>
> The Middle Ages require more study . . . than any previous volume. So many countries, and so many aspects, and so many diverse cultures—Roman, Christian, Byzantine, Judaic, Mohammedan; and each demands expert treatment, with such knowledge and accumulation of details as are required for proper interpretation and vivid presentation. If you would only help me!—if we could advance arm in arm to the goal! How about preparing a chapter on Jewish life in the Middle Ages? . . .

Alas, I was not equipped to write that chapter, but I helped, with a double love, to gather the data for it, and I undertook nearly all the job of classifying the thousands of slips he had piled up to give that big volume its diverse learning and vitality.

Will's pessimism never lasted long, for good fortune kept coming to him. About this time he heard of an offer, for sale, of some forty volumes of Arabic classics in French or English translations. (They included the famous histories by al-Makkari, al-Masudi, and al-Tabari.) These, he felt, were just what he needed for his study of Islamic literature. He submitted an offer of a hundred dollars for the set. The University of Southern California also bid for the set; and when the librarian heard that Will was a competitor he wrote him a letter of friendly advice: the university could always outbid him; why force up the price? The university would buy the books, and set them aside in a private room for Will's use until a date to be agreed upon. It was so done, and for a time Will went almost every day to that glorious library, and took down by hand batches of notes for those wonderful Islamic chapters in Volume IV.

Will and I had one of our longest tiffs during that winter of 1946. Formerly our battles had been over finances, and they had been settled by Will's surrender. Now they were based upon our contrary backgrounds and tastes: I, a city cat, was a wild and adventurous spirit, eager for a varied and exciting life; he, thirteen years older, was an addict of books and peace. He loved the countryside, raved about woods, fields, mountains, trees, birds . . . , and sniffed with ecstasy the fragrance emanating from plants, and from the manure that adorned the road; while I, stifled by the silence of our walled-in home, missed the bustle and danger and variety of Manhattan streets, the prattle of Greenwich Village tearooms, the wild utopias and neckties of artists, poets, and radicals. So, though I had been charmed at first sight by our Casa della Vista, I now found this hilltop isolation intolerably boring, especially when Will was on his lecture beat. I became gloomy and irritable, and this had some mutual cause-and-effect relation with my duodenal ulcer. I was *un*fit to be tied.

Finally Will proposed that I should go to New York alone, stay with Flora and Mary, get my fill of those sights and sounds, those "movers and shakers" of the world, that so fascinated me; and that I should look around for an apartment that could house him, his books, and his notes. If I found such, in a tolerable spot and at tolerable cost, he would sell the Los Angeles house and move to Manhattan; if, he said, Mark Twain had written amid the intermittent clangor of the El, so could he. His surrender conquered me; I gave up Manhattan, and promised to be a dutiful chatelaine provided we could spend the summers in Lake Hill. But when Henry and Gladys Janon, our St. Louis friends, came to visit us, and then started back in their car, I prevailed upon them to take me and Blanche Gurski to El Paso; from there we would take a plane to Mexico City, where Dr. Gurski would try to cure my ulcer. Will could not come, for he was committed to lectures in or near Los Angeles. When I reached Mexico City I found several letters from him.

4-3-46

I am already eaten up with loneliness. . . . I'm used to sleeping alone in trains and hotels, but [here] it's a new experience not to have Ariel either in the next bed or fressing in the kitchen while I reach position 41 and finally get to sleep. . . .

I rely on you not to undergo any operation without my presence and consent. There is nothing wrong with you that moderation will not cure. Just avoid fatty substances and highly acid food like meat, fish, citrus fruits, coffee; eat a piece of bread at each meal to absorb the hydrochloric acid in your stomach. I confess that whole wheat bread may be more irritating . . . than white bread. . . . Drink a glass of buttermilk at each meal. . . . You will need a laxative, but please don't take the pills, which injure you; take a tablespoonful of milk of magnesia every morning. . . . Please ask Dr. Gurski . . . to criticize this . . . If I am on the right track you don't need an operation—just a mild diet, which he can prescribe. Always remember that an operation will leave you weak for a year, and will require even more dietetic restrictions. . . .

4-5-46

Louis and Mollie arrived 8 P.M. last night. . . . Already by now Louis has fixed all sorts of things. . . . Partly as a delight for them, but I suspect chiefly to satisfy my own unphilosophical curiosity, I'm taking them to the Bob Hope party this Sunday. . . . Louis gets $375 a month during his present two months' terminal leave [from the Army], and will get $100 a month for three months after that to cushion his "reconversion." Never before has a government treated soldiers so favorably. But the boys who deserve most are under the sod and far away.

The next letter is about the only occasion I can recall when Will had an unkind word for nearly everybody:

4-7-46

. . . Bob Hope's garden party . . . We had our fill of film celebrities. We were shocked to see how these "stars" age a bit more rapidly than those in the sky. I—— looked ten years older than when she . . . : her face drawn, her hair bleached to a disagreeable red, and her head weighed down with an enormous hat that looked like the headgear of the Royal Guards at Buckingham Palace. D—— has a girlish figure, but her face is pinched and wrinkled. . . . It's a great tragedy for these people to reach thirty-five. The belle of the show was little eight-year-old Margaret O'Brien, modest, bright, and pigtailed, selling dolls. Dinah Shore looked tired; and Ann Sothern chatted as amiably as she could with the husband whom (they tell me) she is about to divorce. . . . Bing Crosby was selling holy pictures and statues. He is almost bald, and has a tired and listless expression; all his millions have apparently failed to give him a good stomach or the *joie de vivre* of the simple proletaire knocking a ball around on a corner lot. Ray Milland was the handsomest face on the scene—finely chiseled features, beautiful iron-gray hair, and perfectly sober. [He had recently starred as an alcoholic in *The Lost Week End.*] His wife is a pretty lady with long gray hair. Healthiest and most likable of all was Bob Hope himself—bouncing with good spirits, with a kind word for everybody. . . .

Come home, come home, wherever you are. Everything is forgiven, even your future sins.

4-10-46

Thank you for your letter of the 8th. . . . Your letter says "I am sleeping with Mr. Gurski." I hope that is only a topographical error.

4-13-46

This morning's mail brought a letter from Arthur Upham Pope offering me all sorts of introductions to Islamic scholars in Africa, Egypt, and the Near East, and adding: "When you get to Persia you will be received royally. I shall see to it that you are received by the Shah. You will meet various members of the Cabinet, and be received by the members of the Academy of Science." So brush up your Persian. . . .

I returned to Los Angeles on April 19, and settled down for three months. On June 16 George Brown brought to us the famous industrialist Owen Young, who, on reaching Los Angeles, said (according to George) that the man he most wanted to see in these parts was Will Durant. We profited from his conversation, for Will felt a need to come off his theoretical abstractions and make contact with men of action and practical affairs. But we enjoyed more our growing friendship with Albert Lewin, a prominent film writer and producer for Metro-Goldwyn-Mayer; here was an artistic, imaginative mind that always kept us on our intellectual toes. We had met him and his kindly, gracious wife, Millie, at the table of Harry and Lilian Kaufman in the Carlotta Apartments just below our hill; now we met them in the exquisite home that Richard Neutra had built for them in Santa Monica. Allie loved to get Will into an argument; attacked him mercilessly, and always ended by embracing him. Once, at a party given by Stephen and Ethel Longstreet, Allie accused Will of shameful ignorance; the next morning he traveled I don't know how many miles to knock at our door and beg forgiveness. He became one of our dearest friends.

We had been planning to leave for the Catskills early in July, but we waited till we could celebrate the marriage of another close friend, Fred Blickfeld, to a Puerto Rican lass whom I remember only as Pilar. We were so much attached to Fred that I hated to share him with another woman, but we knew that Fred was suffering from loneliness. I remember his touching comment, after he had toiled another day to beautify his hilly grounds, "Yes, it's good for me to work hard, but it's harder still to have no one to receive its dedication and to reward me with dinner and love."

On July 14 we leased our Casa for three months to a Mr. Winckelmann. Then we set out, with half a hundred books, to drive once more across America. Seven days later we reached Lake Hill, where we found Ethel and Jimmy, Flora and Mary and Mike, waiting for us. Regina Sands came up from New York, and soon "the civilization factory" was humming. For two months Will hugged his wooden ivory tower, making great progress on *The Age of Faith*.

In September we moved to New York, and I had a happy week in my old haunts. We visited Louis and Mollie in their apartment at 7 Montagu Terrace, Brooklyn, where Mollie was already displaying her homemaking artistry. We renewed old ties and made new ones. Arthur Upham Pope introduced Will to the Iranian Institute at 9 East Eighty-ninth Street, and there Will continued his study of Pope's massive *Survey of Persian Art*. We drove out to Arlington, and went with sister Ethel and her husband, Leo Halliwell, to stand before the graves of Will's parents. On September 27 we began the long drive back to Los Angeles, visiting, on the way, sister Leah in Bound Brook and Sam's widow and children in Royal Oak, Michigan. There we divided: Will took a train to East Lansing to spend his promised four days with the juniors and seniors of Michigan State University; I drove to Mount Clemens for a checkup at a health resort; on October 5 I drove to East Lansing and picked up a tired husband. We moved on through rain and shine to engagements in Colorado, Wyoming, Idaho, Utah, and Arizona. A clipping from the Phoenix *Arizona Republic* of October 22, 1946, under a picture of Will in his most benign moment, reports him as having expounded a rather tough philosophy of life:

> Will Durant, . . . discussing The Lessons of History last night, called Utopia "a coward's dream," and expressed a conviction that nations of the world will never cease fighting among themselves until attacked from another planet.
>
> In the opening talk on the 1946–47 Phoenix Town Hall Celebrity Series Durant told the 1,400 Arizonians . . . that the real optimist is the man who likes life on this earth, "whether it ever gets anywhere or not."
>
> He declared that history has shown man struggles, conquers, is defeated, but remains the same: curious, eager, insatiable, invincible, beaten down only to rise, covered with mud, to march on and build again.
>
> The philosopher asserted that mankind has three major drives: the acquisitive instinct, designed to preserve the individual and the family; the reproductive instinct, designed to preserve the species; and the social instinct, or man's desire to live in groups.
>
> He called the social instinct "the weakest in our blood." "The problem of civilization is how to strengthen the social instinct so as to cope with the acquisitive and reproductive instincts."
>
> "The strongest social forces are the family and religion. I do not know of any nation that long survived the death of its moral code. I don't know how long Western civilization can survive the disintegration of its family life or its religious code."
>
> "I can't give you any hope that the last war was the last war. It was just one in a series of bloody enterprises. . . ."

"Sooner or later some fool will find a way to Mars. Then all the school-teachers will spend their vacations there, we will send missionaries, some missionary will get killed, then we'll send tanks and planes. . . ."

"Freedom and equality are not brothers. To check inequality you must limit freedom, as the Russians do. We aim to preserve liberty, even at the cost of a great deal of inequality."

That Will did not change this Darwinian view during the next twenty-two years is clear from the first chapters of *The Lessons of History* (1968). Amid all his cheerful outlook on life this had been his view since his studies of biology in 1913–17.

We reached home on October 22, after driving 450 miles from Phoenix. For a week or so Will buried himself in the medieval past. Then, restless, eager, and quite forgetting his views on the geological leisureliness with which human nature changes, he joined Michael (ex-Meyer) David in a plan to get the Declaration of Interdependence displayed for all young barbarians to read in all the educational institutions of Los Angeles County. Fortunately, the head of the Board of Education, Dr. Stoddard, was a friend and reader of Will's. He had chaired a debate in St. Louis, where Will had opposed a Catholic speaker on birth control, and he recalled with relish that when the Catholic quoted Lincoln to the effect that "God must have loved common people, he made so many of them," Will had answered, "It wasn't God, it was *common people* who made so many common people." Dr. Stoddard welcomed Will to his office, agreed to the plan, and arranged to have Will indoctrinate the principals at their coming assembly. The next problem was how to pay for printing and framing a thousand copies. Mrs. H. David Kroll, our loyal friend from 1943 to this day, sent in a check for a thousand dollars. Soon the bulletin boards of the county's schools and colleges blossomed with the Declaration, and several principals called up to say how warmly they approved the plan. But did the students read that noble document? However, it was not they who needed the Declaration (for the playgrounds already mingled the races amiably), so much as the parents, who coddled their egos with racial hostility and transmitted it to their children.

How to reach the parents? It was now sixteen months since our big splash in the Bowl had spread some edifying eddies through the press; but what had we done to follow up that proclamation? The racial situation in Los Angeles was relatively quiet: the Jews were prospering, the color chasm had not yet yawned in our faces, and the Catholics talked of toleration; why shouldn't we leave well enough alone? But many members of our committee were for action, and we had some itchy dollars in our treasury. If we could not fill that Bowl again we might at least have another dinner-plus-propaganda, just to keep the iron hot. So Michael David, Stewart MacLennan, Maurine Simpson, Will, and other earnest souls planned for January 10, 1947, a gaudy fiesta for the spacious ball-room of the Ambassador Hotel.

We were all agreed that the first step should be to get cooperation from the motion picture industry. Chaperoned by the dangerously pretty Mrs. Marlo Alter, Will visited Mervin Leroy and Walter Wanger, and solicited their aid in securing some cinema celebrities to participate. Nothing came of these visits. From Will's reports I gathered that these executives had become hardened realists, who felt that genteel declarations of philosophical principles would not change the ingrained racial or religious antipathies of the American people. Will's answer to this was: "Granted, but would it not be worth while to discourage the *expression* of these antipathies in words, actions, and laws; just as much more deeply ingrained impulses have been successfully controlled in all but a small minority of our people?"

He went next to the (Protestant) Church Federation of Los Angeles; its executive secretary, Dr. E. C. Farnham, pledged full cooperation. Will did not do so well when he invited Bishop Manning to give the invocation at our dinner, as Archbishop Cantwell had done at the Bowl; the bishop wrote an amiable and illuminating reply:

December 18, 1946

Since your visit yesterday, I have devoted much conscientious consideration to the separate points of the Declaration of Interdependence. What it says of race and color I can most heartily subscribe to.

The religious implications, however, are such that I cannot agree to them without compromising what is dearest to me, my faith. . . . It would do no good service were we to create the impression that truth in religious matters is something relative.

As you so readily understood our position yesterday, we are bound by the law of charity to regard all our fellow men with brother-like love. This certainly we hope is essential to our beliefs. However, the tenets implied in the Declaration are more basic.

I regret very much, therefore, that I cannot accept your gracious invitation to be present at the forthcoming banquet.

Sincerely yours,
Timothy Manning
Auxiliary Bishop of Los Angeles

Will kept on working. He wrote to our leading local scientist, Dr. Robert A. Millikan, president emeritus of the California Institute of Technology, and asked him to make the principal address; the doctor agreed. We used our friendships with Douglas Fairbanks, Jr., and Lion Feuchtwanger to enlist them for brief speeches. Maurine Simpson arranged to have Will meet Harry Mazlich, head of radio station KFWB; Harry responded handsomely by securing Shirley Temple and Margaret O'Brien for our program, and by squeezing contributions from motion picture celebrities. Finally, with the indefatigable aid of the lovely Maurine, we persuaded the mayors of the various communities constituting Los Angeles County to appear together, under the lead of our excellent Mayor Bowron, to give the dinner the sanction of their presence and the pledge of their aid. Dr. C. C. Trillingham, superintendent of the Los Angeles County schools, Rabbi Magnin of Wilshire Boulevard Temple, and Dr. J. Herbert Smith of All Saints Episcopal Church in Beverly Hills completed our program.

Ethel and David and Jim arrived at the end of 1946 to live with us until they should find their own home. Ethel joined with her usual energy and skill in arranging for the Ambassador dinner. Both Will and I spoke on the radio to round up an audience. When the appointed night came Ethel and I went on ahead, having ordered Will to stay home till the last minute, and to keep out of the crowd—for he had a miserable way of kissing every woman friend whom he met, and he might be snared on the way. When he arrived he startled all of us, white and black alike, by entering with our Negro maid Bleeker McGlendon on his arm and escorting her to her seat; I could imagine a hundred Interdependent souls whispering, "Good God! Does he take this business seriously?" It must have been a hard evening for Bleeker.

Otherwise the dinner went well. The Embassy Room (not the ballroom) of the hotel was filled. Mayor Bowron pronounced his greeting. Clyde Marsh, president of the League of Cities, introduced a score of mayors; Shirley Temple read the Declaration persuasively; Dean Stockwell and other starlings performed a skit illustrating human brotherhood; a short film picturing America as "The House I Live In" was shown. Will introduced the seventy-nine-year-old Dr. Millikan, who stressed the theme that "while science has progressed conscience has stood still." Douglas Fairbanks, Jr., and Lion Feuchtwanger spoke with quiet but effective modesty. Will tried to raise the tired diners to sufficient ecstasy to open their pocketbooks. Drs. Farnham and Trillingham pledged support of the Declaration by the churches and the schools. Rabbi Magnin covered our sins and blunders with a final benediction.

Will had almost forgotten, in his work for the Declaration, that he had committed himself to a transcontinental tour requiring fifty-four lectures between January 12 and March 26. On the evening after the dinner he asked the directors to relieve him of the presidency. They objected, but Stewart MacLennan agreed to serve as acting president. As I had refused to remain separated from Will for two and a half months, he arranged with his lecture agent to send me rail tickets to New York. I stayed there from January 21 to February 11. He wrote from Chicago, January 25:

> You gladden my heart by what you say about your hope of doing some of the work on the last volume[s] of my history. We must outline a regular

course of reading for you, and provide you with means, and perhaps secretarial help, to gather and order your material; it is not too soon to begin; nothing would please me more than to put your name with mine on the title page.

We were reunited in Miami Springs February 15. Instead of going to a hotel we spent two days together in the Miami Battle Creek Sanitarium, whose cook knew how to make vegetables fascinating. Then on the eighteenth Will was off again, while I stayed behind to nurse my ulcer. He resumed his courtship in a letter from Columbia, South Carolina:

2–19–47

Ach! it's dreary without you, without your sweet watchfulness over me, and the touch of your hand in mine. Promise me that you will walk in Central Park with me, hand in hand, and feed the animals peanuts (and me too) as we did when we were young and gay. Love cancels time, and gives us eternal youth.

Charlotte, North Carolina, 2-22-47

BELOVED:

I've just received your sweet letter of Feb. 20th. I'm glad you're having a good rest, glad that our kind friends . . . are so considerate and helpful. . . . I am always reconciled to the nature of man by the excellence of my friends.

Here in this hotel you and I, in 1942, experienced our first blackout; about 10 P.M. the lights of the city and the hotel were extinguished, and we sensibly slipped into bed; in the sweetness of your breasts I forgot the war. I could almost bear another war, or any blackouts, to have you near me now. . . .

Watch those ulcers, those gallstones, that appetite! Your body is the temple and only home of your spirit; your soul deserves a body of cleanliness and health. . . . The phone calls me to the next job. I'll do it well for you.

We met again in New York, March 22, when Will reached Pennsylvania Station 2 A.M. after a lecture in Dover, Delaware. At 11 A.M. he was on the platform at Town Hall with a lecture on "Communism and Democracy"; there he had to be good, for his severest critic—myself—was in his audience. Sunday, March 23, was a holiday, but his memoranda for the day suggest no idleness: "West Iranian Institute. At Astor Library study *A Picture Book of Persian Pottery*, and Rivière's *La Céramique dans l'art mussulman*, or consult these at MMA [Metropolitan Museum of Art]. Study art in Morgan Library. Marc Brown recital at Town Hall. Mollie's baby due. Walk in Central Park. Dinner with family." What a holiday!

Marc Brown was one of our dearest and most remarkable friends. Some ten years back, at Lake Hill, he had lived a few hundred yards west of us on Willow Road, and his daily violin practice had provided a pleasant obbligato to our daily work. In New York I persuaded Persinger, a very hard-to-get teacher, to take Marc for advanced study. Marc developed so rapidly that he was able, at Town Hall, to hold his audience in rapture. Now, twenty-three years later, his varied ability gives a score of aides a comfortable living, and his hospitality spoils his friends.

On March 28 we left for Washington, where Ethel and Jim were waiting for us to drive with them to Los Angeles. Ethel drove David's Hudson, hoping to find a buyer for it in California; Will and I drove my Oldsmobile. Each car was loaded with household possessions and other belongings; Jimmy, aged six, lay comfortably in the back seat of the Olds on a pile of clothing so high that he was able to play with our ears as we drove; his pranks made that long drive a delight. David was waiting for us in Los Angeles. The two families lived together for a while, and Will relished Jim's prankish intrusions into medieval studies.

In June I went east to have our friend Dr. Teller operate upon a cyst that was growing on my wrist. Now, for a change, Will preserved some of my letters, and I must expose one or two. From Lake Hill,

June 10, 1947

Recovering here from the piercing and squeezing of this cyst. . . . Maurice drove mother, Flora, Mary and me to Lake Hill Sunday in a terrible rain. . . . I am worried about Jimmy being operated on . . . I feel so helpless so far away from you and I would so love to be near and help. . . . Going up to Lake Hill without you was heartbreaking, . . . especially rummaging about your study, where every piece of substance breathes your spirit. . . .

Who said this? "Scepticism as a natural human philosophy—perhaps as the only natural human philosophy—underlies all the beautiful soft-coloured panorama of pagan poetry and pagan thought. It must have been the habitual temper of mind in any Periclean symposium or Caesarian salon. It is pre-eminently and especially the *civilized* attitude of mind: the attitude of mind most dominant and universal in the great races, the great epochs, the great societies.

"It is for this reason that France, among all modern nations, is so sceptical.

"Barbarian peoples are rarely endowed with this quality. The crude animal energy which makes them successful in business, and even sometimes in war, is an energy which, for all its primitive force, is destructive of civilization. Civilization, the rarest work of art of our race's evolution, is essentially a thing created in restraint of such crude energies, as it is created in restraint of the still cruder energies of nature itself."

And here is what you might like:

"The Protestant Reformation, springing out of the soul of the countries beyond the Alps, is of course the supreme example of this uncivilized force. One frequently encounters sceptical-minded Catholics, full of the very spirit of Montaigne—who died in the Catholic faith—but it is rare to meet a Protestant who is not, in the most barbarous sense, full of dogmatic and argumentative 'truth.'

"So uncivilized and unlovely is this controversial mood that freethinkers are often tempted to be unfair to the Reformation. This is a fault, for after all it is something to be saved from the persecuting alliance of church and state; . . . it is better to be teased with impertinent questions about one's soul than to be led away to the stake for its salvation. . . . Between Calvin on the one hand and the Sorbonne on the other, Montaigne might well shuffle home from his municipal duties and read Horace in his tower. And we, after 300 odd years, have little better to do."

Ah, well—stuff after your own heart, and there, but for a few years of precedence, go you . . . for had not your good friend said it but held his peace and waited for you to catch up to Montaigne, you would have said it, and perhaps equally well! . . .

It is very lonely without you, and I doubt if I shall go anywhere . . . hereafter without you. . . . It is too terribly lonesome to sleep facing the empty bed where you always waited for me no matter . . . what time I came back.

Mother is slowly and sweetly falling away.

Will responded to this on

6-13-47

We received last night your letter of June 10th; and I read most of it to Ethel and David, for it was one of the most interesting letters I have ever received. . . . The quotations you transcribed were firstrate stuff. They sound like Santayana's *Scepticism and Animal Faith*. You will note that ideas seem more reasonable to you than when expressed by me; they don't arouse your instinct for debate. In general those ideas seem true. A combination of freedom of thought for the intellectual classes, with a religion of myth, miracle, and ritual for those whose arduous life leaves them no time to think, seems better than a stern puritanism that stifles the *joie de vivre*; but, as your author also says, it is better to be bothered with puritans than burned at the stake. I find that every creed—even atheism—persecutes when it has acquired power and its power is threatened. To be cut short with the guillotine, or sent to a forced labor camp in Siberia, is the radical equivalent of the auto-da-fé.

It is interesting to see that your author concludes, like your husband, that in times when rival dogmatisms compete for men's souls, and moderation is outlawed by both sides, it's better to live with philosophy, literature, and the selected wisdom and civility of the past—and meanwhile to live with one's family in the simple old delights of marital and parental love—than to exchange murders in the dirty arena of radical or reactionary strife. You know how I was turned to the writing of history because I found that there was no room in the present for the impartial view. Perhaps I fool myself in thinking I was impartial. Possibly I just wanted to be comfortable.

Which reminds me that I am getting mighty lonesome. Yesterday I suddenly pressed Jimmy to me and cried out: "Oh I wish Ariel would come back!" And he asked me, "When is Ariel coming back?" I told him about

256

your cyst, and he understands; and about your family, and your obligations to them. He's more of a delight each day. Two evenings ago, after dinner, he quietly disappeared into the living room, and put on the Capehart; I had filled it full of records not played by us for many years past, but I had had no time to listen to them. I had told him once, in answer to his persistent questions, how to put the machine in operation; he learned it all at one saying; and now we found him sitting quietly in the chair before the phonograph, listening to Mozart, Schubert, and Beethoven, and apparently enjoying them. He will grow up, thank God, to the sound of good music, and will seldom hear jazz here.

He and Ethel and David and your lover join in sending you love; and I add a kiss for your hair, your eyes, your mouth . . .

6-13-47

. . . . Sometimes I'm tempted to fly to you; and if you say the word I will. My book is not my first love; it can wait; life is better than literature. Perhaps the fact that this book is the hardest I've ever written tempts me to lay it down. The everlasting dilemma: to satisfy the scholars and scare away the reader, or to be easier on the reader and sacrifice thoroness and scholarship—I have to wrestle with this problem on every page. It would be so much sweeter to gallivant with you somewhere, and have not a care in the world. You bet that when you come back we'll go off somewhere and honeymoon again. . . .

What you write about Louis and Eric is very pleasant to hear—that the baby is well, and that Mollie and Louis are intelligent enough to yield to the old instinct of parental love, and that Louis is a good daddy. I knew he would be. I'm glad that he's a normal, decent, civilized human being, and not a crazy intellectual such as you married. Our Ethel, too, is a good parent, and handles Jimmy more successfully and easily than any of us. . . .

I haven't left the grounds here since you went away; will leave it tonight to go to Harry Kaufman's concert; expect not to leave it again until I go to meet you. So look for a virgin when you come back.

Will has been for the last fifty years an enthusiastic writer of fan letters—to authors, artists, musicians, even politicians; and no reminder that such masterpieces brought no royalties could discourage him. A sample of these ebullitions was evoked by our friend Harry Kaufman's recital of June 13, 1947.

6-14-47

Dear Harry:

I had great expectations of your concert last night; they were more than fulfilled. I have heard all the famous pianists who have performed in the United States in the last thirty years, excepting only Horowitz. I don't believe that any of them ever surpassed you in mastery of the piano, in gamut of feeling, in range of expression from the most delicate pianissimo and trills to the most complex chords and runs and the most frightful fortissimi. Nor have I ever heard a program so full of honest music, profound and difficult music, such as only an artist of stern conscience and supreme resources would dare attempt in one evening. I spend six years writing one book, but you must have spent forty years making it possible for your powers of nerve, muscle, memory, and technique to give us last evening's feast; I feel that you gave us forty years of your life and asked nothing in return. At the end we were torn between desires—to give you such a number of curtain calls as would express our appreciation, and yet to let you rest; for such a performance must exhaust body and soul for weeks. Nevertheless you gave us three encores; not one of them trivial (as most encores are), but each a masterpiece in its field; and your concluding performance of the Shostakovich piece was technical brilliance transformed into pure delight.

It was an evening that I shall never forget.

Will sent a similar letter to the Los Angeles *Times,* which printed it on June 29.

My letter of June 17 cleared up the puzzle I had given Will as to the author of the long quotation I had sent him.

Wrong guess, darling! I don't know the early Santayana, . . . but the Latter Day Saint [Santayana spent his last years in a convent sanitarium] I am well acquainted with, and he is incapable of the sweet balance and impartial acceptance of elements in Puritan Protestantism such as my quotations show. Neither did Santayana ever really criticize Catholicism, Spain, or the Inquisition. Besides, my quotations do not discuss religion in relation to classes, and their author in general is free of the snobbishness expressed by Santayana in every line of his many-volume autobiography. For my author is our own beloved real Saint and Friend, Powys, in one of his earliest 5¢ Haldeman-Julius booklets, discovered and stolen by me somewhere recently, title "Montaigne, Pascal, and Voltaire," and so simply written as to be preferred by me, at least, to his later mystic and long-winded novels. Still, I am reading parts of *Oriental Heritage* and Powys' *Autobiography* right now, and much prefer you. . . .

You are a glutton—for I have admired you, and audibly, too, these last thirty-five years, and yet you are a jealous god and want no graven image competing, or getting even a little praise. [I don't know what imp of the perverse made me say this. Will a glutton for praise, and a jealous god? Just the opposite. He took criticism in good spirit, and carried to excess his praise of other authors.] But now that you know it is Powys I hope you will . . . forgive me, for that man has not even yet gotten his due. . . . I told you a thousand times I love you more than any one or thing in the world; I think you the finest contemporary stylist, and only quoted Powys because he said so beautifully the thing you have so many times already told me in conversation. . . .

My hand is tired now; I could write so much more, and less trite, but the hand is a drag on the spirit.

Jimmy's operation for tonsils and adenoids threw all world events into the shade. Will described the event with ecstasy:

6-21-47

He behaved like a hero throughout— . . . obeyed all instructions without a hitch, smiled as he was wheeled away to the operating room. David and I and Ethel waited impatiently, . . . sitting awhile, pacing the corridor awhile; I felt 28 years roll away, and I was again pacing the corridor in Fordham Hospital, while you were struggling with Ethel.

Jimmy was gone 40 minutes; then they wheeled him by, all covered except for his nose and mouth; a little blood clotted on them, his breathing heavy. Fifteen minutes later he came out of the ether, cried a little. Ethel, who had prepared for this moment with many days of thought, presented him with a wrist watch, a double ball pen (writes blue at one end, red at the other . . .), crayons, etc; and David gave him a little airplane. I put my head on his legs and told him, "I'm so sorry it hurts you." The doctor came to see Jim 15 minutes after Jim came out of ether; Jimmy raised his little arms to him and drew him down to an embrace. The doctor said no child had ever done that to him after an operation. (I used to do that after an operation, but I chose the nurse.) It was typical of Jimmy. . . .

At 2 we found him awake but subdued; wondering why there should be suffering in the world. Ethel read to him and the three other children who were in the same room, until they were all asleep. The doctor complimented Ethel on the way she had prepared Jimmy, physically and psychologically, for the operation. Ethel has come thru it perfectly; my respect for her is high.

I returned to the attack in a letter from Lake Hill,

June 23, 1947

My God! this house is full of you. Every nook and corner contains sealed and beribboned boxes of love letters, nostalgic and otherwise, in which you talk to me of enemas, fevers, colds, hot and tepid audiences, athlete's foot and hand, arthritis, poison ivy, and a thousand and one aches and sweats—but, thru every letter, and whatever the subject, runs the persistent desire—to be home and at work. . . .

Will's letter of June 23 is an *apologia pro vita sua*—

6-23-47

You certainly played a trick on me with that Powys quotation. You are quite right: Santayana could have written that passage only in his early days; today he seems to be creeping back. . . . John, however, could write that passage even now in his seventies. He has always based his philosophy upon his sense of beauty, rather than upon ideas, and so it remains steady as long as he is sober and sane. He too, like your old partner, has been forced, by the rival fanaticisms of the time, to content himself with a world that can be chosen and formed—the world of scholarship, philosophy, literature, and art. If we are told that ours is an unreal world, and that we are escapists, I answer that it is the only real world, the City of God, of the immortals; the people who pass me in the street are far less real, for their reality is bound up with flesh that will soon die and be forgotten; while Montaigne and Plato and (for us) Powys will always be real, waiting just around the corner for us to come. We cannot be blamed for choosing our company. It is enough that we ventured into the contemporary world in our Hollywood Bowl and Ambassador Hotel affairs; we got our fingers burned a bit by the fanatics of the left . . . and the fanatics of the right; but we are still intact. . . .

I reported on those cyst treatments, and then,

June 25, 1947

Last night I visited Ben Finkel . . . He played for me some of his early and late medieval recordings, and is going to make for you, at my request, a list of all the recordings available for *The Age of Faith*. We listened, only thinking of you, and we spoke only of you. I guess I must have sounded like a love-sick moon-calf. Kiss Ethel and Jim for me. It is midnight now, and time to dream my dreams of my loved ones far away.

I returned to Los Angeles July 13, just in time to face a tragedy: Ethel had lost her love for David, and wanted a divorce. Will opposed it until he saw that Ethel's mind was made up; then he yielded reluctantly, for he liked David, and still sends him affectionate words. David agreed to cooperate and went off quietly to separate lodgings; Ethel left for Las Vegas, and we were glad to take care of Jimmy. On August 1 Will, Jim, and I drove up to Las Vegas to visit Ethel. She had already developed there a friendship with a Canadian gentleman, Gordon Mihell, who was also establishing the residence requirements for a divorce. We liked him at once; he was handsome, clean-cut, courteous, uncontrollably generous; and we were not unimpressed by the fact that he owned a furniture factory in Strathroy, Ontario. We did not wonder that Ethel was charmed by him.

In October we converged on Strathroy to be present at Ethel's marriage to Gordon. I left Los Angeles separately by plane on October 15 to spend a few days with my mother and sisters in New York. Then I joined Will at St. Thomas, Ontario, and we "gave" Ethel to Gordon on October 23. We stayed with them a few days in the beautiful home that Gordon now shared with Ethel and Jim and his own son John. Will's father had been born in Canada; his daughter was now lodged in Canada; history is a fish that sucks its tail.

Back in Los Angeles, I went to work, five hours a day, classifying some thirty thousand slips of material gathered for *The Age of Faith*. As I proceeded my interest in the Middle Ages grew. I, who had not had the slightest preparation, in heritage, schooling, or character, for understanding medieval Christianity, which I knew chiefly as the theory and practice of anti-Semitism—I discovered a dozen bright facets in those centuries of groping through darkness to dawn. Will undertook this volume with almost equal antipathy. In Catholic college and seminary he had been fed the dreariest part of medieval history: the popes, the kings, their conflicts and wars; the Scholastic philosophers and their dreary attempts to rationalize the Christian mythology; the splendor of feudal lords and the sufferings of serfs bound to the soil and imprisoned in superstition; there was little here, it seemed, to attract a man who had struggled for years to free himself from medieval ideas; and Will approached his task almost in a mood of dislike and despair. I, the neophyte, finding gems in that pile of clips, reminded him that those centuries included the wandering scholars, the love-warbling troubadours, the Gothic cathedrals, the story of Abélard and Héloïse, the *Divine Comedy*, and the beginnings of Parliament; and I pleaded with him to do justice to the medieval Jews. Gradually his antipathy to the subject faded, his interest grew. He found a lively starting point in Julian the Apostate; he was surprised by the poetry, science, and philosophy of medieval Islam; he recovered some sympathy for the religion of his youth; he made the medieval Jews live; and he chose a culminating endpiece in Dante. At first he liked nothing in Dante except the idealization of Beatrice in *La vita nuova*, and the music of the terza rima in the *Divine Comedy*. He sympathized with Dante's sufferings, but shrank from the heat of Dante's hates; "If such a man could get into Paradise," he said and wrote, "we shall all be saved." Then he was swept along by the gentle stream of Dante's verse through the "Purgatorio" and the "Paradiso" to that final line that almost summarized his own philosophy and mood— that nothing matters except love.

But this is getting ahead of the story; in 1947 only half of that fat volume had been prepared. Meanwhile there were pleasures and pains that molded our lives. So, on November 15, we had dinner with Thomas Mann and Lion Feuchtwanger in the home of William Singer in Brentwood; and on November 30 we had dinner with Yehudi Menuhin, and brought him briefly to our house. Moreover, we had many an exuberant hour planning, for the following spring, an extensive trip into Europe and Asia. As I was unable to follow Will on the most important part of that tour, he should tell the tale.

CHAPTER XXI

Innocents Abroad

1948

Will:

Our 1948 memorandum book has disappeared, leaving many dates uncertain; but three soiled sheets survive with the itinerary of another lecture tour, January 13 to March 23. Having leased our home for six months to pay for part of our pilgrimage, we rose from New York on Pan American Flight 142, March 24, for Lisbon. We were due there 4 P.M. the following day, but our famous American efficiency failed us, and made our trip a nightmare. Stopping at Boston to pick up a passenger or two, we were delayed by damage to the landing gear. For three hours we shivered in the unheated waiting room. We soared again. We were almost halfway across the Atlantic when one of the four motors died. Soon I noted a long deep banking of the wings; I asked why such a maneuver in midsea; after some hesitation the assistant pilot broke the news: we had turned back to New York. Surely some others must, like me, have secretly wondered: if one motor died could not another fade out, and even a third?

The plane reached New York in the dawn of March 25. The passengers were invited to wait a few hours while another plane could be prepared to really take us to Lisbon. Most of the passengers, having fallen in love with terra firma, canceled their flight. Ariel agreed with me to try again, and this time we had a smooth passage that brought us to Lisbon just twenty-four hours late. Our schedule, nearly all by air, compelled us to compress into one (rainy) day our survey of the Portuguese capital.

We left Lisbon the next morning by TWA. We spent two days in Madrid—one of them in the Prado, the proud, sad echo of Spain's golden age. On the general principle of the American husband that nothing is too good for his wife if she will wink at his escapades—or because I did not feel competent to find my own way through the Peninsula to its historic treasures and sites—I had arranged for a car and a chauffeur to take us through southern Spain, so that all I had to do was to look, feel, and make more slips. Our guide was sternly good and quietly competent; he called our attention to special monuments and views—of course to the *"vista da Toledo"* from its environing hills. So we came to El Greco's home and paintings, and we debated the cause of his elongated style. The cathedrals there and in Seville seemed to us so gloomy, and their sculptures so terrifying, that we were glad to emerge from them into the untheological sunlight and sit at a café table angling for some informed native or tourist who could talk English or French.

One such Samaritan told us where and how to buy tickets for the next bullfight in Seville. We found that spectacle brutal as well as unfair, until we were reminded that the bull had to die in any case, and why not this way, in a ritual that trained matadors and spectators to bravery, rather than through the throat-slitting of suspended cattle in the slaughterhouses of America? When the blood ran freely I turned to concentrate on the women, who all seemed beautiful because they allowed so little of themselves to be seen. Then on to Granada and the lovely filigree of the Alhambra, and to Córdoba and its massive mosque. I was inclined to believe that the Moslem civilization of southern Spain had been superior to the Spanish Christian civilization that destroyed it in 1492, but that in the pursuit of refinement Hispanic Islam had lost the muscle to survive.

On our flight from Madrid to Rome (April 8) Ariel ate a salad which had presumably been bought in Spain. Soon after our arrival she developed dysentery. Our plans had called for me to go by plane to Turkey, Syria, Iraq, Iran, Egypt, and Sicily alone; Ariel loved Rome, and disliked the Moslem Near East. After getting her a doctor, and receiving her orders to be gone, I left the next morning for Istanbul. There I wired her asking her to wire me her condition; soon her answer came, bravely false: "I am fine; complete your work." Later she confided that at that time she was very weak, and could hardly drag herself to the post office to send her telegram. I revisited the mosques of Istanbul, and tried to feel the artistry and passion of Byzantine mosaics; but I found, and still find, them unappealing to a mind that had emerged from theological caves into the sunlight of classic literature and art.

Another flight over the sands brought me to Baghdad. I had been warned not to expect much of it; in 1948 it was a small town with only a few blocks of paved streets; it was hard to imagine that here, a thousand years ago, Asiatic Islam had had its finest period, when Haroun al-

Rashid ruled urbanely, heard poets gladly, and rewarded them as if they were generals. My hotel had an outdoor restaurant overlooking the Euphrates; as I ate I could see one civilization after another passing up and down that historic river.

But my letter of that day forgot Baghdad in the thought that Ariel was in Rome during the exciting election in which Italy was to make up its mind between Stalin and the Pope. I had seen the walls of Rome covered with the rival propaganda, and Ariel told me later how she could hardly sleep while the rival orators amplified their appeals through the streets. Washington was pouring money into Italy and France to keep their afterwar poverty from turning them Communist. Hence my letter of

4-18-48

Your letter of April 13th . . . has given me much comfort. I was happy to read your line—"I am not afraid to be left alone in Rome any more." I am increasingly confident that we were justified in braving all the dire predictions of our friends . . . about terrible doings in Italy on or soon after April 18th. There will be a few blows exchanged at the polls, but every New Yorker is familiar with such enthusiasm on election day. . . . I'm glad you've made some friends; you usually learn to get around. I suspect that by May 6th you will have Gaspari and Togliatti in for lunch.

I am very happy in you.

The peak of this trip, for me, came in Iran-Persia, where the letters of Arthur Upham Pope had opened many doors for me. So I wrote, from Tehran,

4-19-48

. . . A whole delegation of Persian scholars met me at the airport, and whisked me thru customs, passport, and other tribulations in a few minutes. Dr. Issa Sadiq, head of the delegation, is evidently a man of national standing; one look at his white hairs and all officials hurried my passport back to me, and allowed my bags to enter unexamined. He was formerly president of the university here, then minister of education. . . . With him was an official of the Department of the Interior, and Dr. F. T. Gurney, attaché of the American Embassy, and the directors of two museums, and two members of the Ministry of Education. . . .

Everybody here is doing what he can to make things interesting for me. One . . . is taking me for a ride in a government car thru the city; the American Embassy is giving me a luncheon Tuesday and a dinner Wednesday. . . . I wish you could share honors as well as tribulations. . . .

4-22-48

Forgive me for letting two days go without a letter to you. I've been running from one museum to another, amazed at their rich collections of incredibly beautiful decorative art. . . . I must leave the hotel at 9:45 A.M. (it is now 9:38) to go with Dr. Gurney to the Ethnological Museum, then to a session of the Iranian Parliament, then to a luncheon given me by the Minister of Education. Yesterday . . . I visited the School of Persian Arts and Crafts, . . . then visited the Sepahsala Mosque, and the philosophy class of the college there; then the Gulistan (Rose Garden) Palace, and its library of world-famous illuminated manuscripts; in the afternoon . . . the collection of Crown Jewels.

At six I attended a reception given by the Iran-American Society, and made a 20-minute speech on "Persia in the History of Civilization." Dr. Sadiq introduced me, told how he had enjoyed *The Story of Philosophy*, etc. The speech went over well, and was translated into Persian by the son of the former prime minister. Dr. Sadiq was so well pleased that he at once gave instructions to have *The Story of Civilization* translated into Persian. He has also wired Isfahan and Shiraz to entertain me as a guest on my four-day trip to those cities. . . .

Have just come from the luncheon given by Dr. Ali Akbar Siassi, Minister of Education . . . Practically all members of the Cabinet were there, and the prime minister, Dr. Hakimi, several professors, and some members of the American Embassy. Dr. Siassi made an excellent speech in English, and I replied with an extempore effusion. Dr. Sadiq liked this too, and went out at once and arranged to have me received by the Shah tomorrow. Now more than ever I wish you were with me. You would be fascinated by this young king, 28 years old, sitting on a throne more ancient than any other in the world today, and yet [himself] so modern that he pilots his own plane. . . .

As soon as I returned [from buying airplane tickets] the Ministry of Education came to take me to a tea given for me by Dr. Sadiq. A beautiful home, a distinguished gathering of 100 men and women, including again the prime minister, most of the Cabinet, many members of Parliament, several ambassadors, professors, etc.; I was told that everybody of high standing in government, science, literature, or education in Tehran was there excepting the Shah himself. These people do me too much honor; I had no idea I was so immense as these generous souls make me out to be. [Evidently Arthur Upham Pope had blown me up to bursting point.]

Now the day's whirl is over, and I lay me down to sleep, wishing I could draw you by some magic over the seas and deserts to share the Shah—and my bed—with me.

Isfahan, 4-24-48

I wish you were with me to marvel at the blinding beauty of the architecture built here 400 years ago, when Isfahan was the capital of Persia. Something of the old wealth remains, in the form of the finest street I have seen in the Near East—the Chahar Bagh, or Four Gardens—a spacious avenue some three miles long, composed of two asphalt roads and two roads of beaten earth—one for bicycles (numerous here), one for promenades. Miles of bazaars—little shops where men and boys work at the ancient handicrafts, and display their products. . . . Nearly all the women are veiled, on the general principle that imagination is better than reality.

Amid general poverty . . . rise four tremendous and magnificent mosques, their polychrome tile portals, minarets, arcades, and domes gleaming in the sun. . . . The masterpiece here is the Masjid-i-Shah, or Royal Mosque. Picture a portal like the enclosed [card], leading into a large open court with a central pool; on each side of the court 4 portals, twice as high and wide as the enclosed, all covered with tiles—most of them mosaic tile of small inset pieces—in gorgeous colors and the most graceful designs of flowers, or arabesques, or Kufic script—white Arabic lettering on a blue base; vast surfaces of the finest tile work in history. Each of the four portals leads into a sanctuary whose interior is also covered with tiles in a dozen colors and intricate designs. Over one sanctuary rises a dome so gorgeous that it is rated as the most beautiful object in Persia—Pope thinks it the most beautiful in the world. Its surface is also tile, of small bits inlaid in the most exquisite designs. This dome of the Masjid-i-Shah dominates the city, is visible from miles around. I came to Persia to see if this mosque was what Pope claimed—more beautiful than Chartres. . . .

I had a busy day yesterday [in Tehran]. In the morning I had a half-hour of private converse with the Shah—a handsome earnest young king . . . already graying and wrinkled with the care of government, and the fear that agitates all Persia today—that Russia will in a few years pounce down upon Persia's oil wells. . . . We Americans . . . have no idea how this little country, 80% desert, depends upon its oil for revenue, and trembles at the thought of "another Mongol invasion" [like that which] ruined Persia in 1258. . . . All this was on the mind of the Shah, but also he pled for American capital to develop his country, and for social reform to uplift the people [he has now led that reform] . . . I have seldom met a man so intensely absorbed in the responsibilities of his position. The Parliament, however, has severely limited his power.

I had attended the Parliament on the 22nd, and had met most of its leaders. . . . Last night, in Tehran, the American ambassador gave me a dinner at which I had another chance to meet these leaders. . . . Many of the political leaders here are Ph.D.'s; but I believe our Senate would have an equal proportion of educated and able men. . . .

The ministry of education here [Isfahan] is supplying me gratis with car, driver, and guide for all sightseeing, and any other purpose. . . . So I've been well treated, and all that Dr. Pope promised his been fulfilled to overflowing.

Tehran, 4-28-48

A week from tomorrow I shall hold you in my arms. It has been a terrible separation, and I am not sure that all the Near East was worth it. But my job here is done, and well done; I have gathered material and sensations; and in three days I leave for Cairo. . . .

Let me report on my adventures since Isfahan. I told you that I would take the bus for 180 rials ($2.70) to Shiraz (260 miles) instead of hiring a private car (3500 rials, or $52.50). [No plane service available.] I did, but it nearly killed me. When the bus arrived at Isfahan it was all full with thru passengers . . . to Shiraz, except for 4 places at the extreme rear—just over the wheels. I had to take one of those back seats, tho I knew that the road would be rough and the bumps terrific. I underestimated.

We left Isfahan 6 A.M. April 26. The road was paved for 2 miles; then, for the next 207 miles, a mixture of blue stone and dirt, far worse than the road we traveled from Toledo to join the paved road from Madrid to Granada. [Here I drew a jagged line like a frightening cardiogram.] Every 20 seconds a bump that nearly lifted me and two other back-seat miserables to the roof of the car. This lasted till 3:30 P.M., when we stopped for lunch. Lunch meant that some carpets would be spread for us on the patio of a little inn, and tea would be served—nothing else. Fortunately, I had suspected this, and had brought oranges, zwieback, etc. . . . At this lunch I made the acquaintance of a Dr. Hafizi, a physician from the ministry of health at Tehran; he could speak English; and I learned that he is a direct descendant of the poet Hafiz, whom the erudite consider Persia's best. He insisted on changing seats with me [in the bus]; he reached the rear seat first, and left his front seat for me. It was a lifesaver, for when I reached Persepolis my back ached so much that I could hardly rise from the seat; my old spine-trouble had returned.

I was relieved when at last, after a dizzy ride over deserts and mountains, we sighted, at 4 P.M., the majestic columns of Persepolis. There, as you know, Darius and Xerxes built a lordly palace 500 years before Christ. . . . The head of the Persepolis Archeological Mission, Dr. Sham, . . . said he had been instructed to receive me as a guest of the government. . . .He invited Dr. Hafizi to stay with me. . . . The bus went on; we washed some of the dust off our hands and faces, hurried thru the Persepolis Museum, then spent two hours among the ruins—the Hall of Darius, Xerxes' Hall of a Hundred Columns, the Hall of Artaxerxes, etc. . . . We saw beautiful cuneiform inscriptions in marble, 2400 years old, and magnificent reliefs. . . . A nice dinner. Then sleep.

At 6 A.M. on the 27th Dr. Sham drove us over fifty miles of terrible road to Shiraz. That city is all that fame says of it: beautifully situated in hills like our own in California; rich in gardens, roses, grapes, and Omar's "wine of Shiraz," and home of Persia's greatest poets. . . . We visited the . . . mosque of Shiraz—a brilliant gleam of colored floral tiles, and the tombs of Sa'di and Hafiz. One of Sa'di's poems was inscribed over his vault:

> *Do not mourn that Sa'di is in the ground;*
> *Out of the ground many roses will grow;*
> *And how could a nightingale be buried*
> *Without becoming a flower?*

Then Shiraz's showplace, the tomb of Hafiz. It is a little bizetka of marble, surrounded with spacious and fragrant gardens. Dr. Hafizi here behaved with beautiful modesty. He took some pictures of us at the tomb.

Dinner at the home of Dr. Ghorban, Minister of Health, and night at the Shiraz Inn. At 6 A.M. today, a plane thru bumpy air over a thousand mountains to Tehran. Dr. Gurney of the American Embassy met me at the airport. I learned that I am to have dinner Friday with Julian Huxley. Saturday, 7 A.M., I fly to Cairo.

In Cairo I had the pleasure of renewing friendship with Syud Hussein, whom we had known in Los Angeles, and who was now India's ambassador to Egypt. I visited again the gloomy mosques, studied the handsome men and fascinating women (who rarely keep their fascination after thirty), and then eagerly flew back to Rome (May 6). I had canceled the flight that I had planned to take to study the art of Monreale, near Palermo; to this day, I am ashamed to say, I have never seen Sicily except when passing through the Straits of Messina. But I could not leave Ariel deserted any longer.

She had had a full week of enfeebling dysentery, bravely concealed from me in my weeks of dizzy kudos in Tehran; she was still a bit pale and subdued when I came to her; but some substantial meals in Roman *trattorie* and cafés, capped with fruit and wine, and enlivened with the lusty speech of Italian waiters (I can still hear them shouting my order across the room—"*Fagiolini con burru!*")—brought back my gaiety and her native vitality; and we romped over the Seven Hills as if I were not sixty-three and she not fifty. We took long walks in the Borghese Gardens, and in the Galleria Borghese she indulged me as I feasted my sensual eyes on Canova's *Venus Victrix* (Pauline Bonaparte).

Bit by bit, during these days of reunion, Ariel told me how Professor Charles Morey, cultural attaché of the American Embassy in Rome, had befriended her while I was rambling in Iran. We had come to like him sight unseen when we noted his recommendation of *The Life of Greece* in his scholarly *Medieval Art*. On our arrival from Spain he had straightened out our passport difficulties. Learning of Ariel's illness, he or his kindly wife visited her almost daily, took her for drives in Rome, and for a day's outing to Tivoli and Hadrian's Villa—where, with their expert help, she made notes for our united enterprise. They dined us in the quiet of their suburban home, and the former Princeton professor sat patiently and amused through my fumbling talk at the Roman headquarters of the YMCA. Thank you, Dr. and Mrs. Morey, wherever you are, in whatever world.

Our happiness was inflated by a letter received in Rome from the liveliest publisher since Aldus Manutius:

May 11, 1948

Your letter from Tehran was fascinating and inspiring. . . . Your description, ranking Isfahan with Chartres and Reims, comes at a particularly appropriate moment, since Dick just returned from France and England imbued with the glory of the . . . cathedrals. . . . It must be a tremendous experience to do your field work in this spirit—and get the first-hand "feel." . . . When your full series is complete you will have done a supremely important thing in major historical synthesis. . . .

MAX

And from the same hand,

May 17, 1948

Our old friend, Henry L. Mencken, visited me last week, and I thought you would like to know that he spent a good part of his time telling me how tremendously he admired the heroic and monumental work you are doing. He shared completely the sentiments I expressed in my letter to you a few days ago, ranking you way ahead of . . . for the structural majesty of the conception, the sweep of the vision, and the scholarship of the presentation. . . .

MAX

We left Rome by car on May 15 for Spoleto, Gubbio, Perugia, Assisi, Orvieto, Siena, and Florence; by trains to Bologna, Ravenna, Forlì, Rimini, Padua, Venice, Vicenza, Verona, and Milan; in these seats of medieval and Renaissance art we took reams of notes and pictures for Volumes IV and V. Then by the Simplon-Orient Express through Brig, Montreux, Lausanne, and Dijon to Paris. There we spent a week, quarreled with tired concierges, hired a car and driver, and rode on to Chartres, Dreux, Évreux, Rouen; to more cathedrals at Beauvais and Amiens; through Compiègne and Soissons to Reims; there we descended from spires to cellars, and explored the wine industry. Then through Laon, Saint-Quentin, Cambrai, Douai, and Lille into Belgium. As we paid by kilometer, the driver secretly advanced the speedometer now and then; when we asked him to desist, he swore eternal enmity to us and all America. We consoled ourselves with the placid figures of Jan van Eyck, the graceful piety of Rogier van der Weyden, the opulent ladies of Rubens, the rabbis of Rembrandt, the topers of Frans Hals, the sculptured "oldest citizen" of Brussels (a urinating boy), the sitting *Erasmus* of Rotterdam, the waters of Amsterdam, the tulips and the people of the Netherlands.

We flew to Copenhagen, but our scant knowledge of Danish history left us unprepared to appreciate the brave people whose King had defied Hitler by wearing the Jewish badge; we came away chiefly with memories of Tivoli Gardens, its many concerts and its cigar-smoking matrons. We visited Hamlet in Elsinore, and then hopped over the strait to Stockholm. Here we found friends, who guided us through the fascinating waterways of the city. We had read Marquis Child on *Sweden—The Middle Way*, but we still underestimated the achievement of Swedish statesmen in combining capitalism with socialism.

Our plane from Stockholm to Oslo was delayed till 11 P.M., so that we were given an unexpected view, from the air, of the midnight sun. We spent two days in Oslo, whence our sorties into the countryside to help us visualize Hamsun's *Growth of the Soil*. On the flight to England we got some view of Norway's silvery fjords. We landed perilously in a London fog, found our way to the Hyde Park Hotel, and vowed to be *adscripti glebae* for the remainder of the tour.

England was a delight, although it was now impoverished and half destroyed by the war, and the meals it served us were beneficently meager. The London police were so courteous and helpful that we longed to bring them as a saving leaven to New York. After a week in London and a day in Stratford we began a tour of Great Britain. Our driver was a sixty-year-old widower who had lost his wife and all his children to one of Goering's robot bombs; he was the soul of politeness, honesty, and competence, and his pride in England's ability to "take it" kept his courage master of his grief. He drove us through Kent to Canterbury; then back to Rochester and across the widening Thames into Essex and to Cambridge, which seemed to us the most pleasant town in England. Everything there spoke of university life—no mingling of scholarship with motorcars as in Oxford. We visited several of the colleges, and savored the aura of centuries of learning from Erasmus to Newton to Bertrand Russell. We walked into Corpus Christi College, the alma mater of our late dear friend Ed White; his headmaster, Sir Will Spens, was still functioning there, and remembered him. A fragment of Ariel's letter to Ed and Lena survives:

Cambridge, July 15, 1948

So much of old England is destroyed; . . . so much of the beauty still remains, especially the great institutions of learning, the great cathedrals and the Houses of Parliament; enough to put many cities and countries to shame. In Canterbury and Cambridge alone one must keep rubbing one's eyes, for at every step the medieval is spotlessly preserved, and spreads an aura of benign tranquillity over people and movement, elsewhere mad with modernity; to a traveler from across the Atlantic, it is a healing corrective.

We again visited the grounds and chapels of the separate colleges, and felt the warm spirit of Erasmus everywhere, saw again, in stained glass portraiture, all whom Trinity claims or who claim Trinity. We never before realized so clearly that from Henry VIII to you these temples of learning have been an inspiration throughout the ages, in the continuity that is civilization. And tho it seldom rises, may the sun never set, on England.

July 16. We leave Cambridge in an hour, but will never forget it, and are thankful to it that to some little extent we are different now than when we came. [We felt the same way on July 31, 1970, leaving England for what we thought was the last time. (We came again in 1972.)]

We went on to bow in awe before the majesty of the cathedrals in Ely, Peterborough, Lincoln, York, and Durham. Then to Edinburgh, where I pointed out to Ariel the hill on which I had torn my only pants thirty-six years before. Naturally we had warm debates about Mary Queen of Scots. Ariel is the realist in our ménage, and laughed at my tenderness for the forlorn lass, reared in the Catholicism and grace of Renaissance Paris, suddenly cast upon a distant throne amid a sea of ob-Knoxious predestinarians, and suffering the ax upon her (once) lovely neck for having conspired against a rival queen.

Turning south, we dallied fondly in Walter Scott's Abbotsford home—for we too, in our younger years, had traveled through many of the Waverley Novels. Then down through Carlisle and the Lake District, still echoing Wordsworth; and through sooty Lancashire, where the battle of men against machines was still going on. And then into hilly Wales, searching for John Cowper Powys.

Soon after the death of his wife John had taken his Phyllis with him to England (1934), and, a little later, to Corwen, Merionetshire, Wales. We had long forewarned him of our coming, and he had sent us some joyous letters, in his usual slantendicular hand, cramped and curled and over-laid. From them I make out some pertinent passages:

Nov. 4, 1946

Hurrah! Phyllis and I are simply thrilled at the idea of seeing you again. . . . My only offspring—now 44, for he is exactly 30 years younger than his Dad—is a Roman Catholic priest in Bath, and I know he'd be thrilled to see you there as one of his father's most kind and most generous friends. . . .

Has my god-daughter Ethel given you and Ariel any grandchildren? . . . Give her my love, *please*.

And a year later,

Jan. 12, 1948

Will Durant, old friend, and Mistress old friend:
How Phyllis and I will look forward to those Days, July, 1948. Think of your taking rooms at the Owen Glendower!! But listen you won't *have* to *drive* out from there to Cae Coed . . . when you—as indeed it looks from your itinerary—may be suffering from a combined attack of Greek Fire, Roman Fever, Egyptian Plague, French Pox, Dutch "Hollander," Turkish Delight, the Spanish Fly, . . . for it's only a quarter of a mile . . . to the field "Cae" in the wood "Coed." . . .

We have a friend, a "Georgian" Poet called John Redwood Anderson, . . . who lodges in "The Square" just opposite the Owen Glendower Hotel, who is a bit of a philosopher, and a great "Fan" of yours; . . . and your old flighty sparring partner John has no small *kudos* with him from being a former pal of yours. . . .

Your ever loyal and faithful and affectionate Phyllis and John.

On July 23, 1948, we found them in their primitive brick cottage. When they heard us coming down the street John came out and advanced to welcome us, embracing Ariel and kissing me. He led us into the little room where he spent his days and nights, nearly all the time in bed; eating his meals there—mostly of milk and white crackers—and writing there book after book on a pad attached to a board that rested on his raised knees. He was now seventy-six years old but despite—or because of—his ulcer, he had already outlived his younger brother Llewelyn (1884–1939), and was destined to outlive his brother Theodore (1875–1953) and to die at the age of ninety-one. From his prostrate throne John talked with us for hours.

Phyllis, though she looked like a puritan maiden fresh from Kansas fields, had chosen to live with him as his unmarried wife; all through these years of hardship and contumely she had remained by his side, attending with quiet patience to his every want. Lately she had brought her mother and her aunt, both in their eighties, to live in the cottage next door. We were so moved by the poverty of this double household that Ariel quietly made a list of things in short supply—linens, sheets, blankets, and winter clothing. How could two little stoves keep these cottages warm in the sharp winters of northern Wales?

John was at that time writing a book on Rabelais; this most spiritual and stoic of our friends relished a robust humor, and he had written a volume *In Defense of Sensuality*. But he did not fool us; he was sensitive rather than sensual. Burdened with pain, fevered with the ecstatic search and fashioning of words, he had little time for sensual indulgences—the enjoyment of sense pleasure beyond rational measure and social control. His choice of the modest Phyllis, his love for his priest-son, and the rosary that we had seen hanging on a wall in his Greenwich Village room, meant, among other things, that he hungered for the ethical ideals of Christianity. Like Plato, he was an *anima naturaliter Christiana*. There was more purity in his unsanctioned union with Phyllis than in any but a few marriages in Christendom.

I have seldom met a mind that so enriched and illuminated ours. We came away deepened, exalted, and warmed. When we returned to America Ethel made up bundles of linen, warm underwear, stockings, heavy woolen socks, and other items, and sent them to Phyllis from Toronto. Max Schuster and Dick Simon, learning of John's situation, sent him royalties far above the earnings of his books. When the newspapers and broadcasts of the day incline me to despair of mankind, I remind myself that there are thousands of good deeds, every day, which the press and the airwaves find little incentive to record. Only the exceptional is news, and therefore the news is of the exceptional, and should be counted as such in our judgment of mankind.

John welcomed the gifts in a letter to Ethel:

Nov. 15, 1948

Why! Ethel, my dear child, "you were ever a giver, so one gift more, the best," etc.—as that rascally old Humbug of a too facile optimism, Mr. Robert Browning, [says,] whose credo both your Dad and I take with a pinch of attic salt!—But those stockings, shirts, sheets, and pillow cases are wonderful, and Phyllis and I are thrilled by them. . . . None but you, really, my kind friend and ex-ward, could have done this (or ex-godfather, wasn't it?), but never mind that, my *dear friend you are anyway* in the service of Mnemosyne, the Mother of the Muses! . . . It was simply splendid seeing your dear parents again after some fifteen years! Think of that! Your dad was just the same gentle contemplative ironical with a touch of Anatole France in his humorous toleration of the insanities of the human race and a touch of Renan in his wise interpretation of the Middle Ages on which he is engaged. And O my dear child how well I got on with your mother and always shall till I am dead. I can't tell you how entirely my instincts run in harmony with hers! And when I saw their dear figures (so precious and familiar in their peculiar reciprocity) leaving my door together—I thought "I'll ne'er see their like again!" It was a pleasure as rarely comes to a returned wanderer to have them sitting side by side in this room—incarnations of all the best I'd enjoyed in thirty years of *colportage!* . . . Don't ee bother to reply my dear for this scroll is a reply and a deep one!

And to us on the same day a similar letter came, likened by John to "a leaf from November's bare sycamores," and ending with "The gods guard you both." Neither shall we ever see his like again.

While we were in Wales it seemed logical to visit Bertrand Russell, who was living at Ffestiniog. He had invited us in recent letters, and he repeated the summons when we telephoned him from Corwen. So on July 24 we drove out some forty miles, and found him smoking his pipe in rare content, in a room whose walls were almost completely covered with neatly shelved books; here was a library that must be the gleanings of many generations.

Bertrand was now an earl, but there was nothing lordly about him except the confident consciousness of having a mind that moved like a deadly laser among the shams and delusions of his time. This rather awed and frightened me, for I had some romantic fancies of my own. I comforted my pride by wondering whether Russell's sharply quick and decisive thinking, despite his erudition, had ever allowed him to feel the wisdom hiding in the social and moral traditions of the race. But this is ungracious of me after having accepted his tea. He climbed some steps slowly to show us his children; he asked us to remember that he was then seventy-six years old. He lived (1970) into his ninety-eighth year, still leading noble and desperate causes, and sometimes coming out of the contest with glory. I admired him as a miracle among men, but—though I several times met him in friendly debate—I never knew him intimately enough to love him as I had come to love Powys. I believe that Powys was the deeper, subtler, kinder man.

Back in Corwen, we said goodbye to John and Phyllis, and drove out (July 25) toward Shrewsbury. On the way we saw death in a ghastly and ignoble form: a motorcyclist lying in the road, killed, we were told, in trying to pass a vehicle on a hill; he had been catapulted from his machine into the windshield of an oncoming car; apparently he had passed from life to death with merciful suddenness. Beside the road sat two women weeping over shock and undisclosed injuries. We went our way in sober silence.

We found little to attract us in Birmingham, and we passed on to Worcester, Gloucester, and Oxford; there we visited the colleges, and learned to pronounce "Magdalen" in the proper maudlin way. On July 29 we mused among the ruins of Stonehenge, and later felt the grace of Salisbury Cathedral. We liked Winchester better; we stood in awe in that immense nave, where from the portal font one could hardly distinguish the clerics who moved in the distant sacristy. At Southampton we exchanged the Daimler car for the steamship *Queen Elizabeth,* and moved quietly through the inlet into the English Channel and the sea. We reached New York on August 4, after the most extensive and profitable of our ventures in search of the past. We spent the remainder of the summer at Lake Hill, and on September 18 we repossessed our Los Angeles home.

Ten days later, to pay for all this, I set out on another lecture tour. On October 1, in Baltimore, I lunched with H. L. Mencken, and wrote to Ariel that afternoon: "Mencken is 68, simple, bluff, and obviously honest. He filled me with taffy about *The Story of Civilization,* saying he can hardly wait for Volume IV. . . . He is one of those who hide a really generous spirit under a rough exterior. He walked me back to the station, and wanted to carry my bag when we failed to find a red cap." I did not tell Ariel that on that walk Mencken pointed down a side street to a burlesque theater, and told me how often he had enjoyed at least the comedians there, especially "Sliding Billy Watson"—whom I had seen elsewhere slaloming across the stage.

Amid these historical studies I received a faithful report from Ariel, then staying at the Half Moon Hotel in Coney Island.

Oct. 2, 1948

Was handed two letters from you yesterday. . . . It made me dizzy just reading about the chase your merry lecture agent arranged, but you made it with your usual luck and brains. . . . We had more peace and leisure in Europe, stunned as we were by all we saw and heard. I too have been harried and hurried by "friends" and family, and only now, after having gotten the "girls"—Flora, Mary, Sarah—and Mother packed and settled into the car, unpacked and settled into a two-room suite here, am I able to write to you.

My stay of six days at the Sturzes' was very pleasant. . . . Before I leave N.Y.C. on the 22nd I intend to visit them and kiss them goodby and thank them for their most considerate kindness. . . .

I pay $75.00 a week for our two rooms here, but the air and the lovely view of the ocean and the long span of the boardwalk make it all worth while. . . . The summer flies and the fetid flesh are all gone, and the expanse of shimmering moon on the ocean is overwhelming and silent. I went in swimming just before dark, and felt so invigorated and stimulated I looked for you all over the place, and had to content myself with an hour's brisk walk. . . . I knew all the time that you were far away, though always and ever near. So long as it is nice I hope to take a daily dip, . . . and keep trim so that first Ethel and Jim and then you will be pleased with me.

At Cleveland I had a pleasant interlude with Flora's and our son Louis and his wife and baby son.

10-4-48

Louis took me thru the plant that he is rebuilding for the Cleveland *Press*. I never knew he could superintend so complex an undertaking. We may all be proud of him. He's learned the secret I used to preach to him: external modesty, internal pride. We reached his home in time for a good luncheon that Mollie had prepared. . . . As soon as she had finished the dishes she began to prepare dinner; I took pity on her and invited them out for dinner. . . . They're an ideal young American couple. . . . Tell Flora her boy is A-1. . . .

I took Eric for a long go-cart walk, and he behaved like a gentleman, except that he insisted on touching every hydrant, like a Pomeranian. He was a delight all thru the two days I spent with him—prattling, singing, . . . laying his head trustfully on my knee. . . .

Now back to my money-making, and my MS.

A hectic journey brought me to Cedar Rapids, Iowa, where I was rewarded with Ariel's letter. I replied gratefully,

10-5-48

Tho I am here for only a few crowded hours I must tell you how wonderful, beautiful, glorious is the letter you wrote last Saturday, Oct. 2nd, from the Half Moon Hotel. I am glad you and your family are getting the fresh air afterward; I would dry even the salt water from every inch of your body with my kisses. Thank you for keeping yourself fit; it is more than any man can deserve, to have a wife who cheats age with health, and keeps herself sweet and beautiful thru all the years.

Like so many of your letters, this last one is literature. . . . I must treasure it, so that some day, when we are old (i.e., many, many years from now), we may come upon it in a trunk or album, and enjoy it together. [The fates were kind.] Write me another! . . .

Emporia, Kan., 10-7-48

. . . An unusual experience last night. I had addressed the Knife and Fork Club of Salina in 1944 on "What Are the Lessons of History?," but the secretary had deliberately arranged to have me repeat that lecture. Funnier still, his records showed that I had spoken to the same club in 1941 on the same topic. Protesting, I went thru with it; and the memory of the lecture goers is so brief that apparently it all seemed new to them, and all went well. Finally the secretary is coming to hear the same lecture tonight. . . .

Send me one of those Horace Walpole–Mme. de Sévigné letters!

Oklahoma City, 10-11-48

. . . Did a pile of work yesterday; maybe broke the world's record for writing—4800 words—12 big pages. . . . The book [*The Age of Faith*] is getting along, and will be far and away my best.

Dallas, 10-12-48

. . . A fever has come upon me; I work on the book every moment that I am not eating, sleeping, or lecturing; in jerky trains and bouncing buses as well as in hotels; and when the conveyance jars too much for writing I correct the MS. of the next chapter to be transcribed. When I reach Los Angeles I expect to have finished half the second draft; and at Lake Hill I finished two thirds of the first draft. But the chapters still to be written are embarrassingly rich in material, and will resist my high-compression engine.

Austin, Texas, 10-13-48

Your welcome letter greeted me this morning amid a confusion of greetings. Two students met me at the train, three more joined us for breakfast, three reporters came to the room at 8:30, and at 9:30 I had to give a radio interview, . . . for my lecture is paid for by the students, and . . . they begged me help them scare up a good attendance.

At noon a group of faculty members are lunching me, and at 6:15 a Jewish fraternity is dining me—despite Yom Kippur tonight. This is surely my day of atonement. But it is pleasant to see the intellectual eagerness of these young people, and hear the basic questions they ask. This, as you know, is the University of Texas, with 17,000 students. It's a bustling town, full of handsome youths and bobby-sox girls.

Lubbock, Texas, 10-14-48

. . . I had a wonderful audience last night—2500 college students, bright, eager, alert. . . . They gave me the longest "hand" I've ever received; they stayed for half an hour of questions, and then gathered around me with a dozen more questions, and with many books to be autographed. I was exhausted, but content. I wish I could lecture only to college students. . . .

Ariel undertook, on October 22, the perilous task of driving from New York to Strathroy, Canada, for a visit with Ethel, Gordon, and Jimmy, and then on to Saginaw, Michigan, where we planned to meet on October 26. I had advised against the venture, but she enjoyed these bouts with the great god Chance. So I sent her detailed instructions, and added,

10-18-48

Bon voyage! Take care, my precious comrade; resist the speed fever; don't drive at night; get yourself safely into my arms at Saginaw, and then at Los Angeles, and every night thereafter till the Lord writes *finis* on the book of my life. . . .

Slowly, like an old mosaicist, I am putting the 10,000 pieces of medieval life together into a co-ordinated picture. . . .

Pratt, Kansas, 10-19-48

Your letter of the 14th . . . is so beautifully written . . . that I am sending this weak word of appreciation to you in care of Ethel, as a weak substitute for my welcoming arms. A soothing bath will refresh you, and make you, as always, the *élan vital* of wherever you are.

Give Ethel a hug for me, and read some more of *Hiawatha* to Jim. . . . How I wish I could lie beside you while you read, and feast on you and Jimmy's earnest, all-absorbing eyes. . . . If you feel a mysterious squeeze tonight in bed, it's

WILL

Ariel must have read some good literature at Coney Island amid the surge and murmur of the surf. I find among her notes from that fortnight on the beach this: "Remarkable that a book like Gibbon's *Decline and Fall* should have sprung from something so temporary and ephemeral as a man." I was feeling very ephemeral at that time, but I was perked up by a telegram received at Pratt from New York:

Oct. 19, 1948

Just had a most delightful and stimulating visit with Sinclair Lewis in which he spent most of the time singing praises of Will Durant and of *Caesar and Christ* . . . as "a magnificent history of Rome." Agrees enthusiastically with H. Mencken and

M. LINCOLN SCHUSTER

Ethel drove Ariel to Saginaw; I spent October 26 with them; then Ethel went back to Strathroy, and I drove Ariel to Chicago, most of the way with one hand. There, after our usual *agape* meal with Dr. Zurawski, I resumed my barnstorming, while Ariel steered her car bravely to California. At Denver I received a reassuring note that the long trek was nearing its end. I wrote to her,

11-4-48

. . . You undertook a tremendous job, and as usual when you are left to face a man's work, you accomplished it heroically. You and Truman are the heroes of the hour. . . . Having made $16,150 gross on this trip (of which $10,000 will remain after commissions and fares), I can now devote myself to *The A-of-F* and to you with a clear conscience. It will take me a week to catch up with business, then to work! But I am resolved to be a good husband first, a good writer only after that. . . .

We were reunited with each other, and with our home, on November 7. As I convalesced under Ariel's care and smiles, I remembered that audience of two thousand teachers at McCook, Nebraska, to whom, on October 29, I had had to talk on "The Haunts of Happiness"—and only five percent of them married, and half of them hopeless maids; and I thought of the thousands of broken marriages and divided children in an America chaotic with sex unchained; and I blessed the day when I had met, and the day when I had married, this "child of Manhattan," this girl with the abounding zest of life in her, and the courage of lasting youth, and the love large enough to forgive a man all his faults and cherish him through all the years of his interminable senility.

CHAPTER XXII

On to Dante

1949–50

Ariel:

Don't believe my "crafty Doctor" when he talks about senility. He was, as 1948 ended (and as 1970 proceeds) still dangerously sensitive to swelling bosoms and flashing ankles; he still had seven volumes of *Civilization* in his belly, plus some later tomes and this one; and he is clever enough to turn over the pen to me just when he has reached a plateau of months and incidents undeserving of record except to indulge our memories or to commemorate our friends.

Ethel, Gordon, and Jim came down from Canada in February to warm themselves for three weeks in the California sunshine. After they left I wrote to Ethel:

March 11, 1949

The evening after seeing you off we entered the quiet house with a tightening in the throat, for we knew no one [no seven-year-old boy] was asleep in Popsy's study, and no one would awake us in the morning. For a long time ideas would come, be scratched down on paper; we would reach for our usual books toward evening; but for the happy noise of a child visibly growing we would have to wait and dream, and hope that summer comes soon. . . .

Sometime in June Jimmy, now hovering between seven and eight years old, came from Canada to stay for a month with his father, David Easton, who had remarried. I borrowed Jim for a day, and took him for a ride to a friend in Bel Air Estates. From my letter of July 1 to Ethel:

279

In the spacious patio we frolicked around with three little daughters, . . . climbing apricot trees, plum trees, and the most wonderful huge blackberry tree—each berry 1½ inches long—and eating of everything until we all looked like bleeding pigs, for the berries were that red and juicy.

We drove home in time, 4 P. M., for Jim to undress and dive in nude with Daddy for a swim; and here again he had us thanking you and God—or God and you—for he dived and swam fearlessly, and showed us many tricks, and asked us to show him how to swim under water with eyes open. . . . He is learning even that. We had a lovely dinner—no starches, meats, or fats—and he looked and behaved like a Kellogg dream. . . .

Will was now the passionate prisoner of his book. *The Age of Faith* had been planned as a five-year task, but was taking six, and was suffering from gigantism. His letter to one of his publishers shows him in a stage of advanced and troubled pregnancy.

7-4-49

DEAR RICHARD:

Here's hoping you're having a pleasant summer, and that you and Andrea and your lovely children are still living where they can see grass and flowers grow, and hear birds sing. They sing too much hereabouts, and force us to rise at 6 A.M. . . .

I expect, barring illness, to . . . have the complete MS in your hands by March 1st. I trust that this will permit . . . publication by October 15. . . . We should be able to keep the promise that Volume III made to our readers—that Volume IV would be ready in 1950. . . .

It is unfortunate that the book must, by chronology, begin with Byzantine, then go on to Islamic and Judaic, civilization, before reaching the more familiar ground of Western Christian Europe; but if I can get the reader to survive those 300 pages he will realize their necessity for a proper perspective and understanding of medieval civilization.

You will be shocked to learn that the printed book . . . will run to some 1400 pages, and will require two-volume form. Try as I would, and conscientiously have done, I found it impossible to give a just and adequate account of the quadruple medieval panorama . . . in less compass or detail. I felt that we should aim to do a good job rather than make money by skimpy popularization and the shirking of difficult topics like medieval Moslem, Jewish, and Christian science and philosophy. . . .

Remember us to Max when he returns. We have just received a nice letter from him, redolent of Italian vineyards and Roman ruins.

That letter soon required some amendments. First, the publishers persuaded Will that the full final MS could be readably printed in one volume of some twelve hundred pages. It was so done. A two-volume edition was also issued; it sold a tenth of the one-volume form. Second, we discovered an excellent typist, Mrs. Edith Digate, who soon learned to understand Will's handwriting and abbreviations (*d=ed; g=ing;*

Xtn=Christian, civn=civilization, etc.), and had the patience to transcribe with conscientious accuracy the thousands of unfamiliar Greek, Islamic, Hebraic, and Latin names or terms that littered the text. She was so cheerfully competent that I was afraid Will would fall in love with her, for he was ready to fall in love at the drop of a handkerchief or the rise of a hem; but Edith was proud of her own scholar husband, and offered no temptations.

I read in its typed form the chapters on the medieval Jews, and I liked them so much that I gossiped, especially about the section on Maimonides. Some rabbis heard of this, and Will was surprised with an invitation to speak on Maimonides at the Wilshire Boulevard Temple—Los Angeles' leading center of Reformed Judaism. He accepted with some trepidation, which increased when we learned that several rabbis would sit on the stage and be asked to comment on the lecture. But the rabbis were gentle; they confined their public remarks to their pleasure in finding a Christian so familiar and sympathetic with a medieval Jewish thinker. I was especially proud of my William that evening.

In October Will took to the road again for seventeen lectures in twenty-seven days. As usual, he wrote to me almost daily, though he was feverishly at work polishing the final—Dante—chapter in *The Age of Faith*. So, from the Hermitage, Nashville,

10-7-49

Today at last I have a quiet half-day in this fine old hotel, and shall take another look at Dante. Your intercession for him has saved his life, but I still think he is the most disagreeable of the immortals. I revised my Dante chapter yesterday on the train, and found the final page a failure. I'll rewrite it and rewrite it till it's good. . . .

From Omaha my Old Faithful wrote:

10-10-49

. . . In my room at Chicago yesterday I found myself hanging on the wall. There, over the bed, was Norman Rockwell's fine picture of "Freedom of Worship," and alongside of it, framed, my text under my name. I understand that most of the rooms in the Sherman Hotel have two of the four pictures, so that tired drummers can now read themselves to sleep under me. . . .

I shall try to join you in your room at the Markeen Hotel, Buffalo, Oct. 22nd, 7 A.M., if the room clerk doesn't protest against such immoral proceedings.

From the Hotel Sherman, Chicago,

10-14-49

You can't imagine what a pleasant surprise I had yesterday at Alma, 'way up in the north of Michigan. . . . At 5 P.M. the landlady . . . came to call

281

me to the phone. It was Ethel. She and Gordon had driven 120 miles, and had reached Owosso, 50 miles from Alma. . . . At 6:15 they burst into my room. We had dinner together, they accompanied me to my lecture on "The Haunts of Happiness," and Ethel was not displeased to hear me tell the audience about Jimmy's "Even when you're dead you'll remember how much you loved me." Then we went to a reception at the home of a college official; we separated at midnight, . . . and I was driven in the college car to catch a 2:35 A.M. train at Lansing to Chicago. So here I am again; and in a few minutes I must make "The Lessons of Philosophy" intelligible to 1200 businessmen luncheoneers.

I long for you.

I spent a day in Chicago with my old friend Hattie Malkin, and reached Los Angeles October 31; Will, on November 3. Soon thereafter Cobina Wright interviewed me for the *Herald Express,* asking particularly if Will's absorption in his work had caused him to neglect me. I gave quite a different answer than I would have given twenty years before. Cobina's report, printed on November 22, quoted me as saying, "I confess that sometimes I've been a bit jealous, but Will hasn't neglected me; and bit by bit I too have been drawn into the undertaking, and find myself now almost as interested in it as he is." The report continued:

> Working so closely with this philosophical genius was an extraordinary experience for Ariel, who says, "Now I see how a writer has to be an architect in designing the order of his book; a sculptor in molding each part, paragraph, and sentence: a painter in suffusing the narrative with the color of the age and place; and almost a musician in giving rhythm and flow to every line."

We were happy to learn, in January, 1950, that our friends Louis and Hattie Sturz had accepted our invitation to spend a California holiday at our home. We enjoyed their company because they gave us a stimulating example of integrity and dedication, and because their calm and mature judgment had often served as a saving corrective of our leaping judgments and warm emotions. Many a time we had been their house guests; now we would reciprocate with sunshine and "stars." But Louis had been overworking himself, and perhaps the travail of travel had frayed his nerves. Soon after his arrival, as we were dining in a nearby restaurant he felt a chest pain so severe that we hurried him to our home and called a doctor. Louis could hardly believe the diagnosis that he had suffered a heart attack; but the doctor bade him go to Cedars of Lebanon Hospital, where he could recover his strength under constant and expert care. His wife bore this misfortune with her usual quiet courage. Every day we took her to the hospital, where she spent nearly all her working hours at his bedside; and three evenings a week we joined her in her vigil.

During those weeks Will was completing the final draft of *The Age of Faith.* I felt a close interest in that volume, because nearly all the material for it had passed through my hands for classification, and my persistent arguments had played a part in keeping up his enthusiasm for the task, and in giving the concluding chapter a more sympathetic tone. When all the manuscript had been typed, I read every page of it, and then startled both Will and myself by telling him that it was the greatest book I had ever read. Will smiled at my amorous prejudice. But I set to work to advertise the volume wherever I found an opening. I needed no coaxing when Rabbi Nussbaum, of Temple Israel, Hollywood, invited me to speak on *The Age of Faith,* on March 1, in his series of pulpit book reviews. It seemed silly to review a book seven months before its publication, but our friends brought together a tolerant audience for me, and I prated for an hour and a quarter about Julian the Apostate, Mohammed, Omar Khayyam, Maimonides, Charlemagne, Saladin, Abélard, Dante . . . When at last I finished, Geraldine Kroll asked, whimsically, "What made you stop?"

We were brought back to earth by discovering, on March 20, 1950, that our house had been burglarized the evening before, during one of our visits to Louis Sturz in the hospital. Some jewelry belonging to Mrs. Sturz had been taken from the dresser in her room. Our safe had been forced open, and the greater part of our savings had been stolen. Luckily most of these were in the form of U.S. savings bonds, of which we had kept a careful record. When the police came at our call, Will gave them the serial numbers of the bonds and the stock certificates; detectives went to work; and by 5 P.M. of the next day all had been restored. The Los Angeles *Times* of March 21 spread over its front page the ambiguous headline "DURANT LOOT RECOVERED," raising us to a fame that our books would never have earned.

> Two Hollywood detectives, acting on a [bartender's] tip, early today seized a 22-year-old transient, and from his room recovered $314,000 in nonnegotiable stocks and bonds, and jewelry valued at $300, stolen from the home of philosopher Dr. Will Durant Sunday night.
>
> George B. Roden, recently discharged from the Navy, was arrested at 1655 N. Western Ave., where the Durant loot was recovered from the back of an overstuffed chair by Dets. T. T. Belcher and Raymond Keeley.
>
> "It scared me to death when I saw all that money," Roden, who says he comes from Massachusetts, told officers. "I was afraid someone would bump me off for it. I just happened to be going by and saw the people leave. . . . I got into the house by taking a glass out of a window."
>
> Police counted $278,000 in bonds and $36,000 in stocks . . . Included among the jewelry [was] a pearl necklace . . . belonging to Mrs. Hattie Sturz of New York . . . The burglary occurred between 7 and 9 P.M. Sunday while Dr. and Mrs. Durant and Mrs. Sturz were at Cedars of Lebanon Hospital. . . .
>
> Five cars of officers conducted an investigation. Mrs. Durant discovered the mode of entry used by the burglar. . . . Dr. Durant was more concerned about loss of time from his work than about the loss of the nonnegotiable

papers. "They can have material things," he said, "as long as they leave me ten more years of life." It will take him ten years, he said, to complete the remaining volumes . . . in his "History of Civilization." Only a few hours before the burglary he sent his publisher the manuscript for the fourth volume.

It is entitled "Age of Faith."

We were allowed to interview the prisoner. He was almost penniless. We advised the police to release him on parole, but they objected that such lenience encouraged crime; he was sent to jail. Apparently he behaved well; the police called us to inquire if we still wanted him freed on parole; we said "Yes." Our "loot" having been restored, we sent it to Allan Lehman, of Lehman Brothers, and asked him what we should do with it; he recommended selling the bonds (which were suffering from inflation) and dividing the proceeds among five investment firms. We did.

A fragment of my notes indicates a pleasant conjuncture of events. Soon after reading, in typescript, Will's account of *Carmina Burana*, I heard Leopold Stokowski conduct the Los Angeles Symphony Orchestra in Orff's hypnotic setting of these "Bavarian Poems" so piously preserved by Benedictine monks. "The last of the Bowl concerts," I wrote, "ended in a grand blaze. 'Stokey' had the carriage of a dying Prometheus . . . ; the fingers and hands sparkled as of old; in them you could see the showman still lived. . . . A wonderful sight, [but] when you closed your eyes you transported yourself, via the music, to the glorious student days of Abélard or the wandering scholars so eloquently described in *The Age of Faith*." Poor Helen Waddell, who had provided Will with facts, and fired his feelings, about those scenes, was here shamefully forgotten.

Sometimes in the spring of 1950 we rented our home to Sidney Moss, a Los Angeles lawyer. We agreed that he could keep it for at least a year, for we were planning a long stay in Europe gathering material about the Renaissance and the Reformation. We recklessly decided to take a car with us, and keep our schedule open to changing moods and needs. We drove to Strathroy and then to Cleveland to see our children, and then to Lake Hill to spend the summer with my family. On September 25 I moved into the Park Chambers Hotel in New York, and Will went off lecturing.

I continued, wherever I went, to make propaganda for the forthcoming book. My enthusiasm for the book led me to optimistic expectations which Will sought to moderate in a letter from Cedar Rapids, October 16: "Please don't let your sweet wishes obscure your realistic thinking; we shall probably have a *succès d'estime*—favorable reviews but a modest sale. . . . All in all, we can't expect more than 30,000 copies sold by July 1, 1951. . . ."

On October 23 Volume IV—1,216 crowded pages—burst upon a distracted world. That morning in New York I lived in suspended animation until I could find out what Orville Prescott would say about it in the *Times*—for authors awaited this learned reviewer's verdict with almost the anxiety of dramatists and producers awaiting, at Sardi's, the judgment of critics on the premiere of a play. I breathed again when I read that generous and enthusiastic review; and I danced when I read Sterling North's approval in that afternoon's *World-Telegram.* Max Schuster, who had cheered Will on through all six years of gestation, drew up a long telegram, quoting these reviews; read it to me over the telephone, and then sent it, over his name and mine, to Will at Port Arthur, Texas. I have those reviews before me now, twenty years after, and have reread them with shameless pleasure. All in all, *The Age of Faith,* the most difficult of the series to write or to read, received the most consistent acclaim. Some errors were pointed out, but graciously.* We noted that the long and laudatory article in *The Saturday Review* was signed by Sidney Packard, professor of History at Amherst College, and author of *Europe and the Church under Innocent III;* Will was gradually overcoming the reluctance of the academic community to approve of a nonacademic historian.

November, 1950, was for us a hectic month. Every day we consumed reviews. On November 5 Will, Louis Sturz, and Dr. Stone celebrated together their birthdays, which fell a few days apart in that month. On November 22 we delivered our convertible Oldsmobile to the S. S. *Excambion* for transport to Marseilles. The vessel was small; the larger "liners" did not at that time take cars for transport. On the twenty-fifth, Thanksgiving Day, we dined the Kaufman family at the Café Royal. On the twenty-fourth Charles and Hilda Bensley drove us to the pier, and saw us off in style on the *Excambion.* Will took a Dramamine pill and prepared for the worst.

We were sailing the "sunshine route," headed for the French Riviera. On the second day we ran into a storm so severe that nearly every passenger crept into bed. At every roll the deck dipped to within a few feet of the waves; at every pitch the prow sank into the sea as if welcoming escape from so angry a world. Strange to say, Will, usually the first to succumb, held his food, missed no meal, and paced the rolling deck in confidence that the ballast of cargo would check every roll in time. The captain explained that the pitch was more dangerous than the roll; at every pitch a hundred tons of water fell upon the forward hatch, threatening to break it open and swamp the hold. So he slowed our speed to a few knots. We did not urge him to go faster, and we made no complaint when we reached Marseilles on the sixth of December instead of the fourth.

---

* The most serious of many errors (now long since corrected) was the attribution to Marie de France of a lovely poem ascribed to her in Mark Van Doren's fine *Anthology of World Poetry.* A French medievalist reported that he could find no such poem in the extant remains of Marie. The alleged "translation" turned out to be a poem "in the spirit of Marie de France" by Arthur O'Shaughnessy.

We remained cheerful until our Oldsmobile was hoisted up from the hold and lowered to the dock, and we could see what the storm had done to it. The roll and pitch and vibrations had loosened the blocks and bolts that were designed to hold the car unmoved; it had oscillated sufficiently, in those twelve days at sea, to wear the side walls of the tires almost to bursting point. Will drove me and our baggage to the Hotel Bristol, and then off through the hectic city to find a shop that would sell us four suitable new tires. After a day of struggle we discovered an agent who would examine the discarded tires so that we might get some benefit from the international insurance we had purchased in New York. Two months of negotiations passed before our claim was honored.

On December 8 we ventured forth, on tortuous, narrow, and unfamiliar roads, along the Côte d'Azur through Toulon, Saint-Tropez, and Saint-Raphaël to Cannes. There we avoided the majestic, expensive Carlton Hotel, and settled, after much toil and trouble (Will lugging our luggage up two flights of stairs) in the tiny Hotel Cinna, kept by a Madame Genêt who was no relation to Sartre's "Saint."

In Cannes we received a letter from Max Schott describing the terrible storm New York had suffered on the day after our departure, and complimenting us on having escaped it by leaving on the *Excambion*. Another letter was from one whom we had known only through correspondence, and through constant indebtedness to the meticulous scholarship of his magazine *Isis*, and his gigantic *Introduction to the History of Science*. The letter may seem irrelevant here, but it shared with other similar experiences in molding Will's incorrigible faith in man.

Thanksgiving, 1950

Thanks for your gracious letter. My beloved wife died last Saturday—in her sleep. She was utterly exhausted and longing for release. We had been married 40 years, 40 blessed years—without a cloud—except my anxieties about her health, which was never good. Whatever there is in me of goodness and grace I owe to her. Without her, *Isis* would not exist, for during 28 years . . . I was paying its chronic deficits, and that would have been impossible without her abnegation. I was never able to give her jewels, or a fur coat, or a new hat—but she did not care for such foolish things. She was incinerated last Tuesday; the service read by a Quaker was restricted to 1 Cor. 13—then music, Bach, whom she loved. No words about which theologians are always ready to quarrel, . . . but only music.

I am sure you will enjoy your stay in Europe.

With kindest regards,
GEORGE SARTON

After settling down in our two rooms, we toured the town looking for a mechanic familiar with American cars. While Will kept an eye on the repair of our Oldsmobile, I stepped into an old bookstore which had a real *embarras de richesses*—a rich collection in almost complete chaos. I knew that Will had bought the first two volumes of Jules Michelet's *Histoire de France*, and had searched unsuccessfully for the rest. I asked for them now; the lazy salesman found one; I nagged him to look around for more; one by one they were discovered, scattered here and there. At last I held all five—big, double-column, beautifully illustrated volumes. I hurried with them to Will; he embraced them and me with equal ardor. We have always been devotees and defenders of Michelet, though we knew that later historians, safe in their specialties, had criticized his errors and his prejudices, and had frowned upon his eloquence.

We spent an uncomfortable winter in Cannes. We had thought of the French Riviera as an escape from the winter's cold; it had been so proclaimed by Lord Henry Brougham, whose statue still stands near the Cannes *mairie*. Madame Genêt could not or would not heat our rooms adequately; we had to read and write with gloves on, and wrapped in overcoats and blankets; I can still in memory see Will huddled before an old and crowded desk, handling half a dozen books at a time, and warming himself with enthusiasm for the Renaissance.

He had promised that Volume V would cover both the Renaissance and the Reformation, which were to provide the counterpoint of an age that planted its roots a world apart—in the pagan classics and in early Christian theology. As he proceeded he was swept into the ardor of the Renaissance Italians; he found those burning lights more to his liking than the cold heroes of the German and English Reformation; finally he decided to give an entire volume to the Renaissance—and to the Italian Renaissance alone. I felt that this was an error in perspective and proportion after compressing into one volume a thousand years of Byzantine, Islamic, Judaic, Catholic, and feudal history. But the Master had his way, and frolicked for three years in a period and country that he loved with all the passion of a pagan who swooned before sunsets and beautiful women, and with all the piety of a skeptic who was still, below the neck, a good Catholic charmed by steeples, crosses, hymns, incense, and nuns. I take him and love him as he is, a strange and intoxicating mixture of Pygmalion, Alyosha, Erasmus, and (in imagination) Don Juan.

CHAPTER XXIII

Italian Ecstasy

1951–53

Will:

Ariel is right: I surrendered helplessly to the Renaissance, and gave to the three centuries of its Italian phases an affection and enthusiasm quite out of proportion to the 1,086 pages of text which, in *The Age of Faith,* I had divided among a dozen lands and a thousand years. A similar complaint was made by Simon Ramo, scientist and philosopher, who compared me to a musician compressing an accordion: "You squeeze time more tightly as you go along." I pleaded in excuse that as the persons and events dealt with came closer, in time and influence, to our own age, they required a more detailed treatment of their character and effects.

In some measure Ariel and I divided the European Renaissance between us. I buried myself in Petrarch, Boccaccio, Alexander VI, Leonardo, Leo X, Raphael, Julius II, Michelangelo, and Machiavelli, while she consumed with delight every extant word of Montaigne, and spread her love to that gourmet of women, Henry of Navarre and IV of France. Meanwhile, at Cannes, she found a living friend in Alia Bersin, a Russian emigrée, who amused us with her wit and her personal memories of Nijinsky and other stars of theater and ballet. Helpful and generous to both of us were Étienne and Clarita Isch-Wall, who opened their own and other doors to us, and even discovered a local professor who had read one of my books.

Otherwise we found little to interest us in a Cannes winter. The Mediterranean, though beautiful, was cold, and blurred with fog. The motion

pictures presented in the small but numerous theaters were all in collo-
quial French, which I could seldom follow with clear understanding,
much less translate, *currente lingua*, for Ariel. At times she felt keenly her
absence from her children and her sisters. Among her notes I find the
rough draft of a letter to Ethel.

> This is the first time that we spend New Year's Day abroad. Though we
> are sad and lonesome to be so far from family and friends, it is an interest-
> ing experience. It throws us completely upon ourselves, making us all the
> more sensitive to other people and countries—though strange to us, still
> simple and human and quite pleasing. We shall walk the streets until the
> New Year becomes a *fait accompli*; . . . we will climb up into our little
> rooms and go to sleep, and with unbroken continuity dream of you and
> Jim, and hope that this year may be one of understanding and good will
> towards all people everywhere.

We mitigated our loneliness with listening to the radio, which I translated to Ariel as well as I could. I remember especially a broadcast by
Arthur Honegger, in which the composer declared that in his judgment
most contemporary compositions were products of decomposition. The
local casino, besides living on legalized gambling, offered a course of
lectures featuring André Maurois, André Siegfried, and Édouard Herriot.
Only club members were allowed to attend, but Madame Genêt managed
to get me in for Herriot's talk on the poetess Anna, Comtesse de
Noailles. The President of the National Assembly limped in on a cane,
and under a mane of hair surprisingly black for his seventy-nine years;
was this a wig or dye? I treasured one gem from that hour: *"L'été c'est un
couleuriste; l'hiver c'est un dessinateur*—Summer is a colorist; winter is a
designer;—stressing line through the bare branches against the sky; here
was one difference between the romantic and the classic styles.

Sometime during that winter we motored up to Vence, where we had
the luck to meet Picasso. Of our brief conversation I recall chiefly my
remark that the whim of history might make the Vatican a dependency of
a Communist Italy. (In 1948 the Communist Party had almost captured
Italy.) Picasso replied that in this case the Pope would join the multiplying faithful in America. I admired his way of supplying an autograph—a
P followed by a reckless dash; this seemed to me an excellent time-saving
device. However, having been brought up to worship the classic style of
harmonious form and clear significance, I found it hard to see in Picasso
anything more than a genial humorist who wittingly turned masterly
skill to transitory bizarreries; I confess that this view dates me damnably.
More to my taste were the nearby relics of Pierre-Auguste Renoir, who,
even in old age and with arthritic hands, produced work that added life
to life, and humanity to mankind.

After two months of stoic work in chilly Cannes, we rode forth, on
February 22, 1951, to find some warmth in Italy. Our beginning was not

propitious: some patriot, or a lover of vigorous individuality, had, during the night, cut large slashes into our convertible top. Daring rain and robbery (for part of our baggage occupied the rear seat), we moved in awe along the Grande Corniche, through the double jeopardy of *douane* and *dogana* (customs offices) and through San Remo—lovelier then than we found it, choked with tourists, in 1970. Then our Golgotha began: the road for thirty miles was under repair and passable only by repeated miracles; near Savona it was a slalom course weaving between rocks and holes; in Genoa it was a tangle of traffic and a deluge of rain; we had a wet time finding a safe haven for our car and a warm bed for ourselves.

The next morning the sun shone, and it was Italy again. We explored the churches, palaces, and galleries of the once rich and now reviving city; here enterprising merchants and able shipbuilders, with two thousand years of skill and courage behind them, were recapturing Mediterranean—were soon to capture South Atlantic trade.

On February 27 we set out again, along the Riviera di Levante. We paid our respects to Santa Margherita and Portofino, and then drove down the coast through Rapallo to La Spezia, where we stopped to remember Shelley, who had lived nearby and had drowned in the bay. At Ameglia we diverged left to see the quarries of Carrara, where Renaissance sculptors and architects had sought and found incomparable marble. Then through Viareggia to Pisa, where we spent a day in or around the cathedral, the baptistery, the campanile or Leaning Tower, and the Campo Santo. Postponing Florence to our return trip, we hurried south to Rome, where we lived for two weeks in a *pensione*.

From Rome we zigzagged our way north through Viterbo and Orvieto to Arezzo, where we sought out the traces of its most famous son, Petrarch, and its most reckless libertine, Pietro Aretino; here, while Ariel rested her feet, I followed the faded frescoes of Piero della Francesca. We spent a week in Florence, and then directed our baggage- and book-laden car to take us over the Apennines to Bologna.

It was the end of March, and the mountain roads were still likely to be slippery with snow. We shopped around Florence for chains; we found masterpieces everywhere, but no tire chains. Chainless we went forth, praying to Tyche, the god Chance. Soon we reached the snow line; by eleven o'clock we were climbing slowly between walls of packed snow five feet high, imprisoning us on either side; if we should meet a descending car we would have to slide backward to some widened passing spot. Our wheels began to lose grip; we moved more slowly than if we had walked; we wondered what we would do if we began to slip back— wait in a passing place till summer came? But at last, with a prayer turned sigh, we reached the summit, and cautiously descended the eastern slope. When we came to *terra piàna* and a hotel room in Bologna, Ariel embraced me as the new Lord of the Apennines, but she should have reproached me for my recklessness.

Italian Ecstasy

After a restful stay in the Albergo Majestic, cool walks under the arcades, and a contemplative séance in the gloomy cathedral, we turned east to Faenza, Forlì, Rimini, and San Marino; then north to Ravenna and its mosaics, Ferrara and Tasso, Padua and Giotto; then east to Mestre, where we were glad to leave our car and take the boat for a ride between the palaces and under the bridges of the Grand Canal. We remained only three days in Venice, for we had worshiped there before; but we went through again the Palace of the Doges and the Accademia di Belle Arti, and I believe it was on this trip that (by bribing the sacristan to draw aside the curtains that concealed it) we were allowed to see Titian's *Assumption of the Virgin* in the Church of Santa Maria Gloriosa dei Frari.

Back in our car, and taking turns at the wheel, we drove through Treviso, Vicenza, and Verona; we sat in Palladio's theater and heard a concert in a Roman amphitheater; then we headed south to Mantua, for we were enamored of Isabella d'Este, and perhaps even more of Baldassare Castiglione, whose *Il cortegiano* had tried to teach me how to be a gentleman.

On April 18 we arrived at Parma, where again my carelessness brought on an hour of comic tragedy. We drew up our Oldsmobile before the *duomo,* wherein we hoped to see Correggio's *Assumption.* In my hurry, and with my head swimming with sensuous Madonnas, I left the ignition key in its slot, closed and automatically locked all the doors of the car, and ran up the steps into the cathedral, with Ariel lagging behind my sexagenarian pace. I was still in ecstasy as I came out, until I found no ignition key except in the locked car. I tried a dozen tricks to open the door; I failed. One window had been left open some two inches; Ariel inserted her arm, but it was too short to reach the locking pin. I hurried into the town to find a locksmith, but it was Sunday and all shops were closed. I returned to the car, and in the crowd that had gathered around it I saw a tall girl with long slim arms. She volunteered to curve her arm around the narrow opening; her fingertip barely reached the magic button and released the lock. She withdrew her arm; I opened the door, and then I embraced the girl so fervently that she cried out, "He wants to take me with him." Ariel called me back to earth. We sought out the Palazzo Farnese, whose Reale Galleria contained five rooms of Correggio's luscious pieties. All through the Renaissance, sex competed with religion in art and life, and at times they reached a most satisfying synthesis.

On to Cremona, hearing echoes of the Stradivari and Guarnieri stringing and polishing their violins. Then to Milan, where our friends Carlo and Bibi Foà were waiting to welcome us. With them we rested for a week; relived the stories of Lodovico Sforza, Beatrice d'Este, and Leonardo da Vinci; studied *The Last Supper* once more; tramped through the restored Galleria Brera, and sampled the select treasures of the Museo

Poldi-Pezzoli. We drove out some eighteen miles to Pavia, and wandered again in and around the Certosa.

Then over the Ligurian Alps to Genoa, and along their domineering cliffs to Savona, and back over that tortuous, torturing road to San Remo, Ventimiglia, Monte Carlo, and Nice to a day of rest in Cannes in the splendor of spring. Then we took to the road again, along the tree-lined highways of France through Provence to Aix and Avignon. Here we explored the Palace of the Popes and Simone Martini's frescoes, but our hearts warmed rather to the memories of Petrarch at neighboring Vaucluse; there, tradition said, he had composed some of his sonnets to Laura de Noves. We went out of our way, into the Département Drôme, to visit the Château de Grignan, where, in the seventeenth century, Madame de Sévigné had often come to visit her daughter; like her we gazed fondly from that terrace upon the Provence splendor of mountains and green fields; inside was the bed in which the *grande dame* of French letters had died. Then we moved north for a while along the Rhone, through Orange, Valence, and Vienne to Lyons.

After a day there we turned our creaking car northwest to Moulins, medieval home of the dukes of Bourbon. Thence to Bourges, where we saw how well Jacques Coeur, financier, had lived in the fifteenth century; we lingered in the lovely cathedral, and saw some of the best stained glass in France. Then to Chenonceaux's stately château, standing immobile amid the river Cher. Soon afterward I took the wheel, and discovered that my beloved consort (whose skill as a driver had been a saving boon through these arduous months) had been driving for the last one hundred kilometers with the hand brake on. We ventured forward to Tours, where we searched in vain for someone to reline our emaciated brakes. We left our car, and joined a group of Americans for a tour of Tours and a visit to the nearby châteaux. Returning to our Oldsmobile, we proceeded cautiously along the Loire, visited the Château d' Amboise, saw the caves where, we were assured, some poor people still made their homes; on to Blois and its charming castle and château; off the main line to see at Chambord the gem of all châteaux. All the splendors of the Bourbon age recalled my charabanc tour of the châteaux and the cathedrals with Alden Freeman thirty-nine years before. It was borne in upon me, in a lucid interval, that I was now sixty-six years old—still a novice in learning, but officially in decay.

You picture this senior citizen driving from Tours into the tangle and fury of Paris traffic with only one brake—the foot brake—and that on its last threads. In midmaze it died, and I had to drive several miles through Paris to the Palais d'Orsay Hotel in first gear; for I could stop only by taking my foot off the accelerator while in that gear—which stopped the car and the motor too. A hundred angry Parisians cursed me with their horns, but how could I tell them that my car was lacking its most important part? The next day I drove with similar agony along the full length of the Champs Élysées to a General Motors shop in Auteuil.

We did not use the car much in Paris, until we found in Lee Hirsey a good driver as well as a good friend. He knew enough French to return curse for curse in traffic arguments; I can still hear him shouting joyously and recklessly to angry Frenchmen competing for the road, *"Idiot!"*— which in French ends with a resounding *yo!* Lee tripled his worth by bringing with him, now and then, his wife, Sydney, and her sister Marla—two reincarnations of Aphrodite.

For some sixty days we made a home out of two rooms in the Palais d'Orsay Hotel, which had lost its elegance and lowered its prices. I brought to those rooms armfuls of French books and pictures to help me see and feel the age of Francis I and Catherine de Médicis. I discovered the American Library in Paris, and borrowed precious tomes. I learned to use the Bibliothèque Nationale, and bent so long over the fine print of faded treatises that I suffered a nosebleed when I returned to the hotel. I lost no chance to hear French drama of the classic age. On June 1 I heard Gluck's *Orphée* in the Palais de Chaillot, and for weeks thereafter I moved to the memory of "J'ai perdu mon Eurydice." On June 15 we studied an exhibition of "Diderot's *Encyclopédie*" at the Bibliothèque Nationale. On June 17 I drove our rehabilitated car out of Paris to the Abbaye de Royaumont to hear Honegger's *Le Roi David*, which seemed to me a masterwork. On June 22 I struggled to keep up with the lively French of Molière's *École des femmes* at the Comédie Française. On June 30 we climbed into the shaky stands erected before Notre Dame, to see a medieval mystery play—*Le Vrai Mystère de la Passion*. I visited the Louvre almost every other day.

Ariel's comparative innocence of French left me to do most of these explorations by myself. She made some progress by daily attending a class in French at the Alliance Française at 101 Boulevard Raspail; I walked with her to this every weekday in the morning, and went out to escort her back in the afternoon. There she made new friends, and meanwhile she cultivated old ones like Man Ray. She allowed me an occasional escapade, like a visit to the nudities of the Place Pigalle. But I enjoyed even more an afternoon with Lee Hirsey at the bicycle races in Vincennes.

Despite these diverse cultural pursuits I did much writing. There the first half of *The Renaissance* took form. Gustav Payot, dean and prince of French publishers, came to visit us, and, when we returned his visit, fascinated us with stories of Clémenceau and other French heroes, whom he had known through two world wars. I have long cherished the compliment he gave me, *"Vous écrivez l'histoire en philosophe*—It is as a philosopher that you write history." I had dreamed of doing that, but had not dared to think that I had done it.

Our New York publishers, and particularly Max Schuster, had kept in touch with us on our voyages of discovery, and had kept our egos warm with ever fresh compliments. I believe it was in reply to one of these transatlantic bouquets that Ariel sent him a grace note of which only the rough draft remains:

> It is a quarter of a century now that you have stood by Will, pouring into him your enthusiasm and youth, and inspiring him . . . to complete the task he so passionately began so long ago.
>
> I do not know how other publisher-friends behaved to authors, tho I have read, here and there, of some remarkable instances of friendship plus, from Byron and Murray on; but they are so rare and far between—or the public is so little aware of them—that, by comparison, your steadfastness and understanding are as much an inspiration as an historical signpost.
>
> We feel, across space and time, your good wishes, and return them to you and Ray with all our love.

On July 4 we packed ourselves and our expanding baggage into our Oldsmobile, and set out again for Cannes (the steamers on the northern route still refused to take cars). En route we stopped at Troyes to visit the cathedral in which Jeanne d'Arc first met King Charles VII. At Dijon, in the palace of the dukes of Burgundy, and in the monastery at suburban Champmol, we saw for the first time the work of the somber fifteenth-century sculptor Claus Sluter; the tomb of Philip the Bold was among the profounder experiences of our trip. At Beaune the hospital (Hôtel Dieu—"God's House"), completed in 1451, was still a model of cleanliness and beauty; and the nuns who served it moved in silent pride that they had changed neither their rule nor their ideas nor their habit in five hundred years. Grenoble interested us as having rehearsed the French Revolution by its uprising (June 7, 1788) against the aristocracy and the King. Then—more or less on the route made historic by Napoleon's march on his return from Elba—we advanced to Digne, crossed the Alpes Maritimes, and descended through Grasse to Cannes.

On July 14 we sailed from Cannes on the S.S. *Independence.* Our car was raised from dock to deck, and remained exposed on the overnight passage to Naples; the next morning we found that its paint had been ruined by the salt spray. During the six-hour stop at Naples we made one more visit to the Museo Nazionale, and studied Titian's powerful *Paul III.* On July 23 we reached New York, not yet satiated with Europe, but feeling that we had at least begun to fill in the historical and artistic background for *The Renaissance* and *The Reformation.*

At Lake Hill we had the pleasure of entertaining Father Edward Hopkins, a young Episcopalian priest who classified our boxes of notes for Volumes V and VI. He was a scholar in his own right, whose comments on our gleanings gave us a fresh view—a Protestant clergyman sympathetic with the Middle Ages. Ethel came for a long visit, and Jim, almost ten years old, was approaching the age of omniscience. On September

27, from Max Schuster, came a letter that almost atoned for the slow sale of *The Age of Faith* (seventeen thousand in its first nine months, not half of what I had predicted).

DEAR WILL:

We heard the other day that Bill Shirer . . . is a most enthusiastic reader of your . . . *Story of Civilization*. We wrote him to find out if he had the complete set. His reply:

"Yes, I liked the three books in the Will Durant series I have read: *The Age of Faith, The Life of Greece,* and *Caesar and Christ*. Why they did not attract more attention is beyond me. I feel that they are the most underrated books of the generation, much better than Spengler's *Decline of the West* and Toynbee's *Study of History*—though I have only skimmed through the first six volumes of the latter, and perhaps should reserve judgment on it . . ." I am sending him a copy of *Our Oriental Heritage* so that he will miss no part of the . . . set.

As ever,

MAX

I did not take this too seriously; I still think Toynbee the greatest living historian (1970), and *The Decline of the West* the outstanding book of the twentieth century.

We lingered at Lake Hill till September 23, when I had to go off lecturing. I sent Ariel the usual daily bouquet, beginning at St. Louis September 24: "Every year, as we grow dearer to each other, I miss you more than before when I come away on these tours. Unless I hear your voice every hour or so, life loses meaning."

On September 28 I faced the Chicago Executive Club for the tenth time. Among the guests at the head table was the director of Cadillac sales in Chicago. He invited me to come and see some of the new cars. I went, and before I left those showrooms I had bought a sleek blue "Sixty Special" sedan. While explaining metaphysics to dinner clubs I ransacked my wits for a way of excusing my new extravagance to an Ariel who for thirty-eight years had heard me preach economy.

At Buffalo, October 2, 1951, I found awaiting me a letter from Ariel that made me prefer her to Madame de Sévigné and Horace Walpole fused:

What date it is God only knows, but I do know that it is Friday, and five days since we kissed that funny face of yours good-by. We arrived . . . at a lonely homestead still retaining the aroma of your perfume, lotions,* and armpits.

I hope that the autumn that breezes in upon us here [at Lake Hill] also caresses and smiles upon you there, for tho we have had a little rain now and then, we have had many brilliant days, albeit a little triste as the leaves swirl and fall upon earth and road with the abandon of a fallen woman in

---

* I made my own aftershave lotion by mixing alcohol (49 percent) with witchhazel (50 percent) and one of Ariel's perfumes (one percent).

rich decay. But there is wine in the air, and in the grapes, and we have taken this opportunity . . . to put our ignorant but willing hands to the task of making a little wine, so that you will become a "good European" and rejoice with your friends when we are up here next summer.

Take care of yourself, and drop my Ethel and Jim a card now and then, and remember not to forget this little girl you left behind to keep the home fires burning bright, and a tigress in the night.

To this I replied lamely, on

10-2-51

Your letter . . . is a jewel . . . When am I going to have my tigress warming my old bones with her soft body, and curling her luscious arm around my neck? . . .

I picture you all alone at Lake Hill, . . . painting, planting, supervising a hundred details. You function—and so you are happier than when idleness hung like a chain on your spirit. I love you a hundred times more than when I married you, tho I married you for love. . . .

I speak at Fredonia this evening on marriage. You ought to be with me to prove that marriage can be happy.

At Galesburg, Illinois, I found a letter which has disappeared from our savings, apparently because it was passed from hand to hand. I replied on

10-10-51

SWEETHEART:

Your letter of October 6 midnight brought tears to my eyes, it was so beautiful. Those who see you only in your vivacious public hours, and think of you as the life of the party, can hardly guess—even I couldn't—the depth and keenness of sensitivity revealed in that letter. I shall certainly send it to Ethel; it is *not* sad; it is tender and idealistic—just what she needs.

Where did you get that life of Symonds? I've read so much by him, little about him; never knew he died of consumption at 53. How fortunate I am, then! And apparently he never married [?], never had someone to spur him on, and give him a little warming, rewarding love when the day's work was done. I have all that, and am grateful.

A member of the Knox College faculty here just asked me would I not like to take a ride into the countryside. I told him, "No, I have a fever of writing on me, and I must go on scratching." And when I ask myself why I do it, instead of resting on my oars, I perceive at last that it is because I want to deserve the reward of your approval and your love. I shall need them more and more, and shall have to lean on your strength as mine fails.

No, I am no longer a monster of health. Even my lightened suitcase, which I have to carry half the time (redcaps are rare) has weakened my back again, and I doubt if I shall ever again be vertebrally strong. And the almost night-after-night talking, and day-after-day shaking in a conveyance, is harder on my nerves than it used to be. You will find me looking 66 on Nov. 5.

It's all in the game. And if you will, when my job and "Story" are done, write of me as magnificently as you wrote of Symonds, it will be reward enough. I love you more than the world.

In one of her lost letters Ariel enclosed a message from John Dewey. He and we had not met since our dinner together in the apartment of Maurice Hindus at the Mayflower Hotel about 1945. In 1946, having borne nineteen years of widowhood, he married, at eighty-seven, Mrs. Roberta Grant, forty-two. When reporters came to interview him he said to them, with a dry, sly humor that he had sternly excluded from his books, "I know quite well what is the general opinion about old men who marry young women." He was too gallant to explain that Mrs. Grant had for years taken care of him, and that he wished, before his death, to give her his name and his tiny fortune. In 1951, fearing that he would soon be beyond the reach of any words, I wrote thanking him for his long devotion to humane causes and the fine example of his life. He replied in a handwriting almost illegible,

10-4-51

Dear Will Durant:

It was genuinely kind of you to write me as you did. It has been an abiding satisfaction to me that I was able to be of use to you in your professional career. Your expression of appreciation is somewhat over-drawn, but it is none the less welcome on that account. I am glad you have had the recognition you richly deserve—best wishes for its continuance, since it is that of great public service and also especially so at such a reactionary period as we are going through.

Yours,
John Dewey

He died a year later, aged ninety-three.

Ariel and I agreed to meet in Strathroy. My letter of October 19 outlined a scheme for introducing the new Cadillac to her: "I'll be coming by car; someone in Chicago is driving his Cadillac to New York, and is so infatuated with me that he is going via Detroit and will drive me right to Ethel's house—about 6 p.m. Oct. 26 if all goes well. . . . I've bought a nice wedding anniversary present for you." That "someone infatuated with me" was myself, and the car was to be disarmingly offered as an anniversary gift. So, on October 25, arriving in Chicago by sleeper from Cedar Rapids, I picked up the new car and rolled off toward Detroit as joyous as a boy on a prank. On the twenty-sixth I addressed the Michigan Education Association, spent some time with Gene and her children, drove north to Port Huron, talked the Canadian frontier officials into letting me bring in a car without proper proof that I had not stolen it, and at last, tired and a bit worried, as the sun was setting, drew up before Ethel's house, and blew the horn. Soon Ariel, Ethel, Gordon, and Jim came out to greet me, and to ask what had happened to the "infatuated" owner. I unraveled my double entendres, and presented the car to Ariel. She gently reproved me, and forgave me with a warm embrace.

It was a heartening reunion, but brief; I had to leave Strathroy on October 28 to catch at Port Huron a sleeper to Chicago. There, on the twenty-ninth, I took a plane to Dallas, and at Dallas another plane to Odessa, Texas, where I was scheduled to address a teachers' convention the next evening.

Nemesis caught up with me on that long trip from Canada into the heart of Texas. I reached Odessa with head aching, nose and throat choked. On the morning of October 30 I was a sick man, with voice almost all gone. Members of the Teachers' Association, visiting me at the Lincoln Hotel, were appalled at the thought that I might be unable to orate that evening. They sent for a doctor; he prescribed a reckless combination of antibiotics—penicillin, Aureomycin, and Chloromycetin. I took it in all innocence and recovered in time to satisfy those teachers. But when I tried to answer their questions my voice disappeared again; the head began to buzz again; I grew dizzy, and had to sit down. The solicitous committee hurried me to the hotel, and presumed that I would go to bed; but after they had left me I took a taxi and caught a 10:48 P.M. sleeper to Fort Worth. There, on the thirty-first, I took a plane to Chicago, and at Chicago another to Cleveland. I had expected to fly thence to London, Ontario; that flight was canceled by a storm. I was given a room at the Cleveland Hotel. I telephoned to Ethel and Ariel to meet me at London the next morning. They did, and told me that I looked terrible.

Nevertheless I was determined to meet the commitments that I had made (thinking we would go by train) to meet Max and Dick, Dr. Stone, Colston Leigh, and others in New York on November 3. So Ariel and I left Strathroy early November 2 in our "Lady" (as we called the new Cadillac), resolved to get to New York by nightfall, taking turns at the wheel—for with Ariel beside me there were always two men in the car. But near Monticello we ran into a first-class snowstorm; soon we could not see more than twenty feet ahead. We skidded dangerously on the hills; descending one of these, our car revolved beyond control and stalled at a right angle to the road, leaving us with only a prayer that the descending traffic could stop before crashing into us. It stopped, but we gave up the battle. We put up overnight at a hotel, telephoned to cancel our engagements, warmed and cleansed ourselves, and slept. We reached New York on November 4, but I had to leave at once for Norfolk to see if civilization might be saved.

On November 6 I was allowed a half hour with President Truman, who assured me that he kept a volume of *The Story of Civilization* near his bed for nighttime reading. I spent most of our few minutes together arguing that the United States should recognize the Communist government of mainland China as a first step toward the organization of peace, and that we should take the initiative in securing the admission of Communist China into the United Nations and the Security Council. He was unconvinced, but he was gracious enough to send me a letter the next day—

November 7, 1951

DEAR MR. DURANT:

I appreciated most highly your visit yesterday afternoon and was pleased with the suggestions which you made to me. I am not in complete agreement with what you suggest but I hope you will listen to what I have to say tonight over the broadcasting system of the country, and I think you will find that, with the exception of the murderers and crooks in China, we are in pretty close agreement.

The Chinese communists confiscated all our Government property in China, imprisoned our consuls and murdered some of our missionaries, and I am not quite broadminded enough to endorse that procedure. I am hoping you are right that they will not continue to be the tail to Russia's kite, but I've got to see a demonstration of it before I believe it.

I've been very badly mistaken in Chinese Governments. When I became President of the United States I thought Chiang Kai-Shek's Government was on the road to a real reform government in China. I found by experience that it was the most corrupt and terrible Government that China ever had. I am never to be satisfied with a Government that maintains its power by murder and slave labor. I think sometime or other, probably after you and I are being investigated by historians fifty or sixty years from now, there will be a settlement in China—at least I hope so.

Sincerely yours,
HARRY TRUMAN

That same evening I rejoined Ariel in New York. There we rested for a week, except for my oratorical flights to Toronto and Cincinnati. We resumed our pursuit of European art in the Metropolitan Museum, the Morgan Library, and the Frick Collection. Then, on November 17, we began a fifteen-hundred-mile drive to Florida. We could not recapture our Los Angeles home till September, 1952. And Louis, Mollie, and Eric were waiting for us in Coral Gables, where Louis was engineering.

Our first stop was a sad beginning of a winter of misfortunes. My brother Frank, handsomest of the Durants, was bedridden with cancer in Memorial Hospital, Orange, New Jersey. His wife, Phoebe, his daughter Hilda, and my sister Ethel Halliwell were with him when we arrived. The case had been diagnosed as an inoperable tumor blocking the duodenum. Frank was being fed intravenously, and he was already pale and thin. We were appalled by this quick decay of a body that for years had seemed a model of health.

We spent that night with sister Ethel in Westfield. On the eighteenth we resumed our drive, stopping at Gastonia and Greenville, North Carolina, to earn some lecture fees, and at Fort Lauderdale to thank Mr. and Mrs. Van Ameringen for giving our son Louis so admirable a wife. We put up at Dr. Kellogg's Battle Creek near the Hialeah Race Track in Miami Springs. Dr. Kellogg was no more, and good Dr. Jeffrey was in Battle Creek, Michigan; by some unhappy chance the head of our vegetarian paradise was now a Dr. Senese, who loved meat, and guided his favorite guests to the best pizza havens in Miami.

Despite my resolute adherence to the vegetarian diet, and a daily pint of orange juice, I experienced in this citadel of health the severest sickness I have ever had: for a month sciatica pulsed along my right leg. During the day I managed to divert my consciousness from the pain by writing a second draft of *The Renaissance*; reading was too passive a process to serve this purpose; and at night, as I lay in bed with no distraction, the pain had me at its mercy with its spasms. Dr. Senese shot various antibiotics into my helpless bloodstream; they gave me no relief, and may have infected me with new disorders. I could not sleep without a strong sedative; I suspect it was morphine.

Ariel worried that these repeated injections would injure my "precious" brain; she begged me to do without them, whatever the pain or the cost to sleep; I could not. She tried to distract me, during the day, by reading to me from Montaigne, but I found it hard to pay attention. For a time I lost interest in what we called our "civilization job"; when Ariel begged me to go on with my work whatever the pain, I replied (so her ruthless memory tells me), "I don't care if I never hear about civilization again." When I look back upon those weeks I perceive that they must have been as painful for Ariel as for myself.

Dr. Senese multiplied the misery by suggesting that some dental infection was the cause, and recommending that all my remaining teeth should be pulled out and replaced with plates. I yielded, and Ariel drove me to a dentist in Miami. Climbing the one flight of stairs to his office proved too much for me, and I fainted at the top. Two hours later I returned to my hospital bed, toothless, bloody, and uncured.

Finally I decided that I was deteriorating under Dr. Senese's shots in the dark. On December 6 we left the sanitarium and moved to an apartment at 1481 Bay Road, Miami Beach. Ariel's sisters Flora and Mary came down from New York to help her, and we took an apartment for them near ours. I continued the vegetarian diet, but abandoned all medication. Instead, with the help of a cane, I limped downstairs every fair day to sit with my ailing leg exposed to the sun. Whether diet, or the sun, or time, or the absence of doctors cured me I don't know; but soon the pain and the stiffness lessened. I astonished my neighbors by taking a few steps without the cane; a week later I walked to the corner and back; after another week I walked unaided around the block and was greeted on my return like Napoleon after Tilsit.

The scene changes to Strathroy, where, on January 2, 1952, Ethel gave birth to Monica. Seeing that I could now stand on my own legs, Ariel left on January 3 to go up to Canada and help guard the new life. An hour later I sent a letter to greet her on her arrival in Strathroy:

1-3-52

SWEETHEART, ETHEL, GORDON, AND FAMILY:

Flora and I have just gotten back from the station after putting you on the train, and we're already lonesome. Flora is cleaning up the apartment, spraying, and behaving like the saint she has always been since she tried to throw me down the stairs for wanting to marry you. . . .

It's going to be a busy home when that little girl comes in to be its commanding officer. The first month is the hardest; after that we'll be fighting to see which of us has the privilege of pushing her around the town and showing her off. Our pride in begetting and rearing a healthy child is reasonable; it is a widespread accomplishment, but in it we come nearest to the gods—we create; and we come close to the great artist, for we form and mold. It will take a lot of patience from all concerned; but in two years' time the girl will be the pride of the house; in eight years' time she'll be a beauty; in fifteen years' time we'll be worrying about maintaining her virginity.

Ethel, to you above all, congratulations. We have admired the unassuming courage with which you faced the task; the good cheer you maintained thru months of carrying and worrying. We rejoice that it's a girl, and that Jim will have a baby sister. . . .

Jim, we hear good reports about you in everything but your handwriting; please take more care in that. What a Xmas gift your Daddy Gordon gave you! . . . You now will be a big brother. Help your mother as much as you can. And we'll love you till the end of the world.

When Ariel returned to Miami she found me, as she put it, "deep in the heart of the Renaissance." She herself absorbed Montaigne, fell in love with Étienne de la Boétie, and made hundreds of notes that helped when we wrote of those famous friends in *The Age of Reason Begins.* We exchanged visits with Louis Durant and Mollie in Coral Gables, and with Louis Sturz and Hattie in their neighboring cottage. Max Schuster and Dick Simon came down for a week at the Roney Plaza Hotel; and, hearing that my dental plates could now be relied upon, they inveigled me into talking to a group of fellow vacationers on "The Crisis in American Civilization." I deplored the condition of music and art in the United States, and amused Dick by remarking, "I smell the odor of decay."

As the country moved into 1952 the Republican Party, which had not held the presidency in the last twenty years, saw in the popularity of General Eisenhower an opportunity to regain power and stem the welfare-state tide of reform that had been running since 1933. Problem: how to save the Roosevelt-Truman legislation despite the highly probable election of the amiable General. I had a scheme for this, and expounded it to President Truman in a letter of

3-20-52

Dear Mr. President:

It was good of you to take time out from your many obligations and send me that personal reply to the suggestions I made in our conversation last November. I am taking the liberty of submitting some more amateur thinking.

The Minnesota primary indicates that the Republican Convention will be compelled by public sentiment to nominate General Eisenhower. In that case I believe that the Democratic Party would be defeated, its beneficent legislation imperiled, its appointees dismissed.

I suggest that as soon as the nomination of Gen. Eisenhower by the Republican Party becomes probable, you should issue a public statement recommending that the Democratic Party should also nominate him. I know that there would be some difficulties about the platform, but hardly insuperable; . . . platforms are vehicles to office, not vows to eternity.

Since there are many more Democrats than Republicans registered, and since the independent vote usually inclines to the Democratic side, the General would receive considerably more Democratic than Republican votes. This might balance any prior obligation that he might feel to the Republican Party. . . . Such a two-party election of the same man would prevent the defeat of Democratic candidates for state and congressional offices. It would improve the chances of the Roosevelt-Truman legislation surviving a Republican administration. It might keep in office a large number of Democratic appointees with a good record. It would unify the country dramatically, encourage our allies, and give the Politburo pause. It would allow you to retire from the presidency with a magnificent gesture of non-partisan patriotism, incidentally implementing your generous promise to help General Eisenhower to our highest office. It would ensure your election to the Senate if you should care to run. I hope you will, for you would there remain a creative force in our national life.

Would such a plan endanger our party system? It would *adapt* it—to the possibility, on occasion, of unanimous support for a good man. The party system would remain in the states, ready to revive nationally when the world crisis passed. And in a sense it would not suffer interruption on the national scale, since there would be wholesome competition between the parties as to which would give the General the larger vote, and more indebt him to preserve its policies. Union labor, which might have to fight him if there are two candidates, could support him in the reasonable expectation of winning his friendship.

Above all, we should be one nation, stronger than ever, and moving in impressive unity to meet the challenges of our times.

Sincerely,
Will Durant

Italian Ecstasy

Instead of laughing at me the President sent a kindly reply.

March 22, 1952

DEAR MR. DURANT:

I certainly did appreciate your good letter of the twentieth, and was highly intrigued by the suggestion which you made. That certainly would be a precedent breaker and probably be for the welfare of the country.

I have been spending my odd moments, when I have any, reading your history books, and I get a great deal of satisfaction out of them.

Sincerely yours,
HARRY TRUMAN

My personal problems compelled me to leave the country to the politicians. I was just getting back into stride with *The Renaissance* when I noticed an alarming discoloration in my urine. I took Ariel with me to a Miami Beach physician, who diagnosed my trouble as a prostate infection. When he asked for my clinical history, and I told him of the antibiotic mixture—penicillin, Aureomycin, Chloromycetin—that had been given me in Odessa, Texas, a year and a half before, and of my recent sciatica, he suggested that medication, in Texas and at Miami Battle Creek, had poisoned my system, had produced various abnormal reactions, and might produce more. He gave me a penicillin injection, and ordered weekly visits and injections. I departed downhearted. Would the penicillin cure me or make me worse? I submitted to these punctures weekly, but I put more trust in a cleansing diet patiently followed, and enemas two or three times a week; gradually, I believed, this regimen would clear my long-suffering innards from poisoning by prescription. A month later we heard Dr. Selman Waksman lecture on the dangers of prescribing a mixture of antibiotics. How many guinea pigs have been sacrificed to the progress of medicine!

We left Miami Beach on May 1, 1952, and drove to New York, then to Lake Hill. There I submitted my prostate problem to Dr. Cohn, whom I had long admired as a physician, and as an amateur cellist who played in the Sunday concerts of the local quartet. He was also a man of humane feeling; through long hours every day he treated thirty or forty patients, including many poor people who never paid him. He attended Ariel's mother to the end, sitting by her, relieving her pain, and refusing to artificially prolong her life; *"Lassen sie einschlafen,"* he told her children; "let her go to sleep." When I told him that I had high blood pressure he said, simply, "You must take a two-hour nap every afternoon, or you must take drugs." I objected; I could never keep my writing schedule if I spent two afternoon hours in bed; now I believe he was right. As my urine was still discolored, he ordered me to go on with the penicillin injections. I did, and about June 1 my urine cleared up; but I believe it was the diet that cured me, for if it had been the penicillin it would have acted sooner.

After a pleasant summer with our Catskill friends, we sold the Lake Hill house for fifteen thousand dollars to Ariel's prospering brother Mike, and the Oldsmobile for a forgotten price; and on September 16 we left the old manse. (Mike improved the house, and sold it for thirty thousand.) We spent a month in New York; Ariel made propaganda for *The Renaissance* on Barry Gray's radio program, and I made propaganda for Adlai Stevenson in his hopeless campaign against Eisenhower. Some paragraphs from my letter in the New York *Times* of October 7:

> In general the question that we should debate is: Does governmental interference with the economic life do more harm than good? I believe that such interference has been necessary to counteract the disruptive inequalities of human capacity. The exceptionally able man has had his superiority so multiplied by invention, scientific management and a tariffless market of 150,000,000 people that unless government helped the common man, wealth would repeatedly reach a pitch of concentration that would make for revolutionary disturbances or overturns fatal to our Constitution.
>
> The essence of Franklin Roosevelt's statesmanship lay in recognizing that our marvelous capacity to produce must be balanced by widespread capacity to purchase, or else our American system cannot work. He deliberately put the Government on the side of the common man, supported the unions in organizing labor to equalize bargaining power, protected the farmer against a bitter subjection to market manipulation, raised the general standard of living, and—by enabling the masses to purchase as well as produce—saved our American economy from . . . poverty and class war. . . .
>
> Our American combination of capitalism and socialism is far more successful than either the capitalism of our not-so-gay Nineties or the communism of Russia; and this Hegelian synthesis was the achievement of five Democratic administrations.

On October 14 Ariel and I began our long drive west. We stopped for several days at Strathroy with Ethel and Gordon, who were planning to move to California; and we readily agreed to take Jimmy in our car. His lively good cheer turned our laborious trip into a delight. We reached Los Angeles on October 28, and were glad to find that our Casa de la Vista had survived another earthquake. Soon we were at work, with myself scribbling, Edith Digate typing, Jimmy ruining our electrical gadgets, and Ariel managing us all. Ethel and Gordon, with pretty baby Monica, came to stay with us while they equipped a poultry ranch in San Jacinto; in December they and Jim moved there, and every second Sunday Ariel and I drove out some eighty miles to help them gather and grade eggs.

Toward Christmas we received a pleasant but hardly decipherable letter from Bernard Berenson.

Italian Ecstasy

I Tatti, Settignano, Florence, Italy, 12-12-52

DEAR WILL DURANT:

Returning from a longish stay in Rome, I discovered a copy of your "Age of Faith" with a flattering and caressing dedication[?]. I hope some of the butter was of your own churning and not Max Schuster's.

Be that as it may. I am delighted to be in touch with you, and to confess that that whole series of the Story of Civilization is on my bookshelves, and I pick up one volume after the other, and marvel at your capacity for ingurgitation, digestion, and verbal [?]. Your only rival was my dear friend, René Grousset.

Ten years ago I began to write what was to be a book on Decline and Recovery of Form in the Visual Arts from Constantine to Giotto. I wrote two chapters, and then we Americans were attacked by Mussolini, and I had to leave my library, etc., and never was able to take it up again. It would have furnished an amusing lining to your colossal web. . . .

May I dare to invite you to come and see me if you pass near Florence? With best wishes for 1953, sincerely yours,

BERNARD BERENSON

For us 1953 was *The Renaissance*. This Volume V, though it dealt with Italy alone, was to fill 728 pages of printed text; I found myself incurably addicted to leviathans. Instead of complaining that an entire volume was given to one country and only 243 years, Max Schuster inflated the Durant ego with telegrams of soaring praise as he went through the manuscript which we had delivered to him in December, 1952. Ariel, however, was not content with the book, and submitted certain criticisms that had much basis and force. It began well enough, she said, with an interesting chapter on Petrarch and Boccaccio; I could always be relied upon to enthuse about the poet's Laura and Boccaccio's merry ladies and monks, but then I wandered from city to city, like another Baedeker, describing picture after picture until the result was a blur in the reader's memory; and, like an unregenerate Catholic, I whitewashed those scandalous Renaissance popes; this, Ariel felt, was a letdown from *The Age of Faith*. I mourned, but such dissent kept me from quite forgetting my place in the perspective of astronomic and literary galaxies.

In June, after half a year of heavy duty at 5608, Ariel joined some friends who were driving across the continent. My letters to her were those of a lovesick swain:

7-1-53

Everything here conduces to quiet composition, but I find that your absence leads me to sit and mope for minutes at a time; I would be less distracted by your gossipy talks over the phone. . . . Come home as soon as you can. . . .

305

A Dual Autobiography

I'm nearing the end of Chapter I [of *The Reformation*] and will be glad to get it over with. Every sentence in it will be challenged by either the Protestants or the Catholics; only Anatole France or Renan or Voltaire would agree with me, and they are dead. . . .

The woodpile is disappearing under my axe and saw, and I'm piling it up under the shelf in the garage. . . .

7-6-53

. . . So you've gathered up my love letters and old manuscripts. It's sweet of you to put any value on them. What nonsense a man can write in the course of 68 years! If we followed Horace's rule, and let our productions lie hidden from the public eye for eight years, we'd hardly publish anything, and the world wouldn't be the worse for it.

Ariel returned safely.

On September 18 *The Renaissance* burst upon the world. My publishers gave it the usual full-page natal advertisement. To help the book I journeyed to New York to join in the *Invitation to Learning* radio program of October 3 with Lyman Bryson, Geoffrey Bruun, and George Crothers.

The reviews were more favorable than for any other of my books. Sterling North led the way in the *World-Telegram* of September 16 by exalting Volume V above the masterpieces of Jakob Burckhardt and John Addington Symonds; my secret pleasure over this hyperbole was disturbed by the consciousness that Burckhardt's book was a powerful trailblazer, and Symonds' five volumes were a treasure of eloquent scholarship, from which I had taken something for nearly every chapter. In the *Times* of September 20 Francis Henry Taylor, director of the Metropolitan Museum of Art, gave *The Renaissance* his approval; and on the following day, in the same paper, Orville Prescott gave me wings by saying that after thirty years of reading on the Renaissance he liked my presentation best of all. I was happy to find several university professors among my new friends: Moses Hadas. W. T. Jackson, and David Clark of Columbia, Ray Nash of Dartmouth, G. C. Sellery of Wisconsin, Richard Livingstone of Oxford, and Alfonso Cornejo of the University of Mexico.

But a few offkey notes were in the chorus. A critic in the *Rocky Mountain News* (October 4), after a column of praise, added: "*The Renaissance* is not a work of original scholarship"—meaning, I believe, that I had not unearthed any new facts. I should admit this; my aim has been not to add to knowledge, but to promote better and wider understanding of existing knowledge. I lay no claim to originality except in method—"integral history"; and in some measure Voltaire had anticipated this. — Max Freedman, in the Washington *Post* of September 27, after some compliments, seconded Ariel's objections: "His pages are covered with a litany of noble names which fail to evoke the many-sided splendor of the Renaissance. But perhaps the dullness of a mere chronicle cannot be avoided even in a book which limits itself to the Italian Renaissance." Yes, I must admit that there are some dull pages in the book. It is difficult—perhaps impossible—to transform art or music into words, for they move in a world beyond logic or intellect.

Despite its flaws, the book sold faster than the printers delivered copies to the publishers. On September 23 Max Schuster wired us: "Reviews so ecstatic, demand so active, we may be out of stock for a short period, but we're rushing presses night and day." The same fate had befallen *Caesar and Christ*. We mourned the loss of potential purchasers, but we realized that publishing is a perpetual gamble. Meanwhile Max prepared new advertisements by quoting favorable reviews; and if a hostile reviewer carelessly slipped into a word of praise, Max might quote that word, with a twinkle in his eye.

While I was in New York Ariel accepted an invitation from Nat Nassof and his wife, Estelle, to accompany them on a drive to Mexico City. Nat was my senior partner in some realty purchases; a man of great ability and complete integrity. They found room in the car for a good and jolly friend of Ariel's, "Brunie" Colbert. After an arduous drive they left the car at Laredo, and went on by plane to Mexico City. To Ariel there I wrote,

10-7-53

Here's hoping that you have now reached Mexico City safely, . . . and that Estelle and Brunie and Nat are all well. As for me, I'm used up, but pleasantly. . . .

I've just returned from an exciting lunch [arranged by Max Schuster and Bernard Baruch at the Lotus Club] with Baruch, David Sarnoff, Samuel Rosenman, Marshall Field, Gardner Cowles of *Look,* Robert Young of the Chesapeake and Ohio R.R., Joe Barnes of the *Tribune,* Orville Prescott of the *Times* [and Max and Dick]. It sounded like a cabinet meeting, and the topic was whether a new attempt should be made to arrange a disarmament program with Russia. Sarnoff talked brilliantly on that topic. Baruch reminisced of the days when he offered such a program to Russia for our government. Baruch insists that I am his favorite author, and Marshall Field assured me that he is reading *The Renaissance,* and Gardner Cowles wanted an article for *Look*—which I felt I'd better refuse with an appreciative word; time is running out faster than money . . .

On October 8 I left New York for Chicago; there I survived autograph sessions (I had almost said autos-da-fé) at Kroch's and Marshall Field's; then I flew to Dallas and Midland, Texas, to consider "The Destiny of Civilization." I had more or less identified myself with civilization, and Max had quipped that "civilization is in a race between Durant and catastrophe." From Midland I went through the South, speaking at every stop, and reporting to Ariel daily. From Athens, Georgia,

307

10-22-53

. . . I'm already entering the second step in the evolution of my moods in starting a new volume. I'm getting control of the material, . . . am rearranging it to make a more logical and dramatic sequence, and feel that I can do a reasonably good job . . . if I don't spend too much time on theological disputes.

From Lagrange, Georgia,

10-24-53

Your letters of Oct. 18 and Oct. 21 from Mexico are rich in memorable phrases: "Not an inch anywhere left untouched by man, so fertile is the soil and the womb"; "Long after skepticism has put its withering hand all around the world, the Mexican-Indian will walk barefoot on cobblestones to place his offering on the altar." My love, you are becoming the philosopher, while I subside into the historian.

The last engagement on this round was at Ada, Oklahoma. Thence I flew to Dallas and Los Angeles, arriving just in time to slip into my sixty-ninth year. Ariel, bronzed by Mexico's sun, was there to greet me, and to celebrate the fortieth anniversary of our marriage.

As the year neared its end we received an exalting letter from an old friend who had continued to love us through all our differences on Russia:

December 25, 1953

DEAR WILL:
A happy New Year! . . .
I read your book on the Renaissance, and I cannot tell you how greatly I enjoyed it. . . . What a gift you have to summarize a personality, and through him a whole period, in only a "fistful" of words! It is truly one of the most amazing books I have ever read. . . . Nothing escapes your keen eye, not even the littlest detail in the appearance or character of the immense crowd of personages you spread before the reader. . . .
Lots of love and luck to you and Ariel!

MAURICE HINDUS

So encouraged, and fortified with Ariel's love and faith and help, I crept on to *The Reformation*.

CHAPTER XXIV

Luther, Erasmus, and Tillich

1954–57

Ariel:

Now began an argument that divided us, amicably but fervently, for many years: Luther versus Erasmus, revolt versus reform, a brave new start versus a patching of the old garment; you can see from my way of stating the question that I am still in a fighting mood. Not trusting myself to put Will's view fairly, I have asked him to state it again for these pages.

Will:

My feeling was that the Renaissance was an advance for the European mind, while the Reformation was a retreat. The Renaissance, by reviving a mature pagan culture liberated from theology, and by its own experiments in mental and moral freedom, had opened a road to the Enlightenment and the Age of Reason. There were some indications, under Leo X and the relations of Erasmus with the Renaissance popes, that the Church would wink at intellectual freedom in the educated classes (instance Pomponazzi) if these made no attempt to destroy the consolatory, and morally helpful, faith of the poor, the defeated, or the bereaved in a religion of myth, miracle, and immortality. Such a "gentlemen's agreement" would have been a hazy and hazardous truce, but it might have led Western Europe to such an accord between myth and reason as gave Vienna a second golden age in the nineteenth century. There would have

309

been no tearing apart of European civilization, no Massacre of Saint Bartholomew's Day, no Thirty Years' War, and probably a checking of the Inquisition, as under Pombal in Portugal and Charles II in Spain. The Protestant Reformation, beginning as a beneficent resistance to such abuses as the selling of indulgences, went on to reject the Renaissance as pagan, to revert to the gloomy theology of Saint Paul and Saint Augustine, leading to the predestinarianism of Calvin and Knox, the Puritan regime, and the replacement of papal authority with the authoritarianism of the state in religion in Germany and Great Britain. Luther began as a hero in rebellion and ended with subservience to the princes and hostility to the peasants and to reason. Erasmus—a scholar, a Christian, and a gentleman—shrank from outright battle; he preferred a gradual and peaceful reform of the Church from within to a settlement of theological doctrine by the noisy clashing of extremes and bashing of heads. Violent revolt, he thought, would lead, after a generation of chaos and destruction, to a new tyranny differing from the old only in names, phrases, and forms. And I, similarly timid, would have preferred to move from the Renaissance to the Enlightenment, as in France, skipping the Reformation, the German Pietists, the Scottish Presbyterians, and the English Puritans.

Ariel:

I thought all this was the blindness of hereditary prejudice. France did not move from the Renaissance to the Enlightenment; she moved to religious wars and massacre, to the intolerant revocation of the tolerant Edict of Nantes, to the merciless persecution and banishment of the Huguenots, to the murder of Jean Calas, to the bloody terror of the Revolution. The Church would never agree to intellectual freedom; such freedom would sooner or later spread doubt and heresy even among the lower classes, and the entente would collapse. It did so in Renaissance Italy, for the Council of Trent (1545ff.), under Jesuit leadership, adopted the formulas of reaction and oppression instead of compromise and reform. Meanwhile Protestantism, though formally hostile to freedom of the mind, opened the door to modern thought by appealing to reason in the defense and conflict of the new theologies. The Elizabethan Age in England, though Protestant, allowed a flourishing of literature, art, and philosophy. Francis Bacon and the English Deists preceded and aroused the *philosophes* of the French Enlightenment.

Doubtless my tender-minded lover—who always confessed himself a Catholic below the neck—was prevented by his character from entering upon *The Reformation* with the same verve and enthusiasm with which he had begun *The Renaissance*. Even in their final form the first pages of the new book dripped with Catholic sentiment and ex-Catholic nostalgia; when I read them I wondered how long I could keep my truant altar boy from creeping back into the warm, safe womb of Mother Church. However, as his studies proceeded, and he delved more strenuously into the causes of the Reformation, his spirit of fair play moved him; he spent 332 pages exploring and explaining the many factors that had led to the great revolt; and then he summed them up in an overwhelming and conclusive paragraph. He continued to prefer Erasmus to Luther, for the intellectual naturally prefers the philosopher to the warrior; but he made Luther, with all his "warts," a living and lovable man, towering in influence and courage over the timid and ineffectual scholar. Nevertheless I let him hang a reproduction of Holbein's *Erasmus* on my study walls, and I joined him in mute reverence when, in 1948, we saw the great statue of Erasmus, seated in calm thought, surviving amid the rubble of war-ruined Rotterdam.

Max transmitted to us two letters of March 9 and 10, from Dr. Gerrit P. Judd, chairman of the history department, and Herbert R. Herington, professor of history, at Hofstra College, Hempstead, New York, asking Will's consent to their preparing a "one-volume abridgement of Durant, along the lines of Somervell's abridgement of Toynbee." Will thought the idea was premature, and now he feels that it is impracticable. I agree with him, for I am reluctant to see an alien hand operate surgically upon those eight thousand pages, each of which, however dull, bears for me a certain aura from the labor it cost. We had to reject also the request of a "Durant addict" who wished to gather and publish a volume to be called *The Wit and Wisdom of Will Durant*. Time, we felt, revenges itself on the egotism of such compilations.

I had other gods besides Will; he bore with them patiently, and usually joined in my pieties. This was especially true of Walter Lippmann, whose occasional columns we read with deepening respect for his judgment. We met him at the home of Douglas Fairbanks, Jr., in Pacific Palisades. I burned candles to such buried gods as Benjamin Disraeli and John Addington Symonds; I read the five big volumes of Moneypenny and Buckle on Disraeli, and the five volumes of Symonds on the Renaissance. I was touched by the peculiar tragedy of Symonds: a homosexual who married and had four daughters. And I marveled at Jowett's report that in 1886 he (Symonds) published the final volumes of *The Renaissance*, translated Cellini's *Autobiography*, wrote lives of Sir Philip Sidney and Ben Jonson, edited selections from Jonson and Sir Thomas Browne, and contributed the article on Tasso to the *Encyclopaedia Britannica*—all this while he suffered eye trouble and was dying of consumption, of which three of his daughters died in turn. He developed for himself a system of ethics independent of religious belief. He had no gods except the Swiss Alps, which (like a Druid merging with a tree) he worshiped as nearest to divinity. He modestly described himself as a *vulgariseur*—a popularizer; in his heart he knew that he was much more than that, but lesser men took him at his word.

As work on *The Reformation* proceeded, Will felt more and more guilty of having neglected Switzerland and Germany. We had seen Berlin, Leipzig, and Dresden in 1932, but we had never seen Wittenberg, Worms, Mainz, Augsburg, Ulm, Nuremberg, and other cities famous in the history of German religion, politics, or art. More or less reluctantly he began to prepare another European tour. I did not agree to follow him into Germany, for I could not forget so soon what that country had done to my people; but I was glad to get another view of Italy, France, and England, and to visit my family in New York.

So, on April 30, 1954, we took off by train for New York, where we were spoiled by the hospitality of our friends. Two of them, Joe and Lilian Eaton, asked if they might accompany us on part of our trip, and we could not refuse them, though we foresaw some difficulties from their habituation to a standard of living that we could neither afford nor enjoy. The four of us sailed on the *Independence* May 27.

In Naples, dividing the expense, we arranged for a car and a driver to take us through Rome, Orvieto, Siena, Florence, Rapallo, Geneva, Milan, Montreux, Lausanne, and Neuchâtel to Bern. We shall never forget the driver, Giuseppe Esposito, for he was a model of competence and courtesy, putting up patiently with all the whims of the road, the car, the weather, and his passengers. In each city Will revisited the galleries—especially the Borghese, the Uffizi, the Pitti, and the Brera. In Milan we dropped in on Arnoldo Mondadori, who was publishing an especially beautiful edition of *The Story of Civilization* in Italian. In Bern we had lunch with Dr. G. R. Lang, who had charge of the German translation issued by the Francke Verlag. Dr. Lang praised the books generously, but reported that the Germans, still impoverished by the war, would not buy such expensive tomes. We told him of the success that Éditions Rencontre, of Lausanne, was having with their publication of a French translation in three small and inexpensive volumes for every one of the American edition. The suggestion was taken up; a thirty-four-volume edition is now doing very well in Germany and Austria. Similar handy editions are circulating in Denmark, Sweden, Great Britain, and Japan.

From Bern we drove to Lucerne, and then to Zurich. There Will enjoyed an "auto-da-graph" session at the Orell-Füseli Verlag, which had published a German translation of *The Story of Philosophy*; he was surprised to find a line of some thirty readers waiting to have their copies inscribed. While our friends were shopping around for fine watches, we toured the beautiful city and the lakefront. On July 5 our party divided: Joe, Lilian, and I headed south with Giuseppe through Lugano, Milan, and Genoa to Nice, while Will went on by train to Basel and Germany.

At Nice the Eatons left for a visit to Spain, Giuseppe carried me on to Cannes, and there I stayed till it came time to join Will in Paris.

Will:

Parting from Ariel was difficult for both of us, for I had rarely left her alone in Europe, and now for three weeks she was to be manless in Cannes. That evening I wrote to her from Basel, where Erasmus, fleeing from strife into quiet scholarship, had spent his final years.

7-3-54

A quick uneventful ride from Zurich, and here I am, unpacking and washing as if I were on a lecture tour.

My postal from Zurich told you how Dr. [Alfred] Jordi drove me some 90 kilometers out to the birthplace of Zwingli [at Wildhaus]. A little log cabin, about as big as our L.A. living room; thick plank floors, creaking wooden stairs, tiny windows; dark and gloomy within; did such rooms make for a gloomy theology, or did a gloomy theology form characters that would build such rooms? [Or did poverty and hard winters form both characters and houses?]

We returned by a picturesque and longer route, and visited the Grosse-münster (Cathedral) where Zwingli preached. Everything bare inside; just a communion table and pulpit; no pictures or statues or "idols." No wonder the Catholic population is growing even in Zwingli's Zurich—5% in 1900, 45% in 1950; the people want color, idols, imagery, myths, miracles; they hate sermons, and the Protestants substituted the sermon for the drama of the Mass. Only one item of ritual showed the Protestants to advantage—they let the congregation sing. This bothered Erasmus, and might have hurt Mozart's ears, but people love to sing.

It's 30 hours since I left you, and in that time I have subsisted on nuts and raisins and bread and cheese except for soup and compote in a restaurant last night. Now I'm going out for a meal, then to visit Erasmus' tomb, and see his letters in the library, and, if time allows, visit the art museum. . . .

Among the literary relics were the dispensations sent to Erasmus by Pope Leo X in 1517, freeing him from his monastic vows and the disabilities incurred by his illegitimate birth, and allowing him, without obligations, to hold benefices bringing him a thousand ducats a year. No wonder the timid scholar hesitated to burn this bridge of ducats behind him by joining Luther.

An hour's train ride took me to Freiburg-im-Breisgau, in whose cathedral I saw some paintings by Hans Baldung, Lucas Cranach, and Hans Holbein the Younger. Then on to Strasbourg for half a day in and around the cathedral. I sent Ariel a picture card.

7-7-54

I am writing this [sitting] on the curb facing the cathedral. What power and grandeur—more impressive than Notre Dame de Paris, tho less perfect in

313

beauty. Where did they get the money, and the patience, and the science? Goethe described this façade as "frozen music"—too cold a term; it is courage and hope vainly defying time.

On July 8 I spent three hours in Karlsruhe, and then on to Heidelberg, which I described on a card to Ariel as "a lovely town, full of university memories. Here Bunsen invented his burner, . . . and Helmholtz made the eye famous." At Stuttgart I was housed by Louis Sturz's nephew, Lieutenant Colonel Julian Fried, who was serving as physician to American soldiers in the locality. On July 10 he and his lady guided me to Ludwigsburg and the eighteenth-century castle of the dukes of Württemberg. Then to Ulm and Augsburg and their cathedrals, and on to Munich. This once handsome capital had been ruined by World War II, but the great paintings in the Alte and the Neue Pinakothek had been preserved, and were now gathered in one impressive collection.

From Munich I took a sightseeing bus to Garmisch and Mittewald for a look at the Bavarian Alps; and to Berchtesgaden, where Hitler had brooded over his manias. From Munich I went by train to Nuremberg; there the house of Albrecht Dürer, destroyed by our bombs, was being rebuilt to resemble the original. Then to Salzburg, where Mozart took nearly all my day. Then to Bayreuth and Wagner, to Bamberg and its cathedral, and to Würzburg and its archiepiscopal palace, where Tiepolo's frescoes were the highlight of the week. A two-hour ride brought me to Frankfurt, where I browsed in the Goethehaus; then on to Worms, and the Denkmal, or memorial of Luther's historic (or legendary) defiance of Charles V and the Church: *"Hier stehe Ich, Ich kann nicht anders."* On July 19 I had troubles that recalled my lecture tours. So I wrote to Ariel on

July 20, 1954

I reached Mainz last night at 9:30, and found every hotel filled up, largely by residents, as 90% of Mainz was destroyed by Allied bombing. The Königshof Hotel, which I had given you as address, had no letter for me. I carried my bags to four hotels and could find no room. Finally I was advised to take an interurban trolley to Wiesbaden, 10 miles away. So you picture me hunting the trolley, boarding it, . . . reaching Wiesbaden 11 P.M., and finding no room available in the hotel there. I finally persuaded the desk clerk to let me sleep in a little cubicle containing a rough cot, no window, used for the help.

Today, after looking around Wiesbaden, I took the trolley back to Mainz, found your letter, . . . and saw the most frightful sight of all my German trip—a great modern city reduced almost to the level and condition of Pompeii—practically every building (or 9 out of 10) demolished. An American here . . . told me that most of the destruction fell upon Mainz a few days before the end of the war. The famous cathedral still stands, but all its windows were broken. About the only structure left intact is the Gutenberg Museum, where I found several of his earliest printings.

So I am back now in my Wiesbaden cubicle, counting the days and hours till I have you again . . . Tomorrow I spend all day on a steamer down the Rhine—the only part of the trip you would have enjoyed. It will be a rest for my creaking bones.

On July 22 I left the steamer at Bonn, followed the tracks of Beethoven, tried to find Konrad Adenauer, and failed. (Strange to say, I met him later in Los Angeles.) On the twenty-fourth I was in Cologne, where almost everything seemed to be in ruins except the cathedral, against whose sacred walls a rude *Kölner* relieved his bladder. That night, after pacing the station platform anxiously, dull to the advertisements of eau de cologne, I climbed, quite exhausted, into a sleeping car for Paris. The next morning I found Ariel waiting for me in the Palais d'Orsay Hotel. We had grown accustomed to that hostelry—and, to allure us, Voltaire had died only a block away.

Paris, as heartless as any beauty, gave us a miserable month. I have never seen so much rain as in those twenty-five days in which we shivered there, in midsummer, waiting for the sun. We escaped for a day to Chantilly, and found everything delightful, where the second Prince Louis de Condé entertained Racine, Molière, La Fontaine, and Boileau. Back in Paris we splashed from museum to museum and from theater to theater until August 20. Then we fled south to Biarritz, and found more rain. At last, on August 25, we discovered the sun—in San Sebastián, Spain. Thence we made a side trip to the monastery of Montserrat, where Ignatius Loyola sought the Holy Grail.

Bringing the sun with us, we returned to Biarritz and Bordeaux, and moved east (August 26) to Pau, where the lovable Marguerite of Navarre wrote the *Heptameron*, and her grandson Henry of Navarre ruled with dash and flair his principality of Béarn before buying Paris with a Mass to become Henri Quatre of France. To our romantic ardor the château seemed still alive with his gallant spirit and her kindness to Catholic and Huguenot alike.

From that center of enlightenment and grace we passed in an hour to a medieval scene, the most somber in my experience. From my hotel balcony at Lourdes I saw some of the hundreds of sick or dying women, children, and men being wheeled through the streets to gather before the grotto where, they were told, the Virgin Mother of God had appeared to Bernadette Soubirous in 1858. I went down and walked beside them, and soon saw, affixed to the walls of the grotto, the crutches and votive offerings of those who had pronounced themselves cured. I joined the silent file of those who could walk, and passed through the cave and by the healing spring. Emerging, I wandered among the chairs and the beds, and looked furtively at the ghastly faces of the pilgrims. Greater than the horror of their sufferings was the tragedy of their faith. To my still-Christian spirit the collapse of Christianity before science and Mars seemed more tragic than the death of Christ: so many centuries of hope deceived, so many broken bodies and souls appealing desperately to a silent and now vanished God.

We went on to Toulouse, where faith had murdered Jean Calas, and to Carcassonne and its famous wall. At Narbonne we diverged south to Perpignan, and thence, after passbook tribulations, to Barcelona. We took a long walk through the city, and found it surprisingly clean and beautiful. We recalled the report that Albert Lewin had given us of his long stay in Barcelona when filming *Pandora and the Flying Dutchman*: "In the evenings the people would come down from their tenements and dance and sing in the streets. I joined them, and they called me *simpatico*. I came almost to believe in poverty, superstition, and dictatorship, for I had never seen such happy people as these subjects of Franco and the Church."

From Barcelona we took a *wagon-lit* all the way to Cannes, and from Cannes we sailed on September 6 to New York. We visited our relatives, dined with our friends, slept our way to Chicago, picked up a lecture fee from my old audience at the Executive Club, and took the Santa Fe to Los Angeles. There, on October 3, we concluded the most arduous trip we had made since our venture from Harbin to Warsaw in 1932. Home were the sailors home from the sea, and the hunters home from the museums, the cathedrals, and the tombs.

Though the royalties were mounting as foreign translations spread, and as the success of *The Renaissance* brought its predecessors back to life, I accepted ten lecture engagements between October 11 and 28, tempted by the now usual five-hundred-dollar fee; I did not know enough mathematics to realize that one third of this went to my lecture agent, and a third went to expenses and taxes, and the remainder hardly warranted the wear and tear of trains and planes and buses and hotels upon a sixty-nine-year-old assortment of flesh and bones and nerves. Some of my letters survive from that trip, but let them rest in peace.

Ariel:

Looking over my notes for the years 1954–56, I see that I was more appreciative of Erasmus than our debate would suggest. I read *The Praise of Folly*, dipped into the *Colloquies*, and absorbed the volumes on Erasmus by Froude and Preserved Smith. I gathered a heap of excerpts from Erasmus' letters; one of these, dated May 17, 1527, was advice to a young friend who was going to England, but was also a needed caution to my impetuous self:

> You will meet many of the English nobles and men of learning. They will be infinitely kind to you, but be careful not to presume upon it; when they condescend, be you modest . . . They are generous and will offer you presents, but recollect the proverb, Not everything and from everyone. Ac-

cept gratefully what real friends give you. To mere acquaintances excuse yourself lightly; more art is needed in refusing graciously than in receiving. An awkward rejection often makes enemies. . . . Be especially careful to find no fault with English things or customs. They are proud of their country, as well they may be.

By my own predilection for books and scholarship, I should have more readily taken to Erasmus than to Luther, but my final preference was for the man who dared to stand—almost alone—against a powerful and intolerant Church. I could forgive Erasmus for feeling too indebted to the papacy to join in any attempt to overthrow it, and being too fond of the amenities of civilization to let loose the commonalty against the aristocracy; but it was Luther, not Erasmus, who opened a path to the modern mind. I had to admit that Luther, in his later years, and the early Protestants in general, had been anything but friendly to freedom of thought and speech; but it was their rebellion that broke down the fortress of dogma and made it possible for later reformers to appeal to reason.*

The year 1955 slipped by quietly, because we were absorbed in research and writing. Will was so involved with his manuscript that—like Balzac with Vautrin, Lucien, Eugénie, Goriot—he talked of his fictional persons as more real than the vanishing figures and events of the day; Luther, Erasmus, Calvin, Henry VIII, Gutenberg, Rabelais, and Copernicus were more vital, more lasting in their influence, than the politics, prizefights, murders, fashions, market reports, and baseball scores of the daily press. So we buried our heads in the living past rather than the dying present, and did not surface, except at the sound of friends, until Will flew to Reno, October 9, to begin a stint of twelve lectures ending on October 28 with his most insatiable customers, the Executive Club of Chicago. I have his daily letters before me, and can't resist rereading them. Some bits:

Oshkosh, Wis., 10-25-55

. . . I feel that you exaggerate the horrors of growing old. . . . The work we are doing has the advantage of growing in spread and acceptance with time, so that our later years, tho bothered with a pain in the neck or elsewhere, should have the comfort of work well done, and still proceeding.

---

* The brilliant Episcopalian priest C. E. Hopkin, who helped learnedly in classifying material for *The Reformation* and other volumes, appended to the returned material an illuminating note: "I am more and more impressed with bodily well-being as a big factor in the contest between Erasmus and Luther. Luther was a bull,—a beefy, redblooded hulk of a man, whose body was at least equal to his mind. . . . Erasmus' mind overbalanced his body. His lack of physical stamina may help to explain his lack of interest in the common man, his retreat into his own humanistic interests, and his inability to battle established institutions beyond a certain point.—Also for the same reason Erasmus and Luther complement each other: Luther did more obvious good, but I suspect that some of Erasmus' insights are truer in the end.—No closed theological system is ever completely true of human nature. Erasmus' refusal to plunge either way is not all cowardice. Some of it is due to deeper perception; and bodily weakness *sometimes* deepens this perception."

The Reformation will be too long for the reader, but it will be as good a job as any I have done; and as you and I have fought over every page, . . . you shared mightily in producing it. . . .

So I don't worry about age, and wish you too could accept it gracefully, as so natural that to look young at seventy would seem improper and absurd. It isn't youth or age that matters, it is what health we're in, and how interesting and effective is our work. . . .

LaPorte, Ind., 10-26-55

. . . As to my own repute, I really think of it but seldom; what moves me now is to do justice to the subject, not to amuse the reader. I believe that this *Story of Civilization*, which I have by the tail and can't let go, will make its way slowly but persistently, and will be a help to many students for at least a half century. . . . But I suppose no parent can objectively judge his children.

I note from Will's diary that at Chicago he took for his subject "The Evolution of Love." I know that lecture; it was a frank tracing of the development of sex in the plant and animal world: the historical embellishment of physical relations with the psychological results of female retreat and feminine modesty; male idealization of the desired and refused object; aesthetic feelings and romantic sentiment; and, finally, the mutual solicitude and devotion that come not from erotic desire but from long and faithful comradeship. I was told that this learned but risky—not risqué—discourse was warmly applauded by six hundred auditors, half of them women; for Will's coming to the club was traditionally its Ladies' Day.

I was in New York to welcome my sensual idealist when he arrived on October 31. Five days later Max Schuster gave a handsome party in celebration of Will's seventieth birthday. An ensemble played music by Mozart, Beethoven, and Schubert; Max and Ray, Dick and Andrea, Will and I had similar old-fashioned tastes in music. Nearly all our New York friends attended, and telegrams came from several in Los Angeles. Arde Bulova sent Will an elegant little watch inscribed "To Will Durant, the greatest philosopher . . . of our time"; Will hid this, lest the reporters present should remind him that Arde knew much more about watches than about philosophy. The watch has proved more accurate than the inscription.

By November 17 we were back in our Hollywood home. We visited Ethel, Gordon, and Monica in San Jacinto, and Jim at the Webb School in Claremont, where he was making good progress; but for the rest we buried ourselves in *The Reformation*. I ended 1955 with an unusually pious prayer: "In less than a year Will hands his publishers the sixth volume of his history of civilization, leaving only one to go. If God is willing, and with his help, *The Age of Reason* will be done by 1960, and then we will be ready for the Angels' Chorus." None of us dreamed, at that time, that the *Story* would take five volumes more.

Will was always vowing to quit the lecture platform, but I suspect he had come to derive some secret satisfaction in facing and winning an audience, and hearing them applaud. In March, 1956, he succumbed again, though briefly; he undertook an arduous trip for three lectures in or near Seattle. Perhaps the deciding lure was that Seattle has a "Durant Study Club." An elegant letter from its president explains:

March 14, 1956

DEAR DOCTOR DURANT:

It is with great pleasure that we of the Durant Study Club note you will soon visit Seattle.

We hope we are not being presumptuous in thinking you may remember something about our Club. . . . Ten years ago, at the instigation of Mrs. Linton Murray, this Study Club was organized with your list of One Hundred Best Books as a basis of study. . . .

After a period of ten years our members are still interested, and this year are especially so since the program has been taken from your books "Caesar and Christ" and "The Age of Faith."

It is understood that you will be very busy during your stay, and while we do not wish to encroach upon your time, if you could possibly spare a few minutes to receive a committee representing the . . . Club, giving them a message to carry back to the members, we would be very grateful and very happy.

Whether or not we may be granted the above privilege, may we thank you for the very great stimulation we have received from the study of your books, and we hope that your visit to Seattle will be most pleasant.

Wishing you every success in the completion of your work, we are

Sincerely yours,
DURANT STUDY CLUB
Mrs. Max McFayden,
President

As with each of the volumes, Max Schuster sent alleluias when he read the manuscript of *The Reformation.* But he objected to a word in the last paragraph of the preface. This ran as follows:

If the Reaper will stay his hand, there will be a concluding Volume VII, *The Age of Reason,* which should appear some five years hence, and should carry the story to Napoleon. There we shall make our bow and retire, deeply grateful to all who have borne the weight of these tomes on their hands, and have forgiven a thousand errors in our attempt to unravel the present into its constituent parts. For the present is the past rolled up for action, and the past is the present unrolled for our understanding.

Max protested: "Your researches are so vast . . . that I venture to say that you are over-modest in referring to a 'thousand errors' in your attempt.

Please do me a favor, Will, and eliminate this line." Will compromised by changing "a thousand" to "numberless." He was speaking of all the "tomes," and he had covered so many and diverse fields of inquiry that he could hardly expect to remain immaculate; and (as a merciless critic was to show in the case of *The Age of Louis XIV*) he made some serious slips.

I noticed, from his letter of June 11, 1956, that Max had been caught up in the debate between Luther and Erasmus. "The sections on Erasmus," he wrote, "are particularly inspiring and enthralling." Later the controversy divided the editorial staff at "S and S"; one member called up to ask Will's private preference—as if it had not been evident. (He has this moment admitted to me that "Erasmus left little of lasting substance behind him; Luther changed half of Europe." But he refuses to retract those last words of Chapter XIX: "Luther had to be; but when his work was done, and passion cooled, men would try again to catch the spirit of Erasmus and the Renaissance, and renew in patience and mutual tolerance the long, slow labor of enlightenment.")

The final sections of the manuscript were mailed in June, 1956, and then we set off once more for New York and points east. But this time Will went berserk with his royalties. He had grown very fond of my sisters Flora, Sarah, and Mary; indeed they had been endlessly helpful to us and to Ethel; now he decided to reward them with a trip to Europe. He left Mary out (though he was never through kissing her) because she had recently returned from Europe, self-financed, and was familiar with our usual haunts—Paris and Cannes. But he added Ethel and Monica. Ethel's second marriage was breaking up, and she needed some diversion. So on July 3 all six of us sailed on the *France*. Monica, then four and a half years old, became the belle of the boat, prattling, prancing, pretty, and still unsullied by the knowledge of evil. Her gay spirit made us bear with good humor the rough competition for porter and compartment when, at Le Havre, we passed through the *douane* from ship to train.

In Paris we took rooms near one another in the Hotel Palais d'Orsay. In the evenings we ladies went out on the town, and Will's assignment was to work on *The Age of Reason* while keeping an ear open for the age of innocence as Monica, in the adjoining cubicle, babbled her way to sleep. I must confess that one of those nights, while Will husbanded his virtue, we "girls" (as our provider called us) visited one of the topless shows in the Place Pigalle. When, a few evenings later, Will humbly asked my permission to join a "Cook's Tour of Paris by Night," I could hardly object. I sat up till 3 A.M. worrying about his chastity, just as his mother had done fifty-one years before.

It was a full summer for all of us. Ethel and Monica flew off to Oslo and London to see some friends, and later they and I went to Saint-Moritz to see Bibi and Carlo Foà. Then Ethel, called prematurely home, left us with a quick look at Venice, and returned with Monica to New York and California. My sisters were not neglected; on August 10 they, Will, and I left Paris on a bus tour of Italy. We had a pleasant ride along the shady roads of France, and through Geneva and the Simplon Pass to Milan; the French ladies in the group charmed us en route with their amorous or jolly songs; and the guide, knowing the weakness of our bladders, stopped the bus at wayside inns to *cueillir les fleurs*—"pick flowers." We had the pleasure of showing Flora and Sarah the major cities of Italy. We were all returned safely to Paris by August 26. Three days later we left by train for Cannes, where we caught the *Constitution* for New York.

On board, after a convulsive storm, I wrote to my friend Lilian Kaufman a rambling letter,

Sept. 17, 1956

In three days we dock, and once again we will have finished our work in Europe for another volume, . . . only with this difference—this time it is [to be] the last one. . . . After the book is written and printed, sometime in 1961–2, it will be time to decentralize and decompose; but should a few years between these processes be granted us, . . . what should we do then? What should we do in the last and most precious years of our life?—those few years, supposedly the wisest and kindliest and most tolerant and understanding. How use them as tho our life was not writ in water, as tho one handed something, our all, to someone to whom it made a difference? Funny thoughts these, in the midst of a storm rocking sea, where to spew and puke and hold one's head just a trifle above a chamber-pot is a grand feat of the will to survive. But the day after, . . . when on deck the sun shines in all her glory, so innocently shedding light and warmth on all God's children—how alien then is the mood and memory of the night before, and how large and competitive grows the will to live. . . .

It is good to be going home, to be on the last lap of a forty-year job; and, tho getting old and infirm, it is good to be able to love one's fellow men even tho it is hard to understand them. Thank God for our health, our friends and family, and for the country which, by the grace of good fortune, we live in and call ours.

We arrived just in time to receive the galley proofs of *The Reformation*, and to applaud the gallant effort of Adlai Stevenson to unseat the modest General from the presidency. But Will's lecture agent had committed him to another campaign, and on October 8 he left New York for Duke University.

His letter from Durham, North Carolina, showed him as enthusiastic as ever:

Oct. 10, 1956

Sweetheart:

Everything is all right so far! Beautiful days here yesterday and today, and so lovely and spacious a campus, shaded by a thousand trees, that I

321

commiserated with the students who met my train, since heaven would seem a let-down after this earthly paradise.

How they exploited me, those students! Lunch at 12; meeting with the faculties of philosophy and history at four; tea at 5; visit with Prof. Lionel Stevenson (whom you met in L.A.); dinner at 6; lecture at 8; reception by the students at 9:30; "and so to bed." I could hardly resent this big program, these fine youngsters were so enthusiastic, so eager to pump me on anything from Nixon to God. They gave me such a big hand after my talk on "Does Man Progress?" that I thought I must be Adlai Eisenhower. . . .

From Grand Rapids, Michigan, he wrote gallantly,

Oct. 12, 1956

. . . At the airport here I was met by 2 fine men and their wives, who had all read *Transition,* and wanted to know how Ariel was. I told them you were all that I had dreamed of, and more. . . .

It's consoling to know that you are taking care of yourself, and that Flora is guiding her sisters into . . . health. Bless you all, my wife, my sisters, and my brothers.

On October 12 I went up with Mike to take what I thought would be my last look at our old house in Lake Hill. The next day I indited my annual ode to autumn in a letter to Will:

As tho there were no intervening experiences, I woke this morning and looked out of the three windows from my bed, and lo and behold Autumn in all her old glory. . . . Our rich, widespreading maple trees, still full and most beautifully arrayed, and the sun everywhere warming and blessing. I ran out of the house to the front porch, and, with my wild heart beating love with each stroke, I threw kisses at each leaf and tree, millions and millions of them, . . . dead, or dying, or those clinging to dear life a moment longer. It was memorable! Thoughts of you—your many summers passed here, each hour a way of life, . . . until I could see you near me, and felt your presence near and benign. I suppose that house, those mountains and walks, the years of opening and closing; feeding and welcoming family and friends, artists and beggars—these memories, this longest period of continuity establishes for me, chaotic and rebellious as I am, the one unifying background and most important experience. Here, too, our children spent the innocent years of their sweet youth. Even their children made a bowing acquaintance with these same hills and trees, and this old spacious house . . . I rocked again on one of your favorite [rockers], and dreamed I became one with its memories and odors left over in the many years it carried you.

And now, writing to you . . . before a crackling fire, and looking out thru those picture windows, I still see Willow and Lake Hill in the dying conflagration of another summer. I am thrilled, happy, and so sad . . . My desire is fulfilled! I have been here once again, and give it now my farewell and my last thoughts. From now on I belong elsewhere, but always to you.

Will responded from the Morrison Hotel, Chicago,

Sunday, Oct. 14, 1965

. . . Found a thousand conventioneers here—the "United Hod Carriers of America"! In the Palmer House the "Bakers' Association of America" is cooking up its own fracas. Apparently these conventions are excuses for eluding that "unremitting wifely supervision" which I once described as indispensable to the male's avoidance of adultery. . . .

Now the evening is stealing down around my window, . . . and the sweetest church bells I've ever heard are chiming some touching old Protestant hymns, one so beautiful that I cried out, in my silent cubicle, "O God, how beautiful!" As Napoleon said, "I become a believer again when the church bells ring." But they soon stop, and the world proceeds on its agnostic way . . .

I love you more than the world, till death do us part; and then my prefaces and dedications will continue to woo you.

From Milwaukee Will sent me so many reckless compliments that again I began to worry about his fidelity.

Oct. 15, 1956

Each letter [from you] is full of beauty, worthy of the great letter writers who contributed to fill your mental background and form your style. Your comments on "only the *works* of a writer are interesting" are convincing, but perhaps that is because we expect a biography to be full of external events of the writer's body; if it includes the internal events of his mind it can be mighty interesting. The best example I can think of, shame to say, is *Transition*. The mind has adventures profounder than the body's, and a creed lost may be as vital an event as a battle won. . . .

So you are "gently decomposing"? We're not decomposing so long as we are composing worthily. And I think we are doing that. My hand moves the pen in [the first few volumes of] *The Story of Civilization*, but the spirit is *ours,* and the work is a lifelong co-operation. . . .

I literally count the days, every day, that remain before I can lie beside you and feel the soft warmth of your breasts, and your caressing arm around my neck.

Mad about you.

I rewarded this madness by promising never again to disturb the peace of Los Angeles with longing for Greenwich Village or New York. After a day in the Village I wrote:

Oct. 21, 1965

Since writing to you yesterday, . . . I lived a typical New York day, lots of action, motion and commotion, shouting, arguments, . . . but nothing was really said, and less done, and now, thinking it all over, only the sound and fury remain and still ring in the ear. Well, that was once so interesting that it called for more and more, and so we spent much of our youth arguing about it . . . ; but now it was boring and enervating. . . . I visited Romany Marie, deaf but still picturesque, and [a] living organ of the wisdom of half a century of experience. The Village of her day devoured, mercilessly, many vestal virgins, and left them wounded and bleeding in mind and body. . . . Those were the days when fatal attractions sucked us into the Village—or to the Left Bank—a few escaped merely the richer for the experience. . . . Somehow, somewhere, something died, and one was never the same; try as he would, the taint was there to stay. . . .

You said, "Get your belly full of N.Y." And so I did, today, and with it or without it, I can leave it and go home without regrets and without long-ings. I think that I have almost reached the stage when I can take the advice Lao-tze gave to the young Confucius: "Those about whom you inquire have moulded with their bones into dust. Nothing but their words re-main." And so tonight, or last night, I have paid my respects to their ashes and my dead dreams. May I never look backwards in that direction again, except to draw from . . . amongst the embers buried in the mausoleum of youth. . . .

See you again tomorrow, my love.

After a visit with my Chinese friend Sian Mae Chang at the United Nations, I went to hear a series of lectures by Paul Tillich; I sent my notes of these brilliant discourses to Will, who commented on them in a letter of

Oct. 24, 1956

. . . I am glad you made such extensive notes; you must have listened actively. . . . I gathered that Tillich followed Comte in dividing the intellec-tual development of mankind into three periods: (1) the mythological, which personified and deified the causes and processes of events; (2) the metaphysical, which sought for the causes and the meanings of events in concepts and realities not known to science; and (3) the positivist, which seeks to explain all events and phenomena by scientific (i.e., observed and verifiable) processes. Did Tillich realize that this theory of development leads (as in Comte, Mill, and Spencer) to agnosticism? How does he, on this basis, resurrect religion?

The last paragraph of your page 1 implies that Tillich wants a religion without myths. I'm afraid that such a religion would be accepted only by philosophers. The more myths, miracles, and ceremonies a religion has, the likelier it is to meet the emotional and esthetic needs of the people. Reli-gion, like poetry, is an imaginative embellishment of a prosaic reality. It is an attempt to turn a cruelly neutral nature into a sympathetic ally of man.

Will admired Dr. Tillich's learning, but he smiled at Tillich's definition of God as "the ground of Being." "Can you pray to 'the Ground of Being'? . . . No religion will ever live on abstractions. The Doctor's attempt to salvage Christianity supports rather Toynbee's description of our age as the 'post-Christian century.' "

From Tillich's discourse on God I subsided to picture the family which had been a part of me, and I of it, for fifty-eight years, and to which I was about to say what might be a last goodbye:

> Maurice [now the patriarch] is in the next room. . . . Bored in his daughter's house in Larchmont, he . . . comes here to the girls [his four sisters] for a visit. [Widowed,] he is a lonesome soul, . . . broken and silently pleading for a little love and friendship. . . . Harry spreads his motherly skirt over all his chicks, and protects with his blood and devotion all of us. He won't let anybody die before him. . . . Tomorrow Louie is joining the four girls for lunch, and so I will be able to bid him goodbye. . . .

And then I jumped a generation to our grandson in Claremont:

> Write a word to our Jimmy every once in a while. He deserves more friendship and guidance than he is getting from you, . . . and he is all that I had hoped he would be and more, much more . . . I will give him my love and I will be satisfied that he Just Is, and expect nothing in return. . . .
>
> It is natural . . . that I end with a note of love. Love for Jimmy, for you, for Ethel, and for Monica, and from all of us, including again
>
> Your ARIEL

He reached Chicago at 7:20 A.M. October 27, and met my train from New York at the La Salle Street Station at 8:45. We went to the Conrad Hilton Hotel. After breakfast he insisted on taking a prenuptial bath. As was his custom he shouted with shock and delight when he ended with a cold shower. While he stood toweling himself in the tub, I went to him with some question. Pushing aside the curtain, he leaned over to give me a wet kiss. His foot slipped; he tried and failed to grab the curtain rod; he fell across the side of the tub, and lay with his feet in the air and his head at my feet. I helped him rise, and for a moment we tried to laugh at the absurdity. But his laughter was checked with a pain in his right side; every breath hurt; he had broken one or more ribs. I put him to bed, called a doctor, and crept in beside him to comfort him. He tried to embrace me, in an effort to collect what he called "past dues," but the pain compelled him to desist. Dr. Ernest Malter soon arrived, and fitted around Will's abdomen a band that my wounded athlete called a chastity belt. That evening he insisted on escorting me to the train that was to take me to Los Angeles. He himself went off by sleeper to Omaha. There, from the Fontenelle Hotel, he reported:

Oct. 30, 1956

> . . . Your kind hands and heart, and that parting full-lipped kiss, left me happy in my misery. You were right; I was unable to lower the bed [from the roomette wall]; had to call the porter. Took two aspirin tablets; they enabled me to sleep from 10 P.M. till midnight. Then I tossed around sleepless till 4 A.M., and the bouncing train played havoc with my back; I couldn't turn to any other position. At 4 A.M. I crawled inch by inch out of bed, raised the bed [by releasing a spring], and sat up till arrival at 9:30. Managed to shave.

Arrived at this hotel (where no one has ever heard of Fontenelle), found myself dated for luncheon with a score of businessmen—bankers, Republican politicians, and the president of the Union Pacific R.R. But the luncheon was good fortune for me. Dale Clark, chairman of the board of a bank here, took me to a doctor. The phlegm in my windpipe weakened my voice to a squeak, and produced reflex convulsions that were very painful; but I couldn't bring it up; and it looked as if those convulsions would make oratory impossible. But the doctor injected novocaine into the roots of the nerves that went to the injured muscles; the pain disappeared; I was able to cough now, and threw up horrible phlegm black with the zephyrs of Chicago. By that time it was 4 P.M.; my dinner appointment was for 5:30; my lecture for 7 P.M. Luckily the effect of the novocaine was best when I rose to speak; I could breathe deeply, tho with some discomfort, and gave the audience full measure. Back to the hotel at 9, I fell into bed and slept till 2, tossed till 6, rose and shaved. Now the pain is returning and I shall have to go . . . for a second injection. Don't fear after-effects of these injections; they are the same as those given for the extraction of teeth. This afternoon I take the plane to Austin.

I expect that by the time I reach you I'll be a bit stronger and less plaintive. . . . I'll soon be amorous again.

Kissing your feet,
WILL

He went through with his engagements in Texas, and flew to Los Angeles just in time for a muted celebration of his seventy-first birthday. Soon he was rushing into Volume VII, happy to write about Elizabeth and Shakespeare. I, only fifty-eight, had already begun to feel old; but Will rejuvenated me by giving me an ever greater share in our civilization job. As the year 1957 opened I was preparing a "preview" of *The Reformation* for the home of a friend.

We gave very little time to social activities. We stopped attendance at winter concerts, which involved a trip "downtown" to the Philharmonic Auditorium; but we treated ourselves to a good radio-and-phonograph set which enabled us, each evening, to choose our own music program from among the eight or nine FM broadcasting stations in or near Los Angeles. Will read learned tomes, and I read Gibbon, while hearing classical music; when anything especially beautiful came over, Will would put down his book to listen; and sometimes, enthralled, he would extricate himself from the drawing board that straddled the arms of his chair, and would walk with me up and down the room while the music poured over us. I noticed that his taste for Beethoven had declined, whereas he never had enough of Mozart or Bach. His favorite record is still the aria "Laudate Dominum" from Mozart's *Vesperae solennes* (Victor Record C 2736). He became, I think, prejudiced in favor of Mozart over any of the famous B's; Ethel and I had to argue with him for half a year to cut down his spreading chapter on Mozart in *Rousseau and Revolution*.

Fan letters took a bite from his day. They were not numerous—averaging about two a day; but he insisted on answering every one of them, usually returning flattery with some compliment. Latterly I have often snatched such letters from his desk before he could answer them, and have replied to some of them in my own name, or left them cruelly unanswered. I am the tougher member in the partnership.

Having used and abused our 1951 Cadillac through six years, we thought we deserved another, and went prospecting. We seem never to have bought any car but a Cadillac since 1943; we found that a good car is in the long run as economical as a less reliable car that is only half as expensive and half as durable. So in July, 1957, we bought a pretty Cadillac; and only now, after using it for thirteen years, are we thinking of buying another.

We liked this one so much that on August 24 we rashly set out by car to keep our promise to Max Schuster that we would come to New York to assist at the birth and boosting of the new book. On the Indiana Turnpike a heavy blinding rain fell upon us; the windshield wipers stopped working, and my young septuagenarian had to drive for some ten miles in one-yard visibility, often with his head outside the car, till we found a repair shop. We went to Lake Hill first, to see Michael, Flora, and Mary; and there, in the New York *Times* of September 15, I found so laudatory a review of *The Reformation* that I trembled with joy, and cried out, "My cup runneth over."

We passed down to New York City, ate with our friends, and feasted on reviews. Seldom had the critics been so kind; and if, now and then, one voice fell out of tune, I wanted to go at once and demand an apology. Amid the alleluias a real body blow came, in the prestigious *Saturday Review*, December 7, from Garrett Mattingly, professor of history at Columbia University. The amiable scholar began with a carrot and ended with a bludgeon. He smiled at the progressive compression of time in the series, and predicted, with better foresight then either of us had shown, that

> at this rate the next part announced, "The Age of Reason" (Council of Trent to Napoleon I) can scarcely run less than three volumes; even if the events of the last century and a half require six volumes, one can feel sure that the readers who have been with Will Durant all along will buy every volume and read every word, for certainly, so far, his peculiar powers show no sign of flagging. He still parades the pageant of history before his readers with the gusto of a museum director exhibiting his treasures, and he comments on the sins and scandals, the splendors and terrors of his exhibits with a gentle wit and amused tolerance which is at once intimate and reassuring.

Then the blow:

> It is a reviewer's duty to warn that Will Durant's "Story of Civilization" . . . does not represent the state of historical scholarship in the middle of

327

the twentieth century. In fact, though an imposing apparatus of bibliography and footnotes gives the book the superficial appearance of scholarship, and some critics have permitted themselves the term, it is a mistake to talk about scholarship in connection with Mr. Durant's work at all. He has read a vast number of books about history, and has a large fund of information, much of it quite accurate. But scholarship, in historical studies, means the critical examination of evidence and the scrupulous evaluation of sources. In the field of universal history, where nobody can be expected to do all that work for himself, it means at the least, some discrimination as to the scholarly merits of the secondary works used, and some effort to keep abreast of the latest findings of the specialists. In this sense there is not the slightest taint of scholarship about this volume. Having read so widely, Mr. Durant has of course read some authoritative monographs, but he has neglected far more than he has read, and he has taken his facts, his quotations, and anecdotes wherever he has happened to find them, so that whole chapters of his book are invalidated for any serious purpose. Even the basic scheme of this volume and of the previous one is derived from the false dichotomy between the pagan Italian Renaissance and the reactionary, medieval Christian Reformation which scholars began to reject about fifty years ago.

Mr. Durant's public will care very little about this, of course, and who is to say that they are wrong? Their favorite author may be nothing of a historical scholar, but he is a capital storyteller, a constantly readable expositor, a widely read and highly cultivated man, essentially kindly and well-meaning. Time spent with such a person cannot be time wasted.

Who could be long angry with such a critic, who offered some anodyne with every wound? Will gave him a humble reply in the *Saturday Review* of December 28:

Professor Mattingly's reproof for not always going to the original sources gives me an opportunity to restate my purpose in writing "The Story of Civilization." My chief interest, as this title indicated, has been the history of culture; I have merely sketched in the political and economic history of *civilization*—which is the real history of man. States are the transient vehicles and domiciles of civilization; their rise and fall a dramatic and lugubrious record; civilization uses them, and moves on; it "does not die, it migrates." In describing the cultural contributions of each epoch, especially in literature, philosophy, art, and religion, I have recognized an obligation to go to the original sources, to study them at first hand, or see them *in situ*—at the cost of eight trips to Europe, two around the world, and fifty years of work. But I have not felt a like obligation to base my sketch of the political and economic background upon original sources. How foolish it would be for me, having only one life, to repeat for my present study of Elizabeth I the painstaking researches that Froude gathered in his five great volumes on her reign. To expect of a man to write the history of every phase of sixty centuries of human life in the same way in which he would write a monograph on one figure or aspect of one period in one nation is either to be rigorous beyond decency or to object to any attempt at a humanized synthesis of knowledge. I believe that synthesis is needed; that specialist historians may reasonably welcome any sincere effort to bring their results to unity; and that we must labor together lest knowledge become the technical privilege and jargon of a few men isolated from the people.

WILL DURANT

We had to revive ourselves by reading such letters as these from a university president and an ex-President of the United States:

Columbia University, New York,
June 28, 1957

DEAR MR. SCHUSTER:

I am most appreciative of your kindness in sending me an advance copy of Will Durant's "The Reformation," and most interested in reading it. Mr. Durant is a remarkable synthesist. I thought, when I saw this new work, of the comments I have heard students make, to the effect that they would never have passed a general course in philosophy without the aid of Durant's "Story of Philosophy" to pull them out of the confusion into which their independent studies had led. There is no doubt that many budding historians among thousands of others will benefit in a similar manner from this portion of his "Story of Civilization."

With warmest personal regards, and many thanks, I am,

Sincerely,
GRAYSON KIRK,
President

And from Independence, Missouri,

October 4, 1957

DEAR MR. DURANT:

You don't know how much I appreciated your kindness in sending me *The Reformation*. I know that I am going to read it with the greatest of interest, as I have read your other books.

The personal inscription which you placed in it makes it one of the most valuable books in my collection.

Sincerely yours,
HARRY S TRUMAN

Will:

Not having foreseen that *The Reformation* would get so many "rave reviews" (as the Newark *Evening News* called them), and would make the best-seller list now and then, I had committed myself to fourteen lectures en route from New York to Los Angeles. After drawing up directions for

Ariel to drive with Flora to Chicago, I took a sleeping car on September 30 to Norfolk, where I spoke twice on October 1; add a dinner, a press conference, and a post-oratory reception, and I was already half dead after one day. I reported to Ariel: "Norfolk is beautiful, . . . but I miss your prancing step and agile mind." I moved on to Troy (Alabama), then back to Chicago, then to Omaha . . . I reached Madison, Wisconsin, just in time to see the university absorbed in a World Series baseball game between Milwaukee and New York. I remembered my baseball reporting days.

Madison, Wis., 10-10-57

We always thought Wisconsin beautiful, but you should see the view from my window in "Wisconsin Union" (the campus hotel): a glorious shining lake, two miles across, bordered by autumn-gilded trees, and below me a park where some of the 12,000 students here walk hand in hand, boy and girl, in all the glow of free American youth.

Only one thing can rival the attraction of the sexes here today, and that is the thrill of a Wisconsin team beating what they call "those Damyankees." When I arrived two immense crowds were witnessing the final game on television; every Milwaukee blow and Yankee failure was greeted with joy; and all agreed that Milwaukee tonight will be drowned in happiness, Blatz and Schlitz. And it is good.

How can I interest them . . . in "The Lessons of Philosophy"? I'll forgive them if they think of Burdette [the victorious Milwaukee pitcher] while I speak of Plato.

I can't tell you how sweet Louis and Mollie and Eric were to me. Their home and life are idyls of wholesome marriage and parentage. They are anxiously awaiting you.

From Madison I flew to Chicago and on to Dallas. On October 15 I left Dallas by plane for Chicago. We were delayed by bad weather and crowded runways. I fretted, for Ariel and Flora, after a two-day drive from New York, were presumably waiting for me in the home that Louis and Mollie had bought in Evanston. Finally we were allowed to land. I took a bus for a long ride to Evanston; Louis met me; we were happily united, and all seemed well.

The next morning Ariel, Flora and I started off early in the car for St. Louis, where I was scheduled to attend a dinner and then hold forth on "The Psychological Differences between Men and Women." Halfway to our destination I had so severe a stomach attack that we had to stop to let me surrender my breakfast. I felt unsure of myself, and asked Ariel, so soon after a nine-hundred-mile drive, to take the wheel. When we reached the Chase Hotel I felt better, and Ariel and Flora went off to dine with our friend Henry Janon. I took the opportunity to bathe; probably I let the water run too hot; when I came out of the tub I grew dizzy; the room whirled around me; I stumbled into bed. I called the house doctor;

he pronounced my condition a hypertension crisis, and told me that I must stay in bed for several days. I protested, and tried to stand up; acute dizziness returned. I called Henry Janon; soon he, Ariel, and Flora were with me, and Ariel took command. She called the Ambassador Club and told them that I was *hors de combat*; she wired my lecture agent to cancel all my engagements.

Flora was a godsend to us in those days; while Ariel took care of me Flora took care of Ariel. Henry Janon insisted that all three of us should come and stay in his home. As his wife, Gladys, was in Mexico, and his daughters were in boarding school, he and we had the spacious house to ourselves. After two days I was able to cross the room without holding on to the furniture. After two weeks of shamefully slow recovery I felt strong enough to share with Ariel the task of driving from St. Louis to Los Angeles. Each of us drove a hundred miles; but I could feel tension mounting each time I neared the end of my stint; and when we reached Claremont, California, and stopped to visit Jim at the Webb School, I began to feel dizzy again, and Ariel had to pilot us through the traffic of Los Angeles to our home (November 2).

I tried to resume work on Volume VII, but after a few days I felt my blood pressure rising. On November 15 I put myself under the care of Dr. Myron Prinzmetal of Beverly Hills. I told him that I feared the side effects of the drugs usually prescribed for blood pressure; could he recommend a drugless treatment? He did: an hour's physical exercise every day, a five-minute rest near the end of each hour of mental work, and a continuation of my vegetarian diet. On this regimen I improved sufficiently to fill a long-standing engagement for our friend Ethel Longstreet, in the Beverly Hilton Hotel on December 4. I survived that ordeal, but I have not lectured since.

It was my good fortune that while I was beginning to disintegrate, Ariel was contributing more and more extensively to *The Story of Civilization*. For months at a time she absorbed herself in some phase of the varied subject—the French salons, Montaigne, La Rochefoucauld, Gibbon, Horace Walpole . . . ; and many of the notes and reflections that she wrote during these studies found their way into the successive volumes of our enterprise. I was impressed by the courage with which she marched through all the six volumes of Hume's *History of England*; she recognized its inaccuracy and partiality, but she was fascinated by the style, and by this second example (Voltaire's the modern first) of history being written by a philosopher. Gibbon she accompanied from beginning to end without skipping—which is more than I was ever able to do; I was astonished to find her following faithfully all those early-Christian "heresies" and disputes which I—sated with theology in my seminary days and nights—passed over hurriedly as completely dead for our times.

I believe Ariel took more fervently to Montaigne than to any other hero in our pantheon. I have before me the thick batch of her notes for our chapter on Montaigne in Volume VIII. I find in them many juicy items that did not get into print.

> Montaigne was a Frenchman, [but also] a Renaissance man of the rejuvenated . . . Greek and Latin tradition. The Catholic Reaction pushed him indoors, so to speak, but did not change him. . . . If Montaigne ever had idealism and enthusiasm, . . . his early classic training left no signs of them. . . . He wished to be a free man but not a rebel; everywhere to respect the customs . . . and religion of the people. . . . Now that ardor had been replaced by experience it would be possible, with mutual tolerance, to meet on neutral ground. . . . Montaigne is the father of us all.

As *The Age of Reason Begins* progressed I saw that it was a cooperative labor, and that simple justice required that the title page should bear both of our names. Ariel had never asked for this. When she learned of it she vowed to dedicate herself to the work. Now we proceeded hand in hand, topic by topic, volume by volume, united as we had never been before. It was as if our marriage had received a second consummation.

CHAPTER XXV

Growing Old

1958–61

Will:

One by one we lured Ariel's family to come and share with us the bright warmth of Southern California. Smog had not become more than an occasional nuisance, and we had not yet learned that the almost daily sunlight was part cause of its worsening. Brother Harry came in 1957, after forty years of work in Manhattan's humid summers and winter storms; Flora, having returned to the East after my recovery, came back in 1961 with sister Sarah to live in an apartment just a mile from our hilltop; Mary and her husband, Max Schwartz, came a year later. They have all been a comfort to us and to one another in sickness and health; we see one another almost every day; and I have often rejoiced to find that I married the whole family.

Our friends were almost as vital to us as our relatives. Eric and Marie Scudder had won our affection thirteen years before, when Eric gave his legal learning and acumen to the Declaration of Interdependence; many a time we benefited from his considered judgment. Even earlier, in 1943, we had met Mario Chamlee, once a star in the Metropolitan Opera Company; he and his gentle wife, Ruth, were now teaching the art of song in their Hollywood Boulevard house; their modesty was a lesson to me. Many other musicians exchanged vows of friendship with us: Italo and Katherine Montemezzi, Edmund and "Daisy" Burke (he once a famous baritone at Covent Garden), Joseph and Katherine Schuster, John and Ruth Vincent, Meredith Willson, and—most intimate of all—Harry and

Lilian Kaufman. Harry is gone, but I can still see and hear his educated fingers weaving a web of sparkling silver threads from the sonatas of Scarlatti. Later we enjoyed the hospitality of Joseph and Bessie Levy, and through them we met Dr. Elmer Belt and his wife, Ruth, whose example and guidance lighted our way. We renewed our twenty-year-old love affair with UCLA through friendship with its successive chancellors—Vern Knudsen and Franklin Murphy. "Ferd" Mencacci, logistics expert in the Army, helped us to understand generals; Charles Luckman helped us to understand the audacities of contemporary architecture; and Robert Sutro patiently taught us the elements of finance. Our closest Los Angeles friend, Frederick Blickfeld, was gone, but he had left us his daughter Anita, her mate, Mladin Zarubica, and their beautiful and sprightly children. Later came Victor DeLucia, one of the kindest men I have ever met. Who, gifted with such friends, could say a harsh word about mankind?

At their tables, as well as our own, both Ariel and I put on weight. I had to loosen my belt to let 145 pounds breathe. Dr. Prinzmetal rebuked me, and promised that my blood pressure would fall if I reduced my weight; I brought this down to 125, where it has remained till today (1976); and probably this has helped to ease my hypertension. Ariel developed gallstones and a duodenal ulcer, which at times made her miserable and checked her usually bright spirits. I tried to play doctor to her, and wrote out a detailed regimen guaranteed to cure every ill; nevertheless, on May 14, 1958, Ariel surrendered her gall bladder to surgery. We have found that half a glass of buttermilk after each meal or "snack" can keep the ulcer calm.

On April 1 we had the pleasure of meeting a scholar who had become vice-president of India, Dr. S. Radhakrishnan. We exchanged bouquets: I told him how much I had pilfered from his *History of Indian Philosophy*, and he assured me that among India's students the favorite method for getting a view of Indian history and culture as a whole was by reading *Our Oriental Heritage*. On the next evening we heard Aldous Huxley speak at the Beverly Hilton Hotel on the dangers of our being subconsciously indoctrinated by our television masters, not only in promoting sales, but also in inducing attitudes of mind. We had a chat with him, but found him hard to thaw. Sometime later his home—just a hundred yards from that of our daughter Ethel—was destroyed by a forest fire that for a time threatened all Hollywood; we kept ourselves ready at any moment to go and rescue Ethel and Monica. Aldous lost, in that fire, many manuscripts over which he had labored for years. He died soon afterward.

The great event of 1958 was Jim's graduation, with heaps of honors, from Webb School in Claremont. As his distant progenitor I was invited by Headmaster Thompson Webb to give the commencement address on June 7. It was a charming occasion: a bright afternoon; an open-air gathering of some fifty graduates with their relatives and friends, and myself as wisdom purveyor to youths who had not yet adopted the principle that everyone over thirty was intellectually dead. I was surprised and inflated when half a hundred newspapers printed the address in full. In September Jim entered Pomona College, Claremont, from which he graduated in 1961.

Meanwhile Ariel and I, preparing a volume that would cover all aspects of European life from 1558 to 1642, found many a lack in our knowledge of English and French events and scenes. After we had enjoyed a full summer of music at the Hollywood Bowl we left Los Angeles on August 28, 1958, spent three days in New York, and sailed on the *Queen Mary*, September 3. We made several forays into the evergreen English countryside. Douglas Fairbanks, Jr., a knighted hero of World War II, secured admission for us to a sitting of the House of Commons. We went twice in the month to Oxford, and spent recklessly on books that we feared we could not find in America. On September 23 Ariel sent to Harvey and Marda Brown a letter of which the rough draft survives. (I transcribe it now in London, July 21, 1970.)

> Today we have spent another happy day in London. We went once again, perhaps for the last time, to the British Museum. I was stunned by the beauty of that vast dome, and it was magnificent to see housed beneath it 7 or 8 million books, mss., and letters. We muffled a gasp of delight as we came face to face with letters from most of the great [English] men of letters of the last 400 years. You feel them suddenly come alive, and, for the moment, breathing and contemporary. The gods have signally favored this little isle with the kiss of wisdom, and now, like Periclean Athens, it can never die. We cannot leave London without expressing our gratitude. In 1948 we saw the city in its desolation; now we see it in its brave magnificence, almost all its [physical] wounds healed, its powerful architecture revealing the masculine courage of its people, and its people honorable and courteous, . . . its government—under whatever party or provocation—keeping its head and manners. We have been happy here, and will always remember England, 1958.

After a day at the World's Fair in Brussels we spent three weeks in France, following the traces of Catherine de Médicis, Henry IV, Richelieu, Descartes . . .; disgracefully we neglected to go to Bordeaux to gather some relics of Montaigne. Day after day, in Paris, I rode or walked down the Avenue de l'Opéra to the Louvre, and steeped myself in the art of France. I visited the Gobelin tapestry factory in Paris. We tramped through a dozen museums. We went out once more to Versailles and Fontainebleau (I had been there forty-six years before). We rested for a while in Cannes, returned to New York, and reached our Los Angeles home on October 29.

I was touched by a friendly letter that awaited me from a Jesuit professor of philosophy in Loyola College, Baltimore:

A Dual Autobiography

September 18, 1958

Some twenty-five years ago, I read your autobiography,—your years at St. Peter's College, Jersey City, the crisis about your graduation, your year at the Seminary. And as I read I thought, in the end, in spite of all, Will Durant will receive the last Sacraments in the Catholic Church. For even at that time I could see you mellowing just a bit. And I remember the one Jesuit who appealed to you, Father (to me, Marley) Collins, S.J. . . .

Why do I write this letter? First, because I've remembered you at Mass for twenty-five years—that you will do whatever God may inspire you to do. Perhaps you'll say, "But I don't believe in your God, and I don't like any form of organized religion." O.K., so what? I can still pray for you. It won't do you any harm!

But there is a second reason why I write you. I've taught Scholastic Philosophy for twenty-two years, and I can appreciate your "Preface to the Second Edition" [of *The Story of Philosophy*]. . . . Let me quote Page 11: "The total omission of scholastic philosophy was an outrage, forgivable only in one who had suffered much from it in college and seminary, and resented it thereafter as rather a disguised theology than an honest philosophy."

Will, to me this means that we Jesuits have failed you! Except perhaps for old Father Collins. Do you remember him? Will, he taught me Physics in 1919, when I was preparing to enter the University of Pennsylvania. . . .

Will, my older confrères gave you much. They taught you language and literature, and, such as it was in your younger days, science . . .

My last reason for writing to you: This year I'm running an honor course for the first twenty-five students in the Junior year, out of 190. Among the books they will read, and discuss with me, is your *Story of Philosophy*. . . .

You need not answer this letter. I just wanted you to know that we Jesuits are your friends. . . .

Very sincerely yours,
JOSEPH A. D'INVILLIERS, S.J.

The good father has continued to write to me, even to this year 1976, forgiving me one book after another, and still praying for my salvation. I have always answered him affectionately. If a man is good, differences of ideology should be no bar to friendship. Probably we are both wrong in our ideas and right in our feelings.

Just when our family was getting ready to alleviate my seventy-third birthday I disrupted all plans by having what I mistook to be a heart attack. I shall never forget the patience and devotion that Ariel showed in those days. She called Dr. Rexford Kennamer; an ambulance came, and I was carried to the Cedars of Lebanon Hospital. For three days Ariel kept close to me; for three nights she slept on the floor or on a cot beside my bed. After a dozen tests of everything about me, the verdict was that I had suffered nothing more dignified than a severe gastric disturbance, which did not speak well for my vegetarian diet; I explained it as an echo of the dysentery I had recently contracted in Cannes. Soon I was at work at the same old reckless rate.

We paid some penalty for having escaped the slushy winters and steaming summers of New York: comfortable in the Hollywood hills, with more stars beneath us than were visible above, we missed the stimulating company of other writers, such as we could have heard in New York, at publishers' receptions or at the meetings of the National Institute of Arts and Letters. In 1959 I was elected a member of the Institute, and at its request I sent it some material for an exhibition of the various stages through which a page of *The Reformation* had gone—from classification slips to first, second, and third drafts, to galley proofs and page proofs to published form. I noticed, from the Institute's catalogue of members, the names of William Carlos Williams, Reinhold Niebuhr, Arthur Miller, and others, whose conversation and criticism might have corrected and enlightened me had I been privileged to meet them. Later on, when some first-class writers came to live in Southern California, I had a chance and let it pass: Allan Nevins, Irving Stone, Robert Nathan, and others invited me to join a club which they were forming for occasional meetings of masculine minds, but I was too fond to Ariel to accept.

That Ariel could have kept pace with such elite company was evidenced by her performance at the Severance Club. I had often addressed this discussion group, and Ariel had listened stoically to ideas which she had often heard before. After much coaxing from the club's president she agreed to occupy the rostrum on August 14, 1959, with a talk which she entitled "From Innocence to Repentance." She reviewed her childhood, with its hardships, escapades, consolations, and ideals; she told, with fine delicacy, of her love affair and marriage; and then she surveyed, with humor and sympathy, what sixty-one years of experience had done to her youthful dreams. I was in the audience. I was proud of her delivery, her style, and the logical form and sequence of her discourse; at the end I could hardly keep from embracing her. She received the most sustained and enthusiastic ovation in the memory of the club.

The last fragment surviving from that year is a letter to Max Schuster telling him that the rest of the *Story* was to bear Ariel's name as well as mine. It noted, too, the death of one of our oldest and closest friends, Dr. Abraham Stone, July 3, 1959.

By this time it had become evident that Volume VII, like Volume V, was coming apart, that it could not, without squeezing the life out of it, carry the history of civilization down to 1789, much less to Napoleon. We had been captured by what we called "the English ecstasy" (1558–1648); Elizabeth I had taken forty-five pages, Shakespeare twenty-three, Bacon fifteen; and there remained James I and the Puritans and Charles I; the Golden Age of Spain with Cervantes, El Greco, Velásquez, and Philip II;

France under Henry IV, Richelieu, and Montaigne; the Low Countries with Rubens and Vandyke, Rembrandt and Frans Hals; Russia with Ivan the Terrible and Boris Godunov; the Thirty Years' War with Gustavus Adolphus and Wallenstein; science with Galileo, philosophy with Descartes; how could we force all that wealth into what would remain of the volume after the Elizabethan Age had received its due? Reluctantly and yet with secret joy, we determined to gamble with senility, and spread Volume VII into two. We knew that some critics, even friendly ones, would wonder at our extending the scale of treatment as we went along; we could only repeat that each age, as it came closer to our own, *tended* to have a richer content of significance and influence for us, and required a more intimate inspection for understanding. So we told Max that our *Story* would have eight stories instead of five (as originally planned), or six, or seven. Having announced Volume VII as *The Age of Reason*, we were now compelled to re-entitle it (lamely enough) *The Age of Reason Begins*. I would take a chance on that patient and mysteriously empowered heart of mine to go on expanding and contracting for five years more—till I should be seventy-nine.

Ariel:

My own heart must have beaten faster in those days when I felt myself received into full partnership. I devoted myself more completely than before to the common cause. I accumulated thirty-nine galleys of notes on the French salons, and almost as many on Montaigne. We continued to debate points of interpretation and allotment of space; Will yielded to me on some matters, but I recognized him as my master, and was content that the last form of our work should bear the grace of his style and the wink of his wit.

The puritan element in me was occasionally shocked by his French-Canadian humor, as in the story that ends page 12 of *The Age of Reason Begins*; but I recovered, and I joined in his relish of Sir Walter Raleigh's displeasure with the disclosures of his son (footnote to page 53).

I had found it difficult to follow Will in his threnodies over the poets, artists, condottieri, and popes of the Italian Renaissance; but I rivaled Will in enthusiasm for the Renaissance in England and France. My notes abounded in glimpses and praise of the English humanists, and of the intellectual currents stirred by Francis Bacon. I was fascinated by Henry IV, and for a year Montaigne was my god.

Who did the housework while I pored over the heroes and heroines who were to give life to Volume VII? I did. My sisters had apartments a mile or so away from us; they liked level land, and had no car to take them up or down our hill. Once a week, for eighteen years, Laura Nelson came to help keep our quarters clean, but I did all the shopping and the cooking, and attended to the cars. I found it hard to make vegetables interesting day after day, and to keep my vegetarian husband properly supplied with proteins; he eased this problem by munching shelled peanuts between meals, and, latterly, by condescending to eat chicken or fish once or twice a week. He was not hard to please; and when I succeeded in making rice pudding he embraced me as if I had written a symphony. We lived simply. Neither of us smokes. Will took care of his own study, and made his own bed; at times he wanted to help me with the dishes, but here I found him more of a nuisance than a help. Until 1967 he worked all day in his spacious library on the second floor; but after our six-o'clock supper (our main meal was at noon) he joined me in my ground-floor study, and we worked together. We were grateful for our good fortune in being allowed to earn our living—and something for our relatives—by writing books that might help young students for some years to come.

We had ceased to make political noises. We rejoiced to see how cordially the American people welcomed the visit of Khrushchev, and his conference with President Eisenhower at Camp David, and we mourned when that interlude of good feeling was ended by the downing of an American reconnaissance plane inopportunely flying over Russia. Strange to say, a general, become president, kept the peace, while Democratic presidents (whom we had voted for) led us into war; and the American economy languished under a Republican president favorable to business, while it prospered under Democratic presidents opposed by the business community; the reason, of course, was that the wars in Europe and Korea had been a boon to American industry. In any case Eisenhower, in 1960, was ending his terms as a *roi fainéant*, and the United States was throbbing with the game of choosing his successor.

That year was darkened for us, at times, by the passing of our friends. The first to go (on March 14) was Gustav Payot, whom we had admired as a philosopher among publishers. In the same week Dr. I. Percival Gerson died, after serving for many years as the beloved president of the Severance Club. On July 30 Richard Simon died, ending the famous, creative partnership that he had formed with M. Lincoln Schuster in 1924. He had been the business leader of the firm, and our relationship with him had been less intimate than with Max; but we had enjoyed his constant loyalty and kindness. And on November 17 our former friend and opponent Upton Close was killed in the crash of his car in Mexico.

I got away from Will and *Civilization* in February, 1960, to join my old chum Hattie Malkin for a week in Scottsdale, Arizona. I had there another good comrade, Dr. Collice Portnoff, who had won high repute for many years as professor of English literature in the state university at Tempe; and through her I made a precious new friend in Louise Kerr, the uncrowned queen of Scottsdale. On this outing I was interviewed by an excellent reporter, "Maggie" Savoy; I quote from her piece in the Phoenix *Arizona Republic* for March 13, 1960:

Still very much the imp, Ariel Durant [sixty-two years old] bounces around the conversation, gossiping familiarly of Montaigne, and Catherine de Médicis and her weakling sons, and "rare Ben" Jonson, and Francis Bacon, the man who "rang the bell that called the wits together," and of Shakespeare, quite as though they still exist.

"And they do," she sparkles. "They live for me, and for millions of others all over the world. When I am immersed in a personage of history I live with him, eat with him, laugh and cry with him. Will once said sadly to a friend, 'I have lost my wife to Disraeli.' Not surprising—Disraeli was a bewitching man; he bewitched Queen Victoria too . . . You do not invent history, nor do you apologize for it. You recognize forces behind facts, and instincts and desires behind actions; and you record these in vignettes which you try to make alive and understandable."

Will sent that interview to Max Schuster, along with the news that he was pregnant with triplets:

March 19, 1960

DEAR MAX:

Ariel has been taking over the job of Meet the Press. Here is her latest: a pretty good performance. I've never been able to find so competent a reporter. . . .

I am flirting with the idea of dividing *The Age of Reason* into three, instead of one or two volumes. I have nearly completed the second draft of the period from 1558 (accession of Elizabeth I) to 1648 (Peace of Westphalia); it makes 750 manuscript pages—which would make 600 printed pages; and it has been cut down as far as I can without weakening the adequacy or the vitality of the narrative. I have written 650 pages of the first draft of the period from the Peace of Westphalia to the death of Louis XIV (1715), but have some 240 additional pages to write about that period . . . The third part, covering the age of Voltaire (1715–89) will make another 600 printed pages.

Instead of printing 1680 pages in two volumes, we might publish *The Age of Reason Begins* (1558–1648) in September, 1961 (ready for you Dec. 1, 1960); *The Age of Louis XIV* (1648–1715) in September, 1962; . . . and *The Age of Voltaire* (1715–89) in September, 1964. . . . It means taking additional chances on Old Man Reaper staying away from my door. . . . Let's think it over. . . .

We did, and the triplets became quadruplets.

We regularly arranged our hunting expeditions in Europe for periods when enough first draft had been written at home (with three thousand books at hand) to keep Will busy, when abroad, compressing this into second draft in the intervals between gathering material for future volumes. So we left Los Angeles April 20, 1960, visited our friends in and around New York, and sailed on the *Queen Elizabeth* for Southampton. In London we always stayed at the Washington Hotel; it was moderate in its charges, and was not infested with flunkies; the chambermaids looked upon us as old friends, and provided Will with a big table on which he could spread out his manuscripts, his dictionaries, and his peanuts.

On May 5 Douglas and Mary Lee Fairbanks gave us a pleasant party at their home in "the Boltons" (an ellipse of sumptuous residences around a pretty church patinaed with time). So many titled Britishers came that Will, in a gay and impish moment, challenged one gentleman, "I'll bet I have more titles than you have"; and he won by reciting the titles of his published books. The handsomest guest in the gathering was Henry Fonda—but only next to Douglas himself.

A week later Douglas took my husband (who had never gambled on anything but health and time) to lunch at White's, the citadel of stylish gambling. We were astonished to find, on our walks in London, so many ornate houses devoted to this wishing game. The British, friendly to freedom, thought that what could not be prevented should be legalized and taxed.

Will spent most of two days at the Victoria and Albert Museum and the Science Museum, much to the profit of his chapter on the Industrial Revolution in Volume X. On May 11 Will McQuitty, who had written scholarly books and had helped prepare the film *A Night to Remember* (the sinking of the *Titanic*), drove us and our friend Edith Russell (oldest survivor of that tragedy) through many historic spots out to his home and gardens at Mote Mount, where his wife, Betty, entertained us with a simplicity which obscured the fact that she was a scholar and a distinguished writer.

On a bright Sunday, May 15, Harvey and Marda Brown drove us out to Hampton Court, Windsor Castle, Eton College, and Twickenham. There we visited Horace Walpole's Strawberry Hill château, and I saw where my epistolary idol had fashioned his letters and nursed his gout. We noted the relics of Alexander Pope; we dallied as delighted spectators at a game of bowling on the green; how much more pleasant this seemed than the weary slinging of balls in an underground alley. On May 18 we took a train to Bath for a second visit, and studied its architecture, its Roman remains, and its echoes of Gainsborough and Beau Brummel. That night we cheated the Channel by slumbering in a *wagon-lit* while a boat ferried it to France.

In Paris we stayed at the Hotel Lutetia on the Boulevard Raspail; we were watching our pennies, and regretted that on an earlier tour we had allowed our travel agency to deposit us at the extravagantly expensive Plaza Athénée. Max and Ray Schuster were now in Paris, and lavished their hospitality upon us, even to taking us, at Will's request, to the Lido Cabaret. On June 1 we left Paris by train for Cannes. There we stayed for two weeks at the old Gray d'Albion Hotel. I made Will's breakfast in our room, always of the same mixture: an orange, then a bowl of nonfat milk covering a sliced apple and banana, and a piece or two of whole-wheat bread. His lunch was also taken in the room: fruit, bread, raw vegetables, cheese or nuts, salad, milk. Dinner we usually ate at a restaurant facing the Croisette. During those two weeks Will must have worked ten hours a day on his manuscript. On June 15 we embarked on the *Cristoforo Colombo* for New York. On July 5 we were in our usual Box 956 for the opening of the summer season at the Hollywood Bowl.

Through the spring, summer, and fall of 1960 John F. Kennedy waged his well-organized and well-financed campaign for the presidency. We favored Hubert Humphrey against him in the primaries, and then Adlai Stevenson at the Los Angeles convention. When Kennedy won we were faced with a choice between a handsome young Catholic, supported by Catholic unity and his father's fortune, and Richard Nixon, who, till that time, had consistently followed the conservative Republican line of allying the government with the major business interests of the nation. It was hard for me, who, like Will, had looked upon Franklin Roosevelt as the redeemer of the American way, to give my vote to Nixon; but it was still harder for me to vote for a man who was pledged by his creed to put his Church above the state. Some secretly cherished memories of the warmer and lovelier elements in Catholicism left Will more open than I could be to the attractive qualities in this young Apollo offering to devote his agile mind and proven courage to the task of leading America between the Scylla of reaction and the Charybdis of Communism. Will hoped that Kennedy's Harvard education and associations had raised him, however privately, above the intolerance of the ancient faith. He felt that a Democratic administration would preserve the reforms with which Franklin Roosevelt and Harry Truman had mitigated the dangerous concentration of wealth in America; and he feared that the men who were financing Nixon would force him to follow the principles of Harding and Coolidge. We debated these matters through the long campaign—I passionately, Will diffidently. I still do not know how he voted, and I have never asked him. Our differences were subdued when that bright spirit was snuffed out so cruelly after nearly all America had come to love him.

The Catholic problem touched us again when Konrad Adenauer, Chancellor of the Federal Republic of Germany, visited Los Angeles, and the German consul general invited Will to be among the representative citizens who were to meet and eat with *Der Alte* (March 19, 1960). Will welcomed this opportunity to study at close range a man of action and affairs. He had long admired the political skill of this apparently irremovable and irreproachable leader; now he came away with the thought that part of Adenauer's practical wisdom lay in his steady adherence to Catholicism, which helped him to keep the support of half the population of West Germany. Soon the difference in birth rates would make that nation predominantly Catholic, and the Church would recover another of the lands once Protestant.

As I was past the child-bearing stage, I could do nothing about this, and I settled down to work on *Civilization*. I emerged for a moment on October 31 to share the podium with County Supervisor Ernest Debs in dedicating the San Vincente Public Library. Five days later we celebrated Will's seventy-fifth birthday. The United Press asked him to tell its clientele how he felt on rounding out three quarters of a century. He replied:

> How sharp of you to notice that this recluse will come of age on November fifth. To reach seventy-five without succumbing to diseases or their cures is now so common an event that it deserves scant attention. The real wonders of the age are men like Winston Churchill, Bernard Baruch, Bertrand Russell, and Somerset Maugham, who verge on ninety and yet are still clear and strong in their thinking.
>
> You ask me to send you a "birthday message." The older I become the fewer messages I bear. In my present condition of normal disintegration I know as many questions as before, but not half so many answers. If I live to be ninety I may at last realize that I am a drop of water trying to understand the sea.
>
> One gift of age is reconciliation. You learn to accept and forgive. You perceive that since the basic challenges of life remain the same from generation to generation, from century to century, our basic responses remain the same; consequently progress repeatedly improves our means without altering our ends. You don't expect human nature to change appreciably in the foreseeable future, and you are grateful that it is not worse. After reading the papers and looking at television, the motion pictures, and the stage, I am astonished to find so much kindness around me, so many reasonably happy marriages, so many children who are not delinquents but delights. After studying history for sixty years, and coming out of it with my hair singed with wars, massacres, Inquisitions, superstitions, famines, and plagues, I am grateful that I have not yet been burned at the stake.
>
> Every effort has been made to poison me with smog, antibiotics, and radiation, and I may be canceled out at any moment by some marvelous bomb; but I will take my chances with the present as against the past. I believe that the same intelligence that split the atom will find some way of ending our blundering and blustering hostilities with the mutual consideration and brave compromises indispensable to peace.

On September 6 *The Age of Reason Begins* was submitted to the judgment of critics and public. We seldom breathed until we could feel that we had earned permission to proceed with our work. As if sensing our parlous condition, Max Schuster hastened to send us, on the book's natal day, a seven-page telegram, characteristically enthusiastic, assuring us that we might breathe again. Never had the critics been so generous to us: Prescott in the daily *Times*, Hutchens in the *Herald-Tribune*, Bruun in *The Saturday Review*, Barkham for the Saturday Review Syndicate. *Time* and *Newsweek* concurred; and, sweetest of all, Dennis Brogan, in the *Times Book Review* (September 10), hailed our offering as "a feast not merely of information but of judgment, beautifully organized by a humane and liberal mind [I did not mind this singular 'mind'], . . . an exercise in scholarship in the grand manner." This was the height from which we were fated to fall in 1963.

Max urged us to come to New York and accept some of the many invitations to radio, television, or newspaper interviews. We could not resist the temptation to go and sip our success at the fount of literary fame. We left home September 7 by train, but with a soaring sendoff from the Los Angeles *Times* through a generous review by Robert Kirsch. In Chicago we picked up the New York *Times* of September 6, in which Orville Prescott, the Lord Chamberlain of metropolitan literary critics, said of the *Story*:

> As an introduction to, and a survey of, world history, this series is invaluable. Enormous in scope, exact in scholarship, lively, entertaining, and brightly written, it is illuminated throughout by the light of Dr. Durant's own mind. A skeptic and a rationalist, he is prejudiced only against prejudice, intolerant only of intolerance. His own bluntly challenging opinions give bite and savor to his work. His command of English is impressive. His style ranges from the epigrammatic to the stately.

But Orville found some fault with *The Age of Reason Begins:* "Durant is definitely in trouble when he comes to Shakespeare. Dismissing 'Twelfth Night' and 'A Midsummer Night's Dream' as almost worthless, he fails completely to appreciate their poetry and their humor." I am inclined to agree with the critic. Will, though he loves great poetry, is too rationalistic to care about such gossamer fantasy as Shakespeare wove into his dream.

We reached New York in a state of euphoria that proved impervious to any hostile critique. We gorged ourselves unphilosophically at the tables of Max and Ray Schuster, Irwin and Hattie Sturz, Albert and Millie Lewin, Bernard Baruch and Charles Korn. Our publishers arranged a dinner at the Four Seasons Restaurant; the air conditioning there so chilled our California blood that Baruch insisted upon wrapping his sweater over Will's shoulders, while he himself donned a topcoat. Will still has that sweater, for Baruch refused to take it back.

After nineteen days of drinking kudos we left New York and returned to our hideout in Hollywood. It took us some time to subside into the daily tasks of research, classification, composition, revision, and cooking; but soon we were caught in the glamour of the Sun King and France's golden age, blissfully unsuspecting that Volume VIII was to be the unluckiest of all. I turn over to my mate the story of that chastening.

CHAPTER XXVI

Indicted

1962–63

Will:

Ariel was now working almost as many hours a day on our *opus intermi-nabile* as I was. She left the house early every morning to join her three sisters and her brother Harry at breakfast; she shopped for our living necessities, returned about ten o'clock, helped to answer the mail, shielded me from phone calls and visitors, read and made notes for our concluding volumes, and prepared our noon meal. Usually, at home, she shared my vegetarian dishes, which required little preparation. After lunch I took an hour's nap; then I worked for an hour or more in the garden or at the woodpile, or I walked down to Hollywood and Vine for some rendezvous with Ariel and "les girls"; by 4 P.M. we were back at work on the book. Between meals I munched some shelled peanuts, sent to us periodically by the James Gardners of Tyrone, Pennsylvania. At 6 P.M. we had our evening meal, normally composed of a thick vegetable soup, whole-wheat bread, some raw vegetables, some fresh or stewed fruit. After dinner we worked in Ariel's study, within sparring distance of each other.

Ariel and I differed in outlook and temperament. She thought that I overvalued reason and allowed too little to feeling and imagination. She was inclined to mourn the evils in man's nature and politics, while I celebrated the many good or great men and women whom we had met in life or history, and the many reforms that had been enacted since our youth. She smiled at what seemed to her the almost religious enthusiasm with which I concluded the chapter on Spinoza in *The Age of Louis XIV*. She accepted, I rejected, Spinoza's determinism; however, we agreed in accepting his view of the duplex unity of matter and mind.

Our differences were useful in our work. My rationalism naturally drew me to make careful studies of Francis Bacon, Descartes, Hobbes, Spinoza, Locke, and Hume. Ariel's sentiments fortified her in her long study of the women who organized and moderatored the salons of modern France; most of the material, in our volumes, about Mesdames de Rambouillet, de Tencin, Geoffrin, and du Deffand, and Mademoiselle de Lespinasse was precious grist that she brought to our mill. Largely because of her work we were able to present, in greater fullness and depth than in any other general history, the creative role of women in giving French civilization its bisexual charm.

Ariel felt that we should not interrupt our studies to answer fan mail; we compromised by dividing the pleasant task between us. Letters like this from Fresno, California, obviously called for a reply:

Jan. 15, 1962

Dear Friends:

Almost thirty years have passed since I and my wife were snowbound at Shaver Lake in the Sierras. We had plenty of time, and a few good books. Among these were Wells's *Outlines,* Carrel's *Man the Unknown,* the complete works of Darwin and Spencer, Renan's *Life of Jesus,* Wells and Huxley's *The Science of Life,* and Durant's *Story of Philosophy, Transiton,* and *The Mansions of Philosophy.* Since then I have built up my library to several hundred titles, including all, or nearly all, of the works of Herodotus, Plutarch, Gibbon, Guizot, Symonds, Parkman, Prescott, Motley, Irving, Beard, and, of course, *The Story of Civilization.* . . .

My purpose herein is not to praise your writing. The mere fact that every book you have written, except *The Age of Faith,* just finished, has been read and reread several times. . . . I have, I believe, won the right to comment on your work, and to suggest some changes in your plans, which have deviated from the original as laid down in VI.

The Story of Civilization, as it now stands, offers no . . . theory of social evolution. Your personal predilections have been well screened behind your thousands of witnesses; you have said nice things about institutions which you have rejected; you admit, in the introduction to *The Reformation*: "I know no more about the ultimates than the simplest urchin in the street." If I were asked just what Will Durant believes, or disbelieves, I could not produce a paragraph *explicitly* stating your position. . . .

Gibbon must be, as Bacon suggests, chewed, swallowed, and digested. After him would come Mommsen, Ranke, and, if I may be so bold, Will Durant. . . .

I protest your apparent plan to break off the narrative with *The Age of Voltaire.* . . . I think that you and Ariel should plan to bring up the narrative to, say, 1905. . . .

Indicted

The Introduction to *The Story of Civilization* is, in my opinion, your most noteworthy contribution to the philosophy of history. . . .

Ed Steen

We were moved by this praise from so alert and discriminating a reader. We replied,

Jan. 25, 1962

Dear Ed and Mrs. Ed:

We have accepted your letter of the 15th as a stimulating challenge. How happy we should be to continue our story beyond 1789! . . . But tho Ariel is still young and strong, her mate is stumbling toward 77. We are finding the material for Vol. IX (*The Age of Voltaire*) so rich, so demanding of time and study and space for exposition, that I'll be at least 80 before it is finished; and it would be foolhardy to reckon on six years of relative health sufficient to do justice to the subject [the nineteenth century] and the reader. I already feel that I am losing steam, that the fine frenzy, after thirty years, is petering out.

As to revealing my own philosophy, I think (tho here Ariel agrees with you) that the historian should keep his own opinions out of the story except by indirection; his function is to narrate, not to pontificate. His selection of material will sufficiently reveal his bent. Tho Gibbon's frequent pricks at Christianity (*after* Chapter xvi) give his incomparable history additional piquancy, I feel that he would have done better to state the significant facts as he saw them, without personal comment. However, I must confess to having intruded myself into the narrative now and then, as in the first paragraph of Chapter xix of *The Renaissance*, [and] the last paragraph of Chapter xxxv, and page 939, of *The Reformation*. And we are planning to end *The Age of Voltaire* with an Epilogue on "Some Lessons of History," which will sum up our tentative conclusions.

So hang on; don't desert us; we want to feel, as we two work together, that you two are looking over our shoulders, spurring us on. We will not let you down.

Sincerely,
Will and Ariel

Not all Jesuits were my enemies. Some, like Father d'Invilliers of Baltimore, wrote to me repeatedly without a word of reproach, or any appeal for my return to the Church. From my alma mater, however, came a gentle reminder that I had better come to Canossa before the Reaper mowed me down.

Jersey City, March 29, 1962

Dear Mr. Durant:

Your brief word of grateful memory [of my Jesuit teachers in 1900–07] arrived at St. Peter's. It reminded me to do something I have many times thought of doing. . . .

347

In 1933 or -4 I read your articles on Communism in the Saturday Evening Post. The grace and dignity of your writing have come back to me every time I read your name. . . . How much, I thought, such a man could do for the glory of God, and in gratitude for such a gift. What a strong right arm he could be for the Church, which has so many talented enemies.

You are in the not remote future to finish your busy life. There is still time to do much for God and His Church. With God's grace you can come to see again much that has been hidden from you for so long. . . .

This is to ask you to have the faith and courage to get back to the Sacrament of Penance in contrition and sincerity, and without delay. Even if you can write no more, just to proclaim your return to the Church will do much good and make much reparation. There is much joy in heaven over one man's repentance. Will you let me help you return?

Of course this letter is entirely between us.

Pray much, and may God bless you with His grace in abundance.

We must preserve the author's privacy by omitting his name. It was a kindly letter, and I am sure that I gave it a courteous answer. It is a comfort to know that two good Jesuits have been praying for me.

By June 1, 1962, the complete typescript of *The Age of Louis XIV* was in the hands of our publishers. Max Schuster took it with him to his summer home on Long Island Sound. It has been our good fortune to have a publisher whose intellectual interests are at least as wide, and whose artistic sensibilities are at lesat as keen, as ours. I believe I have mentioned his kindly habit of sending us, almost at the outset of each manuscript, a telegram calculated to lift us up to the next rung of our climb. So, on June 8, we received a message that fortified us against the ill winds that were soon to buffet us.

DEAR WILL AND ARIEL:

Redoubled and ecstatic congratulations on *The Age of Louis XIV*. I am reading it by day and by night, by land and by sea. It stirs me so deeply, inspires me so greatly, holds me so irresistibly that it requires brute force to tear myself away from it for sleep and for food, even for a few minutes to write out this telegram. . . . I must confess after finishing your magnificent opening chapter I instinctively turned first to [the chapter on] Spinoza, . . . the high point of a book of great heights. But he is hard pressed by the reigning queens of the salons. . . . What a liberal education to be taken backstage to eye-witness the making of the modern mind. . . . Devotedly, gratefully, affectionately,

M.L.S.

We answered at once,

6-8-62

DEAR MAX:

What a generous and juicy telegram! You know that Ariel and I need a lift now and then; and nothing spurs us on so much as your approval.

348

We're having the toughest time of our lives with *The Age of Voltaire*; we find it more difficult to cover that century in a manner forgivable by scholars and yet digestible by collegians, than we [did] to cover a millennium in Vols. II, III, or IV. . . . Here we are at page 1070 of the first draft, and not half through. We were just beginning to lose breath and courage, and I was beginning to feel my age, when your message told us that we mustn't let you down.

We especially appreciate your restraint in not mentioning the dull parts in *The Age of Louis XIV*. We found it beyond our ability, in the time allowed us, to make some topics "exciting" without resorting to popularizing techniques that would make the judicious grieve. In the case of Spinoza our aim was to give an honest analysis of the profoundest of modern philosophies, even tho we knew that some readers would find it a hard nut to crack. Meanwhile these volumes are filling in the awful gaps in *The Story of Philosophy*.

Ariel has chosen Switzerland as a hideout where we can put together the second draft of Part I of *A-V*. . . . She is finishing the sixth and last volume of Gibbon. We are enjoying Confucius' scheme of forgetting, in the absorption of study, our normal and gradual disintegration. Don't be shocked if, when you see this Old Man of the Mountain again, you find that time has written its signature on his face.

Our love to you and Ray.

WILL

On August 9 we left the comforts of home. We visited Louis and Mollie in Evanston, embraced Max and Ray and many other faithful friends in New York, and studied, in the Morgan Library, Voltaire's scandalous correspondence with his niece. On August 16 we sailed on the S.S. *France*. We refreshed our memories of eighteenth-century relics and landmarks in or near London and Paris. In Geneva we saw Voltaire himself; in full equipment of wig, silk shirt, long coat, short pants, and cotton stockings, he sat writing at a desk in the Musée et Institut Voltaire; true, he was here in firm wax rather than in frail flesh, but so lifelike that, as we came upon him at the turn of a corridor, we were startled to gasping, and waited for him to speak. We met him through the courtesy of the Musée's director, Dr. Theodore Besterman, who offered us the riches of the Institut in early editions of the *philosophes*, and agreed to read our nascent *Age of Voltaire* in typescript and catch our errors in transit. It was an exciting afternoon.

Geneva, of course, not only gave refuge to Voltaire; it had given birth to Rousseau. But it banished him, too, and we followed his tracks to Môtiers-Travers, where he found protection under Frederick the Great; and we came upon many relics of him in the little museum at neighboring Neuchâtel. Back in Geneva, we took the lake steamer to Montreux, and renewed with Michael and Doris David the warm friendship that had begun in Los Angeles eighteen years before. We followed them to their hideout in Clarens, hearing Rousseauian echoes as we went, for in that idyllic vale he had placed the central scenes of *Julie, ou La Nouvelle Héloïse.*

Near Clarens is Vevey, and there another old friend was turning exile into paradise. We broke in upon Charlie Chaplin unannounced, and found him absorbed in preparing his autobiography. He read some pages of the manuscript to us, and we renewed our suggestion that he let Max Schuster sponsor its American editon. He led us on a tour of his new estate, which stands on a hill between towering mountains and the placid lake. Two days later (September 17) we met at his table the representative of his British publishers, and were happy to hear this gentleman second our recommendation of Simon and Schuster. I note a memo made by Ariel of those meetings: "Charlie has outwitted all his enemies. Rich, successful, amiable father with a young and cheerful wife. He is courted by the Swiss bankers and the Communist dictators. All the notables coming thru wish to be presented or to renew their friendship with him."

After some peaceful days at Montreux we took the long train ride to Cannes, glimpsing the Rhone every now and then. We visited old friends, and meanwhile, in our room overlooking the Mediterranean, we made good progress rewriting *The Age of Voltaire.* On October 19 we sailed on the *Independence* for New York; we were especially fond of that boat, and of her sister ship the *Constitution,* because, on nearly all our trips with them, luncheon was served on the spacious afterdeck, in *plein-air* jollity. We made our annual pilgrimage to the Durant reunion on the shady grounds of my sister Ethel Halliwell in Westfield, New Jersey, stopped between trains at Chicago with Sam Lesner (prize-winning cinema critic), and then rode on to Los Angeles.

In the mail awaiting us was a thoughtful letter that expressed the most disturbing moral dilemma of our time:

October 28, 1962

Dear Mr. Durant:

My son, Timothy, was two years old today. Like other children of his age, he spends his waking hours finding new sights, new sounds, new things to do . . .

He is a fine boy, healthy and glad to be alive, and I hope that one day he will grow into a strong and considerate person, a good citizen, a boon to mankind. But he must have a chance—as must other millions of Timothies across the globe.

He is so little now, and his life is so simple and full of joy that I think we often forget his significance; and we forget about the day when he will inherit the things we leave behind—the material things, the social systems, institutions, literature, music—the hundreds of things man has labored for thousands of years to achieve.

Soon he will ask of peace and of war. And this is my dilemma, for what then will I tell him? What can I say of the common man's role in the give and take of world events? How can I show him the way to peace . . . when I myself do not know it? Should I tell him I am helpless, and that he, too, must be? Should I say that the matter is not one for simple men? That it is out of our hands, to be decided at levels far above us?

I address this question to you, a man of great significance and accomplishment, and I sincerely hope that you can take the time to mail me a reply: How can I and other men of my standing work concretely for international peace?

For the Timothies everywhere I ask this.

> Respectfully yours,
> LEONARD V. FULTON

I gave him an honest answer, but, as I look now at the copy Ariel made of it, I see how lame and inadequate it was.

> *11-27-62*

DEAR LEONARD:

Your thoughtful letter is a challenge that I cannot meet. I dream of the time when a president of the United States will feel safe in applying to international relations the same code of morals that we ask of individuals— when, for example, he will not ask of Cuba or Russia anything that he is not ready to offer from America. But, as Machiavelli argued long ago, a nation cannot afford to apply the moral code to its relations with other states; for there is no guarantee that other states will respond in the same spirit, and there is no system of international law that will protect the "good"state against the "bad." Consequently states remain in a "state of nature"—i.e., a condition before law and order came to human communities. In that state there are no rights, there are only powers, and each national unit strives to protect itself by increasing its power through trade, diplomacy, and war. Until a responsible international law is established and enforced, the history of the major states will be a conflict of powers.

Within this limitation I think President Kennedy has done very well. He has refused to be stampeded by the warmongers, but he has taken vigorous action when he thought that the security of the United States was threatened. And he appears to be exploring patiently the possibility of mitigating the cold war. Khrushchev has amiably [!] co-operated by withdrawing his offensive weapons from Cuba, and by compelling China to halt its invasion of India. Meanwhile we are developing peaceably in America a compromise between capitalism and socialism, uniting the productive stimulus of the one with the mutual aid of the other.

So I am grateful, and though I am a vegetarian, I ate turkey on Thanksgiving Day just as a symbol of gratitude.

My regards to Timothy.

> Sincerely,
> WILL DURANT

My fondness for my sisters Ethel and Eva shared in sustaining my tenderness for the lost faith of my youth. Eva had become a nun in 1913. Fifty years later her convent in Jersey City arranged a modest celebration of her "golden anniversary," I ventured to join in the celebration with a small gift and a letter:

3-14-63

DEAR SISTER:

Fifty years of service as a Sister of Charity!—that is really an immense gift to mankind. Those patient and comforting nuns in our schools and hospitals are the highest expression of Christianity. I remember with grateful affection the Sisters who bore with me in my conceited youth: Sister Margarita, who was my teacher in Kearny, and whom I used to visit many times after she was transferred to Hoboken; and Sister Celeste, who welcomed me in her convent at Passaic, and gave me a motherly hug despite my intellectual escapades; and many other nuns who had learned not only to serve but to forgive. If the sacrifice of the self is the perfection of the self, you and your sister nuns are the salt of the earth.

Will you accept the blessings of an old heretic? And let my faithful wife join in them? We too will have an anniversary this year—our golden wedding anniversary.

Lovingly,
WILL

Sister Rose Marita answered

March 24, 1963

DEAR WILL AND ARIEL:

How kind and thoughtful of you to remember me so generously on my golden anniversary. Your note and enclosed gift are deeply appreciated.

I have much to be thankful for as I approach this date. God has been very good to me in many ways. I was seriously ill once in all these years. I still carry a heavy schedule—five French classes daily. I'm happy to be kept busy.

I would love it, Ariel and Will, if, when you are in New York again, you would take a few minutes to cross the river and visit me at St. Michael's.

God bless you both for your kindness to me.

Sincerely,
EVA

In this same week I received another touching appeal to come down from my intellectual pride and humbly return to the Catholic Church:

March 23, 1963

DEAR MR. DURANT:

. . . Though I have never met you personally, I feel I know you quite well—through your literary children—even better than some people I know

352

personally. I was first introduced to you while in the seminary, by way of your *Story of Philosophy,* to which my priest-professor referred quite often. . . . I was immediately impressed. . . . I proceeded to procure a used copy of *Transition,* which I have read several times. I have covered large parts of *The Life of Greece, Caesar and Christ,* and *The Age of Faith.* . . .

I cannot conceive of the story of philosophy and the story of civilization being presented in a more thorough, scholarly, palatable, brisk, and delightful manner than you have done—with one important exception! . . . How regrettable that . . . latent on every page of your writings is a fundamental agnosticism. I am sure you are not an atheist, but your only credo that I can detect is: nothing is certain but uncertainty.

I believe it is in *Transition* where you state that it takes more courage to doubt than to believe. Bishop Sheen has said almost the contrary: "It takes more courage than brains to know God." Doubt is a kind of intellectual suicide whereby the mind rejects the very truth for which it was made and naturally inclines. . . .

In the preface to *The Reformation* you state: "Even the trust in reason is a precarious faith, and we are all fragments of darkness groping for the sun. I know no more about the ultimates than the simplest urchin in the streets." But the simplest urchin has a basic belief in God that puts the sophistries of the intelligentsia to shame.

It is this certitude, this positive statement of the true philosophy and the true religion, that is missing from your writings. And what an omission! I am convinced that it is no exaggeration to say that you could have been—and in God's providence could still be—the twentieth-century Augustine or Aquinas. The world today needs such a man so badly. God has given you the intellectual equipment to do a tremendous work for His Mystical Body [the Catholic Church]. You need but to unite yourself completely with him in faith and hope and love.

Won't you give serious consideration once again to the Mother Church of all Christendom in which you and your ancestors worshipped? . . . Why not arrange for some discussions with either Fulton J. Sheen of New York or Father John A. O'Brien of the University of Notre Dame . . . I'm sure that both of these men would be ready, willing, able, and anxious to talk with you. . . .

Christ's arms are extended to embrace you once more in the sacrament of the Eucharist! Christ longs to bestow His sacramental kiss of forgiveness upon you once more in the sacrament of Penance! Don't let Him down! . . . It is the lost sheep that the Good Shepherd seeks. Mr. Durant, come back home!

With prayerful best wishes to you and Ariel, that God will guide and strengthen each of you, I am,

Sincerely yours,
JEROME WELCH

I regret that I answered this fervent letter so curtly,

3-27-63

DEAR MR. WELCH:

Thank you for your beautiful letter of March 23rd. I feel the difficulties of unbelief as well as those of belief. But I trust that the good Lord will accept intellectual conscience as well as the humility of faith.

Sincerely,

WILL DURANT

More to my mood was a very pleasant meeting which we had with Arnold Toynbee before his lectures at our friend Jim Fifield's Congregational Church. We exchanged courtesies: I told the amiable scholar how indebted I was to his *Study of History,* and he countered by saying that he was reading our *Story of Civilization* with keen interest. I found it easy to like him; no one would have suspected, from his simple bearing and modest speech, that he was the most famous historian of our time. I was impressed by his hope that a merger of the great religions might restore hope, inspiration, and a moral order to Western civilization, and I had to admit that many religions had begun, like Christianity, as an amalgam of preexisting faiths. But I was still suspect of all supernatural creeds, and could not forget the obscurantism and intolerance of Catholicism in the days and places of its power.

Another side of the picture appeared in a letter from an anxious Protestant:

2-18-63

DEAR DR. DURANT:

. . . Sometimes I wish I had never read your books. . . . How simple and easy life would be if I had never been brought to realize some of the "facts of life" as you have brought them to light; how easy it would be to take matters for granted, . . . and not be really concerned! But having been reading your books for years and years—I am not the same person.

My most important problem right now is CATHOLICISM vs.—all of us. We just recently organized a chapter of P.O.A.U here in Minneapolis (Protestants and Other Americans United for Separation of Church and State). . . . On page 368 of the paper-back copy of *The Pleasures of Philosophy* you say: "By the year 2000, if present tendencies continue, this will be your country." (To Matthew—the Catholic.) Page 369 [Matthew speaking]: "Protestantism is doomed. Look at its decay; it has broken into ten thousand fragments," etc. Right, right.

Dr. Durant, is our struggle of no avail? Are we going to admit it is a lost cause? . . . I may be presuming on you to ask for your reply. But—to one who gets up at three o'clock in the morning to read Will Durant as an answer to my many problems,—please.

Next to the rise and fall of *The Age of Louis XIV* the great event in our lives in 1963 was our association with *The Fall of the Roman Empire.* The matter began with a cable from Madrid, signed by two old friends from Ariel's Greenwich Village days.

Oct. 24, 1962

DEAR WILL AND ARIEL:

Hello from Spain. Samuel Bronston Company preparing to shoot remarkable film title the Fall of Rome. This is no ordinary spectacle; enormous definitive film dramatization as conceived by Anthony Mann. . . . Mr. Mann, a disciple of yours, voiced a sincere desire to have you associated with film; wishes you write film foreword. . . . Mr. Mann willing to fly L.A. to discuss project with you. . . . I fervently hope you say yes. . . . Regards from Mr. Mann and Lou and Jane Brandt.

This message came to Los Angeles when Ariel and I were in New York, and was forwarded to us by sister Mary. We have no record of our reply to Lou Brandt, but on October 30 Paul Lazarus, executive vice-president of Samuel Bronston Productions, called at the Park Chambers Hotel, and talked with Ariel. She asked for further information, and Paul (whom we soon learned to like and trust) wrote,

October 30, 1962

MY DEAR DR. DURANT:

. . . I am sending you herewith a copy of our script on *The Fall of the Roman Empire* together with a brochure which will convey to you some of the facts on our production.

When I talked with Mr. Anthony Mann in London today he expressed the hope that you and I might meet, so that I might convey to you some of the magnitude and scope of our project. . . . Meanwhile I can assure you that the basic promise of our production is borne out by parts of your own "Caesar and Christ," which Mr. Mann and others in our organization have read with the greatest of interest.

We will begin shooting in Madrid on January 7th. We are planning to reconstruct the entire Roman Forum just outside of Madrid. . . .

We would hope that you would consider the possibility of allowing us to utilize your services as consultant. We would also like to weigh with you the possibility of your writing a prologue for our film. . . . Please be assured that we do not mean this to be taxing on your time or your strength. If, in the course of the enterprise, you would find it possible to spend some time with us in Spain we would, of course, be delighted. . . .

On the way to Los Angeles I read Paul Yordan's script. It was brilliantly done, and dramatically effective, but it took so many liberties with history that I felt that I had better withdraw from any connection with the film. So I wrote on

Nov. 10, 1962

DEAR MR. LAZARUS:

I have read nearly every word of *The Fall of the Roman Empire,* and I have given much thought to your letter of October 30th. I hasten to send you my conclusions, lest you should make a trip to the West Coast merely to talk with me.

I recognize that a motion picture, like even the best historical novels, must, for dramatic purposes, and for wide public reception, take some liberties with history. I am afraid that some of the divergences will meet with criticism.

1. The character and reign of Commodus were comparatively minor factors in the fall of Rome. I have listed on a separate sheet some of the factors that entered into the decline and fall.

2. Lucilla, in history, was not [as in the script] a devoted lover of Livius Gaius Metellus, but a rather loose lady who, early in the reign of her brother Commodus, had already a second husband; "imitated the manners of Faustina," her audulterous mother; was surrounded by a "crowd of lovers," and hired an assassin to kill her brother. This conspiracy having failed, she was "first punished with exile, and afterwards with death." (Gibbon, *Decline and Fall of the Roman Empire,* Everyman's Library ed., Vol. I, p. 86.)

3. Commodus died not on Livius' sword (as in the script), but drugged by poison and then strangled by a wrestler (Gibbon, 95). . . .

I take it for granted that Mr. Yordan has sought to reduce the fictitious elements in his script to a minimum consistent with commercial viability. But it would be unwise for me to lend my name to the production in any way. I must remain an anonymous friend, and I am sure that I can rely on you and your associates to respect my reluctant decision. Purely as an anonymous friend I have sketched the enclosed "Prologue" both as a possible introduction to the picture and as an attempt, in its final paragraph, to disarm the critics by making some apologies to history. You are welcome to use part or all of this Prologue, but do not ascribe it to me.

WILL DURANT

My desire to remain uncommitted was shaken the moment Ariel led Anthony Mann into my study in Los Angeles. I had imagined motion picture directors to be tough dictators as ready as Newton to give laws to stars. But here was a gentleman—of fine figure, handsome face, open countenance, modest manners, courteous speech, and artless but ensnaring charm. He had brought with him his copy of *Caesar and Christ;* his knowledge of the book softened me. Everything would be done, he assured us, to bridge the gap between Yordan's script and historic fact; but I should remember that Paul had been commissioned not to write history but to fashion a play capable of holding, through three hours, the attention of millions of auditors. I promised to reconsider.

I had long since made it a rule not to make any important decision until after a careful discussion with Ariel. I found her inclined to accept the proposal: it would open up a new world of art and life to us, and a new land—for we had never had our fill of Spain. I accepted.

We sailed on our old friend the *Independence* April 30, 1963, debarked at Algeciras, and slept our way over southern Spain to arrive at Madrid on May 7. That evening I spoiled Anthony Mann's dinner by presenting to him a sheet listing the various causes which historians had assigned for the fall of the Roman Empire in the West. A few days later I warned Samuel Bronston that his majestic enterprise might be faulted for its historical license; he assured me that he would do his best to reconcile the play with history. But I had seen the costly realistic reproduction of the Roman Forum as setting for a part of the picture, and had witnessed Sophia Loren and Stephen Boyd laboring to present the love story that was to relieve the scenes of war. I realized that it was too late to alter the script except in minor detail; and Ariel and I, softened by almost imperial luxury, adjusted ourselves to making the best of a delightful experience.

On May 23 we flew to Rome, and there, on and off, we watched Sophia Loren at work, and marveled at the humility and patience with which this proud and busy woman went through the same scene again and again till Anthony Mann was satisfied. I told her that her big black eyes were enough to seduce any man, but she was too absorbed in her task to spare a moment to seduce me, and Ariel pulled me out of the fire. On June 2 our service with Bronston Productions ended, and we flew on to Milan.

The reader may recall what happened to *The Fall of the Roman Empire* when it reached the screen. Alas, what a fall was there, my countrymen! I had expected the critics to question the historicity of the film, and had steeled myself to being blamed; instead they condemned the picture on artistic grounds—too overwhelming a display of temples, spectacles, and battles; "spectaculars" had become too common, had lost their lure; and the enormous debt that the producer had incurred—partly through generosity to his employees—left his vast organization bankrupt. We had not had much contact with Samuel Bronston, but we had come to like him, and we mourned his fate.

In Milan we were further spoiled by the hospitality of Carlo and Bibi Foà. With Carlo accompanying us as interpreter, we visited the lordly mansion that housed the publishing firm of Arnoldo Mondadori, which had given our *Storia della civiltà* the handsomest of all its editions. We had long marveled at the care and expense that had gone into the translation and printing of these massive volumes, with their fine typography and innumerable illustrations. When I asked the aging paterfamilias of the firm how he managed to find purchasers for such expenseive tomes— then priced at fifteen thousand lire each, or twenty-five dollars, he answered, "There are many well-to-do Italians who will buy these books as treasures to be passed on to their children." His son Alberto brought us the page proofs of *The Age of Reason Begins* in its Italian dress; he was having difficulty translating the clumsy title; we agreed that he should call it *L'avvento della ragione—The Coming of Reason*—a much better title than mine.

After a visit to the restored Galleria Brera, we left Milan for Cannes by the TEE—Trans-European Express—one of the many European trains that now equal or surpass our best American trains in comfort, cleanliness, safety, and speed. On June 22 we boarded the Cunard S.S. *Mauretania* (I had sailed on another *Mauretania* fifty-one years before). We were mystified that we had been assigned not to the simple room for which we had paid but to a more spacious room on the main deck. We suspected that some angel had intervened; and, behold, there soon peeked into our cabin a man with a massive head, ruddy cheeks, and eyes ever alert with wonder and concern. It was Max Schuster. Having learned of our plans for the westward voyage, he had canceled his airline reservations and embarked on the *Mauretania* at Genoa, resolved to share at least sixteen meals with us in eight days.

At table, or in his cabin or ours, we brought ourselves up to date with each other. We told Max that Volume IX, imitating Volume VII, was bursting into two. Max, all enthusiasm, drank to the forthcoming twins; and then, after our stomachs had learned to roll and pitch and vibrate peacefully with the ship, the three of us debated and planned how that revolutionary eighteenth century was to be divided between those hostile twins Voltaire and Rousseau, whose rolling and pitching had unsettled the intellectual and political world.

We reached New York July 2, courted our friends and comforted our relatives, flew to Los Angeles on July 8, and were in our usual seats, the next evening, at the summer seasons's opening of the Hollywood Bowl. In the premonition that flaws would be found in Volume VIII (already in the hands of reviewers) we sent the typescript of Volume IX to Dr. Besterman, head of the Institut Voltaire at Geneva, asking him to correct any mistakes he might find in the 1,139 manuscript pages, nearly every one of which contained half a dozen possibilities of error.

The Age of Louis XIV was published in September, 1963. Robert Kirsch gave it a handsome sendoff in the Los Angeles *Times*. In the New York *World-Telegram* of September 11 John Barkham was of the opinion that "the quality of the series . . . grows better with the years—the prose pithier, the judgments more mature, the insights more mature. . . . The Durants embrace all history—political, military, economic, artistic, intellectual—in a single, tightly integrated narrative which glows as it informs."

Then, in *The New York Times Book Review* of September 15, came the most devastating review that ever fell upon us. It was by J. H. Plumb, professor of history at Cambridge University, England, and author of an excellent biography of Sir Robert Walpole. We quote the review:

> Over 40 years ago Will and Ariel Durant planned to write the story of civilization from its beginnings to the present day, a grandiose task con-

ceived on a heroic plan. Volume after volume has appeared, this being Volume VIII, covering the years 1648–1715. They rest on the shelves of thousands of libraries and are daily plundered by hundreds of students in search of easily digestible introductions to their weekly work. General readers also have found the diet offered by the Durants very much to their palate. And there must be tens of thousands of Americans whose idea of human history from Ancient Egypt to Louis XIV is derived from these books. More is the pity! The foundations of their history are as shoddy as the superstructure is glamorous.

"The historian," they write, "like the journalist, tends to lose the normal background of an age in the dramatic foreground of his picture, for he knows that his readers will relish the exceptional and will wish to personify processes and events." This describes their own methods admirably. A brief, superficial sketch of religion in France is followed by potted biographies, skillfully written, of Pascal, Bossuet, and Fénelon, interspersed with an equally potted and equally high-painted account of the religious and educational reforms at Port-Royal. Similarly, in the section on literature, a quick glance in the manner of an encyclopedia, is cast at literature in general and is immediately followed by a chapter on Molière and shorter pieces on Racine, La Fontaine, Boileau, Mme de Sevigné, La Rochefoucauld, La Bruyère. Science and philosophy are personalized in the same way.

Here and there are chapters devoted to the main stream of events—the wars, the revolutions, the development of those countries that the Durants consider peripheral to their theme. For them the torchbearers of European civilization in this age are France and Britain, and these countries dominate their long book. The panorama of personalities moves at a splendid pace: as soon as the interest of the serious reader is likely to flag, the subject changes. No effort is called for: like a television series, it doesn't matter much at which episode you start. The result is like cheese spread—good color, little taste, easy to use, boring in bulk, and infinitely remote from the true product. . . .[Errors of fact] stud this book like stars in the heavens on a frosty night. But there are worse faults than errors of fact.

The Durants ignore almost completely and in the most astonishing way the work of professional scholars. This volume reads as if A. R. Hall had never written about the Scientific Revolution, as if Christopher Hill had published nothing on seventeenth-century England, nor C. V. Wedgwood, nor Andrew Browning, nor John Kenyon, nor Peter Laslett, nor the host of scholars, British and American, to say nothing of those French writers, who have illuminated seventeenth-century studies during the last 50 years.

The Durants' idea of a leading authority is very quaint. They quote what they state to be the leading French authority on the Revocation of the Edict of Nantes, by which Louis XIV threw the Protestants out of France. The leading authority turns out to be a bitter anti-Catholic Huguenot propagandist writing in 1697, quoted, however, not directly but from Buckle's "History of Civilization" published in 1861! Two admirable monographs on the effects of the Edict of Nantes, have been published in America in the last five years. The Durants seem unaware of either, as, indeed, they seem unaware of the activity of most professional historians.

Worse than their ripe errors of scholarship and their wanton ignorance of professional studies is their basic attitude to the historical process. They reduce everything to a softminded pulp. Tough thinking is totally alien to their work. Everything is gloss, smoothed away, made inevitable; science, philosophy, literature march scarcely impeded for a moment up the broad smooth path of progress. The entanglements of the age of Louis XIV in the feudal past of Europe, both socially and intellectually, is ignored; the conflicts between classes, the impact of commercial and agrarian revolutions on the structure of states, might never have taken place; the whole rhythm and flow of history is reduced to a collection of personalities.

Historical analysis is a concept that appears not to have occurred to the Durants. Take one of the greatest factors in the cultural and economic life of Europe in the age of Louis XIV—its involvement in Asia which Europe ensnared in its spider's web of trade and power; about fifty lines of description are devoted to this out of a quarter of a million lines in the book itself. And, there is little or no discussion of either the causes or effects of this extraordinary development. Rarely do the Durants display any sense of historical realities, any concept of what life was really like or of the forces that molded the past.

To expose the shortcomings, no matter how heinous, of aging historians may appear somewhat brutal, but this book is unworthy of the traditions of American scholarship. It is also dangerous for it is so facile that the unwary will be first ensnared and then misled. The gross faults of such a book cannot be overlooked.

Our first feeling about this sweeping indictment was that it was cruelly indiscriminate. Had the book no virtues at all to put in the scale against its faults? Were all the other seven volumes to be condemned, sight unseen, because some errors had been found in the eight hundred pages of this one? Was this professor of history out to fight a war against non-university competition? (I could not tell him that Professor Hocking had asked me to join the Harvard faculty, either in history or in philosophy.) But when I came to specific charges I was dismayed to find that I could not locate, in the mass of my used notes, my source for placing the Convention Parliament of 1689 in Coventry on February 1 instead of in Westminster in January. On other alleged errors I felt that I could defend our work, and I wrote to the *Times* the following letter, which was printed in the *Book Review* of October 6:

> In reviewing our "Age of Louis XIV" (Sept. 15) J. H. Plumb charges us with a tendency to "personify processes and events." This is true. We believe that in the last hundred years history has been too depersonalized, and that statistics have replaced men in the story of mankind. History operates in events but through persons; these are the voice of events, the flesh and blood upon which events fall; and their human responses and feelings are also history. We aim not so much to personalize history as to humanize it, as James Harvey Robinson urged historians to do. Perhaps our experiment in combining history and biography has gone too far to-

ward biography. Frankly, we too are more interested in persons than in things.

Mr. Plumb thinks that our method, dealing with so many events and personalities in so many nations, condemns us to superficiality. It may be so, but we do not believe that the chapters on Molière, Milton, and Spinoza, or the sections on Pascal and Swift, are superficial; we trust that the reader will judge for himself. The reviewer complains that in this book "the panorama of personalities moves at a splendid pace; as soon as the interest of the serious reader is likely to flag, the subject changes." That too is true. He adds that "no effort is called for" on the part of the reader. But many a reader has accused us of making him think. If the chapters on Hobbes, Spinoza, and Leibniz do not compel thought, our vanity must have clouded our judgment.

Nevertheless Mr. Plumb has caught us in a serious error. We wrote: "At the request of the provisional government he, William III, summoned the Lords, Bishops, and former Members of Parliament to meet at Coventry. The Convention that assembled there on Feb. 1, 1689, declared that James had abdicated the throne by his flight. It offered to crown Mary as Queen and accept William as her regent" ("Age of Louis XIV," p. 297). This passage, says Professor Plumb, "contains five major blunders. The Convention Pariament was elected, not summoned. It met at Westminster in January, 1689. It did not offer the crown to Mary, nor to make William regent."

As to the first point, the "Cambridge Modern History" (Vol. V, Ch. X, page 249 of the 1934 ed.) reads: "On the news of James's second flight William had—at the request of the Lords Spiritual and Temporal, the members of Charles II's Parliaments, and the Common Council of London— assumed the administration. *Following their instructions,* he issued a circular to constituent bodies, requesting them to elect representatives for a Convention." Did the Convention "offer the crown to Mary"? Our text did not say that, but that the Convention would have been willing to crown Mary as Queen, and make William regent—for, as Mary was daughter of the deposed King, legitimacy would have been preserved.

Says Sir Winston Churchill, in his "History of the English-Speaking Peoples" (Vol. III, page 6): "Loyal Tories were alarmed by the prospect of disturbing the Divine Right in the Stuart succession . . . An obvious solution which would please many Tories was the accession of Mary . . . The suggestion that William should be regent on behalf of James was rejected in the Lords by only 51 votes to 49." That the offer of a regency was open to William is obvious from his blunt refusal: he "declared publicly, at the beginning of the month, that he would return to Holland unless he were chosen King jointly with his wife, with the whole administration vested in himself" (Cambridge Modern History," V, 256). Our text continues: "It (the Convention) offered to crown William as King and Mary as Queen; they accepted (February 13)."

We must admit, however, that "Coventry" instead of London is a grievous mistake. We must have had some reason for naming Coventry, but our source eludes us now, and there is nothing left for us on this point but to plead guilty.

The reviewer adds that "the Durants ignore almost completely . . . the work of professional scholars." We have gone over the Bibliography that occupies pages 723–32 of "The Age of Louis XIV," and find that we used the works of Aaron, Acton, J. W. Allen, John Ashton, Beard, Bell, Bourgeois, Bowle, Bryant, Bury, Butterfield . . . to a total of some 49 professional scholars out of a total of 322 sources consulted. If we have not used the monographs of the younger scholars it is because through long experience we have found that they add little to the standard authorities beyond some minor corrections of date, place, wording, or emphasis.

We can understand how professional scholars who devote their lives to some special subject, limited in time and place, should feel a certain distrust of those who seek to bring the major events and personalities of history into a larger perspective and synthesis. . . . We knew that eight volumes covering so many countries in all aspects of their life through seventy centuries would commit some errors of detail. We had hoped that specialist scholars would look with approval upon serious and painstaking efforts to bridge the gap that was more and more dividing them from the general public, and that (as many have done) they would point out our errors in a spirit of helpfulness rather than of hostility.

Meanwhile, we shall go back to work, chastened and subdued, but not yet dead.

WILL DURANT
ARIEL DURANT

Through this unhappy month we might have borne with some wavering in our publishers, but they proved their faith in us by almost daily letters, and by their wide circulation of some of the many favorable reviews that were coming in. Some professors were on our side. From the College of Arts and Sciences at Rutgers State University:

Sept. 27, 1963

DEAR MR. AND MRS. DURANT:

. . . I am sure I speak for thousands of your readers in expressing my indignation at the *Times* review of your latest book. . . . I was amused by how the . . . academic historian slipped in referring to your "offered to crown Mary as Queen" when he said "it did not offer the crown to Mary." Your phrase well summarized Parliament's recognition that Mary had become Queen by James's flight; the reviewer twisted your meaning, unintentionally but carelessly. I am sure the rest of the "errors" (claimed to be found in your book) were mostly of equally debatable, or at least minor, character.

My wife and I read your histories aloud with tremendous pleasure and profit. . . . We are looking forward equally to your next volume.

Sincerely yours,
SIMON N. WHITNEY

A professor of history at State University College, Fredonia, New York, sent us a kindly word:

Indicted

October 11, 1963

I have recently read the bitter and unjustified "review" of your new book
. . . in the *Times*. I should like you to know that I have read, and drawn on
information, in your volumes in *The Story of Civilization* for many years,
and I consider the books to be beautifully written, stimulating, and filled
with extraordinary richness of detail and interpretation.

I suppose it gives some sort of pleasure to petty critics to attack the
efforts of the few creative writers that we have. Please do not permit them
to disturb you. I (and thousands of others, I am sure) continue to be proud
of your splendid work.

> Sincerely,
> DANIEL ROSELLE

The weeklies gave us a triple flagellation. *Newsweek* for September 16
described *Louis XIV* as "not so much history as a compendium of historical fragments" [I had thought the book will organized]; it objected to our
way of humanizing history with vignettes of leading individuals, and it
smiled at the way "the Spinozoic Durants linger for 37 loving pages"
over our favorite philosopher. "The Durants resemble nothing so much
as the writers of those paperback trots that help college boys to get
through Humanities I." In the *Saturday Review* for September 21 Leo
Gershoy, of New York University, praised our style, but gently reproved
us for putting too much stress on "the Great Debate between faith and
reason," and for describing dramatic individuals instead of economic
groups. *Time* for September 27 thought we gave too much space to
"poets, philosophers, and men of science," and too "little space to . . .
the great outward thrust that sent 17th-century Englishmen, Frenchmen,
and Dutchmen around the globe"; however, "Durant is at his best in his
cogent, detailed discussion of that oddly reactionary heretic, Baruch Spinoza." (Spinoza was two centuries ahead of his time in reconciling science, philosophy, and religion, in seeing mind and body as the inside
and outside of one and the same reality, in defending democracy and
toleration, and in expounding an ethic independent of all supernatural
belief.)

The Worcester *Telegram* and the Atlanta *Journal*, both of September 15
and therefore untouched by the Cambridge professor, praised the book
with an abandon that should have made me blush. Said Nelson Hayes in
the *Telegram*: "Brilliantly written, full of insights into man and his nature, . . . these seven volumes—and presumably the two that are to follow—are, after Toynbee's, the greatest single work of history written in
this century." Herbert Kupferberg, in the New York *Herald-Tribune*,
hailed our opus as "a magnificent series of books, perhaps the most
remarkable premeditated historical project carried out by one man [and
his wife] in our day. Like its predecessor, *The Age of Louis XIV* is studded
with vivid characterizations, flashes of urbane wit, and observations on
human conduct that are almost epigrammatic."

We had to wait till September 28 to get the verdict of Orville Prescott in the daily New York *Times*. He entitled his piece "In Defense of the Durants," but we were not quite absolved:

> The Durants go grandly marching on. "The Age of Louis XIV" is the eighth volume in the massive and monumental series Dr. Durant began nearly 30 years ago. In the last two volumes Mrs. Durant is given credit as a collaborator. The industry that has gone into this enormous project is formidable. The wit and literary skill are admirable. And now, although Dr. Durant will be 78 in November, two more volumes are announced. Seldom has a fine feat of popularization of learning won such well-deserved success. But it is necessary to understand what kind of books these are and for whom they are intended. Some learned historians have failed to understand. They point out, correctly, that the Durants did not consult the most recent historical monographs and even neglected some major works of recent scholarship. And that they made minor errors of fact. These oversights, however, are venial. In a work of professional scholarship written for scholars they would be fatal. But in a many-volume work written to introduce non-specialist readers to the past, and particularly to the culture of the past, such failings are of small significance. What matters is the vast amount of information to be found in these books, the vigor and grace of their prose, the provocative opinions of the authors, whose point of view is always skeptical, rational and humane. Professional historians who lament that the reading public knows little history and that too many of their own books are wretchedly written should welcome rather than denounce authors who, because they write it very well, can attract hordes of readers to history.
>
> Like its predecessors, this huge volume is primarily social and cultural history with only small space devoted to politics and wars and less still to economics. It is the essence of a civilization that primarily interests the Durants, not its mechanics. So they roam rapidly over religion, customs, manners, morals, costumes, architecture, decoration, art, literature and philosophy. And also education, science, medicine, superstition and magic. . . .
>
> It seems to me that the Durants have allotted excessive space to the philosophers and that on the whole this volume (and its immediate predecessor also) lacks the authority and the stylistic verve of the earlier books. Even so, this is an intelligent and useful book and occasionally a controversial one.

As the bitterest attack upon *The Age of Louis XIV* had come from England, so our final absolution came in the prestigious London *Times Literary Supplement* of February 13, 1964, under the title "Thinking History":

> One of the most remarkable enterprises in modern historiography, unduly neglected in this country, is the American series of volumes by Mr. and Mrs. Durant on "The Story of Civilization". They began in 1927 and the first volume on ancient Asiatic civilization appeared in 1935. Since then seven other volumes have appeared. They carry the story, chronologically,

to Louis XIV, and two more projected volumes will complete it to the French Revolution. Mr. Durant is now aged 78 and a much larger share of the work is borne by his wife, who was formerly a pupil. Resting on the twin assumptions that the history of mankind is entrancingly interesting and that it can and should be interestingly told, their massive work has attracted a wide public in the United States and accolades from even professional academic historians. It undoubtedly deserves wider attention in this country, for its approach is universalist, its scope comprehensive.

It is a feature of the Durants' historical approach to lay special emphasis on literature and philosophy, both for their intrinsic interest and cultural importance, and as reflections and revelations of the character of a society or a period. This emphasis makes the latest volume, on the years 1648–1715, particularly rewarding. Whether dealing with France or England as societies, or with the "intellectual adventure" of the scientific revolution as a whole, they find here a rich mine of cultural endeavour and achievement. Their versatility is no less remarkable than their erudition. What they say about Molière and Dryden, Newton and Locke, Spinoza and Leibniz may not always be highly original and could at times be more profound. But it is mostly accurate and thoughtful, and is based on a firm grasp of standard authorities; unfailingly it suggests cross-currents and interconnections which must be the life-blood of any such general synthesis. The authors define civilization as "social order promoting cultural creation"; their purpose is to write "integral history—to cover all phases of a people's activity in one perspective and one unified narrative", and they achieve much success in their massive undertaking of *vulgarisation* in the best sense of that abused word.

The underlying question continually recurring as one reads the flowing prose of some 800 pages, is whether a public in need of such instruction will endure the task of absorbing so much historical material. The synthesis is skilful, the passage smoothed by literary art; even so who but a scholar earnest to the point of professionalism will stay the whole course? Although it could be said that the resulting bulk is either too vast for its purpose or too synthetic for the specialized student, there must be room and need for historical synthesis at all levels and on differing scales. On its chosen scale, this work has few if any rivals.

Who shall say which of the two English reviewers was right?

Love kept us going in those dubious days. On October 31 we celebrated our golden wedding anniversary with our children, grandchildren, and close relatives. When Ariel asked me to propose a toast I merely altered one word of those that my mother had spoken at her own anniversary: "I thank God for having given me this good woman to take care of me these fifty years."

Three weeks later John F. Kennedy was assassinated by one or more of those many men who live on the threshold of insanity, waiting for the winds of religious or political hatred to topple them over into heedless, headlong crime. The young President had offered to a dilatory Congress a series of measures designed to extend civil rights and educational opportunities to millions of exploited or neglected Americans; and he had graced his office with an aura of culture and good manners that could have inspired the rising generation if he had been allowed to add political maturity to his personal charm. In revulsion against this ghastly murder the American people took on the burden of guilt, and tried to atone by idealizing the remarkable family to which he had belonged.

Perhaps it was as part of that revulsion—or was it only a sign of my waning vitality and growing age?—that I wrote, shortly after that tragedy, a little dirge entitled "Have We Too Much Freedom?" It was sent out across America by the Associated Press; I insert it here as it appeared in the Washington *Star* for December 22, 1963:

May I raise my head out of the 18th century and speak my piece about the 20th?

In the period which I am studying—the last decades before the French Revolution—the individual was struggling to liberate himself from ancient traditions, congealed creeds, and despotic states. Therefore he idealized freedom against order, the new against the old, "genius" against discipline; and when his rebellions succeeded he tried to establish constitutions that would weaken the state and the church, and strengthen the rights of the individual.

The attempt failed for a time in France, because a quarter-century of war re-established discipline and monarchy; it succeeded in America, and Jefferson gloried in a government that would govern as little as possible.

Throughout the 19th century in England and America, and after 1870 in France, the aim of law, in large part, was to protect the individual against the law, to make it difficult to arrest a suspect or to convict an innocent man. Most of our literature and social philosophy, after 1850, was the voice of freedom against authority, of the child against the parent, of the pupil against the teacher, of men against the state.

Through many years, like any unplaced youth swelling with genius, I shared in that individualistic revolt. I do not regret that rebellion; it is the function of youth to defend liberty and innovation, of the old to defend order and tradition, and of middle age to find a middle way. But now that I too am old, I wonder whether the battle I fought was not too completely won. Have we too much freedom? Have we so long ridiculed authority in the family, discipline in education, rules in art, decency in conduct, and law in the State that our liberation has brought us close to chaos in the family and the school, in morals, arts, ideas, and Government? We forgot to make ourselves intelligent when we made ourselves free.

Should we be free to commit murder and escape punishment on the ground of "temporary insanity"? Have our parole boards been too gentle, humane, and approachable? Should we be free to sell, to any minor who has the price, the most obscene—the most deliberately and mercenarily obscene—book of the 18th century, while we deplore the spread of crime, unwed motherhood, and venereal disease among the youth?

Should divorce be so easy that marriage loses its function of promoting sexual order and family discipline? Should advertisers be free to multiply their sales by pictures of violence, or by persuasive propaganda for products officially branded as injurious? Should a few old men be free, by accident of seniority, to obstruct Government by preventing Congress from considering measures recommended by the president?

These are difficult questions, requiring careful thought, and I have no dogmatic answers to any of them. I know that severity of punishment does not always prevent crime—though I believe that surety of punishment would deter it. I know how hard it is to say who should judge what is right or wrong, obscene or decent, and where censorship should stop once it has begun. I realize that the old moral code, designed for an agricultural society in which marriage came early, children were assets, and the family was the unit of economic production, is inevitably breaking down in an industrial and urban society where marriage is deferred, children are liabilities, the individual and the corporation are the units of production, and the protective anonymity of the individual in the city crowd hampers the functioning of public opinion as a moral check and stimulus.

But with all these excuses and doubts, public opinion has been guilty of criminal and cowardly silence in the face of growing crime, moral disorder, and deteriorating taste. We have been afraid to speak out lest we be considered old-fashioned and incapable of adjusting ourselves to changing norms and ways. We tolerate, and allow our children to be formed by, pictures that habituate them to crime and violence, to the cheap heroism of flaunting a gun, and to taking the law into their own hands. We patronize products sold by appeals to the lowest common denominator of the public mind. We make idols of screen celebrities who deliberately break up home after home. We give not only money but honors to writers who peddle sexual stimulation. We pass in wonder by some of the modern art exhibited in some of our museums, and we dare not speak out against it as turning our stomachs with the odor of decay. Our ears are deafened and insulted by cacophonous music, but we fearfully recall that Beethoven was condemned by traditionalists, and without protest we go to be deafened and insulted again. We hear the wits laugh at the old copybook maxims, and we haven't the nerve to say that those maxims are still true.

Let us speak out. Let public opinion resume its function as an indispensable aid in transmitting standards and transforming the savage into a citizen. We shall be charged with hypocrisy, because we too are sinners; the sins of our past will be exhumed and flung into our faces; we shall be called timid and senile reactionaries. Yes, we are guilty with the rest; we have been silent too long; and part of our tardy righteousness may well be due to the lessened flow of sap in our flesh. No matter; let us speak out. Let us say, humbly but publicly, that we resent corruption in politics, dishonesty in business, faithlessness in marriage, pornography in literature, coarseness in language, chaos in music, meaninglessness in art.

It is time for all good men to come to the aid of their party, whose name is civilization.

The riot swelled.

CHAPTER XXVII

European Safaris

1964–65

Ariel:

My poor William took a long time to recover from that murderous review and its many echoes. It was some consolation that the Book-of-the-Month Club had taken *The Age of Louis XIV* as its selection for August, 1963, and had sold 150,000 copies; we trusted that many of these would be read, and that the book would make its way. We had to forget it now, and worry about *The Age of Voltaire*.

I was never satisfied to see that volume so untidily divided from its successor. Politically it covered only England, France, Germany, and Switzerland, 1715–56, but the survey of science, philosophy, and religion continued to 1778. The senior partner of the firm answered that the basic theme of this Volume IX was the conflict between Christianity and the *philosophes,* and that this "great debate" could not be split, like the political history, at the coming of the Seven Years' War (1756). Perhaps, too, Will wanted to unify this volume around Voltaire and the revolt against the Church, while Volume X (1756–89) would hinge on Rousseau and the dawn of revolution. He thought of the two books as combining to make a substantial (1,989 pages) history of Europe in the eighteenth century.

The seventy-nine-page chapter on "The Scientific Advance" was out of my line, but I was very much concerned with the discussion of Voltaire as historian. Two of my favorite books at that time were A. J. Black's *The Art of History* and A. L. Rowse's *The Use of History*. I could not agree with Will that Voltaire had long preceded him in writing "integral history"—covering and uniting all phases of human activity in a given period. The *Essai sur les moeurs* gave a few incidental pages to literature, but hundreds to politics; the biographies of Charles XII and Peter the Great were naturally political; only the wonderful *Siècle de Louis XIV* (even our title had been preempted) gave substantial sections to art and literature, but rather as appendices to the political record than as integrated currents in a united narrative. But I must not let my *esprit de corps* lead me into derogating from the incredible achievements of the fascinating imp of Ferney.

Our chastened vanity was revived by news that the Huntington Hartford Foundation had chosen us for its 1963 award in the field of literature. Probably our friend John Vincent had something to do with this, for he was the able director of the artists' colony maintained by the foundation in Pacific Palisades. Huntington Hartford himself had sent us the thousand-dollar check on December 24, 1963, but the formal award was made at a dinner in the central hall of the colony on January 10, 1964. We were honored by the presence of Max Eastman, Raymond Kendall, Charles Luckman, Franklin Murphy, Paul Jordan-Smith, James Taylor, and their wives, and many of the resident artists, with John and Ruth Vincent as host and hostess. I made a speech brief enough to quote:

> May I indulge myself in a moment of retrospect?
>
> I was born toward the end of the century, and was barely thirteen when I met my teacher—my husband-to-be. From a barefoot tomboy to the present, this little old lady has come a long way, the whole gamut, you might say, from innocence to repentance.
>
> All in all, Will and I have been lucky, and have had more than the proverbial seven good years. We have been the other half of each other for over fifty years. And if I ask myself what it is that has bound us and made us one, I cannot express it better than by saying, "It was because he was he, because I was myself." And because some inexplicable power had decreed an indissoluble union dedicating us to our work.
>
> Celebrating now a half century of marriage and history, I thank Mr. Hartford and Dr. Vincent for including me in this award. It will be an added incentive, beautifully timed, toward the completion of our *Story of Civilization*.
>
> In the name of history, thank you.

Will spoke more abundantly, and more optimistically then I believe he would speak today. Some excerpts:

> I thank Mr. Hartford for his generosity not only to Mrs. Durant and myself but to so many enterprises that his beneficent influence will long be felt in America and in the world. I thank Dr. John and Mrs. Ruth Vincent who, I suspect, had a quiet and gentle hand in these proceedings. I thank Ariel for her patience with me while I took half a century to learn the art of husbandry—if I may add a new meaning to that word.

None of the nine volumes so far completed of *The Story of Civilization* could have been written without her help, and none of the final four without her active and painstaking collaboration. These have been happy years for us, working separately each day, working together each evening, reading the same books, sometimes aloud to each other, comparing notes, arguing interpretations, preparing the manuscript, correcting proofs, and breaking our united heart over an unfavorable review.

When we look back over the thiry-five years in which these books have kept us from other mischief, and ask ourselves what lessons we have learned from the complex record of so many cultures—rearing their heads proudly for a time, then disappearing from history—it is hard to avoid the conclusion that the only certainty in life, individual or national, is death. . . .

There is no escape from that somber picture except to say that in states, as in families, death is life's way of renewing itself in fresher forms. After all, we would not wish to live forever; even perfection would become a bore if long continued. The meaning of life is that we may fulfill ourselves, contribute our part to the whole, and be content to leave immortality to the nation, or to the species, or to life; so the more we contribute, the less we die. You elect ones—poets, historians, composers, artists, together with the statesmen, scientists, philosophers, and saints—provide the heritage that goes on. Each of you may say with Horace, *Non omnis moriar*—I shall not entirely die.

In like manner the worth and meaning of a civilization is not that it may linger on forever, but that in its tenure of life it may welcome, increase, and transmit the human heritage. In that sense a great civilization does not die, it migrates; it picks up its values and passes on to a new habitat and a rejuvenated form. So the civilizations of the Near East and Crete passed down into Greece; Greek civilization—its poetry, drama, science, philosophy, religion and art—crossed the Adriatic to Italy and Rome; Roman civilization—its Greek heritage, its laws and language and roads and forms of government—became part of the Greco-Roman inheritance of Italy, Germany, France, and England; the European heritage enters into the stream of American life; we are to Europe what Rome was to Greece. As the death of the individual organism is the rejuvenation of life, so the death of a civilization is the rejuvenation of history . . .

Despite the incorporated homicide or suicide called war, despite the crimes of individuals, the natural conflicts of domestic parties and national ambitions, I believe, after fifty years of studying history, that man is physically, mentally, and morally better, on the average, than at any time in the past; that our poverty, so disgraceful amid our unprecedented wealth, is not so shameless as the slavery that supported an enfranchised minority in Periclean Athens or Augustan Rome; that our marital chaos and moral laxity are no worse than in the England of Charles II or the France of LouisXV; that more good books are being published than ever before and more widely read; and that art will soon rise to a new level of self-discipline and social significance.

I mourn the ugly slums of our cities and the distress of those who cannot find work for their hands to do; but I see realized around me, in an unparalleled proportion of our people, such a spread of home ownership, family income, physical comforts, educational opportunities, political freedom, and scientific powers as would amaze and gladden our Founding Fathers if they could return to see what their progeny and their institutions have done. I am proud of our universities, and I look to them to protect America from the recrudescence of superstition and intolerance. I acclaim the statesmanship that is seeking and finding alternatives to nuclear war. This time, this moment, is as good as any that ever bryant, and is incomparably more wonderful.

But, you remind me, life is short, and we shall die before we can give full form and measure to our dream. Ariel and I could join you in that lament; how grateful we should be if we could carry our history down to our own exciting time and include the America to which we owe so much! Yet we remember Goethe's advice: *Entsagen*—renounce; accept with good cheer the limits within which you are allowed to work. Others will carry on.

As for me, I am thankful for the years and health that I have had, and I shall be content with a few years more. I rarely think of death, nor do I resent it; it is the wisest of life's inventions. When it comes, I hope I shall have the wits and grace to look back gratefully upon life and say to my children and grandchildren, "It was good."

On April 23, 1964, we left Los Angeles again, and pushed eastward, with friendly stopovers, until we found ourselves in London. On May 6 we were admitted to the box of the sergeant at arms in the chamber of the House of Commons; it was a tame session on minor issues, but the day was brightened by the unexpected entrance of Sir Winston Churchill, leaning heavily on an attendant's arm. I believe he was then ninety years old (despite cigars and whiskey), and had but another year of life left to him. I quote from my notes of the day:

> The question hour was very democratic. Her Majesty's Loyal Opposition fired away, and were answered concisely and promptly, . . . while the judge, with gray wig and stole, kept order, so that only one or two rebuttals were permitted before the gavel came down. All in good order, without excessive levity or gravity—while across the bench, on his usual Tory seat, Winston Churchill slept, his great dome of a bald head bent over his chest, soundly oblivious but in his right place, quietly decomposing. To me this is England, this sacred earth. . . . We did right to come here again, and once again breathe the air of England, and feel the undaunted spirit of her people; to see another English spring, greener and more loved than any spot on earth.

The next evening was almost as thrilling, at least for me. Sir Douglas Fairbanks, Jr., knighted for his bravery in World War II, and his Lady Mary Lee, rosily beautiful despite the enmity of time, had invited some of their friends to meet us. We were a bit shy, surrounded by so many titles and accomplishments: Sir Arthur Bryant, knighted for his books on

English history; Sir Alan P. Herbert, famous for his *Punch* humor and a distinguished career in Parliament; Sir Steven Runciman, author of classic books on Byzantine civilization and the Crusades; Herbert Agar, winner of the Pulitzer Prize in 1933; John Crosby, alert columnist for the *Tribune* of New York and Paris; Hamish Hamilton, publisher; each of them with his lady. Lady Alexander Metcalfe, daughter of Lord Curzon, was pleased to find that we had been much helped by her father's volumes on Persia. Most renowned and most modest of all was Sir Laurence Olivier, who exchanged notes with Will on theatrical history and colonic irrigation. All these men and women gave us many a lesson in carrying distinction with simplicity.

After another visit to the British Museum we took the boat train to Paris. There Will went almost daily to the Louvre, almost every night to the Théâtre Français or the Opéra—and at least once to the Place Pigalle to see if the French girls were developing bosoms. Also, I find in my notes:

> Will made his (usual) pilgrimage to the Gardens of the Tuileries, where he patted, oh so lovingly, each buttock and thigh of the female statues; . . . it took a long time, since he had to find the special ones he remembered above others. It was a sad farewell we took of the ladies left shivering in cold marble, the wind blowing the leaves all around, and the sky overcast and bleak, the Seine gray and misty, almost looking the way we felt. . . . Even in the face of age and decay Will remained an unrepentant and voracious lover.

On May 20 we left by sleeper for Cannes. I had begged for three weeks' stay there, for I thought we would never come again, and I had some dear friends, like old and ailing Alia Bersin, to whom I wished to say an unhurried goodbye; Will's liability to hypertension made it doubtful that we should ever undertake an overseas trip again. Meanwhile he worked on Volume X, content in a bright room in the Gray d'Albion Hotel. There we received a comforting letter from Sir Cedric Stanton Hicks, who had won international repute by recognizing, long before most of us, the problems of ecology:

> *Woodley,*
> *Glen Osmond,*
> *South Australia*
> *June 1, 1964*

> Dear Friends—
>
> For that is how my wife and I feel towards you both, because you have lived in my study for many years between the covers of your books. We were both delighted and honored to receive your letter in the midst of your busy search for atmosphere and situation with which to weave the basic colors of your final tapestry of western civilization. . . . We hope that you will both be spared to complete this gigantic task. . . . How delightful it

was to read your reference to British historians and their opinion of your work! How very typical of that world of analytical finesse and critical acrimony. . . . What makes the Durant story is the human element, the all too prevalent frailties, the poetry, the art, the music, the lust and the nobility, and ever and ever the common people, living, lusting, loving, sorrowing, working, and dying. What a cavalcade! What a toccata and fugue! . . .

On June 23 we sailed on the *Independence* for New York. We reached Los Angeles on July 7, just in time to join our new friends Frank and Laura Quittner in the box that we now shared with them at the Hollywood Bowl.

We followed with some concern the contest between Lyndon Johnson and Barry Goldwater for the presidency. The men and women who had engineered the Senator's nomination, and were the chief financiers of his campaign, were frankly in favor of enlarging the war in South Vietnam, and of heating up the cold war against China and Russia; they were eager to rid the government of all obligations for the "welfare state," and of that Bill of Rights which had set the United States on the road to a real democracy. We took no part in the turmoil, feeling confident of Johnson's victory; but as the national temperature rose Will thought he should stand up and be counted; and he took the opportunity to suggest some Democratic arguments. Our American economy, he wrote,

> evolves peacefully out of a devil-take-the-hindmost license into an orderly freedom regulated by the community will through law and the state. Liberty grows out of order, and generates disorder unless it is checked; it is an indispensable stimulus and a perpetual peril. It must be periodically limited to prevent its passing from stimulation to disintegration.
>
> The same is true of the concentration of wealth: it is inevitable and dangerous. Clever people must be left free to make profits, else they will not (with some saintly exceptions) bestir themselves to their economic best. But if this clever minority is left completely free it will soon possess so much of the community's wealth, privileges, and powers as to arouse divisive envy in the majority. All men are born unequal and unfree, and they become more unequal with every increase in the complexity of the economy—its processes, finances, management, and tools. The welfare state is an attempt by statesmanship to keep this natural inequality from growing to the point of social disruption.
>
> History has never known so stimulating an economic system as ours, but unless the average man's power to purchase goods keeps pace with his repeatedly multiplied power to produce them, the system will periodically balk, and production will slow down to let consumption catch up. Theoretically such a recession is incurable; for the lessening of production throws men out of work, their reduced purchasing power throws more men out of work, and so on through a cycle of deepening poverty and chaos. Should the fortunate among us look upon this process with smug indifference, and allow the displaced workers to flirt with revolution?
>
> We faced such a situation in 1932; we might face it again if we adopted

the lazy view that most of these workers are lazy fellows who prefer to be unemployed. Presumably some of them are; but obviously many of them are victims of automation, or some other economic change over which they had no control. Many others are in distress through sickness or old age; they feel the high cost of medicine, and suffer from the decline of the family and mutual aid; and that decline has been due chiefly to the individualism, and geographical wandering, of the job. Here, obviously, the community must come to the help of the family. So—and because we insist on dominating the world—our taxes grow.

I too begrudge paying so much of my income to the government, but I perceive that my income is made possible by the stability of the state and the wide distribution of wealth. Doubtless there is considerable malfeasance in the handling of state and federal funds; I know of no government in history that was free from corruption; we are like that. We must protest against it in others, and daily check it in ourselves; but it would be childish to imagine that the "outs" are more virtuous than the "ins."

I conclude—with thousands of our ablest and most enlightened businessmen—that the welfare state, within limits, is not an evil but a boon. With its help capitalism has mitigated the excesses of greed that disgraced it in the sixty-four years that followed the Civil War, and has spread wealth, comfort, opportunity, education, and even happiness, far more widely than ever before. The experience of Europe confirms this conclusion: England, France, Italy, and Western Germany have accepted the welfare state, and their economy has prospered beyond any European precedent.

It is good for the rich that the state should help the poor—through schools, hospitals, medical care, parks, recreation facilities, unemployment insurance, accident compensation, veterans' benefits, and other forms of relief. It is good for the city dweller that the farmer should be helped to face the disadvantages caused by the perishable nature of his products and the superior organization of the groups that intervene between him and the consumer; for industry would languish if the purchasing power of the agricultural community were seriously reduced. It is good for all of us that the state should regulate banks, commerce, communication, transportation, utilities, civil rights, minimum wages, and the sale of drugs. The state can be a curse when it is a tool of tyranny or exploitation; it can be a blessing when, realizing Rousseau's ideal, it becomes the agent of the general will.

I believe that our government, with all its human faults, has reached this stage in America; and I am confident that the electorate will not wish to turn the clock back upon the economic progress, the political moderation, and the humane compassion of our time.

Max Schuster sent a copy to the President, who (or some ghost writer) replied:

October 28, 1964

DEAR MR. SCHUSTER:

Thank you for sending me Dr. Will Durant's article, "The Basic Issues of the Campaign."

The article is both trenchant and eloquent, and I am very pleased to know that a man of Dr. Durant's wisdom and erudition feels as he does about the meaning of this election. I am referring the article to the appropriate individual, with the hope that it can be used to further our efforts.

Sincerely,
LYNDON B. JOHNSON

On November 3 the President was re-elected. Soon he sent to Congress his historic proposals for the "Great Society," and then he began his long journey to Golgotha via Vietnam.

That week Will entered his eightieth year. On December 15 we made our annual pilgrimage to Pasadena to hear Richard Lert conduct the *Messiah*. I accepted gratefully the tribute that Handel had paid to the prose and poetry of the Old Testament, and joined Will in thankfulness for all the good fortune that had come to us in our little corner of the world.

We were now getting fan letters from several continents, and invitations to lecture for absurdly high fees. Will excused himself on the ground of his "rickety bones," though he still pranced around, or chopped wood, as if he admitted only half of his eighty years. Several offers came to me, and Will urged me to accept them if only to break the monotony of our daily routine. I refused to leave him overnight, for his susceptibility to hypertension continued till the *Story* was finished; but I succumbed to the temptation to address the San Fernando Valley Branch of the American Association of University Women on April 10, 1965. I came out alive.

I must confess that I could not stay put so long and so contentedly as Will. His many lecture tours, and their remembered tribulations, had left him with a distaste for travel. But when we had nearly completed the first draft of *Rousseau and Revolution,* and as the second draft could be written anywhere, he agreed, as he said, to "roll and pitch" once more. So on April 30, 1965, we sailed on the *Constitution* from New York on its leisurely voyage to Cannes. Several shore excursions were arranged, and we signed for all of them. At Casablanca we joined a motor tour to Rabat, the capital of Morocco; at Palma we visited the cells once occupied by Chopin and George Sand; at Naples we took an exciting drive to Pompeii, Amalfi and Sorrento; at Genoa we bounced over the waves in a motorboat for a second visit to Santa Margherita, Portofino, and Rapallo. At Cannes we were happy to entertain our Pasadena friends Edmund and Daisy Burke, who were refreshing their memories of the days, long ago, when he had toured Europe as baritone star in operatic performances with Nellie Melba. With my ailing friend Alia Bersin I visited her relatives at the Pension Rodnoi in Les Issambres on the Riviera.

We met many old friends in London. Lilian Kaufman, of Los Angeles, was at the Ritz Hotel in Piccadilly; she knew a hundred musicians, and alerted us to the fact that Alfred Wallenstein, once the director of the Los Angeles Symphony Orchestra, was to conduct the London Philharmonic in Festival Hall. We went, and had a pleasant visit with the modest maestro and his ever lovely wife, Virginia. On June 16 we rode out to the Old Vic and saw Sir Laurence Olivier in *Othello*; after the performance we went backstage to thank him; he embraced me, and left on me some of the black ointment that he had not yet removed from his arms and face. On the seventeenth we paid another visit to the British Museum, hunting relics of the English authors who had a place in our Volume X. On June 20 we boarded the speedy S.S. *United States* at Southampton; on June 25 we were in New York; on July 6 we were home.

Now, while daily immersed in *Rousseau and Revolution*, we waited anxiously to see what the critics and the public would do to *The Age of Voltaire*. That volume was the most dangerous of all, for its central theme was the increasingly bitter duel between philosophy and religion. (It was not yet, as it would become in the nineteenth century, between science and religion.) Leading the attack were David Hume in England, Frederick the Great in Prussia, and, in France, the hotly anticlerical *philosophes:* Voltaire, Diderot, d'Alembert, d'Holbach, and La Mettrie.

Will tried to stand aside from the conflict, for he felt an obligation to record without prejudice the battle of personalities and ideas; nevertheless he echoed the decibels of history—the comparative noise-making of the combatants—in giving prominence to the embattled philosophers, and above all to the endlessly interesting Voltaire. I took no share in those lively chapters, for though my own people had nurtured Christ and cradled Christianity, it had suffered so much from unforgotten persecutions that I could not pretend to impartiality. Will, however, had developed some doubts about his own skepticism; and in the concluding "Epilogue in Elysium" he had tried to moderate the iconoclasm of the book's protagonists by putting into the mouth of the liberal Pope Benedict XIV a surprisingly vigorous statement of the case for religion.

Granted that religion was rooted in myth and mystery, and had grown with soothing ritual into a not-to-be-questioned creed; yet what alternative did science or philosophy or history offer to such consolatory beliefs? Had not the apparent victory of the scientists, the historians, and the philosophers deposed the God who had been the very staff of life to the poor, and a pillar of support to the moral code that had helped tame the savage hunter into law and order, morality and civilization? Would philosophy or education or statemanship ever succeed in establishing an effective moral code without the aid of religious sanctions and beliefs? And if they failed, and religion continued to fade, would Western civilization lapse into a chaos of sexual laxity, political corruption, mutual violence, and a common, consuming despair? Could it be that all that enthusiastic slaughter of irrational creeds had undermined the secret foundations of civilization itself? Will repeatedly broached these problems to me—so often, indeed, that sometimes I worried lest he should suddenly leave me and disappear into a monastery.

When *The Age of Voltaire* was published in September, 1965, we were surprised to find that hardly anyone paid much attention to that brooding epilogue; no reviewer (except in the Catholic periodicals) seemed bothered by the decline of supernatural beliefs, and none agreed with Will that the continuing conflict between philosophy and religion was of deeper consequence than the contest betwen Communism and capitalism. Most of the critics remained uncommitted on the subject, so that the import of the book was dimmed. Nearly all the reviews were favorable, none was enthusiastic. We had not expected our book, with its long account of "the attack upon Christianity," to be recommended by professors, but we were pleased to hear, from fan letters and other sources, that our volumes were listed as supplementary readings in many colleges. We were aware that we had lost favor with some literary leaders in the East, partly by our move to California, partly by our criticism of Russia, and doubtless by the flaws in our work; but that barrier too was breaking down, as evidenced by our election to the Institute of Arts and Sciences and, later, by our receipt of the Pulitzer Prize. In our own bailiwick—Los Angeles—we were accorded all the kudos we could stand; the Authors' Club, in 1965, gave its annual award to *The Age of Voltaire*.

I upstaged Will for a moment at the end of the year. On November 16 I received the following telegram:

> For the fifteenth consecutive year the Los Angeles *Times* will honor outstanding Southern California women whose distinguished achievements have earned the respect and admiration of our community.
>
> Because of your significant contribution and important accomplishments I am both pleased and honored to inform you that you have been named a Los Angeles *Times* Woman of the Year for 1965. Your award will be presented formally . . . on December 13 in the Harry Chandler Auditorium. . . . I ask that you keep your selection confidential until the event. . . .
>
> OTIS CHANDLER, PUBLISHER

How could I keep this a secret for four weeks? Of course I told Will, who shared my happiness; and I telephoned my thanks to Robert Kirsch, head of the literary department of the *Times*, for I guessed that it was he who had submitted my name. On December 13 Will escorted me to the festivities. Several other women received awards: Anna Bing Arnold for philanthropy, Dr. E. Margaret Burbridge for science, Dr. Marian Gallaher for medicine, Julie Andrews for her work in the cinema . . . Each of us was presented to the audience by the head of the corresponding department of the *Times*, and each of us received a gold cup from Mrs. Dorothy Chandler, who had founded the awards fifteen years before. Mr. Kirsch introduced me with a summary of the Durant collaboration. I knew how much of this honor I owed to Will, and I confessed my debt in the briefest speech I have ever made: "For this high honor and privilege I wish to thank Mr. Chandler and Mrs. Chandler, whose wonderful newspaper and indefatigable labors have so greatly contributed to raising this city to universal acclaim. I wish to thank Mr. Robert Kirsch for his abiding faith in me. And always I thank my teacher, friend, and husband, Will Durant, for fifty-two years of happy marriage to him and history."

But enough of me. I leave Will to tell the story of how we marched up to the Bastille and collapsed with its fall.

CHAPTER XXVIII

Symphony Unfinished

1966–67

Will:

We had long since been gathering material for the tenth volume of our *Story*. Putting that material into shape had been our chief concern since (early in 1964) we had submitted the second draft of *The Age of Voltaire* to daughter Ethel for her helpful criticism and immaculate typing. Indeed, when, in the preceding fifty years, had we not studied Rousseau's books and calamities, Voltaire's partriarchal years, Frederick the Great's battles and philosophy, Catherine the Great and Madame de Pompadour, Mozart and Schiller, Kant and Goethe, Reynolds and Gainsborough, Boswell and Johnson, Gibbon and Goldsmith, Beaumarchais and Mirabeau, Marie Antoinette and Louis XVI? These and their times had been part of our meat and drink for half a century.

And now how could we bring together intelligibly and vividly in one volume all these and other giants of 1756 to 1789, with their origins, surroundings, and effect? These figures, and the ideas they represented, were still in the public mind and interest of Europe and America; we were still living under the sign of Voltaire and the illness of God, of Rousseau and the death of monarchy. We could not ignore them, and yet it would be impossible to say anything about them that had not been said abundantly before. Should we merely mention them as the inessential embroidery of politics, statistics, and war, or should we give each of them, and his country and people, an honest, impartial, and adequate survey, no matter how much the mountainous result would burden the reader's mind and arms? We sacrificed the reader.

Ariel worked on this absorbing venture more than on any of our earlier tasks. She continued to do most of the research on the women who provided the more gracious themes of our composition; of course she had the last word on Mesdames Geoffrin and du Deffand and Mademoiselle de Lespinasse. We studied Goethe *pari passu,* locked in interest and aim, except that after strenuous sampling of *Faust,* Part Two, Ariel left that melodious confusion to me. Neither of us, however, missed a word of Eckermann's *Conversations with Goethe;* the Privy Councilor was not always fascinating, but upon every subject he shed the light of eighty years. Ariel had long preceded me in studies of Catherine the Great and Laurence Sterne, and I could never keep abreast of her addiction to Horace Walpole. She knew Gibbon, footnotes and all; her own notes on *The Decline and Fall* and Gibbon's various autobiographies would make a volume of themselves. She had read every published line of Boswell before I reached that faithful, thirsty scribe. I marvel that she found time for all these studies amid the varied chores of the home. Among her notes was one that might have served for many a twilight: 'This is the end of the day—eventide—and I am so tired that I will sit and do nothing but watch the fading light mysteriously become night. . . . I am weary—weary with the satisfaction that I have accomplished the thousand and one trivia of the fleeting day."

Our divergent tastes led to many a spirited debate. Ariel did not value Goya as highly as I did; she frowned upon my voting him fifteen pages, and made me improve them with her shears. She loved Mozart, but felt that I had lost perspective in giving him more space (twenty-nine pages) than to Johnson (twenty-seven) or Kant (twenty-one); I replied that I had tried to avoid repeating the material on Kant in *The Story of Philosophy,* and argued that Mozart played a larger part in Western civilization today than the Great Cham, who is almost unknown outside the English-speaking world. Many critics agreed with Ariel, and suggested that Volume X might have been easier to handle and to read if my enthusiasms had not swelled it to 1,091 pages. I promised never to do it again.

I believe it was in June, 1966, that we wrote the presumably last page of *The Story of Civilization.* Instead of feeling relief at the end of nearly forty years of labor, we were rather somber over the thought that we would no longer have this task as a constant and steadying companion, which would tell us, each morning, where our work lay, and would fill each day with substance and meaning. We felt as if we were deserting readers who had toiled with us over every page, and had in many cases bidden us go on. I wrote the concluding envoi, but Ariel rejected its final paragraph as too sentimental. She composed an alternative last page, and I accepted it at first sight. Her hand was at the wheel when we came to port.

During those terminal years our egos were sustained by the friends who opened their homes to us, and by readers who wrote from almost every country except Soviet Russia, Communist China, and their dependencies. Precious corrections came to us from India and Japan. In January, 1966, Walt Cranon sent word that the labor unions of Otero County had set up in their Labor Temple at La Junta, Colorado, a "Durant Library" with our books as a nucleus. A letter from England enclosed a copy of an appeal to *Life* magazine to get us the Nobel Prize. *Life* did not print the letter, and we did not get the prize, but we received, as a consolation piece, a nice letter (dated November 22, 1966) from a real Nobel-man, world-famous physicist Werner Heisenberg, telling us: "I have studied in your 'Age of Voltaire' with very great profit and pleasure."

On June 30, 1966, Max Schuster, aged sixty-nine, retired from the firm that he and Richard Simon had founded in 1924. He and Dick had revolutionized the publishing of hard-cover books by risking large sums on large-scale advertising, thereby reaching a larger public; and the success of *The Story of Philosophy* owed much to these bold acts of faith. Max had long planned to write or edit some books under his own name; often he talked more like a student and scholar than like an enterprising businessman; now he was free for travel and research, and for the exploration of his magnificent library.

His successor, Leon Shimkin, had been with the firm almost from the beginning; as its treasurer he had managed its financial relations with us, and we had long benefited from his business acumen and his integrity. In 1939 he and three others had founded Pocket Books in the belief that books would reach a wider audience if in America—as long since in France—they dispensed with costly bindings. Now he united Pocket Books with S and S, and talked of the time when *The Story of Civilization* could be published in small volumes available to anyone rich enough to buy a meal. It was just like him, when he learned that Ariel and I were contemplating another "farewell tour" to Europe, to offer to pay our expenses out of company funds. How could we refuse? (We had spent some seventy thousand dollars of our own earnings on travel, mostly for research.)

We left Los Angeles on August 24, 1966. On August 27 we spent a happy day with Louis, Mollie, and Eric in their new nest in Cos Cob, Connecticut. Louis had found a promising berth in New York, and Eric was already a sophomore in Williams College. On the twenty-ninth Mollie and Eric drove us to Norwalk, where we visited Bern and Billie Dibner and their beautiful Burnby Library. That afternoon we crossed into New York State to Mohegan, and renewed old bonds with Eva and Joe Brandes and other survivors of Ferrer Association days. Ariel's diary notes:

We talked about old times, ideals, and friendships. It felt good to be fifty-three years younger again, to submerge our aches and pains in the lush memories—somewhat embellished and idealized—of the time when we were brave, pure, and original. How like our "impossible" youngsters of today, who frighten and antagonize us. So history repeats itself; only the actors grow old and decay; the process is eternal.

On August 30 Leon Shimkin sent a car to pick us up at Mohegan and take us to his summer home in Pound Ridge, New York; there we fell in love with his wife, Rebecca. On September 1 we delivered to Leon all but the final chapter of *Rousseau and Revolution*, and celebrated with his staff of highly capable aides a new marriage of the Durants with S and S. On September 4 we went out to Sands Point, Long Island, and spent a day with Max and Ray Schuster. On Labor Day, September 5, brother Michael drove us out to another reunion of the Durant clan in Westfield, New Jersey. On September 8 we sailed on the S. S. *United States* for Southampton.

On September 14 we settled down, as usual, in the Washington Hotel, in Curzon Street, London. Ariel's diary that evening was overly darkened by her wrong guess that we would never see England again.

England, London, the English people continue to obsess and possess us as we are ever conscious of finishing our "Story" and their part in it. We and they are slowly going down together—we in a few years, they in a few hundred . . . We are both finished, dying, and have this in common: we both leave what was best in us, a reminder that we were once alive. Sounds funny, doesn't it, equating our puny selves with Shakespeare's England; forgivable only because we love it so much that in our mind and heart, dwelling upon it so long, we have become one with the thing we love. This is our own leave-taking of England. . . . I feel quite mellow. We now must turn in other directions far removed from the motives and history that have imprisoned us for many years.

Ariel commented on the ethnic discoloration of urban Britain:

London is not only polyglot, it is polychrome. English shopkeepers are in a minority, and restaurants are in the hands of Near Easterners, Far Easterners, Arabs, Africans, Armenians, Cypriotes, Hindus, Italians, sprinkled here and there with Jews. Only the exclusive clubs are still overwhelmingly Nordic—perhaps. To her Commonwealth peoples England gave too many of her native sons, leaving herself open to invasion from without and below. . . . My sympathies have colored my thoughts.

We never stopped wondering at the number, fresh beauty, and stately trees of London's parks, so carefully nurtured, so invitingly open to all who sought an hour's escape from the stones and maelstrom of the city. So Ariel:

We walked across Green Park to Buckingham Palace to St. James' Park, along the lake—gently floating ducks and geese. Across the bridge to Birdcage Walk, opening out upon Big Ben as he struck twelve. . . . As far as the eye could see, all that was noble or ancient in London's history basked in a soft autumn sunshine half subdued by English mist. We stood on Westminster Bridge and looked long and reverently, taking mental note. The English people were still the salt of the earth, tho a little run down . . . in the twilight of empire, repeating step by step the . . . fall of Rome

We cultivated our old friends in London, and found new ones in Paris (September 27). Brenda Helsen, a California woman of great beauty and bountiful spirit, had married Count Lorenzo de Morelos, whose modesty and manners long concealed from us his wide culture and business skill. Brenda was a member of the Book-of-the-Month Club, and through it she had been exposed to *The Story of Civilization;* she developed so generous an affection for those painful tomes that she placed them at the crown of her library; and when a French translation appeared in thirty-two volumes she bought them all as an heirloom for her son Carlos. Through her we met Comte Fernand de Saint-Simon, collateral descendant of the famous duke whose voluminous memoirs had helped to give a contemporary touch to *The Age of Louis XIV* and *The Age of Voltaire.* We were impressed by noting how these scions of ancient lions had gone out into the economic jungle and earned their bread by the sweat of their brows.

On October 1 we took the Train Bleu for Montreux, feasting our eyes, along the way, on the green fields and hills of France. With Michael and Doris David we took two coach tours. One was to the St. Bernard Pass, to get a Pisgah view of Italy; when we had spiraled our way to the peak we found nothing of Italy except impenetrable mist. Far more pleasant was our trip to the medieval village of Gruyère, famous for its ancient castle and its *living* cheese. En route we had lunch at Gstaad, which remains in my memory as one of the loveliest, cleanest towns I have ever known.

On October 8 we left Montreux for Milan. We arrived in a heavy rain, but our old friend Carlo Foà met us with two umbrellas and a Fiat car, and took us to his apartment, which we remembered as a treasury of precious books. His talented wife, Bibi, had spent a fortune on this library of literature, history, music, and art. Of all our nonprofessional readers I think she was the most learned, familiar with the best productions of Italian, French, English and American writers, poets, and philosophers—in their own languages. Her praise went to our heads, and made us forget that we had defined philosophy as perspective.

We would have stayed with Carlo and Bibi for the rest of our time in Europe, and could have taken the boat at Genoa, but Ariel had agreed to spend a week near her beloved Alia Bersin. So, on October 10, we rose before waking and caught the 6:25 A.M. Trans-European Express, which swept us by clean electric power over the Alps to Genoa, Savona, San Remo, Nice, and Cannes to Saint-Raphaël; thence a car took us to the Pension Rodnoi at Les Issambres. There, in a quiet week near the sea, we caught up with our work schedule. After another week at Cannes we sailed on the *Michelangelo* to New York. On November 5 we reached Los Angeles.

Ariel has a worried note in her diary at this point: "Will is glad to be home; shrinking and withering away; looks more gentle and spiritual . . . Why did we really [have to] go to Europe this time?" I had no consciousness of shrinking or withering, after all those minestrones on the *Michelangelo*. Moreover, Ethel had arranged a birthday dinner; our daughter and grandchildren gathered about us, and I did not find it unpleasant to be eighty-one.

We began the year 1967 with a nasty task: we drew up at considerable length a list of additions and corrections for *The Story of Civilization*. We brought the history of India, China, and Japan down to 1950; to our account of Crete in *The Life of Greece* we added the emendations made possible by the decipherment of Minoan scripts; and inserted into *Caesar and Christ* an account of the Dead Sea Scrolls. We took advantage of the corrections proposed by critics, friends, and foes. We asked our publishers to have the changes inserted in all future printings, and we arranged them so that they would require no change in pagination or binding; even so it has been, or will be, a costly operation for S and S.

In January we were surprised by a call from Chet Huntley of the National Broadcasting Company: might he come out with a television crew to interview us about the demise of the *Story?* Of course we agreed. He came on January 15, trailing a maze of wires and a truckload of miraculous machines. As these purred and whirred and we posed and smiled, Chet asked was it true that *Rousseau and Revolution* had been completed? We showed him the last page of the manuscript. At his suggestion Ariel read into the microphone the concluding paragraphs. On January 31 the interview appeared on the morning *Today* program; and that evening, more briefly, we found ourselves on the *Huntley-Brinkley Report* of world-shaking news. Those few moments brought us a delectable panegyric from Manuel Komroff, who had been our friend and fellow scribe through strikes and bombs, ideologies and reviews, for fifty-five years:

Jan. 18, 1967

DEAR WILL AND ARIEL:

There you were as big as life on TV tonight and I cannot tell you how nice it was to see you.

And on top of this BEST CONGRATULATIONS.

You have single handed accomplished what whole academies have failed to do. And what is more you have done an outstanding piece of scholarship, perhaps the most outstanding ever accomplished in America. This is my sober judgment and I stand on it and ready to face all challengers. Truly it is a great piece of work.

I do not know how it would feel to do a work so long protracted and have it come to an end. Will you feel relieved? Will you be lonesome? Does the freed prisoner miss his chains?

We miss you.

Odette joins me in sending you our best love.

Ever your old friend,
MANUEL

The fragrance of that bouquet may have lingered long enough to temper the comic tragedy that brought me to Cedars of Lebanon Hospital on March 2, 1967. On February 28 I blew my nose too strenuously, and splashed blood over my handkerchief. I lay down with my head hanging back over the pillow; after some ten minutes the bleeding stopped. When I told my friend and physician Rexford Kennamer about this he suggested that I should go to Dr. ——, specialist, and ask him to cauterize the blood vessels in my nose. I did, on March 1; the procedure was painful, and I believe it injured those arteries or capillaries or veins. That night, without perceivable reason, the bleeding resumed, more abundantly than before. I called the specialist; he thought it useless to make the long trip from his bed to mine; instead he bade me go to the emergency station in the Medical Building at the University of California at Westwood, Los Angeles. We had a long wait before a taxicab came; then an eight-mile ride with Ariel, while with one hand I pushed cotton up the bleeding nostril and, with the other, applied an ice bag to my nose.

About 2 A.M. on March 2 we finally, after much searching, found the receiving room in that bewildering maze called the Medical Center of UCLA. I took my turn in a line of patients as impatient as myself. At last my turn came, and a brutal but efficient young doctor came, and stuffed both nostrials with cotton (shoving the wads up as if he were riveting bolts). He took my blood pressure, found it to be 220, and bade me get to a hospital at once. At 6 A.M. Ariel went with me to Cedars of Lebanon, where Dr. Robert Feder, cool and competent, inserted into my nasal passages a tube designed to press upon the blood vessels and retard the flow sufficiently to allow clotting. I tossed and rolled in that bed till March 8. Through those six days and nights Ariel remained beside me.

To make up for my loss of blood Dr. Kennamer ordered one or more transfusions of blood; it took me several weeks to acclimatize this blood to its new environment. Various antibiotics were given me, and some morphine to ease my discomfort, quiet my questions, and help me sleep. I became delirious in my sleep, and muttered absurdities which Ariel clinically recorded; I have those notes before me, and I am shocked to find what a medley of nonsense had been stored up in my neural apparatus.

That sickness proved a blessing in many ways. Perhaps the loss of blood had eased a pressure that might have caused a cerebral lesion. I had received a warning that I had better reform the fast life that I had been living with my pen. One especially pleasant result of the mishap was Ariel's firm decision that I must no longer climb stairs five or six times a day to my second-story study (I had long been a second *Story* man); now she turned over to me her cozy first-floor study, put a comfortable bed in a corner of it, had our gardener bring down my desk and table and reference books and rocking chair (with the big flat arms to hold my writing board), and so she let me in on the ground floor of our partnership. She made her own study out of the adjoining living room, which had for years remained almost unused while we groped our way through centuries; there she has her desk, her special books, and her cot. An open passage connects the two studies; we talk and dispute with each other through it, and sometimes visit one another, at any hour of day or night, to compare notes or rub noses. It has been for me a very happy demotion.

On returning from the hospital we found a thick batch of galleys waiting to be corrected; they represented the first quarter of Volume X. I was still groggy with all the medication that had been shot into me, but the task helped to fill my convalescent days. After I had corrected those sheets Ariel went through them carefully and found some sixty errors that I had missed. On March 29 a telegram from Leon Shimkin informed us that the Book-of-the-Month Club had chosen our final leviathan as its selection for August, and was planning a national campaign to offer the ten volumes of the *Story* at fifteen dollars a set. Ariel and I thought we were making a financial sacrifice to reach a wider audience, but in the long run this new way of selling books proved a financial windfall for us and the tax collector.

On March 24 we received an invitation from the White House to attend the dinner which President Johnson was planning to give for the visiting President of Turkey; we excused ourselves on the score of ill health. I had not liked our government's policy in Vietnam, but I thought that Lyndon Johnson was doing his sincere best to meet a very ambivalent situation, on which his judgment was at least as good as mine, and his information immeasurably superior. I felt that his critics had passed beyond reasonable and healthy dissent to disgraceful excesses of vituperation.

In July the race problem in Detroit flared into a riot in which some infuriated blacks burned down several acres of property, and some hungry blacks engaged in a revel of robbery. Many alarmed whites called for more vigorous control by the police and the National Guard or the Army; some demanded immediate retaliation. In a speech (July 28) admirable in substance and tone, the President appealed to the nation to avoid any extreme reaction, and to continue patiently the processes of amelioration. I was so moved that I sent him a telegram: "Thank you for your address of last night; it was an inspiring example of courage, wisdom, and humanity." He replied,

August 2, 1967

DEAR DR. DURANT:

I cannot tell you how grateful I am for your message of last Friday.

I know that you and Mrs. Durant have explored many of the struggles between chaos and order that have occupied men since the beginning of time. You know, as well as any man or woman, the tangled web of rights and wrongs that emerges from those struggles. The current torment in our cities is no different.

I am greatly strengthened by your words of commendation; when and if you feel moved to write to me again with your thoughts on this grave matter, I shall be just as appreciative.

Sincerely,
LYNDON B. JOHNSON

In September, 1967, *Rousseau and Revolution,* six pounds strong, burst upon the world. The reviews were all favorable; *Time* was especially generous, and set the tone. We were charmed to find, in the news columns of the New York *Times* for Tuesday, September 12, a substantial article entitled "Durants' History Reaches Its End"; on that day we shared the limelight with pitchers and presidents. In that same week the *Times* ran an editorial congratulati.ong us on having completed (?) our rash enterprise, and arguing that the wide circulation of these volumes hardly accorded with the view that the Americans are a materialistic people. The Chicago *Tribune* also crowned our collapse with a complimentary editorial; and in our own neighborhood Robert McClure, editor of the Santa Monica *Outlook,* called "the work of the Durants the best historical writing of our time." Fondling such bouquets, I had the feeling of a man reading his own obituary, or smelling the flowers on his grave.

In November Georges Fischer and half a dozen electronic wizards from station KNXT came to immortalize us for a day on the television screen. For three days we were subjected to sharply intelligent questions on history, philosophy, religion, and what Ariel called our progress from "innocence to repentance." Then for the first time I learned that Ariel had married me not for love but to free herself from her family. I recovered from that blow when she smiled; for when Ariel smiles the sun, the moon, and the stars all come out at the same time. The result was shown for an uninterrupted hour in a local broadcast on January 19, 1968, and was repeated in February, 1969.

That transfiguration into film seemed to close our career. Nevertheless we were still in good health, and not quite ready to die. We cast about for new blank books to fill, and soon we were pregnant with three books.

CHAPTER XXIX

Finale

1967–68

Ariel:

For an hour we were tempted to yield to a hundred appeals and undertake an integral history of the nineteenth century. We had already filled boxes and file-cabinet drawers with notes on Europe and the Americas, 1789–1900. But the overwhelming fascination of that period—in five continents—in politics, revolutions, social organization, racial movements, scientific discoveries, industrial technology, religion, morals, literature, philosophy, music, and art, frightened as well as attracted us; how could we do justice to these diverse developments and their protagonists, still fresh in educated memories, still living in daily influence? Perhaps if Will had kept to his earlier plan of writing a history of the nineteenth century only, he could have brought that off successfully in a lifetime; but now that he was eighty-two such an enterprise would have tempted the gods to chasten him with disaster. Besides, were there not already in existence a hundred thousand books about the nineteenth century, a hundred thousand more about the French Revolution, two hundred thousand about Napoleon? What could we add to that embarrassment of riches except some new order and synthesis?

A more reasonable challenge came from letters and critics: "What have you learned from your survey of history?" "Is there any evidence that men—or their leaders—have ever learned anything from history, or are human actions motivated by impulses older than history, and tarnished as ever by their origins and results?" "Can the study of history be any-

388

thing more than an amusement, an asylum for tired hearts and minds?" So we wrote *The Lessons of History*.

It was to be a small book, easy to handle and to read, and yet facing without evasion some of the most uncomfortable questions of our time. What role had differences of race played in history—and does history support the view that some races are genetically superior to others? Was Carlyle right in exalting, or Marx in belittling, the role of exceptional men in history? Has religion proved itself indispensable to social order, or has it been an oppressive and retarding force in the development of mankind? What has happened in the past when a great religion has lost its hold upon human behavior? Has any society found it possible to preserve moral character or social order without the help of supernatural belief and a surveillant god? What has been the result, in the past, of permissive moral codes like that which prevails in sections or sectors of America today? Why is it that poverty has persisted despite all advances in technology and production? Have revolutions ever been successful, or have they always replaced oppressors by oppressors? What forms of government have fared best in history? Was democracy made impossible by the natural inequality of men, and was war made inevitable by deep-rooted tendencies to violence? Have there been any successful socialist regimes? Is progress real? Why do civilizations die? Is ours dying?

Here was a program for a year or a decade, and a morass for reckless feet. But to attempt it was a debt of honor, and we had promised to write no more leviathans. So my Don Quixote, with my minuscule help, set out to answer all these questions within a hundred pages and one year. By the time *Rousseau and Revolution* came from the press *The Lessons of History* reached the publishers.

We took a rest, but we found resting dull. What should we do now to guide and dignify our days? Here we did not hesitate, for through our years of exile from the present we had promised ourselves, when the *Story* was finished, an unfettered frolic of reading in contemporary literature. We knew that brilliant things were being done by the writers of our time while we were meandering in the past, but we had remained ignorant of them except by vacation snatches of Hemingway, Gide, and Mann, and some sorties into the night with Eugene O'Neill. Now we were free. We threw ourselves happily into Yoknapatawpha with Faulkner, into bullfights with Hemingway, into the cutest obscurities with T. S. Eliot and Ezra Pound. We charted for ourselves a reading tour all the way from Mississippi to Moscow.

At first we were innocent of all intent to write about these heroes. But, midway in Faulkner, Will confessed that reading seemed too quietly dull and supinely passive compared with making a serious study of each author, of his life, character, work, and philosophy of life, and then telling the world what we thought of him. Almost clandestinely he wrote essays on Faulkner and Hemingway. Ethel and I read these sheets, and told him that they were not up to par; that they added little to what others had said, and that those authors, who had worked hard at their trade, deserved a wider and deeper study before he had any right to judge them. He humbly agreed, then challenged me: "Let's both of us read these writers carefully, compare our notes and reactions, and see if our composite product merits print." I am not at all sure that we succeeded, but that is how *Interpretations of Life* came to be.

It kept us enchanted, wherever we went, through 1968 and '69, despite another sally into politics. Some of it was written in February, 1968, when we were the cottage guests, in Scottsdale, Arizona, of Mrs. Louis Kerr, a woman who has never ceased to astonish us by the richness of her endowment in character, mind, and art.

In March, 1968, Long Island University invited us to receive honorary degrees, at its commencement on June 4. I was pleased, for I have never worn a degree, while Will had carried two of them for half a century; now he submitted to the "third degree." Then it occurred to me that if we went to New York we should be only three thousand miles from Europe; why couldn't we do our work while pitching and rolling to Europe and back?

So we left Los Angeles on April 10, and sailed from New York on the S.S. *United States* April 17. We missed Douglas Fairbanks in London, but his Lady Mary Lee entertained us with her unfailing vitality and grace. On May 4 we were in Paris, navigating the Seine on a *bateau mouche* with Brenda de Morelos as our hostess. She brought with her Mary Blume of the Paris *Tribune*, who interviewed us patiently whenever Will could take his mind off the historic sights that passed us quietly by. Were there, he asked, any flying buttresses that could compare with those of Notre Dame?

I believe it was on May 6, 1968, that I was surprisingly involved in the revolt of the students at the Sorbonne. Leaving Will contented in his work, I took a taxi to visit my old friend Man Ray on the Left Bank. It was now some fifty years since our first meeting. I did not care much for his collages, and he did not care much for our books; we ignored each other's prejudices, and got along very well. When I left his studio I found myself between a squad of advancing helmeted gendarmes and a mass of ecstatic students resolved to reform their university and the state. I worked my way cautiously to the Seine and prayed for a taxi; when at last one came the driver explained, through our language barrier, that he would have to take me a mile or more out of my way before we would find a bridge which we would be allowed to cross; and, true enough, as we went on, I saw bridge after bridge blocked by police assigned to keep the rebels from the Right Bank.

When I reached the Grand Hotel I found Will asleep in bed. I was beginning to undress when, about 11 P.M., the telephone startled me.

"I am Lloyd Garrison, Paris correspondent of the New York *Times*," said the voice. "I have just received a cable announcing that Will and Ariel Durant have been awarded the Pulitzer Prize for *Rousseau and Revolution*. The *Times* has commissioned me to see you at once and ask you to say a word about this new honor."

"But," I replied, "Will is asleep; can't you wait till tomorrow morning?"

"We are here in the hotel lobby; it would be cruel to send us away emptyhanded."

I woke Will with the news: "We have received the Pulitzer Prize." He mumbled a word of appreciation and turned away to resume his slumber. "Two reporters are in the lobby, asking to be allowed a few moments' interview."

"All right."

A few minutes later Garrison and his associate were at the foot of the bed, and Will, sitting up in his pajamas, and groggy with sleep, answered questions about the woes of the world. Garrison radioed a jolly account of the interview to the *Times*, but Mary Blume wrote a still better piece for the Paris *Tribune* and the Los Angeles *Times*.

The next day the Comte de Saint-Simon gathered a group of French leaders in politics and letters to further turn our heads with lauds and wine. On May 8 he used his special entree to take us through as much of the Secret Archives at Versailles as our legs could stand. Here Jules Michelet, whose *Histoire de France* had been Will's standby for centuries of French history, had brought decaying records to life and light by his patient researches and his impassioned style; here was the table at which he had studied and written. I sat in his chair, and pretended that I too had written immortal history.

On May 10 we convened at the American Library in Paris, where Will made a pretty speech telling how much we owed to France. Olivia de Havilland met us there, and she, Brenda, Lorenzo, Saint-Simon and his lovely, modest wife motored by detour to a bridge where we crossed to the Left Bank, and slowly made our way along platoons of police to the restaurant where the famous actress had arranged to have us fed. The student revolt was still in progress; we felt quite heroic in venturing into these streets still echoing with the watchwords of rebels eager to replace injustice with chaos; but we quite forgot the revolution when Olivia entertained us with her memories.

We bade a fond farewell to our friends, and caught a few hours of sleep before rising early the next morning to take the train to Montreux. We spent a day there with Michael and Doris David, rode on to Milan to enjoy the hospitality of Carlo and Bibi Foà, and passed to eleven days of quiet in Cannes. There we were joined by our St. Louis friends Henry and Gladys Janon and their daughter Patricia Benson, charmingly modest and happily pregnant. Will at once fell in love with the unborn babe, who now is saddled with Will's names. On May 26 we sailed on the *Michelangelo*, and on June 3 we reached New York.

On June 4 we were taken to Brooklyn to receive our honorary degrees at the commencement exercises of Long Island University. At the faculty luncheon that followed I made a jolly speech which, Will told me, left him both jealous and proud. We came back to our hotel just in time to receive a telephone message from Michael Korda telling us that on that day Simon and Schuster had received the Carey Thomas Award for "creative publishing," specifically for *The Story of Civilization.* Once again our cup ran over.

After an evening with Marc Brown, a day at Cos Cob with Louis, Mollie, and Eric, and an afternoon at Westfield with Will's relatives, we entrained at Newark and stopped at North Philadelphia to see our oldest friend, Ed White, who had lent us, fifty-four years before, the interest-free money to buy our first home. We found him weak from a heart attack, but making a good recovery under the care of his wife, Lena, lively and lovable at seventy-four. It delights Will to see such loyal aging couples, experiencing the full return on the mutual fund of their trust; at any moment I expect him to burst out in a song, "The Old-Time Marriage Is Good Enough for Me." Then on to Chicago and Sam Lesner and Esther and Hattie, and at last, June 13, to Los Angeles and Ethel and her husband, Stan, and her children, Jimmy and Monica, and my faithful sisters and brothers Flora, Harry, Sarah, Mary, Max.

By this time the quadrennial contest for the presidency was beginning to excite us. We followed the unique campaign of Senator Eugene McCarthy in the primaries for the Democratic nomination; we sympathized with his views, liked his quiet manner of public speech, and were glad to see so many college students finding in him some reason for faith in political procedures as a substitute for competitive destruction. We were not surprised when the Republican convention nominated Richard Nixon; our hopes were pinned on the Democratic convention that met in Chicago on August 26.

We were shocked by the television pictures of the riots that broke out there in that week. Since photographers and reporters were naturally drawn to the most dramatic incidents, we received the impression that the police had responded with intemperate force to what had begun as a peaceful protest against machine politics and the war in Vietnam. But when we read of out-of-state leaders, frankly pledged to revolution, infiltrating the crowd and urging it to violence in action and speech, we could understand how the patience and discipline of those harassed bluecoats had broken down into uncontrolled fury and indiscriminate assault.

We turned with hope to the reports of the convention, which the police had been ordered to protect from external attack. We knew that Senator McCarthy could not be nominated; it was too much to expect the delegates—nearly all of them party "regulars"—to cripple their campaigns by repudiating the President. We were sorry that Hubert Humphrey had felt obligated to support all the policies of Lyndon Johnson, but we knew the pressures generally laid upon a vice-president to support the head of his government. Will through many years had followed Humphrey's career in Minnesota and in Congress, and had not forgotten the courageous and steady liberalism of his policies; it seemed reasonable to believe that the Vice-President, if elected, would continue and extend the humane and farseeing legislation with which Mr. Johnson had distinguished his first administration. We joined in feeling that the Democratic convention, with all its lusty chaos, gave due hearing to the views of the McCarthy minority, and that Humphrey won the nomination without unfair play.

Will now resumed his kingmaking. If Senator McCarthy would lead his followers into support of Mr. Humphrey, the Democratic Party might overcome the handicaps created by the President's policy in Vietnam and by the disorders attending the Chicago convention; it would be led by two proved liberals to undertake a further extension of the progressive legislation that Franklin Roosevelt had begun and that Harry Truman and Lyndon Johnson had continued. So he wrote to Senator McCarthy,

September 3, 1968

DEAR SENATOR:

After considerable thought on the recent contest for the Democratic nomination, I should sum it up by saying that you won a remarkable and historic victory. No informed American, of course, expected you to win the nomination; the President's set-up and control of the non-primary delegates made that impossible. But (1) you gave the conscience of America an educated voice, and dared to propose the subordination of governmental policy to moral principles. (2) You gave youth a chance to come out of the streets and make itself heard in political action. (3) You aroused America to the ignominy of letting national decisions be made by political machines still imprisoned in the nineteenth century. (4) You won a moral victory even in the Vietnam plank in the Democratic platform, for though that document could not afford to repudiate the President, the substantial vote for your minority version revealed the impact that your highly civilized campaign had made upon the American mind. And (5) you put yourself in a position to determine the result of the coming election.

For it is you, and not Gov. Wallace, who hold the power to elect or defeat Mr. Nixon and his Southern strategy. Only you can prevent the domination of the next Congress by conservatives who plan to meet our urban crisis with the latest and largest guns, and to replace the liberal legislation of your party with a police state. All you need do, to elect a reactionary administration, is to do nothing. All you need do to elect a Democratic administration, and to give it the liberal and progressive direction, is to advise your millions of dedicated followers to accept their defeat as only apparent and temporary, and to help Hubert Humphrey to a victory that would be due to them and to you, and would commit him to a policy of humanitarianism and peace. LET HIM OWE HIS ELECTION TO YOU. Encourage him to revive the liberalism that characterized his Congressional career. I believe that America would be inspired and heartened by the sight of your foresight and generosity.

And if, despite your forgiveness and support, Mr. Humphrey should be defeated, you would emerge untarnished, a living and honored voice of liberal and pacific hopes, and the natural future candidate of a united party grateful for your wisdom and your loyalty.

Sincerely,
WILL DURANT

The Senator replied,

September 12, 1968

DEAR MR. DURANT:

I appreciate hearing from you and having your recommendations.

I recognize your loyalty to the party and your regard for the Vice President and for me, but the issues I raised were, I think, somewhat different from intra-party issues, and I must reserve judgment somewhat longer.

With best wishes,

Sincerely yours,
EUGENE J. McCARTHY

The Senator probably felt that his divergence from Mr. Humphrey on the Vietnam problem was too vital to be silenced. He finally accepted the position here proposed, but so late that by that time most of his followers had committed themselves to repudiate the party's candidate. If the move had been made earlier the Vice-President would probably have been elected.

Our family now went ardently to work in the Humphrey campaign. Daughter Ethel, already on the Democratic headquarters staff at Los Angeles, visited prosperous friends and persuaded them to contribute to the treasury of the campaign. She arranged to have me speak at small gatherings, and together we raised many thousands of dollars. To the largest of these groups we brought Will as a captive lion, and his oratory so captured the audience that a goodly sum was pledged. He spoke for Humphrey over radio KNX. He composed for me "A Message to McCarthy Democrats," which I used in an appeal to a liberal organization called Women For. And he wrote for the campaign a blast which should have brought Humphrey in by a landslide:

A WORD FOR HUBERT HUMPHREY

by Will and Ariel Durant

Normally we do not mingle in the rough game of politics. But in this presidential campaign we are in danger of turning our backs upon all that

394

America has done since 1932 to remedy the defects of our economic system while keeping the productive zest of individual enterprise.

For in truth we have witnessed almost a revolution in these last 36 years. The living standards of our people have been raised far beyond any precedent in history, even beyond the hopes of our radical youth. Education has been opened to all, even through college, with only a token payment of tuition. The pains of old age have been eased with Medicare and Social Security; and medical aid has been given to the poor of any age. Home ownership has been extended to millions of families. We have fought poverty as vigorously as the high birth rate of the poor has allowed. Seventy million men and women have found jobs in our expanding industries. Our country and our cities have been crossed by new and magnificent roads. We have broken down many of the political inequities that closed to some minorities the avenues to peaceful reform. We have brought hope, and at last we are bringing birth control, to the ghettoes generated by the movements of population across the oceans and across our state lines. And we have maintained freedom of speech and dissent, even to dangerous limits, during the most unpopular war in American history.

In almost all these forward movements Hubert Humphrey has played a leading, constructive, creative part; for thirty years he has led liberal ideas into functioning legislation. In only one matter we could not agree with him—on the war in Vietnam, and on that matter he has come as close to our hopes as is possible without a disastrous repudiation of the President who still controls the finances and machinery of his party. . . .

Our hearts go out to Hubert Humphrey. We have never known in our lifetime, and rarely in our studies of history, so moving an example of a good man fighting for a good cause against so many obstacles thrown up against him by his supposed friends as well as by his declared enemies. He is fighting to preserve the fruits of a lifetime of dedication. The moneyed men who supported Mr. Johnson in 1964 have closed their pockets against his self-sacrificing Vice-President; he is forced to campaign almost entirely on his debts, his courage, and his incredible energy.

Now, if ever, is the time for all good men and women to come to the aid of their party. Never, since Hitler, have the forces of reaction and bigotry been so strong as in America today. See them gathering around Gov. Wallace and Mr. Nixon: the Ku Klux Klan, the American Nazis, the race bigots, the enemies of civil rights, the frightened octogenarians who plan to meet our urban crisis not with jobs and schools but with the latest and biggest guns.

They must not win. We will fight them to the dawn of Election Day, and then again. We will oppose our devotion to their hate. The antedeluvians have united against Hubert Humphrey, and have left him almost penniless amid the worst accumulation of difficulties that any candidate in our history has ever faced. He has to depend upon us, upon those lovers of light and liberty whom through all his years in Minnesota and in Congress he represented and defended. No man since Franklin Roosevelt has done so much as Hubert Humphrey for the progressive programs that were on the way to cleanse and improve American civilization. His selection of Edmund Muskie as his running mate and potential successor shows where his heart lies.

Let us forget our wounds, unite our forces, recapture the leadership of the Democratic Party, and commit it to policies of humanitarianism and peace. Infuse into this campaign your vitality and fervor. Inspire the hesitant and tired ones by the drama of your energy and your devotion.

Don't despair. We have seen many miracles in our life times; we hope to see one more. Perhaps it is your help and your gift that will turn the tide and bring hope and victory to these two good men fighting for you and for us.

A shorter form of this was sent to the press, and appeared in the New York *Times* for October 27.

Two days later the Vice-President sent Will a birthday greeting: "November 5 is going to be a significant day for many of us, but I seem to recall that it also marks the celebration of your 83rd birthday. I simply wanted to take a moment to wish you a wonderful day and many, more more years of good health and happiness. . . ."

During that exciting week we met Mr. Humphrey at a reception arranged for him by the local campaign committee. He looked so exhausted that we were moved when he told Will, "Don't work so hard." At another gathering we were happy to hear Senator Muskie praise *The Lessons of History*. That little book had been published in September, and had been forgotten, even by ourselves, in the ardor of the campaign. The reviews were all favorable, but hardly enthusiastic. It is slowly making its way.

The election came on November 5; all the country quit work to celebrate Will's birthday. The defeat of our candidate did not surprise us. We sent him a pledge of our undiminished admiration and our growing affection. He replied,

December 3, 1968

DEAR WILL AND ARIEL:

I am grateful for your warm note. I think the campaign was worth while—that we may have done the country's spirit some good even in defeat.

I know I don't need to tell you how much your friendship and support mean to me—now, as always.

Sincerely,
HUBERT H. HUMPHREY

CHAPTER XXX

Requiem

1969–70

Will:

All through that campaign, and till October, 1969, we worked on—and diverted ourselves with—*Interpretations of Life*. We began it as an amusement, and then submitted to it as a challenge. We tried to progress from the careless simplicity of the earlier chapters to such conscientious and substantial essays as those on Proust, Sartre, and Thomas Mann. We did not expect the book to arouse any enthusiasm among established critics, for we were invading, without proper visa, territory that they had made their own by years of cultivation. But we were already absorbed in our reckless safari into our own time.

February 16 was a dark day. We had gone to the home of the famous cellist Joseph Schuster, at the invitation of his angelic wife, Katherine, to join several others of their friends in listening to a domestic rehearsal of the program he was preparing for his next international tour. His performance of a Tchaikovsky sonata for cello and piano was a stirring revelation of feeling, beauty, and depth. Then Joseph began a piece by Beethoven. Suddenly he stopped, and said simply, "I don't feel well." He carefully laid his cello on the floor beside him, sat back in his chair, closed his eyes, and died, apparently without pain. Poor Katherine was now a mixture of terror and good sense; she bade us stay away from those who were trying to revive her husband, and she summoned their doctor (and ours), heart specialist Rexford Kennamer. He came at once, carrying pulmotor apparatus. It was of no avail.

The next morning we sent the widow a word of condolence:

Feb. 17, 1969

DEAR KATHERINE:

It was a beautiful and peaceful death—a soul almost literally carried off on the wings of song. We are reminded of Keats's wish to die in ecstasy over a nightingale's "high requiem"—"to cease upon the midnight with no pain."

All the pain is left for you to bear. We rejoice that you are strong; that you have such rich memories of toils and triumphs shared; and that a fine son and daughter-in-law are near you to comfort you, and to receive the love that your nature craves to give.

Please tell us if we can help you in any way.

Lovingly,

WILL AND ARIEL DURANT

I shall never forget Ariel's quiet words as we signed that letter: "I trust that when my lover's turn comes he will find so kindly a death."

My turn could have come a month later, for on March 23, 1969, I had another troublesome nosebleed. The flow of blood was faster and fuller than on a similar occasion two years before; it came suddenly while I was lying quietly in bed at night; it had nothing to do with blowing my nose; apparently it resulted from hypertension. I hoped to stop it without waking and alarming Ariel; I stuffed my nose with cotton, which I pressed upward with the eraser end of a pencil; but the blood merely changed its course by coming down through the mouth. I woke Ariel; she called Dr. Feder, who bade her take me to Cedars of Lebanon Hospital; we repeated the experience of 1967—helpless patient and patient wife. After three days of mechanical contraption, blood transfusions, morphine sedation, and precautionary antibiotics, the bleeding stopped; and on the fourth day we were back home, sobered from our ecstasies by these new intimations of mortality.

June of 1969 was a busy month for us. Dr. Norman Austin, president of the University of Akron, had asked us to address the graduating class, and accept two more degrees, at the commencement on the fifteenth. We agreed, for the fee would cover the expenses of a week with our friends in New York. After we had so committed ourselves we were approached by the director of the Buckley School in Sherman Oaks, California: would I address the graduating class (which included our granddaughter, Monica Mihell) on June 13 at the Bel Air Hotel? I had done a similar stint in 1958 for the Webb School of Claremont, when grandson Jimmy graduated; I could not refuse a like performance for his sister's school, though it would require us to fly to our engagement in Akron. I enjoyed the Buckley commencement; many of our Los Angeles friends attended; I was at my best, and Monica rewarded me with a hug.

On June 14 we flew to Cleveland, rode to Akron, and had a restful night in Dr. Austin's home. The next day we established a precedent by giving a cooperative commencement address: Ariel spoke with impish humor on "The Generation Gap," and bridged it so quickly that she received a standing ovation. My own contribution was merely an elaboration of the material I had presented at the Buckley commencement two days before. When we had received our applause and degrees President Austin, by an act of merciful courtesy, escorted us from the platform, so that we might be spared the ordeal of listening while diplomas were handed out to two thousand graduates.

On June 16 we flew to New York and began ten days of reunion with friends still bound with us across the Continental Divide. Louis and Mollie had made a cozy nest in Cos Cob; S and S were prospering under Leon Shimkin; brother Mike drove us to Westfield, where we found my sister Ethel, seventy years old, and my one surviving brother, John, eighty-seven, both in fair health—though John, like me, was subject to nosebleeds. Finally a sumptuous sendoff by Marc Brown, and we were on our way to Chicago and the Lesners, to Los Angeles and home. We embraced our children, paid our bills, resumed our places at the Hollywood Bowl, and exhumed our past for confession and display.

We repeated ourselves in 1970: we wrote, talked, and ran over the earth. A book is like a quarrel: one word leads to another, and may erupt in blood or print, irrevocably. And one speech leads to another. Word had spread that Ariel could charm an audience, and she was now getting more invitations to oratory than I was. The Young Women's Christian Association of Phoenix asked would she address its members on February 26. She agreed, for we had already arranged to spend that week in nearby Scottsdale. So we sallied forth on February 22 in our aging (1957) Cadillac for a two-day drive into thriving Arizona. Ariel's address received her usual standing ovation from a large audience. We returned to Hollywood exalted.

Ripon College must have heard of our eloquence in Akron; President Adams invited Ariel to give the commencement address on May 16. To the offered fee was added another lure: she would be one of five women who on that occasion were to receive honorary degrees for having made outstanding contributions to American life. The others were Margaret Chase Smith, four-term senator from Maine; Mary Ingraham Bunting, president of Radcliffe College; Maria Goeppert Mayer, a Nobel Prize winner for physics; and Elizabeth Yates McGreal, winner of the Newberry Award for children's books. A third consideration was that Eric was about to marry the sweetheart he had brought back from Finland; couldn't we come to their wedding? Of course we could.

One temptation leads to another. Were my creaking joints up to another "farewell tour" to our European friends? I voted to risk them. We could do second draft of this book on board ship or in Cannes or Lugano. We reserved a room on the S.S. *Raffaello* from New York May 23; that melodious name, echoing beauty and grace, was itself a lure. In Milan our devoted Bibi had died, leaving her Carlo desolate; we would go to comfort him. Hearing of these excuses, our pretty granddaughter, Monica, suggested that this was a good time to carry out our oft-repeated pledge to take her to Europe; might she join us at Cannes after completing her first year in college? This would require her to fly from Los Angeles to Nice, risking her young life; she laughed at our fears; her mother favored the adventure, and paid Monica's expenses to Cannes.

On May 15 we flew to Oshkosh, and were driven thence to the pretty town of Ripon, alleged birthplace of the Republican Party. At the commencement I was one of a thousand proud relatives who watched as faculty and graduates, somber in cap and gown, filed past, two abreast, led by President Adams, six feet tall, and Ariel, five feet one. Her address so pleased Senator Smith that on her return to Washington she secured consent to have it read into *The Congressional Record.*

We flew on to New York, and fond Eric and Tiina in the throes of love. Their marriage had been postponed for a month; we could not attend, but we left them the thousand-dollar check that Ariel had received for her Ripon address.

Then news came that the *Raffaello* had collided with a tanker, and would be out of service for two weeks. We could not wait for her to recuperate, since we had promised to meet Monica at Nice on June 2; and no scheduled sailing would take us to Europe on time. So on May 23 we flew from New York to Paris in six hours; on the twenty-fourth we flew to Nice, and that evening we slept in Cannes; it took our heads and stomachs twenty-four hours to adjust themselves to the change of time. Monica, delayed by an air controllers' strike, arrived in Cannes six hours late, tired and happy.

Difficulties developed. Monica was eighteen, and was feeling her oats; I was eighty-four, and had spilled nearly all my oats; the generation gap yawned between us. The saviors of the situation were George Zachary and John Waller, two handsome gentlemen, who lived only a few blocks from us in Hollywood, and had fallen from the sky into Cannes to take Monica—and often ourselves—to "cautious and secure" places on the Riviera; Monica was happy, and all five of us began a friendship which is growing day by day.

Parting from George and John was sweet sorrow, but Carlo Foà was waiting for us in Milan. He took Monica to see what remained of Leonardo's *Last Supper,* and we cooled our ideologies by calculating whether the pigeons in the Piazza Duomo outnumbered the statues on the ornate cathedral. I was impressed by the crowds—men as well as women—that attended one or another of the many Masses offered on June 14, Sunday, in that vast shrine, and I reckoned that Catholics would still be worshiping there centuries after Voltaire and Nietzsche had been forgotten. On the sixteenth Carlo drove us to Lugano, sometimes at ninety miles an hour—Monica enjoying, Grandpa trembling, Ariel gently moderating us all. I thought Lugano one of the most attractive places I had seen in my wanderings: mountains in silent majesty cupping a placid lake, quiet hotels congenial to incurable scribblers, and, along the miles-long waterfront, a tree-shaded promenade ideal for lovers and octogenarians alike; here I fretted when I saw those lusty youths ogling my Monica.

Then on to Paris and Brenda, Lorenzo, and the endlessly considerate Saint-Simons, and three affectionate meetings with Olivia de Havilland. Both Brenda and Olivia took Monica to their hearts; Brenda and her son Carlos went riding with her (for Monica loves horses); Olivia guided her through museums, and helped Ariel and me to make some progress across two generations.

London too added to our education. Who but the gallant, valiant Douglas Fairbanks guided us in an aftertheater tour of central London, explaining to Monica the historic structures that we passed? He secured us tickets for Olivier's *Merchant of Venice* "in modern dress," but we did not care for the Victorian cutaways and pantaloons and prosaic interiors that replaced the color and flow of Venetian costumes, palaces, and canals.

So, instructed on many fronts, we embarked on the *Queen Elizabeth 2*. We spent three days as the guests of Marc Brown in New York, while Monica flew home to her mother. We found Eric and Tiina happily married and profitably employed. We drove out with brother Michael over the Verrazano Bridge and Staten Island to Westfield and Leo and Ethel Halliwell and a score of upcoming nephews and nieces. On August 11 we were home.

Today, October 31, 1970, is the fifty-seventh anniversary of our marriage. On November 5 I shall be eighty-five—not old enough to be a sage, but ready to finish this book and my life. I speak only for myself. Ariel is still in full vigor and spirit; soon she will speak for herself, and then end, as she began, this fond memorial of trials survived and blessings won.

My greatest blessing now is her continued presence. The sound of her slippered feet moving swiftly about the house is a comforting obbligato assuring constancy. When she sits down to work or talk with me she is a bubbling fount of inspiration and insight. Her gay gossip over her telephone comes muted to my study as part of the music of persisting youth. Our daughter Ethel has been an added blessing, indescribable and unique. I have walked with geniuses (Powys, Russell, Darrow), but never with such delight as when I walked her to school. Her mind is as rich in content, as quick in perception, as fertile in suggestion as any that I have known. She has checked me in errors of fact or judgment innumerable times, and has repeatedly improved our manuscripts in substance or expression. She has borne the challenges and buffets of life with courage and good cheer, and has taken on new responsibilities as if born to the task. Now, when I walk stumblingly, she is always near to help me. I bless, not once a year but every day, the day she came.

All in all, I have had a happy life; I am grateful for it, and would be glad to live it again. But if I were reborn I would not ask for a kinder childhood than I had, nor for a fairer faith. If my second life could learn from the first I would not break away so sharply from that faith, but would move less abrasively to a more stoic and realistic creed. I still prefer a moral code independent of supernatural belief, but I am far from sure that our ingrained individualistic impulses of greed, hatred, pugnacity, and violence can be controlled without the inculcation of supernatural hopes and fears.

Probably my moral battle was eased by some feminine element in my makeup. This weakened my aggressiveness, though it did not reduce my ambition—which was born of vanity and sustained by obstinacy. Perhaps I found it easier than most youths to preserve virginity so long; and the passion to write big books may have drained away some of the energy that might have gone into extramarital sex—though my imagination committed many sins. My modest fires cooled after seventy, and have now reluctantly died out in this year 1970—so that this book ends fitly.

I have entertained at one time or another so many ideas that now seem foolish to me that I cannot be harsh with contemporary youth for cherishing its own delusions. I was a fervent radical in my time, and cannot expect my grandchildren to be conservatives. They will sober down as they grow up; and meanwhile some of their notions may survive the wholesome tests of obstruction and debate. In all likelihood many of the proposals advanced by today's rebels will be peaceably adopted by our government, our educational system, or our society. Consequently I distrust revolution and work for reform. I still believe in progress, but not so confidently as in my declamatory days.

I am still a socialist, but with some cautions. I do not relish the control of economic lives by vast corporations. To keep the benefits and check the power of these mastodons I would favor public ownership of natural resources, including the land and all its minerals, fuels, and other subsoil wealth; also of transportation, banking, insurance, and medical and hospital care. I recognize that invention, enterprise, competition, and the profit motive are the activating forces in any productive economy. I know that we must appeal to the acquisitive instincts if we are to get men and women to toil, invent, save, and invest. I know that capital, management, science, and machinery play a rising role, and "labor" a diminishing part, in production and distribution, and that the excellence of the product—automobile, clothing, razor, wine—is largely due to the competition it must meet in the marketplace. The desire to eliminate struggle and competition—success and failure—from our economic life is an un-Darwinian dream. I will not join in the condemnation of science and technology; certainly they need more public responsibility and control; but only they—chastened by the humanities and directed to communal ends—can cure the evils they have caused.

Since government can be despotic—can be more terrible a monster than any corporation—I would insist on a real and active democracy as so necessary to a tolerable socialism that if I cannot have both of these I would make my peace with such a regulated capitalism-plus-welfare-state as we have in the United States today, despite its brazen affluence and political corruptions and amid minority desolation. I welcome the active, watchful, initiative citizenship contemplated by John Gardner's Common Cause. Moreover, my brand of socialism would allow private enterprise to compete with the government in postal services, education, banking, transportation, insurance, and medical care—subject to regulation wherever the public interest would be endangered. So our government allows telegraph companies to compete with the Post Office, and the British government allows commercial television to compete with the British Broadcasting Company.

I interpret our moral laxity today as an excessive reaction to the excessive puritanism and prudery of our Victorian ancestors; and I believe that, like its opposite, it will be brought to an end by its own excess. History—in literature, art, and government as well as in morals—tends to an alternation between liberty becoming license and authority becoming tyranny. The moral laxity of Hellenistic and Roman "paganism" was followed by the restraints of early Christianity; the laxity of the Renaissance—in the Italy of Leo X, the France of Francis I and Henry IV, and the England of Elizabeth I—was followed by the Counter-Reformation in Italy, Pietism in Germany, Calvinism in Switzerland and Scotland, Jansenism in France, and Puritanism in England and America; the relaxing of life and letters under the Stuart Restoration was followed by moral and literary discipline in the "Augustan Age"; the exaltation of liberty in Revolutionary France and the England of Byron and Shelley was followed by the monarchical and Catholic reaction in France and the Victorian Age in England . . . On this analogy we may expect the current age of indulgence to be followed by an age of authority, discipline, and restraint—perhaps in literature and art as well as in words and politics.

I am still an agnostic, with pantheistic overtones. The sight of plants and children growing inclines me to define divinity as creative power, and to reverence this in all its manifestations, even when they injure me. I cannot reconcile the existence of consciousness with a deterministic and mechanistic philosophy. I am skeptical not only of theology but also of philosophy, science, history, and myself. I recognize supersensory possibilities but not supernatural powers. I doubt philosophy when it is metaphysics, and psychology when it becomes Freudian psychoanalysis. I doubt physicists when they explain the atom, astronomers when they explain the stars, geologists when they date the strata, historians when they explain the past. I know that my own work is flawed, and that our laborious masterpieces will be superseded as knowledge grows and vistas change.

I accept death as a necessary clearing of the way for fresh life; like style it is the removal of the superfluous. I live on in the fond belief that Ariel and the children need me. I trust that when the Reaper finally gets me they will recognize his rights and his patience. I ask my doctors not to prolong my existence artificially when they and my family agree that I am physically finished and mentally dead.

Life has been kind to me; but after so many years, so many volumes, so much dressing and undressing, so much love given and returned, it will be time to sleep.

POSTSCRIPT, 1977

Ariel:

Despite those compliments and invitations, the Reaper continued to pass us by. Soon we were repeating the experience of 1968—reading for pleasure, with no clear purpose or visible result. Again we lusted for the pen, for the daily guidance of a plan and a goal, for the consuming industry of studying and describing another period of history in its time and place and in all the major aspects of its life. We had been frightened by the terrors of the French Revolution, and by the enormity of Napoleon; now, encouraged by another bill of health from Dr. Kennamer, and by a hundred appeals or challenges from readers or reviewers, we resolved to see and picture Europe as a whole in another span of time. Never had we found so fascinating a subject, nor any on which it was so difficult to be dull. We worked at the enterprise night and day through four years, and delivered the manuscript—eighteen hundred typed pages—to Simon and Schuster in August, 1974. Then we treated ourselves to a relaxing cruise, on the *Michelangelo*, to Genoa, Istanbul, Sochi (in Soviet Georgia), Beirut, and back through Genoa and Cannes to New York. For a year we waited, in semi-animation, for *The Age of Napoleon* to go through the press. On November 3, 1975, after costly mishaps and delays, it reached publication, and we looked anxiously for the reviews.

When the first one came—on November 2—by our dedicated enemy, Professor Plumb of Cambridge University, it seemed to be an irreversible sentence of death. It condemned *The Age of Napoleon* as an utterly worthless popularization of history, a loose concatenation of "potted biographies," comparable to *Portnoy's Complaint*. Will took the blow in somber silence. If this was to be the general verdict of the critics we should have to count our whole literary life, through half a century, as an immodest waste of time.

We were restored to hope by many friendly letters—some from univer-

405

sity professors—denouncing Dr. Plumb's masterpiece of mayhem; and still more by a near-unanimity of favorable reviews from all parts of the United States. The Book-of-the-Month Club made *The Age of Napoleon* its selection for January, 1976, winning for us an added audience of 100,000 readers. The United States Senate, on a motion by Senator Humphrey, voted us a scroll of recognition and applause. The government of France sent us two medallions in appreciation of our fond recording of French civilization. Crowning all, in January, 1977, came our own government's award, to each of us, of the Presidential Medal of Freedom.

Let me end on this buoyant note. All in all, despite some stimulating setbacks, we have been among fortune's favorites through sixty years. We have been allowed to earn our bread while celebrating the creative men and women who made history forgivable by enriching our heritage and our lives. Once again, probably for the last time, we bid our readers a grateful goodbye. But we are not really leaving them. They can always find us between the covers of our books.

Index

Index

Index

414

Index